D1093333

BLOOD ROSES

BLOOD ROSES

THE HOUSES OF LANCASTER
AND YORK BEFORE
THE WAR OF THE ROSES

KATHRYN WARNER

HIGH LIFE HIGHLAND	
3800 18 0079046 5	
Askews & Holts	18-Jan-2019
942.03	£20.00

First published 2018

The History Press
The Mill, Brimscombe Port
Stroud, Gloucestershire, GL5 2QG
www.thehistorypress.co.uk

© Kathryn Warner, 2018

The right of Kathryn Warner to be identified as the Author
of this work has been asserted in accordance with the
Copyright, Designs and Patents Act 1988.

All rights reserved. No part of this book may be reprinted
or reproduced or utilised in any form or by any electronic,
mechanical or other means, now known or hereafter invented,
including photocopying and recording, or in any information
storage or retrieval system, without the permission in writing
from the Publishers.

British Library Cataloguing in Publication Data.
A catalogue record for this book is available from the British Library.

ISBN 978 0 7509 8554 3

Typesetting and origination by The History Press
Printed and bound by CPI Group (UK) Ltd

CONTENTS

GENEALOGICAL TABLES

1. ROYAL HOUSE OF ENGLAND AND THE LANCASTERS

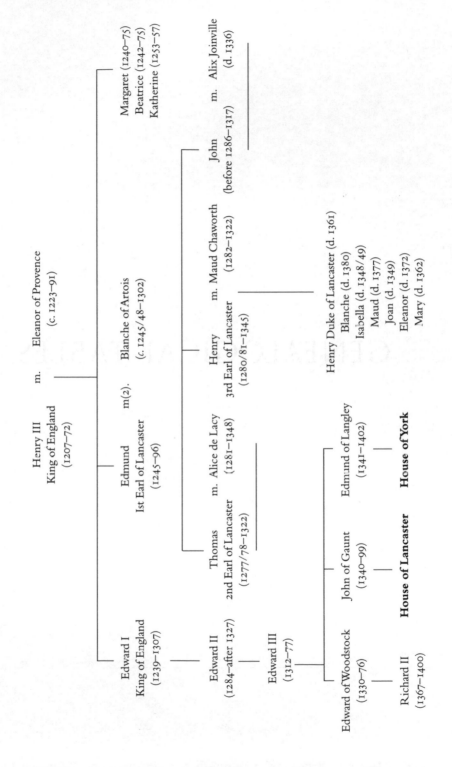

2. FRENCH CONNECTIONS

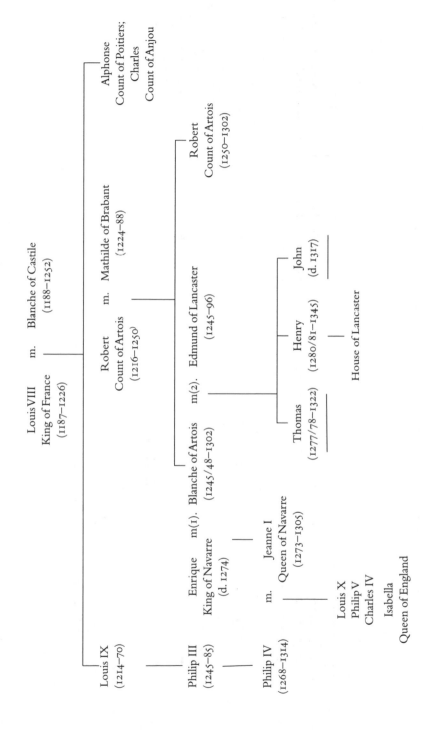

3. CHILDREN AND GRANDCHILDREN OF HENRY, EARL OF LANCASTER, AND THE WAKES

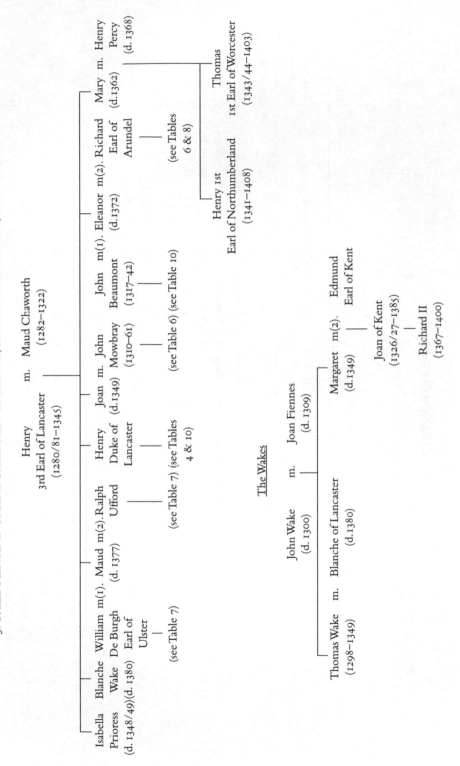

4. DESCENDANTS OF JOHN OF GAUNT

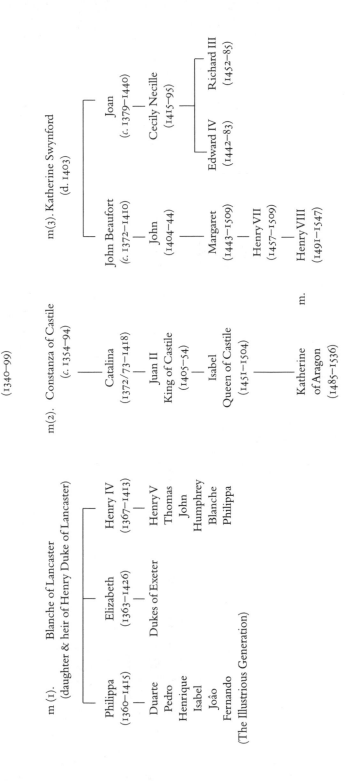

Edward III
(1312–77)

John of Gaunt
2nd Duke of Lancaster
(1340–99)

m (1).   Blanche of Lancaster
(daughter & heir of Henry Duke of Lancaster)

Philippa   Elizabeth   Henry IV
(1360–1415)   (1363–1426)   (1367–1413)

Duarte   Dukes of Exeter   Henry V
Pedro   Thomas
Henrique   John
Isabel   Humphrey
João   Blanche
Fernando   Philippa
(The Illustrious Generation)

m (2).   Constanza of Castile
(c. 1354–94)

Catalina
(1372/73–1418)

Juan II
King of Castile
(1405–54)

Isabel
Queen of Castile
(1451–1504)

Katherine
of Aragon
(1485–1536)

m.

m (3).   Katherine Swynford
(d. 1403)

John Beaufort   Joan
(c. 1372–1410)   (c. 1379–1440)

John   Cecily Necille
(1404–44)   (1415–95)

Margaret   Edward IV   Richard III
(1443–1509)   (1442–83)   (1452–85)

Henry VII
(1457–1509)

Henry VIII
(1491–1547)

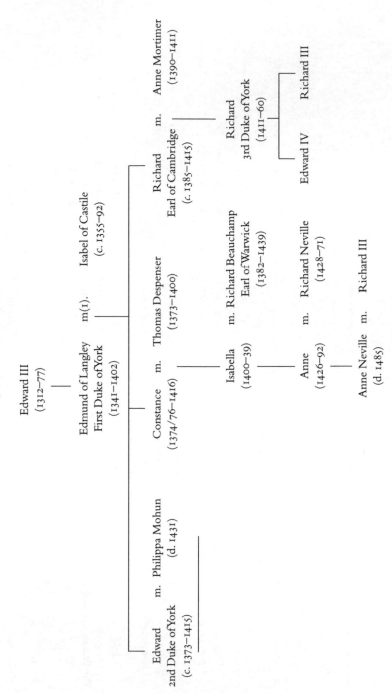

5.THE HOUSE OF YORK

Edward III
(1312–77)

Edmund of Langley   m(1).   Isabel of Castile
First Duke of York   (c. 1355–92)
(1341–1402)

Edward   m.   Philippa Mohun
2nd Duke of York   (d. 1431)
(c. 1373–1415)

Constance   m.   Thomas Despenser
(1374/76–1416)   (1373–1400)

Richard   m.   Anne Mortimer
Earl of Cambridge   (1390–1411)
(c. 1385–1415)

Isabella   m.   Richard Beauchamp
(1400–39)   Earl of Warwick
                   (1382–1439)

Richard
3rd Duke of York
(1411–60)

Anne   m.   Richard Neville
(1426–92)   (1428–71)

Edward IV   Richard III

Anne Neville   m.   Richard III
(d. 1485)

6. MOWBRAYS AND ARUNDELS

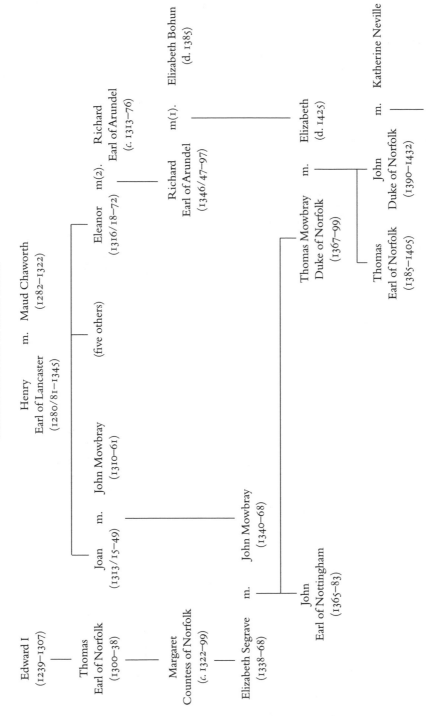

7. CLARENCE, MORTIMER AND VERE

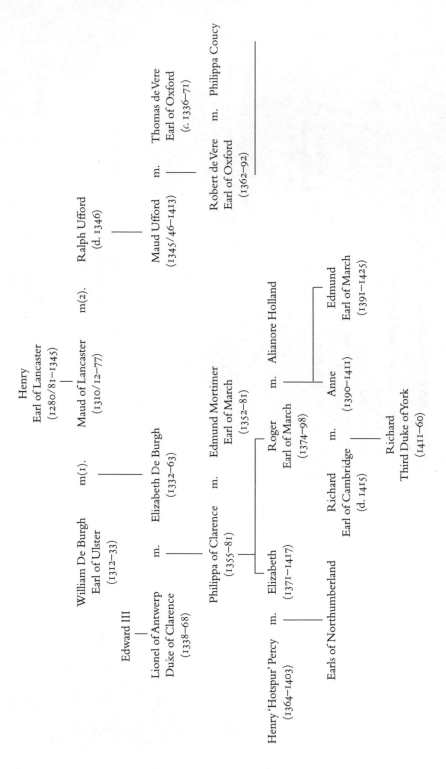

8. ARUNDELS, HOLLANDS, STAFFORDS AND YORKS

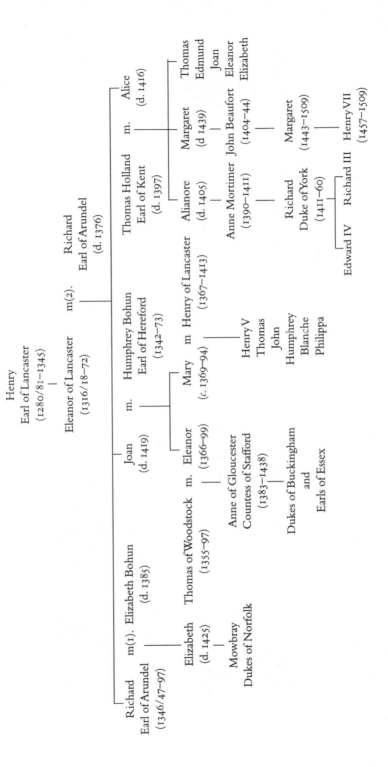

9. CHILDREN AND GRANDCHILDREN OF EDWARD III

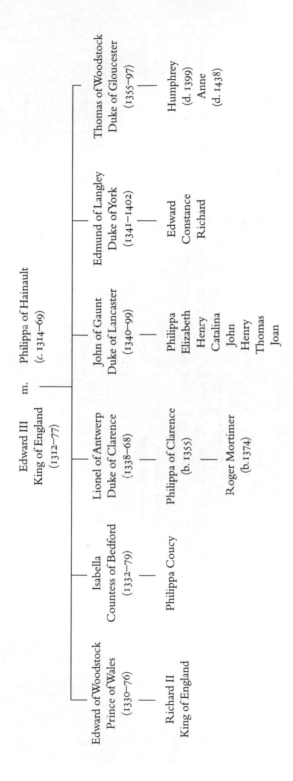

Edward III
King of England
(1312–77)

m.

Philippa of Hainault
(c. 1314–69)

Edward of Woodstock
Prince of Wales
(1330–76)

Isabella
Countess of Bedford
(1332–79)

Lionel of Antwerp
Duke of Clarence
(1338–68)

John of Gaunt
Duke of Lancaster
(1340–99)

Edmund of Langley
Duke of York
(1341–1402)

Thomas of Woodstock
Duke of Gloucester
(1355–97)

Richard II
King of England

Philippa Coucy

Philippa of Clarence
(b. 1355)

Philippa
Elizabeth
Henry
Catalina
John
Henry
Thomas
Joan

Edward
Constance
Richard

Humphrey
(d. 1399)
Anne
(d. 1438)

Roger Mortimer
(b. 1374)

10. THE BEAUMONTS

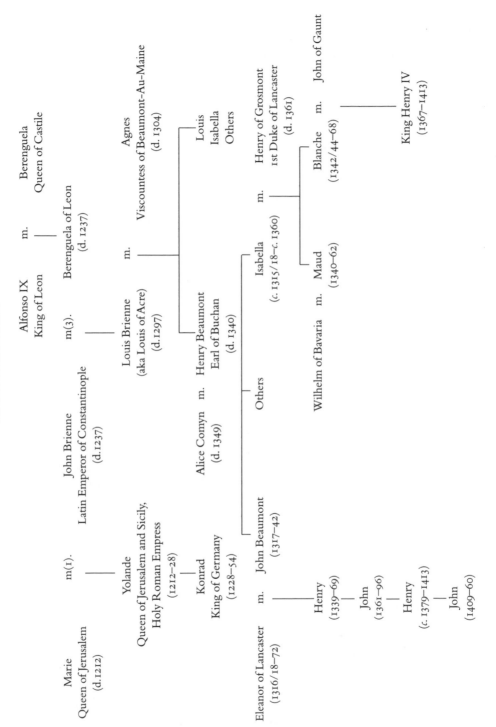

INTRODUCTION

I n the middle of the fifteenth century, two branches of the English royal family began a decades-long series of conflicts known to posterity as the Wars of the Roses. They were the Houses of Lancaster and York, and *Blood Roses* tells their story before they became deadly rivals. The symbol of the House of York was a white rose, and that of the House of Lancaster a red rose, hence the modern name for the series of wars between them and the title of the present book.

The House of Lancaster was founded in 1267, when Henry III created the earldom of Lancaster for his second son Edmund, and the House of York in 1385 when Richard II bestowed the new dukedom of York on his uncle, also Edmund. The book opens in 1245 with the birth of Edmund of Lancaster, first Earl of Lancaster, and closes in 1400 with the accession of the first Lancastrian King of England, Henry IV, and the murder of his cousin and predecessor, Richard II. One of Richard II and Henry IV's first cousins was Edward, second Duke of York, whose heir was his nephew Richard, third Duke of York and later the Yorkist claimant to the throne as the senior descendant of Edward III's second son. Henry IV, his son Henry V and grandson Henry VI were descendants of Edward's third son, and the decades of war between the two rival branches of the royal family were ultimately caused by the question of whether the descendants of Edward III's second son in the female line should take precedence over the descendants of his third son in the male line.

PART I
1245–96

PART I

1243–96

DRAMATIS PERSONAE

Edmund of Lancaster (b. 1245): fourth child and second son of Henry III and Eleanor of Provence; first Earl of Lancaster and founder of the House of Lancaster; also Earl of Leicester and Steward of England

Henry III (b. 1207) and **Eleanor of Provence** (b. *c.* 1223): King and Queen of England; Edmund's parents

Aveline Forz (b. 1259), Countess of Aumale in her own right, heir to the earldom of Devon: daughter of William Forz, Earl of Aumale (d. 1260), and Isabella Redvers, Countess of Devon (b. 1237); marries Edmund of Lancaster in 1269

Blanche of Artois (b. *c.* 1245/48), Dowager Queen of Navarre, Countess of Lancaster: marries Edmund as his second wife in *c.* late 1275, and the mother of his children; niece of Louis IX, King of France, and widow of Enrique I, King of Navarre (d. 1274)

Robert, Count of Artois (1216–50), son of Louis VIII of France and brother of Louis IX, and **Mathilde of Brabant** (1224–88): parents of Blanche of Artois; grandparents of Edmund's children

Jeanne I, Queen Regnant of Navarre, Queen Consort of France (b. 1273): only child of Enrique I and Blanche of Artois; stepdaughter of Edmund of Lancaster; marries Philip IV of France

Thomas of Lancaster (b. 1277/78): eldest child and heir of Edmund and Blanche; half-brother of Queen Jeanne; second Earl of Lancaster

Henry of Lancaster (b. 1280/81): second child of Edmund and Blanche; heir of his childless brother Thomas and ancestor of all the later Lancasters; third Earl of Lancaster

John of Lancaster (b. before May 1286): obscure third child of Edmund and Blanche; spends almost all his life in France

Edward I, King of England (b. 1239): eldest child of Henry III and Eleanor of Provence, and his father's successor on the throne; Edmund of Lancaster's brother

Margaret (b. 1240), married to King Alexander III of Scotland, **Beatrice** (b. 1242), married to Duke John I of Brittany's eldest son John, and **Katherine** (b. 1253, dies young): Edmund and Edward's sisters

Leonor of Castile, Queen of England (b. *c*. 1241): daughter of Fernando III, King of Castile and Leon in Spain, and his second wife Jeanne of Ponthieu; marries Edward in 1254; Edmund's sister-in-law

Richard of Cornwall (b. 1209), Earl of Cornwall, elected King of the Romans (i.e. Germany) in 1257: brother of Henry III, and Edmund of Lancaster's uncle

Henry of Almain (b. 1235) and **Edmund of Cornwall** (b. 1249): sons of Richard of Cornwall; Edmund's first cousins

Simon de Montfort, Earl of Leicester (b. *c*. 1208): French nobleman married to Henry III's youngest and only surviving full sister **Eleanor** (b. 1215); Edmund of Lancaster's uncle by marriage; has five sons, Henry, Simon, Amaury, Guy and Richard, and one daughter, Eleanor, who marries Llywelyn ap Gruffudd

Louis IX (b. 1214), King of France: married to **Marguerite of Provence**, sister of Eleanor, Queen of England; uncle of Blanche of Artois, and Edmund of Lancaster's uncle by marriage

Philip III (b. 1245), King of France: son of Louis and Marguerite; first cousin of both Edmund of Lancaster and Blanche of Artois; married to Isabel of Aragon (d. 1271), then Marie of Brabant (d. 1321)

Philip IV (b. 1268), King of France; son of Philip III and Isabel of Aragon; marries Edmund of Lancaster's stepdaughter Jeanne I of Navarre in 1284

Alexander III, King of Scotland (b. 1241): marries Edmund's sister Margaret in 1251

Margaret of Scotland, Queen of Norway (b. 1261): eldest child of Edmund's sister Margaret and Alexander III; marries Erik II of Norway in 1281

Margaret 'the Maid' of Norway (b. 1283): only child of Margaret of Scotland and Erik II; her grandfather Alexander III's heir; betrothed to her cousin Edward of Caernarfon in 1289

Edward of Caernarfon (b. 1284): fourth but only surviving son of Edward I and Leonor of Castile; heir to the English throne and later King Edward II; Edmund of Lancaster's nephew

Eleanor, Joan of Acre, Margaret, Mary and Elizabeth (1269–82): surviving daughters of Edward and Leonor; Edmund's nieces

John (b. 1266–71), **Henry** (1268–74) and **Alfonso of Bayonne** (1273–84): elder sons of Edward and Leonor

Robert Ferrers, Earl of Derby (b. *c.* 1239): enemy of Edmund of Lancaster, who takes his earldom of Derby in 1269; married to Marie de Lusignan, Edmund's first cousin; his sister Elizabeth Ferrers marries Dafydd ap Gruffudd

Henry de Lacy, Earl of Lincoln (b. 1250/51): son of Edmund de Lacy and Alesia di Saluzzo; grandson and heir of Margaret de Lacy (née de Quincy), Countess of Lincoln in her own right; long-term friend and ally of Edmund of Lancaster; marries Margaret Longespee, Countess of Salisbury in her own right

Alice de Lacy (b. 1281): daughter and heir of Henry de Lacy and Margaret Longespee; marries Thomas of Lancaster in 1294; Edmund's daughter-in-law

NOT THE KING OF SICILY

⸺◦◦◦⸺

On Monday, 16 January 1245, either in London or at the Palace of Westminster, Eleanor of Provence, Queen of England, went into labour for the fourth time. Her husband Henry III had already decided that the child should be a boy and ordered monks to stand outside Eleanor's birthing chamber and chant about St Edmund, a king of East Anglia murdered by the invading Danes in 869 and later canonised. The king had 1,000 candles placed around the shrine of the murdered Archbishop St Thomas Becket in Canterbury Cathedral and another 1,000 in the Canterbury church of St Augustine, specifically to ensure the queen's safe delivery. Queen Eleanor did indeed give birth to a boy, who was duly named Edmund after the holy murdered king. A delighted King Henry paid for a robe of expensive samite, a kind of silk, for Queen Eleanor's purification (a ceremony held forty days or so after birth) and for another robe for Edmund's christening, and offered an embroidered chasuble, which cost him 5 marks, at the high altar of Westminster Abbey in gratitude. The king also paid 25s to Master Walter Elenches and his fellows for singing *Christus Vincit* before the queen during her purification forty days after Edmund's birth.[1]

In the boy's own lifetime and long afterwards, his name was spelled Esmon, Edmon, Eymon, Emon or Esmoun and was probably pronounced

'Aymohn', and the nickname for boys and men called Edmund was 'Monde'. Henry III and Eleanor of Provence's son Edmund is often known to history by the nickname 'Crouchback', though the reasons behind this name are somewhat mysterious, and it is generally thought nowadays to mean 'crossed back' with reference to his Crusade to the Holy Land at the beginning of the 1270s. Then again, many or even most European noblemen of the age went on Crusade and none of them gained the nickname 'crossed back' because of it, and there seems no particular reason to believe that Edmund was famously more pious than anyone else of his era. The nickname Crouchback appears not to date to Edmund's own lifetime, but to have been given to him in the late fourteenth century, almost 100 years after his death, when his descendants were claiming the throne and a tale that he was Henry III's elder son but was put aside in favour of his brother Edward I because of his physical disability was invented. There is no reason whatsoever to suppose that Edmund was hunchbacked or suffered from any other kind of deformity, and none of his contemporaries so much as hinted at it.[2]

Edmund was the royal couple's second son, following Edward in June 1239, and hence was the 'spare' part of the proverbial 'heir and the spare'. He also had two older sisters: Margaret, born in September 1240 and named after their aunt the Queen Consort of France, and Beatrice, born in June 1242 and named after their grandmother the Countess of Provence. Curiously, although Queen Eleanor was still only about 21 years old at the time of Edmund's birth in early 1245, she had no more children with the sole exception of Katherine, born in November 1253, almost nine years after Edmund, who died at age 3½ in May 1257. There may, of course, have been miscarriages or stillbirths which we do not know about.[3] Edmund was born in his father's twenty-ninth regnal year; aged 37 at his second son's birth, Henry III had become King of England as a 9-year-old in October 1216 when his father, King John, died suddenly the year after being forced to sign the Magna Carta. In January 1236, after a long series of false starts in attempting to find a suitable bride, Henry married Eleanor of Provence, who was probably only 12 at the time and about sixteen years his junior, and whose elder sister Marguerite was already married to Louis IX of France. The third Provence sister, Sancha, married Henry's brother Richard, Earl of Cornwall in November 1243, fourteen months before Edmund's birth.

The Provence sisters were the daughters of Ramon-Berenger, Count of Provence, who died on 19 August 1245 when his grandson Edmund was 7 months old, still only in his 40s. Edmund's paternal grandmother Isabelle of Angoulême, widow of King John and the Dowager Queen of England, also died not long after his birth, on 4 June 1246. Her eldest child Henry III ordered 'divine service daily' to be said at Marlborough Castle in Wiltshire for her soul on 31 August.[4] Within months of Isabelle's death, five of her nine children from her second marriage to the Count of La Marche, the Lusignans, had made their way to England to be greeted with enormous generosity and affection on the part of their half-brother Henry III.

As is almost always the case with children of the Middle Ages, even royal children, little is known of Edmund's upbringing and childhood. By 1246, the year after his birth, he was living at Windsor Castle with his older siblings and was officially in the care of Aymon (or 'Eymo') Thurbert, constable of Windsor and guardian of the king's children. A special area near the north corner of the castle had been constructed for the royal offspring in May 1241, before Beatrice and Edmund were born: it consisted of a chamber next to the chapel with its own fireplace, and another chamber two storeys high, with two fireplaces. Two men called Hugh Giffard and Peter Wakering received 100 marks (£66) for looking after the royal children at Windsor in May 1246, and silver cups, dishes, sauces and an alms-dish were purchased for the children's use that October.[5] Edmund's nurse was called Pernell, wife of Clement Foliot, and he had his own cook called Master William. His sister Beatrice, two and a half years his senior, was looked after by Agnes Eversle, and their brother Edward by Alice of Luton.[6] Although there is no direct evidence for it, the likelihood is that both Edward and Edmund learned to read and write: their first cousin Henry de Montfort, born in late 1238 and just a few months Edward's senior, wrote out his father Simon's will in his own (very neat and legible) hand on 1 January 1259.[7] It is also probable that Edmund learned to speak English as well as French, his first language (or rather, the dialect of French used by the medieval English elite, which in modern times is called Anglo-Norman); his brother Edward could speak English.[8] The royal siblings must also have learned Latin.

Edward, who had been given a long-dead Anglo-Saxon royal saint's name even more unfashionable than his younger brother's – had Edward been anyone other than the King of England's first son, he would have been teased unmercifully for his hilariously outdated moniker – was five and a half years older than Edmund, and heir to their father's throne. The boys' names reveal how much Henry III venerated St Edward the Confessor, the King of England who died in January 1066 and was canonised as a saint ninety-five years later, as well as St Edmund. In early 1247, perhaps to mark his younger son's second birthday, Henry gave an expensive gold cup to contain the Host to the abbey of St Edmund's in Suffolk, and later that year told the sheriff of Suffolk to 'feed as many poor … as can be found in his neighbourhood' on St Edmund's feast day.[9] This is just one of countless examples of Henry III's huge generosity in helping the poor.

Edward, Margaret, Beatrice and Edmund had the great good fortune to be born into a close-knit and loving family. Whatever Henry III's failings as a ruler, he and Eleanor of Provence adored their children, and all of them except perhaps Edward when he was older basked in it. When 7-year-old Edward became seriously ill in the summer of 1246, the queen insisted on staying with him at Beaulieu Abbey in Hampshire for three weeks, despite the prohibition on women living within a Cistercian house and regardless of the monks' immense displeasure at her presence. The king's huge relief at his son and heir's eventual recovery is demonstrated by his spending over £30 to feed the poor in his great hall at Westminster 'for the love of him who made the king's son safe and sound'. Henry also paid a chaplain in Dover Castle in 1246 to celebrate divine service daily 'to preserve the king and his household from sudden death', which suggests that he was preoccupied at this time with serious illness, and this was mere weeks before his mother Isabelle of Angoulême passed away. His younger son Edmund was also ill several times in 1252–53 and was attended by three of the queen's physicians. The boy was also bought a kind of barley sugar, perhaps simply because he had a sweet tooth rather than for medicinal purposes.[10]

When the royal couple heard that their elder daughter Margaret was being denied access to her young husband, the King of Scotland, and even being held in something closely resembling captivity, they themselves rode all the way to Edinburgh to set things right. Margaret was so determined to give birth to her first child in the company of her mother in 1260/61 that she probably lied to her husband and the Scottish nobles about the progress of her pregnancy to achieve it.[11] The second daughter Beatrice and her husband John of Brittany voluntarily spent much of their time at the English court, and several of their children lived in England for most of their lives. When little Katherine, the surprise daughter born so many years after her siblings, died in May 1257 at the age of 3½ – she was mute and perhaps also deaf – the king and queen grieved so much they became deathly ill.[12] In later years, Eleanor of Provence also demonstrated much warmth, affection and concern for her grandchildren. Among many other examples, she herself raised her grandson Henry (one of Edward's many children) and was with him when he died at age 6 in 1274, and in 1290, near the end of her life, begged her son Edward not to take his little son Edward of Caernarfon to the north of England as the air was bad and would make him ill.[13]

As well as his older brother and sisters, Edmund had plenty of cousins. There were the two sons of his uncle Richard of Cornwall, Henry III's younger brother: Henry, known to history as Henry of Almain (meaning Germany, as Richard of Cornwall was elected King of Germany in 1257), who was born in 1235, and Edmund of Cornwall, who was born at the end of 1249 and as well as sharing Edmund's name was his first cousin on both sides, as their fathers were brothers and their mothers sisters. Next came the many sons and one daughter of Henry III's youngest full sister Eleanor and her husband Simon de Montfort, Earl of Leicester, a French nobleman who had arrived in England to seek his fortune in about 1230 and succeeded beyond his wildest dreams by marrying no less a person than the king's sister. The Montfort boys were Henry, Simon, Amaury and Guy, plus the much younger Richard and the only girl, named Eleanor after her mother. Henry III's other two full sisters, Joan the Queen of Scotland and Isabella the Holy Roman Empress and Queen of Sicily, had died in 1238 and 1241 respectively, only in their 20s; Joan left no children, and Isabella had only one child who survived into adulthood, Margarethe von Hohenstaufen (d. 1270), Countess Palatine of Saxony and landgravine of Thuringia. Henry III, always a generous giver of charity and aid to those in need, fed hundreds of poor people on the anniversaries of his sisters' deaths every year.[14] Seven of the king's nine younger half-siblings, the Lusignans, from his mother's second marriage, had offspring of their own, and Henry III also had numerous other half-siblings who were the illegitimate children of his father King John. Edmund's mother's elder sister Marguerite and her husband Louis IX of France were raising a large family, including the future king Philip III, and the youngest Provence sister Beatrice married Louis IX's brother Charles of Anjou in 1246 and gave Edmund several more first cousins including a king of Naples, a queen of Hungary and a titular emperor of Constantinople. In a pleasing piece of symmetry, the four sisters married two sets of brothers, and all four were, famously, to become queens.

Royal life in the early 1250s, the first years Edmund would be able to remember, proved eventful. Edmund's uncle by marriage, Louis IX, had departed from France in 1248 for Egypt with his younger brothers Robert, Count of Artois, Alphonse, Count of Poitiers and Charles, Count of Anjou, to lead the Seventh Crusade. (Henry III also took the cross in 1250, though ultimately never went.) Robert of Artois was killed in action at Mansourah in February 1250. His son and heir Robert the younger was born several months after his death, and he also left a daughter, Blanche, who one day would marry Edmund. At Christmas 1251, Edmund's sister Margaret married King Alexander III of Scotland; she was 11 and he was 10. The amount of food provided for the wedding feast in York was truly staggering: 68,500 loaves of bread, 60,000 herring, 25,000 gallons of wine, 7,000 chickens and 170 boars, among much else.[15] Among the items Henry III purchased for his daughter's wedding, and for her life in Scotland afterwards, were a gold cup, a gold chalice and six gold spoons, and 20 marks' worth of books for her chapel.[16]

In 1251–52, the intense rivalry between the king's numerous half-siblings, the Lusignans, and the queen's numerous uncles, the Savoyards (brothers of Eleanor of Provence's mother Beatrice of Savoy), spiralled out of control, and chronicler Matthew Paris commented on the hostility between the two powerful alien factions at the English court. Henry III's anger with Queen Eleanor over her meddling in politics reached a peak when he exclaimed, 'How high does the arrogance of woman rise if it is not restrained?' and packed his wife off to Guildford in Surrey.[17] The royal couple did eventually reconcile, though this argument between his parents and the endless squabbling among their kin – as well as the happier occasion of his sister's marriage to young Alexander of Scotland – were perhaps among Edmund's earliest memories.

Far to the south, Alfonso X inherited Castile and Leon, two of the four kingdoms of medieval Spain, from his father Fernando III in May 1252, and immediately set about trying to expand his territory northwards. Claiming that his great-grandmother Eleanor of England had been given the large and rich duchy of Aquitaine in the south-west of France as her dowry on marrying Alfonso VIII in 1177, Alfonso X incited a rebellion there in 1253 with a view to invading and taking over the duchy. The Duke of Aquitaine was none other than Henry III, King of England, who had inherited it from his father King John and John's mother, the redoubtable Eleanor of Aquitaine (also the mother of Alfonso's great-grandmother Eleanor of England, Queen of Castile). An elegant solution presented itself to Henry: he had a 14-year-old son, Lord Edward, heir to the English throne, and Alfonso had a half-sister Leonor, aged 12. He proposed that Edward and Leonor should marry, whereby Leonor would one day become Queen of England and Duchess of Aquitaine, and hoped that Alfonso could thus be persuaded to give up his claim to the duchy. And so it came to pass.

Queen Eleanor therefore departed from England on 29 May 1254 with her elder son Edward the bridegroom and her younger son Edmund, now 9 and leaving his homeland for the first time (though certainly not the last). No fewer than 300 ships were required to carry the royal party from Portsmouth to Bordeaux.[18] Edward was born into a large family and was also marrying into one: his soon-to-be wife Leonor was the twelfth of her father's fifteen children and had eleven brothers and half-brothers. Her mother, Jeanne de Ponthieu, was French and Countess of Ponthieu in northern France in her own right, and married the widowed Fernando III of Castile and Leon in 1237 when he was 36 and she about 17. Somewhat peculiarly, Jeanne had been married by proxy to Henry III in 1235 and Henry wrote to her father soon afterwards to arrange a time and date for her to be crowned Queen of England, which all had to be sorted out by the Pope before their children could marry. Leonor, Jeanne and Fernando's second child, was born probably in late 1241.[19] She and Edward married in Burgos in northern Spain on or around 1 November 1254, at the monastery of Las Huelgas which had been founded by her great-grandparents Alfonso VIII and Eleanor of England. Leonor's young brother-in-law Edmund was in attendance as well as her half-brother Alfonso X, who knighted the young groom before the ceremony, though her mother the dowager queen, Jeanne, did not attend, having left Castile under something of a cloud following a dispute with her stepson Alfonso X over her dower. Edward and Leonor began building their own large family around 1260; it is difficult to establish precisely how many children they had, though it was at least fourteen and perhaps more.

Not long before the English royal family's departure from England in May 1254, the papal nuncio in England, Alberto di Parma, had formally offered 9-year-old Edmund the throne of Sicily. Edmund's aunt Isabella, Henry III's second sister who died in 1241, had been the third wife of one of the most fascinating men of the European Middle Ages: Frederick II, Holy Roman Emperor and King of Sicily. Frederick was known to his contemporaries as *Stupor Mundi* or the Wonder of the World. On his death in 1250 Frederick left Germany and his northern territories to his eldest son Konrad (whose mother Yolande was Queen of Jerusalem in her own right), while Sicily ultimately went to his illegitimate son Manfredi, whom he had appointed regent of the kingdom.[20] Frederick had a long-standing battle with the papacy; several popes had excommunicated him, officially deposed him as emperor and even, so he said, attempted to poison him, and they continued this vendetta against his son Manfredi. Pope Innocent IV had previously offered the throne of Sicily to Edmund's uncle, Henry III's younger brother Richard, Earl of Cornwall. Ever the realist, Richard declared that he might as well attempt to reach up and seize the moon. Thrilled at the thought of his second son ruling in Sicily, however – and the kingdom of Sicily in the thirteenth century covered much of the Italian mainland as well as the island – and somewhat lacking in practical common sense, Henry III eagerly accepted on Edmund's behalf. On 25 May 1254 he had a great seal made for Edmund as King of Sicily and, eighteen months later, the papal nuncio di Parma formally invested the boy with the kingdom by putting a ring on his finger.[21]

Two major obstacles stood in the way of Edmund's glorious reign as an Italian king: the person of Manfredi (the Wonder of the World's son) and money. Henry III went before his barons and asked for their support, both military and financial, in the venture. Seeing no possible advantage to themselves of paying to take armies halfway across Europe merely so that a child could become King of Sicily, the English magnates refused. Despite this setback, Henry and Queen Eleanor refused to give up and persisted for years in their grand dream of seeing their boy ascend a throne in distant southern Italy. Their efforts included dressing the then 12-year-old Edmund in Apulian clothes and parading him before Parliament in 1257, which, not entirely surprisingly, failed to move the English magnates to action on his behalf. One wonders why Henry ever thought it might, and whether the adolescent Edmund found the experience as embarrassing as it sounds. Pope Alexander IV presented Henry with a bill of a staggering 135,541 marks, or more than £90,000, for his campaigns against Manfredi, who in the meantime had upgraded himself from regent to crowned King of Sicily. This, in modern terms, is equivalent to billions of pounds, and represented three years' government revenue in England. And all for nothing; despite Henry's insistence on his son being addressed as 'king of Sicily' and sending a letter on Edmund's behalf to the Pope in June 1257 dated 'in the second year of his reign', and despite Edmund himself sending a letter as late as March 1261 asking his Sicilian subjects to prepare for his arrival, he never laid eyes on the place.[22]

As part of the king and queen's deeply felt desire to gain a crown for their younger son, in April 1256 negotiations took place for Edmund to marry the widowed Queen of Cyprus.[23] Her name was Plaisance of Antioch, and she was the daughter of Bohemund, Prince of Antioch and Count of Tripoli, and the widow of Henry I 'the Fat' de Lusignan, King of Cyprus. She was about a decade Edmund's senior, and the mother of and regent for Hugh II of Cyprus. This also came to nothing, as did negotiations in 1257 for Edmund to marry Manfredi of Sicily's daughter, Constanza.

2

ROYAL CONNECTIONS

⟨⟨⟨⟩⟩⟩

I n late 1254, Edmund visited his uncle-in-law Louis IX in Paris with his parents Henry III and Eleanor of Provence. Also present were Edmund's aunts, Queen Eleanor's three sisters – Louis' queen Marguerite, Sancha, Countess of Cornwall, and Beatrice, wife of Louis' youngest brother Charles of Anjou – and their mother Beatrice of Savoy, Dowager Countess of Provence and the only one of Edmund's grandparents he ever met. The royal visit was, by any standards, a roaring success, and a magnificent spectacle. Louis exclaimed to Henry, 'Have we not married two sisters, and our brothers the other two? All that shall be born of them, both sons and daughters, shall be like brothers and sisters.'[1] Thibaut, the teenage King of Navarre in northern Spain, who married Louis and Marguerite's daughter Isabelle a few months later, was also in Paris. He, Louis IX and Henry III jointly held a splendid feast which was attended by French magnates and bishops and eighteen ladies of the rank of countess or above. Henry impressed his hosts by feeding large numbers of the poor and making numerous lavish gifts to the French court.[2] On the English royal family's departure from France, Louis presented Henry with an elephant, and in February 1255 Henry ordered the sheriffs of London to make a building in the Tower of London 40ft long and 20ft wide 'without delay' for the animal.[3] Although her presence is not mentioned, it is possible that Edmund's future wife

Blanche of Artois met the royal English guests, including Edmund. She was Louis IX's niece, her mother Mathilde was the widow of Louis' brother Robert, and some years later she married Thibaut of Navarre's brother and heir Enrique, so it makes sense that she would have been there.

After the royal family's return to England, Edmund and his older sister Beatrice continued to live at Windsor Castle with a chaplain, a clerk, a washerwoman, six valets and a cook called Master Godwin. With them lived their baby sister Katherine (born in November 1253), the king's niece Marie Ferrers (née de Lusignan), whom Henry III affectionately called 'Mariota', and Henry de Lacy, heir to his grandmother Margaret de Quincy's earldom of Lincoln. Henry was born in 1250 or 1251 and was half-Italian via his mother Alesia di Saluzzo, and four decades later his daughter would marry Edmund's eldest son. Edmund and Beatrice's older sister Margaret, married since the age of 11 to Alexander III, lived in Scotland, though Henry III bought blue cloth for a cape for her in November 1254 and a silver ewer in February 1255, and in July 1253 had asked Alexander to give his wife permission to visit her mother Queen Eleanor (it was not forthcoming). Another resident of Windsor Castle was Edmund's half-uncle Guy de Lusignan, one of the king's nine younger siblings from his mother's second marriage, who lived in a tower of the castle overlooking the town.[4]

The married Edward, now 16, returned to England from Spain and Gascony in November 1255, and Edmund was sent to Dover to meet him. Edward's wife Leonor had arrived in England for the first time a few weeks before, and offered a gold buckle at the Westminster shrine of St Edward the Confessor, the king's favourite saint, after whom her husband had been named.[5] Little Katherine, Edward and Edmund's sister, died at the age of 3½ in May 1257. Her grieving father the king paid over £50 for her funeral at Westminster, which 12-year-old Edmund must have attended, and 70 marks for a 'silver image' to place on her tomb. The image may have been of St Katherine. The little girl's tomb still exists in Westminster Abbey, though was displaced from its original location after the death of Richard II's queen, Anne of Bohemia in 1394.[6]

Edmund never gained a crown, but in 1257 his uncle Richard of Cornwall did. The kings of Germany, almost uniquely in Europe, were elected and not hereditary, and were chosen by seven powerful electors: the archbishops of Cologne, Mainz and Trier, the King of Bohemia, the

Count Palatine of the Rhine, the Duke of Saxony and the margrave of Brandenburg. Richard's chief rival was his nephew Edward's brother-in-law Alfonso X of Castile, and Richard finally won the battle by virtue of having more money with which to bribe the electors than the Castilian king. He and his wife Sancha of Provence set off to be crowned at Aachen in May 1257.

In 1266, Edmund's uncle by marriage Charles, Count of Anjou, would manage to take the kingdom of Sicily which Edmund's parents had so desired for him. Much closer geographically to Italy than Edmund, much older and more experienced, and with the wealth of his wife Beatrice's county of Provence and her influential uncles of Savoy behind him, Charles invaded Italy, defeated and killed King Manfredi at the Battle of Benevento, and was crowned King of Sicily. Charles had Manfredi's 16-year-old nephew Konradin publicly beheaded in Naples, imprisoned Manfredi's wife Helena Angelina Doukaina for the rest of her life, and had their four young sons imprisoned and blinded. The whole venture began atrociously and ended badly – Charles of Anjou ended his life ignominiously expelled from his kingdom with his son and heir in captivity – but it did have the happily romantic result of making the youngest Provence sister Beatrice as much of a queen as her three older siblings, which for some later writers was really all that mattered.

Richard of Cornwall, King of Germany, was to spend little of the remaining fifteen years of his life in his new kingdom. Events in England proved more pressing. Carried away with the romance of his youngest sister Eleanor marrying the dashing young French nobleman Simon de Montfort in 1238, Henry III had given permission for them to wed clandestinely but almost immediately came to regret it, and Richard of Cornwall led a brief baronial revolt against his brother, provoked by his fury over their sister's secret marriage. Simon de Montfort and Eleanor named their first son, born in late 1238, after his uncle the king, but tensions broke out at the ceremony following Queen Eleanor's purification after the birth of her son Edward the following year, and Henry III and de Montfort were to have an uneasy relationship for decades. De Montfort was given the inhumanly difficult task of ruling over Gascony, the larger part of Henry's duchy of Aquitaine, and was put on trial in England in May 1252 over his failures there. He was acquitted, but the whole procedure did nothing to smooth his relationship with his brother-in-law the king, and in the 1250s he quarrelled with both Henry's half-brother William de Valence (one of the Lusignans) and Queen Eleanor's mighty uncles from Savoy.

In July 1260 King Henry brought more charges against Simon de Montfort, and in 1258 was forced to consent to the Provisions of Oxford, a series of reforms and limitations on royal power proposed by de Montfort and twenty-three others. One hugely important and far-reaching reform was the proposal that three Parliaments be held every year, and the Provisions of Oxford also placed the king under the authority of a small council of fifteen men. The Provisions were sent out to all the sheriffs of England in Latin, French and English. These astonishingly radical reforms, which removed all the king's executive power from him, would soon be overturned and it would be hundreds of years before anything similar was seen again.

The king's second son Edmund was in France with his parents between November 1259 and April 1260 – he passed his 15th birthday abroad – when Henry III met Louis IX and thrashed out the terms of the Treaty of Paris, signed on 3 December 1259.[7] The English kings' control of much of south-west France caused endless strife between themselves and the kings of France in the Middle Ages, and Henry and Louis attempted to repair the damage with their treaty. Henry III gave up his and his heirs' claims to the Duchy of Normandy, which his father King John had lost to Louis IX's grandfather King Philip Augustus of France in 1204, as well as Anjou, Touraine, Maine and Poitou. In return, Louis recognised his right to hold Gascony. Edmund made an official notification that he 'accepts the said peace and that he has sworn on the Gospels to observe it'.[8] By the standards of the day the treaty was a triumph of diplomacy and good sense, and healed long-standing wounds between the two kingdoms, but unfortunately in the long run it made matters worse, as it stated that the English kings had to travel to France to swear homage to their overlord for their French lands every time either a king of England or France succeeded to the throne. This required the English king, albeit in his capacity as Duke of Aquitaine and not as the ruler of a sovereign nation, to kneel to the French king. (The kings of Scotland, who held lands in England, were in the same awkward position.) Henry III's elder son and heir Edward was opposed to the treaty, and he and his successors loathed the ceremony of homage they owed to the King of France and did all they could to delay it or even wriggle out of performing it.

Henry III, Queen Eleanor and Edmund spent Christmas 1259 at the French court, and Eleanor gave gifts of rings to her sister Marguerite the Queen of France, Marguerite's daughter Isabelle the young Queen of Navarre, Eleanor and Marguerite's sister Beatrice of Provence, Countess of Provence and Anjou (and future Queen of Sicily), and many others. They were still in France on 11 January 1260 when Louis and Marguerite's eldest son Louis, heir to the throne of France, died at the age of not quite 16, leaving his brother Philip as their father's heir. The King of England acted as one of the pall-bearers, and Edmund must also have attended his cousin's funeral in Royaumont Abbey. His elder sister Beatrice of England's wedding was postponed for a few days out of respect, though such was the cordial affection between the royal families of England and France that the grieving parents chose to attend their niece's wedding.[9] After their return to England a few months later, Henry III bought his second son a palfrey horse at a cost of 10 marks, and Edmund wrote to his putative subjects in Sicily asking them to prepare for his arrival there.[10] Neither he nor his parents had completely given up on their Sicilian project yet, though nothing ever came of it.

Seventeen-year-old Beatrice of England married John, son and heir of Duke John I of Brittany, on 22 January 1260 in France, and Edmund's other sister Margaret and her husband Alexander III, King and Queen of Scotland, came to England on a royal visit later in the year. Chronicler Matthew Paris wrote that Queen Eleanor loved her Scottish son-in-law as though he were her adopted son.[11] When Eleanor was pregnant with her youngest child Katherine in July 1253, Henry III had asked Alexander to allow Margaret to come south to keep the queen company while he himself sailed to Gascony; although permission was not given, this is yet another example of the English royal family's closeness.[12] In 1260, Queen Margaret of Scotland may have pretended that her first pregnancy was less advanced than it actually was in order to remain in England with her mother and give birth there. The 19-year-old Alexander III returned north in November 1260, not before holding his father-in-law to a solemn vow that Margaret and her child would travel to Scotland after her purification ceremony, and that in case Margaret died in childbirth, the infant would be sent to Scotland to his or her father.[13] Alexander and his nobles were understandably alarmed at the prospect of the future King of Scotland being born in England under the jurisdiction of the

English king, and potentially kept there as a hostage. In the end, the child born at Windsor on 28 February 1261 was a girl, named Margaret after her mother. Little Margaret of Scotland was probably not Henry III and Eleanor of Provence's first grandchild, as Edward and Leonor had likely had one or two of their numerous offspring by then, but she was the eldest to live into adulthood. Not to be outdone, Queen Margaret's younger sister Beatrice gave birth to her first child five months later, on 25 July 1261: the future Duke Arthur II of Brittany.

Edmund's aunt Sancha of Provence, sister of his mother Eleanor and married to his father's brother Richard of Cornwall, died on 9 November 1261 only in her early 30s, and was buried at Hailes Abbey in Gloucestershire, which Richard himself had founded some years before. She left her only surviving child Edmund of Cornwall, not quite 12 at the time. Sancha had a quieter personality than her sisters, and even though she was the Queen of Germany, her death barely caused a ripple; Richard himself was not even present at his wife's deathbed.

3

BARONIAL WARS

—⟨oɜɜɔo⟩—

I n late 1261 when Edmund was almost 17, Henry III considered a marriage for him with a daughter of Guy Dampierre, the long-lived Count
of Flanders – Guy was born in the 1220s and lived until 1305 – and
asked the advice of his recently widowed brother Richard of Cornwall,
King of Germany. Nothing came of it, however.[1] Edmund went overseas
again with his brother Edward and father the king in July 1262, seeking
the support of Louis IX against the 1258 Provisions of Oxford, which
would, as far as Henry III was concerned, intolerably limit his powers.
Edmund's mother the queen and his sister-in-law Leonor of Castile,
Edward's Spanish wife and the future Queen of England, also went. One
of Leonor's attendants on the journey was Edward's former nurse Alice of
Luton.[2] While the royal party was in Paris in September 1262, a serious
illness broke out among Henry III's household which killed dozens, and
Henry and Edmund themselves were badly affected. Edmund was sent
home to England to recuperate, and the king only recovered his strength
very slowly.[3] On 10 January 1263, six days before his 18th birthday, Edmund
was given custody of the lands of the recently deceased Earl of Devon,
Baldwin Redvers, who had died childless in his 20s. He was one of the
sixty or so victims of the serious illness which struck the English royal
family and court in September 1262.[4] In October 1260, Edmund's brother

Edward had been granted custody of the lands and the marriage rights of the children and heirs of Redvers' late brother-in-law William Forz, Earl of Aumale or Albemarle, and in August 1263 Edmund himself was given the rights to the marriage of Forz's widow Isabella, Baldwin Redvers' sister and heir.[5] Edmund later married Redvers' niece Aveline Forz, fifth but only surviving child of Isabella and William Forz.

The political situation in England slowly deteriorated as two rival political factions formed, the royalist party and the baronial party, the latter led by Henry III and Richard of Cornwall's brother-in-law Simon de Montfort, Earl of Leicester. Originally Edmund's elder brother Edward, who had turned 21 and thus officially come of age in June 1260, took the side of his uncle de Montfort against his father the king and made a pact with him in October 1259, but later switched sides and was to become his father's loyal supporter. The unpopular Queen Eleanor, while sailing on her barge on the Thames between London and Westminster on 13 July 1263, was pelted with rubbish and filth by a mob and had to be rescued by the mayor. Edward's utter fury at this insult to his mother resulted in his slaughter of men fleeing from a battlefield where he faced his uncle de Montfort the following year, for no better reason than the men came from London. Edward's brother Edmund was appointed as custodian of the great castle of Dover on the Kent coast in June 1263 as civil war loomed, but went abroad with his parents and his elder brother that September, and remained on the continent with the queen after Henry III and Edward returned to England, aiding his mother in her attempts to raise mercenaries to invade England and help Henry against his brother-in-law de Montfort. Edmund was to remain outside England until October 1265, and therefore played no role in the momentous events of 1264–65. Problems also arose in Wales in the 1260s, when Llywelyn ap Gruffudd, Prince of Wales, led a Welsh revolt on the lands of the English baron Roger Mortimer of Wigmore (Llywelyn's first cousin) and prepared for a more general uprising. Edmund was appointed as the captain of his father's forces, at least nominally – he was, after all, still only a teenager – but Llywelyn retreated into the impenetrable fastness of Snowdonia beyond the reach of Edmund and his men.

Both English political factions, royalist and baronial, agreed in 1263 to subject themselves to the arbitration of Louis IX of France, and Henry III left England for the French court on 28 December 1263.[6] Louis settled the matter in the Mise of Amiens on 23 January 1264, and probably predictably given that Henry III was his brother-in-law and a fellow king, found entirely in favour of Henry and annulled the 1258 Provisions of Oxford. Such a one-sided and unfair settlement naturally enough did not appease Simon de Montfort and his baronial allies, and left them with little choice but armed rebellion. The reasons behind the barons' wars of the 1260s are highly complex, but dissatisfaction with the king and with the favouritism he showed towards his Lusignan half-brothers were chief among them, as was the considerable amount of money the king wasted trying to gain the crown of Sicily for his younger son Edmund. Among Simon de Montfort's allies were Sir Hugh Despenser, justiciar of England, whose grandson of the same name would become notorious as Edward II's powerful and despotic favourite a few decades later, and Gilbert 'the Red' de Clare, Earl of Gloucester and Hertford. Gloucester was born in September 1243, so was barely even into his 20s, and was unhappily married to one of Edmund's countless cousins, Alice de Lusignan. Their marriage – arranged in February 1252 when they were both children – would be annulled many years later, and Gloucester would marry one of Edmund's nieces instead.[7] When Gloucester's father Richard died in 1262, Henry III gave his widow Maud (née de Lacy), Gloucester's mother, a dower which unfairly included several of Gilbert's chief lordships, and this was a factor which pushed the belligerent young earl in opposition to him. Gloucester's younger brother Thomas de Clare was, however, a close ally of Edward and his father the king.

Fighting broke out in February 1264, and a few weeks later Henry III raised Simon de Montfort's siege of Rochester Castle in Kent and captured Tonbridge in Kent and Winchelsea in Sussex from the rebels. On 14 May 1264, when Edmund and his mother the queen were still abroad, the royalist and baronial forces fought each other at the Battle of Lewes in Sussex. Simon de Montfort's two eldest sons, Henry and Simon, were among the leaders of their father's army and acquitted themselves well, but on the other side, neither Henry III nor his brother Richard of Cornwall was much of a battle commander. Henry's son Edward was, but he was so busy bravely and honourably chasing down de Montfort's contingent of soldiers from London (who were fleeing from the battlefield on foot) and slaughtering them – all to avenge the Londoners' insult to his mother the year before – that he only came back to the battlefield hours later to find the battle lost and his father Henry III and uncle Richard captured, and his half-uncle Guy de Lusignan dead. (Richard of Cornwall, no less a person than the King of Germany, was humiliatingly taken prisoner while hiding in a windmill.) Edward had no choice but to surrender, and spent the next few months in comfortable captivity, as did his father and uncle, while Simon de Montfort, Earl of Leicester and his sons and allies ruled the kingdom in their stead. Edmund and his mother the queen remained overseas. At some point in 1264 or 1265, Simon de Montfort the younger (probably born in 1240, and Edward and Edmund's first cousin) tried unsuccessfully to abduct Edmund's wealthy future mother-in-law Isabella Forz (née Redvers), Countess of Devon, with a view to marrying her. Isabella fled to Wales, claiming that de Montfort had chased her around England with horses and arms.[8]

In May 1265 Edward escaped from captivity in Hereford with the aid of the Earl of Gloucester's brother Thomas de Clare, and Gloucester himself switched sides and joined the young heir to the throne against his former ally the Earl of Leicester. Edward raised an army, and on 4 August 1265 met his uncle's forces at Evesham in Worcestershire. Edward's younger brother Edmund was not present, being still outside England, and neither was their cousin Henry of Almain, though this counted for nothing six years later when two of de Montfort's sons killed him in revenge for what happened to their father on 4 August 1265. Evesham proved to be less a battle than a slaughter and was an overwhelming victory for the royalists, and the great Earl of Leicester himself was killed, along with his eldest son Henry de Montfort (he who had beautifully written out his father's will a few years before) and his close ally Sir Hugh Despenser. Guy, the fourth son, managed to escape from the battlefield, and Simon, the second, arrived with reinforcements just in time to witness the grotesque spectacle of his father's head going past on a spike. The Earl of Leicester's body was desecrated, and Roger Mortimer of Wigmore, a great baron of Herefordshire and the Welsh Marches who was a close ally of Henry III and his sons, sent de Montfort's head and testicles as a macabre gift to his wife Maud Braose at their castle of Wigmore. Guy de Montfort fled overseas and was joined later by his older brother Simon the younger after Simon managed to escape as well, and Henry III's sister Eleanor, Montfort's widow, also left England and spent the remaining ten years of her life in voluntary exile in France. Louis IX and Marguerite of Provence treated her, a woman who was the daughter and sister of kings, with the utmost respect and honour.

Less than three months after Evesham, on 26 October 1265, Edmund received the lands of the late Simon de Montfort from his father, and was styled Earl of Leicester from January 1267 onwards. He also became Steward of England, another title once held by Simon. Edmund did not return to England until 30 October 1265, four days after the grant, with his mother, the queen.[9] It remained for Henry III and his sons to try to reconcile the remaining Montfortians, though one man not trusted by either side was Robert Ferrers, Earl of Derby. Ferrers was born around 1239 so was almost exactly Edward's age, and in 1249 when they were both children, he married Marie 'Mariota' de Lusignan, one of Henry III's many half-nieces and Edward and Edmund's cousin. Ferrers' father died in 1254 when Robert was 15, and custody of his lands was given to Edward. Edward was feuding with Robert Ferrers in the mid 1260s; before the Battle of Lewes he attacked Ferrers' Staffordshire castle of Tutbury and ravaged his lands, and after Lewes, Ferrers in turn attacked Edward's lands in Cheshire and Derbyshire. Henry III thanked Ferrers' tenants on 22 May 1266 for 'having left the ways of levity of the said Robert and given their adherence to himself and his first-born son'.[10]

On 28 June 1266, Edmund received supposedly temporary custody of the earldom of Derby, which in 1269 was stolen from Robert Ferrers and given to him permanently in a particularly unpleasant piece of legal underhandedness. Edmund's brother Edward had Ferrers kidnapped and imprisoned and only released on a promise to pay the impossibly large sum of £50,000 to get his lands back, which in modern terms would be equivalent to a high-ranking government official taking away your property and promising to return it provided that you hand over £10 billion in cash by the end of the quarter.[11] Ferrers was violent and unpopular, and had switched sides during the conflicts and hence was trusted by no one, but that was no excuse for taking his patrimony away from him, and the earldom of Derby had belonged to his family since 1138. Of course, he defaulted on the impossible payment, and so he and his family lost their earldom forever by the doing of the king's son with the full knowledge of the king and his other son Edmund, beneficiary of this unpleasantness. Edmund's cousin Henry of Almain, Richard of Cornwall's elder son and heir, was also involved.

As late as December 1301, Robert Ferrers' son John was trying to claim his rightful inheritance from Edmund's son Thomas. Edward, by then King of England for almost thirty years, spitefully forbade John to pursue the claim by threatening him with 'forfeiture of all he can forfeit'. He ordered him to appear before King's Bench to explain why he was pursuing the case (as though the king did not know).[12] In 1318, Edmund's son Thomas hired a chaplain to say masses for the souls of five people: his parents, grandparents Henry III and Queen Eleanor, and Robert Ferrers, so perhaps he had a guilty conscience.[13] Robert Ferrers' great-nephew Henry, Lord Ferrers of Groby, was a close associate and ally of Edmund's second son and ultimate heir, Henry, for many years, so perhaps Henry was in some way attempting to make amends for what his father and uncle had done.

Although they and their descendants certainly held the Ferrers lands, neither Edmund nor his sons Thomas and Henry added 'Earl of Derby' to their list of titles, preferring to call themselves 'Earl of Lancaster and Leicester, Steward of England'. It is doubtful whether they thought of themselves, or were considered by others to be, earls of Derby. During the reign of Edmund's nephew Edward II, one chronicler still referred to the earldom of Derby as 'the earldom of Ferrers', so even fifty or sixty years later it was still strongly associated with Robert Ferrers and his family.[14] Edward II himself also called it 'the earldom of Ferrers' in October 1324.[15] In May 1322 Edward II referred to his uncle Edmund as 'late Earl of Leicester and Derby', but this is very rare, and occurred in a letter appointing the custodian of a forest formerly owned by Edmund's second wife Blanche of Artois, who between 1276 and 1298 held all the Ferrers lands as dower from Edmund.[16] Edmund's grandson Henry of Grosmont, first Duke of Lancaster, was created Earl of Derby in 1337 during his lifetime of his father (Edmund's second son Henry), and the title was given to Grosmont's 10-year-old grandson the future King Henry IV, heir of the Lancasters, in 1377.

4

THE FIRST LANCASTER

On 30 June 1267 came the grant which gave Edmund and his dynasty their name: the brand new earldom of Lancaster, the town in north-west England which gives its name to the county of Lancashire and is its capital, and which in the twenty-first century has a population of about 50,000. He also received the Welsh lordship of Monmouth and a gift of the so-called 'Three Castles' in Wales: Grosmont, Skenfrith and White Castle.[1] Edmund's grandson Henry, first Duke of Lancaster, was almost certainly born at Grosmont, and Edmund's great-great-great-grandson Henry V, second of the three Lancastrian kings of England, was born at Monmouth. Edmund appears only to have styled himself 'Earl of Lancaster' almost ten years later, in December 1276, and received other lands from his father and brother including the Staffordshire town of Newcastle-under-Lyme and the castle and town of Pickering in Yorkshire. Edmund served as high sheriff of Lancashire between 1267 and 1269, a position held in later years by his two eldest sons, grandson and great-grandson-in-law. By now, Edmund also owned the magnificent castle of Kenilworth in Warwickshire, once a royal castle which Henry III had given to Simon de Montfort in 1253. The Montfortian garrison holding out there under siege – a siege in which Edmund himself took part as commander of one of the four royal battalions – for six months from June 1266 had finally been compelled to surrender on 13 December 1266 as they had almost run out of food, and three days later Henry III granted the castle to his second son.[2] This was probably the longest siege of a castle in English history. Within a rather short time, Edmund had become a landowner of great importance: the inquisition into his holdings taken shortly after his death reveals that he held property in 632 separate locations in twenty-five counties in England and Wales, and owned fourteen castles.[3] His descendants increased this already massive inheritance, and Edmund's grandson Henry, first Duke of Lancaster, owned lands in no fewer than thirty-four of the thirty-nine historic English counties at his death in 1361.

Edmund briefly visited France in early June 1267 when he attended the knighting of his cousin the future King Philip III of France, second but eldest surviving son of Louis IX and Queen Marguerite. Perhaps Edmund saw his future second wife Blanche of Artois when her brother Robert, Count of Artois, entertained him during the visit; like Edmund, the Artois siblings were first cousins of the King and Queen of France's children. Philip of France was now 22 years old and was almost exactly Edmund's own age, just a few weeks younger (born on 30 April 1245). That autumn, Edmund arranged some jousting tournaments with his brother Edward and their cousin Henry of Almain, after his return to England.[4] Their aunt Beatrice of Provence, Queen of Sicily, died on 23 September 1267, the same month as the late King Manfredi's German nephew Konradin took up arms against her husband Charles of Anjou, which resulted in the boy's public beheading a year later. Like her older sister Sancha, Beatrice was probably only in her early 30s when she died, and her widower Charles wasted little time arranging another marriage for himself.

To the utter fury of her older sisters Marguerite, Eleanor and Sancha, their father Ramon-Berenger had left the county of Provence to his fourth and youngest daughter Beatrice in its entirety on his death in 1245. Generations later, their descendants were still trying to win a share of the county. In May 1286 Queen Eleanor of England bequeathed her claim to Provence to her Lancaster grandsons, the sons of Edmund, with the consent of Edmund and his brother King Edward. In early 1322, shortly before his death, Edmund's eldest son Thomas of Lancaster was still trying to get hold of a share of Provence from his second cousin Robert, King of Sicily and Count of Provence (grandson and heir of Beatrice of Provence and Charles of Anjou), using Pope John XXII as an intermediary. John XII wrote to Robert of Sicily and Provence on Thomas' behalf, but rebuked Thomas for failing to speak courteously enough of the Sicilian king.[5] Thomas' cousin Edward II, another grandson of Eleanor and heir of the third sister Sancha, also wrote to King Robert in 1323 asking for a share of Provence, though nothing came of it.[6] As late as October 1366, 121 years after Ramon-Berenger's death and eighty years after Eleanor of Provence's bequeathing of her rights in Provence to her Lancaster grandsons Thomas and Henry, John of Gaunt, husband of Edmund of Lancaster's great-grand-daughter and heir Blanche of Lancaster, asked for the 1286 bequest be inspected and confirmed.[7]

Crusading fever was in the air in northern Europe in the late 1260s. The Sultan of Egypt, al-Baibars, and his forces had been busily capturing Antioch and other Crusader towns and fortresses, and the Christians of the Holy Land begged European rulers for aid and support. In April 1268, Pope Clement IV absolved Henry III from a previous vow to go on Crusade if he sent his second son Edmund instead.[8] Edmund, his brother Edward, their cousin Henry of Almain, their uncle William de Valence, Gilbert de Clare the Earl of Gloucester, John de Warenne the Earl of Surrey, and numerous other young English noblemen took the cross and vowed to go to the Holy Land on 24 June 1268.[9] Louis IX, who had already spent years on Crusade in Edmund's childhood, desired to go again, and on the second occasion he took his son and heir Philip and Philip's half-Spanish, half-Hungarian wife Isabel of Aragon with him as well as his brother Alphonse of Poitiers and sister-in-law Jeanne of Toulouse, his son Jean Tristan, and his daughter Isabelle and her husband Thibaut, King of Navarre. Leonor of Castile also decided to accompany her husband, and Edmund and Edward's sister Beatrice to accompany hers, John of Brittany.

But before the adventure of Crusade came the adventure of marriage for Edmund of Lancaster. On 9 April 1269 at Westminster Abbey, Edmund married an heiress named Aveline Forz, who was only 10 years old to his 24 (she was born in Burstwick, Yorkshire on 20 January 1259, and spent part of her childhood in the custody of Sir Ralph Bray, Constable of Scarborough Castle).[10] Aveline's father William Forz, who died in May 1260, was Count of Aumale (or Albemarle), and her mother Isabella (née Redvers) was the heir to her late brother Baldwin, and received the earldom of Devon and the lordship of the Isle of Wight after his death in September 1262. Henry III had considered the possibility a few months before of marrying

Edmund to the widowed Isabella (b. 1237) herself, though in the end he married her daughter.[11] Aveline's four older siblings were all already dead by 1269, and marriage to her was intended to give Edmund a fourth earldom and extensive lands on top of the ones he already held, plus the promise of yet another when his mother-in-law died.

Three days before the wedding, Edmund's mother the queen promised to pay £1,000 each to Aveline's mother Isabella and to Isabella's mother Amice, Dowager Countess of Devon and sister of Richard, late Earl of Gloucester, for the marriage.[12] Rather amusingly, the queen's letters patent contained the phrase 'if it shall happen that [Edmund's] courage should change so that after espousal he should abandon the said Avelina during her life, and take another wife … '. Edmund did not abandon Aveline, but of course she was far too young to consummate the marriage for a few years, and he spent a long time, until the end of 1272, outside England. A few weeks after Edmund and Aveline's wedding, Edmund's cousin Henry of Almain, elder son and heir of Richard of Cornwall, married Constance of Béarn, whose father Gaston was a restive and troublesome subject of Henry III in Gascony.

A few months after his wedding in Westminster Abbey, Edmund returned there with his family, including his sister and brother-in-law Margaret and Alexander III, King and Queen of Scotland, to attend the ceremony when the bones of St Edward the Confessor were moved there and reburied. Henry III had been rebuilding the abbey church for decades, and the chapel he had had constructed for the Confessor was finally ready. Edmund met his sister Queen Margaret at St Albans and was of the important men of the realm designated to attend his brother-in-law the King of Scotland, and carried the bier containing the saint's bones to their splendid new resting place on 13 October 1269, St Edward's feast day, with his brother, his father the king and his uncle Richard of Cornwall.[13]

Finally the time came to depart for Crusade, and Edward, with his brother-in-law John of Brittany and John de Warenne, Earl of Surrey, left England on 20 August 1270. Edmund of Lancaster himself seems not to have travelled with them but to have remained in England until early 1271.[14] His brother missed the planned meeting with their uncle-in-law Louis IX, who had sailed for Tunis rather than the Holy Land in support of his brother Charles of Anjou, King of Sicily. The King of France died near Tunis on 25 August 1270, five days after his nephew Edward left England, probably of the dysentery cutting a terrible swathe through his army. Over the next few months the French royal family trailed slowly home, and the years 1270–71 took an astonishingly heavy toll on them. As well as Louis, his eldest daughter Isabelle, Queen of Navarre, and her husband Thibaut died, as did Louis' daughter-in-law Isabel of Aragon, who briefly reigned as Queen Consort of France as the wife of Philip III and who was the mother of the future Philip IV, Louis' brother Alphonse, Count of Poitiers, Alphonse's wife Jeanne of Toulouse, Louis' 20-year-old son Jean Tristan, and his 16-year-old daughter Marguerite, Duchess of Brabant. Louis IX's widow Marguerite of Provence, who had sensibly remained behind in France after taking part in her husband's earlier crusade, lived on; she outlived her husband by a quarter of a century, and also outlived all but three of her eleven children. Her son Philip III succeeded his father as king, while in the small kingdom of Navarre between France and Spain, Enrique I succeeded his childless brother Thibaut, with Blanche of Artois, Louis IX's niece, as his consort.

Despite the massive setback of his uncle Louis' death, Edward decided to press on to the Holy Land, disregarding his father's request to return to England, and travelled there via Sicily and Cyprus. While his and Edmund's cousin Henry of Almain was passing through Sicily, Henry took the chance to pray at the church of San Silvestro in Viterbo, and was followed there by his cousins Simon and Guy de Montfort, second and fourth sons of his uncle the Earl of Leicester, killed at the Battle of Evesham in 1265. Guy, a stronger and altogether more violent personality than his older brother, stabbed Henry to death in the church on 13 March 1271 in revenge for his father's murder (even though Henry of Almain, like his cousin Edmund of Lancaster, had not been present at the Battle of Evesham). Simon de Montfort the younger died later in 1271 near Siena, 'cursed by God, a wanderer and fugitive'.[15] Guy, the only de Montfort brother who inherited his father's charisma and chutzpah, survived and even thrived after his 1271 excommunication for Almain's murder; he served Charles of Anjou, King of Sicily, and married the daughter of an Italian count. Anastasia, the elder of his two daughters, was an ancestor of Edward IV's queen Elizabeth Woodville (d. 1492), and thus de Montfort blood returned to the English royal family in the fifteenth century. Guy's luck ran out when he was captured in 1287, and he died in about 1291 in a Sicilian prison. The third de Montfort brother Amaury, who had joined the Church, died in about 1300, and the fifth and very obscure brother Richard appears to have died young in France. Eleanor, the only de Montfort daughter, married Llywelyn, Prince of Wales, though was captured by the notorious pirate Eustace the Monk on the orders of her cousin Edward I on her way to wed Llywelyn, and spent some time in comfortable confinement before being allowed to proceed with her wedding in 1278.

Leonor of Castile gave birth to her and Edward's latest child at Acre in the Holy Land in the spring of 1272, and called her daughter Joan; she is usually known to history as Joan of Acre, and later married Gilbert 'the Red' de Clare, Earl of Gloucester, who was nearly thirty years her senior. Edward survived an assassination attempt by Sultan al-Baibars in Acre on his 33rd birthday, 17 June 1272, and the knife used to stab him was kept and was still held in the English treasury at Westminster in the early 1340s.[16] Although he and Edmund did not yet know it, their uncle Richard, Earl of Cornwall and King of Germany, had died on 2 April 1272 at the age of 63. He had never recovered from the murder of his elder son Henry of Almain at the hands of his de Montfort nephews, and suffered from a stroke in late 1271. Richard's heir was his younger son Edmund of Cornwall, child of the late Sancha of Provence; his third marriage to the German noblewoman Beatrix von Falkenburg, who was about forty-five years his junior, produced no children. Edmund of Cornwall married Margaret de Clare, sister of Gilbert 'the Red', Earl of Gloucester, in October 1272, but it turned out to be an unhappy and childless match which ended in annulment.

Another death that Edward and his wife Leonor only learned about much later was that of their eldest son John, whom they had left behind in England in the care of Richard of Cornwall and who died aged 5 in August 1271. Edward, when he heard of the deaths of both his eldest son and his father much later, made a remark which seems callous even by the standards of the age, to the effect that he mourned his father's loss much more than John's as he could have more sons but never another father. One wonders if this flippant remark came back to haunt him in later years when he lost another two sons in childhood, and had to deal with the possibility of his throne passing to a daughter. Little John was never heir to the throne as he died in the lifetime of his grandfather Henry III, though if he had survived to adulthood he would have become King John II of England in July 1307 on the death of his father Edward.

On 16 November 1272 at Westminster, King Henry III himself finally slipped away at the age of 65, to the background of a London mob outside his palace noisily demanding the election of a new mayor.[17] He had been little more than a cipher for the last few years of his life and is probably one of the least-known kings of England, yet reigned for fifty-six years, the fourth-longest reign in English history behind Elizabeth II, Victoria and George III. Hardly anyone would place Henry III high on the list of best English monarchs, but he should be remembered for his great rebuilding of Westminster Abbey in the new Gothic style; the work he commissioned was not finished until centuries after his death, but much of what still exists today dates from Henry's time. He was buried at Westminster Abbey, the first of many English kings to be buried there down the centuries, and his funeral was attended by his queen Eleanor of Provence and the great English magnates including Gilbert de Clare, Earl of Gloucester; John de Warenne, Earl of Surrey; and Humphrey de Bohun, Earl of Hereford. None of Henry's children, Edward, Margaret, Beatrice and Edmund, were even in England at the time of his death. Edward, far away in the Holy Land, was now, though he did not know it, King of England.

5

THE KING'S BROTHER

───⊗⊗⊗───

Thre are hints in a couple of letters from Pope Gregory X shortly after Henry III's death in late 1272 that all was not well between the royal brothers Edward and Edmund: Gregory asked the new king Edward on 30 November to be 'favourable to' Edmund and show him 'brotherly kindness', and wrote to Queen Eleanor on the same date asking her to 'promote and preserve affection between her sons'.[1] If they had had some kind of row, however, it cannot have been a serious one, and Edmund remained a loyal supporter of his brother for the rest of his life. Edmund of Lancaster left the Holy Land in May 1272 – historian Walter Rhodes pointed out rather unkindly though accurately that he 'did little or nothing there' – and arrived back in England around 6 December, three weeks after the death of his father. He visited his mother Eleanor of Provence, now the dowager queen, a few days later.[2] In late 1276 King Edward I was to empower two men to 'bind him [the king] or Edmund, Earl of Lancaster, his brother, to go on the next passage to the Holy Land', but neither Edmund nor Edward would ever go on crusade again.[3] Edmund may have consummated his marriage to Aveline Forz not long after 20 January 1273 when she turned 14, and they were given possession of all her lands in seven counties on 2 February that year as she had come of age (21 for men but only 14 for women, or 15 if they were not yet married).[4]

On 14 January 1273, Louis IX's niece and Edmund's future second wife Blanche of Artois gave birth to a daughter called Jeanne, who would be her only surviving child with her first husband King Enrique I of Navarre.

Before Jeanne of Navarre was a year old, on 30 November 1273, her father Enrique came to an agreement with Edward I that she would marry Edward's second son Henry, then 5 years old and heir to the English throne (as his elder brother John had died in 1271).[5] Just a few months later in July 1274, however, King Enrique died at the age of about 30, and the baby Jeanne succeeded as Queen of Navarre in her own right. The widowed Queen Blanche, worried about the kings of Castile and Aragon casting their beady eyes on her vulnerable baby daughter's kingdom, left Navarre in 1275 and took Jeanne to the safety of the French court and the protection of her cousin Philip III. The French king was as eager as Edward I to snap up the great heiress for one of his sons, and Jeanne was duly betrothed to Philip (b. 1268), the king's eldest son from his first marriage to the late Isabel of Aragon and heir to the French throne. The planned union between Jeanne of Navarre and Henry of England never came about, and Henry died in October 1274 anyway. Edward I made the future marital arrangements for their children with King Enrique of Navarre while in his duchy of Aquitaine, where he and Queen Leonor were then staying, travelling back to England from the Holy Land in leisurely fashion. Their third son Alfonso was born in Bayonne in the far south-west of France in November 1273 and named after his uncle and godfather Alfonso X of Castile, and their second surviving daughter Joan of Acre (b. spring 1272) did not return to England until 1278, staying in northern France with her grandmother Jeanne, Dowager Queen of Castile and Countess of Ponthieu.

Rumours flew around England in 1273–74 that Edward I might never return to his kingdom, and sometime in 1273 an armed uprising – about which little is known – took place in the north of the country. Edmund of Lancaster, with his long-term ally and companion Henry de Lacy, now Earl of Lincoln, and a few others, besieged the manor of Chartley in Staffordshire which was one of the few properties his adversary Robert Ferrers had been allowed to retain when his patrimony was taken from him. Edmund and the others were pardoned for 'any deaths caused' during the siege almost ten years later, in December 1282.[6] Gilbert de Clare, Earl of Gloucester, was less than impressed, writing 'it does not seem that there can be tranquillity in the land, nor is the king's lordship worth anything if the people of the land can assemble forces like this in times of peace'.[7]

Edward and Leonor of Castile finally returned to England on 2 August 1274 and were crowned king and queen at Westminster Abbey on 19 August. Although their sister Margaret, Queen of Scotland, attended, it seems that Edmund of Lancaster boycotted the ceremony following a row with his brother over who should carry the great sword of mercy, Curtana, during the procession. He is not mentioned in the list of magnates who were present, and also fell out with his brother over Edward's refusal to make him hereditary Steward of England, as he had requested.[8] The king, however, soon forgave his brother for this snub, and Edmund forgave his brother for his, and on 21 October 1274 Edward pardoned Edmund some debts so evidently they were on better terms by then.[9] This is another example of how Edmund and Edward could sometimes quarrel and fall out but always managed to mend things in the end, and the overall pattern is one of affection on both sides and immense loyalty on Edmund's, and a normal brotherly relationship which sometimes saw mutual irritation but which never broke entirely. Relationships between royal brothers in the Middle Ages could often be hostile and acrimonious, and it is much to Edmund of Lancaster's credit that he remained loyal to his older brother for the rest of his life.

Two deaths struck at the English royal family in the last months of 1274. The king's second (but eldest surviving) son Henry died in October at the age of 6, at Guildford in Surrey in the custody of his grandmother, the Dowager Queen Eleanor of Provence, leaving his 11-month-old brother Alfonso of Bayonne as heir to the throne. And Edmund of Lancaster's wife Aveline Forz died on 10 November 1274, still only 15 years old.[10] She may have borne twins, or she may have been pregnant twice: the chronicler Nicholas Trivet (who wrote his work at the request of Edward I's daughter Mary) says she and Edmund had two children, though neither of them survived – not surprisingly, given Aveline's extreme youth. A custom called the 'courtesy of England' allowed a man to keep all his wife's inheritance in his hands until his own death, provided they had at least one child together who drew breath. As Aveline's children, assuming Trivet was correct that she had them, did not live, her lands should have reverted to her heirs, who in 1275 were named as five distant cousins, instead of to Edmund.[11] Her mother Isabella (née Redvers), however, gave them to Edward I on her deathbed in 1293, surely with some coercion involved.[12] Aveline was buried in Westminster Abbey in a magnificent ceremony conducted by the Archbishop of Canterbury, and many years later Edmund was buried next to her, even though he had been married to another woman for twenty years and had three children with her. This perhaps suggests that his feelings for Aveline went beyond mere desire for her lands, and that he genuinely mourned and missed her. Their tombs can still be seen today.

In January 1275, two months after his young wife's death, Edmund of Lancaster turned 30. As though losing Aveline and the young heir to the throne, Henry, was not enough, death continued to stalk the English royal family in 1275. On 26 February Edmund lost his sister Margaret, Queen of Scotland, who was 34, leaving her widower Alexander III and their three children, Margaret, Alexander and David. Less than a month later their other sister Beatrice followed her to the grave, at the age of only 32. Beatrice never became Duchess of Brittany, as she died in the lifetime of her father-in-law John I (who lived long enough to see the birth of his great-grandson, the future John III – grandson of John II and Beatrice and son of Arthur II, in 1286). Her sixth and youngest child Eleanor of Brittany, a future abbess of Fontevrault in France, was born in 1275 and Beatrice may have died as a result of childbirth: she was perhaps already seriously ill on 23 February, a month before her death, when her husband received permission to grant land to various chaplains in return for celebrating divine service for Beatrice's soul and his after death.[13] The chronicler Thomas Wykes commented that the Queen Mother Eleanor of Provence grieved terribly at losing her two daughters in such quick succession, though her grief was somewhat tempered by the joy she took in their children.[14] And in April 1275 Edmund's aunt Eleanor, widow of Simon de Montfort and the youngest and only surviving of King John's five legitimate children, died in France where she had lived in exile for the previous ten years. She had taken vows as a nun at Montargis Abbey south of Paris, a foundation of her late husband's sister Amice, who was its abbess.

Edmund of Lancaster left England for Navarre soon after 25 November 1275, and sometime between 18 December 1275 and 18 January 1276, a little over a year after Aveline Forz's death, married for the second time.[15] His bride was Blanche of Artois, Dowager Queen of Navarre, who held the county of Champagne during the minority of her toddler daughter Jeanne, Queen of Navarre and Countess of Champagne and Brie in her own right. Blanche's father Robert, Count of Artois, had been the brother closest in age to Louis IX and died in action at Mansourah in Egypt in February 1250, when Blanche was between 2 and 5 years old (she was close to Edmund's own age and much older than Aveline Forz). Her mother Mathilde, who lived until 1288, was the daughter of Duke Henryk II of Brabant in the Low Countries and his first wife the half-German, half-Byzantine Marie von Hohenstaufen, a granddaughter of two emperors. Mathilde of Brabant's sister Maria, Blanche of Artois' aunt, was probably betrothed to Edmund of Lancaster's brother Edward in 1247, at least informally, and in 1256 was beheaded for adultery by her husband Duke Ludwig of Bavaria. Blanche was named after her paternal grandmother Blanca or Blanche of Castile (d. 1252), the powerful Queen of France who ruled as regent for her underage son Louis IX and who was a granddaughter of Henry II of England and Eleanor of Aquitaine. Blanche of Artois had known tragedy: she and Enrique of Navarre had a baby son who fell from the battlements of Enrique's castle at Estella, and died.[16] Her daughter Jeanne, or Juana, was the first queen regnant of Navarre (though she rarely if ever visited her kingdom after she left it as a toddler) but certainly not the last: Jeanne's granddaughter reigned as Jeanne II, and later in the Middle Ages came Blanca, Leonor and Catalina. The last queen regnant of Navarre was Jeanne III, whose son Henri de Bourbon became King of France in 1589.

King Philip III of France was a first cousin of both Edmund of Lancaster and Blanche of Artois, and his mother the Dowager Queen Marguerite of Provence actively promoted the marriage of her nephew and niece-in-law. They made an entirely suitable couple, and Blanche brought Edmund control of the rich county of Champagne until they sold it to Philip III in 1284. They may have met for the first time in 1267 when Blanche's younger brother Robert, Count of Artois, entertained Edmund during his visit to France to attend the knighting of the future Philip III.[17] It is even possible that the couple had met much earlier, as children in 1254 when Edmund visited Paris and the court of Louis IX with his parents. Count Robert of Artois was not pleased about his sister's marriage to Edmund, supposedly because Edmund's brother Edward, the King of England, had no love for his cousin the King of France, but the St Albans chronicler states that Edmund and Blanche had heard good reports of each other and were mutually attracted.[18] Another chronicler, writing a century and a half later, claimed that Blanche had a love affair with the baron Roger Mortimer (d. 1282), and that at a jousting tournament held at Kenilworth in 1279 sent him barrels of gold coins 'like a latter-day queen of Pamphylia in love with Hector'. Mortimer, meanwhile, supposedly wore a jewel on his armour in Blanche's honour for the rest of his life (only another three years).[19] A love affair seems extremely unlikely, though does make a pleasantly romantic story, and Roger Mortimer did hold a tournament at Kenilworth in 1279 at which Blanche of Artois gave him wine barrels filled with gold.[20]

The newlyweds spent a few months in France after their wedding and were in England – presumably it was Blanche's first time there – by 9 June 1276. Edmund dowered Blanche with a third of his lands, as was customary, including all the lands formerly of Robert Ferrers, and Edward I confirmed the grant on 29 October 1276.[21] For the rest of his life Edmund travelled very regularly between England and France, and was said to be 'going to the parts of Navarre' on 26 July 1276 only a few weeks after he had returned to England. He was in France by early September 1276 and remained there until the spring of 1277, and went overseas yet again in early 1278.[22] Edmund was summoned on campaign against Llywelyn ap Gruffudd, Prince of Wales, in late 1276, and was 'going to the March' in April 1277 shortly after his return from France. He led an army into South Wales, with the Marcher lord Sir Payn Chaworth as his second in command; Chaworth's niece and heir Maud later married Edmund's second son and ultimate heir Henry. Edmund took the opportunity to go on pilgrimage to St Davids, returning to England on 20 September 1277 for a few months before he headed off to France again.[23]

Edmund of Lancaster and Blanche of Artois' eldest child Thomas was born in late 1277 or early 1278, two years after their wedding. The name was an unusual one in the royal families of both England and France at the time, so the couple perhaps named their son in honour of Thomas Becket, a saint much revered by English royals of the thirteenth and fourteenth centuries. On 9 September 1298, Thomas' uncle Edward I stated that he 'considers [Thomas] as of full age' and allowed him to have possession of his father's lands.[24] This demonstrates that Thomas was not yet 21 years old on 9 September 1298 and thus was born after 9 September 1277, though probably not too long after. His name may indicate that he was born on or around 29 December 1277, as Thomas Becket was murdered on 29 December 1170 and this date became his feast day, though this is only speculation. The townspeople of Leicester gave 5 marks to the 'messenger of the Lady Queen of Navarre after her delivery' of Thomas, though it is difficult to date this entry more precisely than sometime in Edward I's sixth regnal year, 20 November 1277 to 19 November 1278.[25] The Inquisition Post Mortem (IPM) of Thomas' father-in-law the Earl of Lincoln in late February 1311 says that Thomas was then '32 and more' or 33 years old, which fits well with a date of birth at the end of 1277 or beginning of 1278.[26]

Thomas of Lancaster must have been born in England or another territory ruled by his uncle Edward I, as birth in his mother's native France, outside the allegiance of the King of England, would have caused legal problems when it came to inheriting his father's lands and earldoms. This would happen to his father Edmund of Lancaster's great-grandson Henry Beaumont, born in the duchy of Brabant in late 1339 and heir to his father and grandmother's lands in England, and Edward I's grandson Edward III had to change English law in the early 1350s to accommodate Beaumont's birth overseas. Edmund of Lancaster was given protection to leave England on 8 January 1278 and on the 10th appointed two attorneys to act for him during his absence, which perhaps indicates that his son Thomas had already been born by then. Edmund probably did not return to England until October 1278, perhaps later.[27] Thomas was followed by a brother who was named Henry after their late grandfather Henry III and who is generally assumed to have been born sometime in 1280 or 1281. Thomas had no surviving legitimate children and Henry eventually inherited their father's lands and titles, without legal difficulties, and therefore must also have been born in England or in the continental lands ruled by his uncle Edward I. Edmund of Lancaster was in France for much of 1280–81, putting down a rebellion in Provins (the capital of Brie, between Paris and Troyes), though was in England in May 1280 and May–June 1281.[28] Perhaps he returned to England when his wife gave birth for the second time, and Henry of Lancaster was thus born in either May 1280 or in May or June 1281, though we cannot know for sure. Edmund and Blanche's third son, John, was born sometime before May 1286 when the three Lancaster brothers are named on record for the first time.[29] John of Lancaster spent almost all his life in France, held lands there, married there and was probably born there, and hardly ever appears in English records. He was presumably named in honour of Edmund's grandfather King John (d. 1216), though one might have expected one of the Lancaster brothers to be named Robert after their maternal grandfather Robert, Count of Artois. Thomas and John of Lancaster left no surviving legitimate children, and Henry of Lancaster, the second brother, was the ancestor of the later Lancaster dynasty.

Edmund's brother Edward I and his wife Leonor of Castile were also busily producing children throughout the 1260s, 1270s and into the 1280s. They had four sons and at least ten daughters, possibly more, though all but six of their children died young, including one named Berengaria after Leonor's grandmother the Queen of Castile and Leon. By the late 1270s, their surviving children were Eleanor, born in 1269; Joan of Acre, born in 1272; Alfonso of Bayonne, born in 1273; Margaret, born in 1275; and Mary, born in 1279. Elizabeth of Rhuddlan, born in August 1282, and Edward of Caernarfon, born in April 1284, completed the large royal family. Edmund of Lancaster was given authority in March 1279, as Count of Champagne, to claim the northern French county of Ponthieu for his sister-in-law Queen Leonor.[30] Her mother Jeanne, Dowager Queen of Castile and Countess of Ponthieu, had just died, and Leonor was her heir and now Countess of Ponthieu in her own right. Edmund was sometimes referred to as 'count of Champagne' in English records, beginning in February 1278, and his wife Blanche was always called 'queen of Navarre'.[31] Champagne was a hugely rich county and nicely added to Edmund's already sizeable income. During his absences in England, Champagne was ruled for him by John of Acre, grand butler of France and one of the sons of John Brienne, King of Jerusalem and Emperor of Constantinople.[32] John of Acre's great-niece and great-nephew would marry two of Edmund's grandchildren in 1330. Edmund spent most of 1278 and early 1279 in France, but probably attended the wedding of his cousin Eleanor de Montfort, only daughter of the late Simon, to Llywelyn ap Gruffudd, Prince of Wales, on 13 October 1278.[33]

6

MARITAL ARRANGEMENTS

⚬⚬⚬

Edmund sent a letter to his brother the king on 15 May 1282, from La Ferté-Milon between Paris and Reims in Champagne. He stated that he had heard how 'the Welsh have commenced a war against' Edward, and that he would hasten to put his affairs in Champagne in order and return to England to aid his brother, as soon as he received permission from King Philip III to leave.[1] Edmund's loyalty to his older brother is very apparent in the letter: he stated that he was willing to do whatever Edward wished him to do in order to support him. Edward I had been pushing English influence in Wales for years, and battling against its prince, Llywelyn ap Gruffudd. On 21 March 1282, Prince Llywelyn's younger brother Dafydd ap Gruffudd and a band of armed followers attacked Hawarden Castle near Chester, captured the constable, Roger Clifford, and killed some of the garrison. In the days following, other English-held castles in North Wales were assaulted and captured in a full-scale revolt. Llywelyn, claiming probably correctly not to have had foreknowledge of his brother's rebellion, found himself in a dilemma, unsure whether to support him or not. After his wife Eleanor (*née* de Montfort), Edward I and Edmund of Lancaster's first cousin, died giving birth to their daughter Gwenllian in June 1282, Llywelyn decided to join his brother. A furious Edward I summoned earls, knights, men-at-arms, crossbowmen and countless others, and set out against them. Some of his brother Edmund's men were assaulted and robbed on the road between Northwich and Chester while they were taking victuals to Wales in October 1282; their horses and carts were carried away.[2]

Prince Llywelyn was killed in an ambush on 11 December 1282, having become separated from his army at the Battle of Orewin Bridge. He is considered the last of the native princes of Wales; officially he was succeeded by his brother Dafydd, but Dafydd never ruled, and was given the full horrors of the traitor's death by hanging, drawing and quartering in Shrewsbury in October 1283. Llywelyn's only child Gwenllian ferch Llywelyn, Simon de Montfort's granddaughter, was sent by her kinsman Edward I to Sempringham Priory in Lincolnshire and was to live out her entire life there, finally dying in 1337 in her mid 50s. Her cousin, Dafydd's daughter Gwladys – niece (via her mother Elizabeth) of Robert Ferrers, Edmund of Lancaster's adversary in the late 1260s – also spent almost her entire life at a convent in Lincolnshire, far from her native Wales. Dafydd's two sons Llywelyn and Owain were imprisoned at Bristol Castle, and Owain ap Dafydd was still alive in captivity there as late as 1325, after which he disappears from written record. Chillingly, in 1305 Edward I ordered that he be kept in a 'wooden cage bound with iron' at night. Edward's son Edward II did not release Owain but seems to have improved his living conditions at Bristol Castle: in August 1325 he confirmed a grant of 7 pence a day to Owain, and paid for his clothes and those of his two attendants. This is the last known record of Owain ap Dafydd.[3]

Queen Leonor was pregnant for at least the fourteenth time when Dafydd ap Gruffudd was executed by her husband in October 1283, and on 25 April 1284 gave birth to her youngest child at Caernarfon in North Wales. It was a boy, named Edward after his father, and the royal couple's fourth son. His birth in Wales was intended as propaganda to hammer home the message of the King of England's conquest of Gwynedd; a previous attempt to have a royal son born in Wales in August 1282 had gone awry when the infant was a girl, Elizabeth of Rhuddlan. Edmund of Lancaster went overseas yet again shortly after the birth of his nephew: on 5 May 1284 he appointed two attorneys to act on his behalf while he was in France. He had returned to England by 1 July 1285, when he sent his proctor Master Elias Petragor abroad to take care of his affairs.[4] Edmund was now 40 years old and had at least two and perhaps three sons with

Blanche of Artois, depending on when John of Lancaster was born. The couple signed a treaty with Philip III of France in Paris on 17 May 1284, whereby Blanche kept her dower from her first marriage to Enrique I of Navarre but had to give up the county of Champagne, as her daughter Jeanne I of Navarre was now in her twelfth year, and the King of France claimed she had come of age. Blanche retained joint possession, with her daughter, of the palace in Paris which belonged to the kings and queens of Navarre.[5] Jeanne married Philip III's son and heir Philip on 16 August 1284, when she still only 11 years old; he was five years her senior. The marriage ensured that the kingdom of Navarre and the county of Champagne would remain under the control of the kings of France until 1328, when Philip and Jeanne's youngest son died and their granddaughter Jeanne II inherited Navarre.

Just three days after the wedding of Philip of France and Jeanne of Navarre in Paris, disaster struck in England when Alfonso of Bayonne, heir to the throne since his brother Henry's death in October 1274, died suddenly at the age of 10. He was buried at Westminster Abbey with his older brothers John (1266–71) and Henry (1268–74), and his sisters Joan (born and died 1271) and Berengaria (1276–78). Edmund's brother had now lost three sons – on this occasion Edward, now 45 years old, is not known to have made a heartlessly flippant remark about being able to father more – and now the king's and Leonor's latest child, 4-month-old Edward of Caernarfon, was the only one left. The little Edward became heir to the throne. Curiously little is known about the childhoods of Edward of Caernarfon's cousins, Edmund's sons the Lancaster brothers, despite their high birth and rank. Edmund and Blanche spent much of their time in France in the 1280s and 1290s, and perhaps their sons did as well, either with their parents or with their half-sister Jeanne, Queen Regnant of Navarre (who spent her entire life in France). Jeanne became queen consort of France as well when she was 12 years old, on the death of her father-in-law Philip III in October 1285. The Lancaster brothers may also have known their and Jeanne's maternal grandmother Mathilde of Brabant, who lived until 1288, and Mathilde's five children from her second marriage to Guy, Count of St Pol, who were their mother's half-siblings.

Amaury de Montfort, third son of the late Simon, Earl of Leicester, and a canon of York, had been released from captivity in 1282 after promising never to set foot in his native England again; he had been captured in 1278 while accompanying his sister Eleanor to her wedding to Llywelyn ap Gruffudd. Amaury audaciously cited Edmund of Lancaster before the papal court, on a charge which remains somewhat mysterious but was probably connected to Edmund holding the earldom of Leicester, formerly in the possession of Amaury's father Simon. A not entirely amused King Edward sent a letter to one of the cardinals on 28 December 1284, asking him to forbid Amaury from pursuing the matter; revealingly, he did not acknowledge Amaury as his cousin as would have been usual and conventional.[6] Whatever Amaury had hoped to achieve, it came to nothing, though perhaps he only wished to embarrass his cousins publicly. His brother Guy was captured during the Battle of the Counts off the coast of Naples on 23 June 1287, and died in prison four years later. This left Amaury as the only surviving child of Simon de Montfort and Henry III's sister Eleanor; he died in about 1300.

Edmund of Lancaster's niece Margaret of Scotland, born at Windsor in February 1261, had married King Erik II of Norway in the summer of 1281. Erik was a few years his wife's junior and only 13 at the time of the wedding, but despite his youth Margaret became pregnant the following year and gave birth to a daughter on or a little before 9 April 1283. The infant was inevitably named Margaret, and her mother Margaret of Scotland, Queen of Norway, died shortly after her birth, leaving King Erik a widower and a father at barely 15 years old. Queen Margaret's brother David of Scotland, third child of Alexander III and Edmund's sister Margaret of England, had died as a child in 1281, and in January 1284 her other brother Alexander also died at the age of 20, married but childless. All three of Alexander III's children were now dead, and his only heir was his granddaughter, the infant Margaret of Norway. Belatedly, having been widowed from Edmund of Lancaster's sister for a decade, King Alexander realised it was high time to marry again and try to beget more children, and in the autumn of 1285 wed the French noblewoman Yolande de Dreux.

On 19 March 1286, the King of Scotland died in a tragic accident: he rode his horse off a steep embankment in Fife during a storm and was found the next morning with a broken neck. His death was a terrible loss for Scotland, and Alexander, who had been its king for thirty-seven years though was still only 44 years old when he died, is remembered as one of the great kings of Scotland. His death ushered in a twenty-year period of uncertainty. The thirteenth century had seen a long era of peace between Alexander's kingdom and his brother-in-law Edward I's, but sadly England and Scotland would be at war for much of the next few centuries. Not surprisingly, Alexander's second wife Yolande de Dreux bore him no children during their very short marriage, which lasted mere months (though she may have been pregnant in 1286; if so, she had a miscarriage or stillbirth). The Guardians of Scotland, surely reluctantly, proclaimed Alexander's 3-year-old granddaughter Margaret of Norway, Edmund of Lancaster's great-niece, as the rightful queen, though the little girl remained in Norway with her father King Erik II for the time being. Edmund's mother the Dowager Queen Eleanor of Provence, little Margaret of Norway's great-grandmother – who surely mourned the sudden and shocking death of the son-in-law she had supposedly loved as her adopted son – retired to Amesbury Priory in Wiltshire in July 1286, where she would spend the last five years of her life. She asked for two of her granddaughters to accompany her, and so Edward and Leonor's fourth daughter Mary, and Beatrice's youngest daughter Eleanor of Brittany, entered the priory in 1285 ahead of her and were later veiled there as nuns. The girls were 6 and 10 years old respectively. Mary had little if any vocation and would spend part of her adult life at the court of her brother Edward II, but Eleanor of Brittany later became abbess of Fontevrault, Amesbury's mother house in France. Shortly before the dowager queen's retirement to Amesbury, her two sons Edward and Edmund and daughters-in-law Leonor of Castile and Blanche of Artois left England on an extended visit to Gascony.

Edmund of Lancaster appointed attorneys during his long absence from England on 28 April 1286, and took a large retinue with him including Henry de Lacy, Earl of Lincoln, his frequent companion since childhood and the grandson and heir of Margaret de Quincy (*c.* 1206–66), Countess of Lincoln in her own right and one of the greatest English noblewomen of the thirteenth century.[7] Henry de Lacy must have fallen ill during the visit to Gascony, as he made a will on or around 25 January 1287 in Bordeaux, which was later cancelled. The earl left £100 each to the poor scholars of Oxford and Cambridge, and made a reference to £1,000 he had deposited at Lincoln Cathedral in case his then 5-year-old daughter Alice did not marry. She would, in fact, marry Edmund's eldest son Thomas.[8] At this time, Alice was not her father's heir, but became so somewhat later when both her brothers died in childhood accidents. Her mother was Margaret

Longespee ('Longsword'), who inherited the earldom of Salisbury from her father William.

Perhaps Edmund's young sons, including Thomas, also went to Gascony with their father, or perhaps they remained in England with their cousins, the king's children. Edward I was attempting to sort out the long-standing quarrel between France and the papacy on one side, and Sicily and Aragon on the other. The late King Manfredi of Sicily's daughter Constanza and her husband King Pedro III of Aragon invaded Sicily in 1282 and took Charles of Salerno, Edmund and Edward's cousin, prisoner. Charles' father Charles of Anjou died not long afterwards, expelled from the kingdom he had captured in 1266. Edward, who turned 50 in June 1289, had an international reputation as a statesman, and he eventually managed to resolve the conflict, in which he had a personal stake: his and Leonor's eldest surviving daughter Eleanor was betrothed to Constanza and Pedro of Aragon's eldest son Alfonso, and he himself was a first cousin of Charles of Salerno.

Edmund of Lancaster's mother-in-law Mathilde of Brabant, Countess of Artois and St Pol and great-granddaughter of two emperors, died on 29 September 1288 while he was in Gascony, and not long afterwards the Pope absolved Edmund of any perjury for not setting out on Crusade again within the time promised, though his obligation to fulfil the vow remained.[9] He was still overseas with his brother on 25 October 1287, returned to England at some point then left again in April 1288, and returned in August 1289 when the king did as well.[10] Seemingly incapable of remaining in the same place for more than a few weeks at a time, Edmund received protection to go overseas yet again on 12 October 1289, a trip he had been planning since 18 August, mere days after his return to England.[11]

After Edward I returned to England in the late summer of 1289, he turned his attention to the important issue of his children's marriages. The 5-year-old heir to the throne, Edward of Caernarfon, was betrothed to his 6-year-old cousin Margaret of Norway, Queen of Scotland, in September 1289, and in April 1290 the king's second daughter Joan of Acre married Gilbert 'the Red' de Clare, the powerful Earl of Gloucester and Hertford. Gloucester's first marriage to Edmund of Lancaster's cousin Alice de Lusignan had been annulled, and their two daughters Isabella and Joan de Clare made illegitimate. Joan and Gilbert's first child and heir, Gilbert the younger, was born a year later, and they also had three daughters, Eleanor, Margaret and Elizabeth, born between 1292 and 1295. The king's third daughter Margaret married the future Duke John II of Brabant in July 1290, and the following month Edward also arranged his nephew Thomas of Lancaster's future marriage. The king's plans for his son Edward of Caernarfon to rule Scotland one day as well as England foundered when the 7-year-old Queen of Scotland, Margaret of Norway, died in the Orkneys in the autumn of 1290 on her way to her kingdom. Her body was returned to Norway and buried in Bergen next to her mother Margaret of Scotland, Edward and Edmund's niece.

Edmund's eldest son Thomas of Lancaster appears on record for the second time in August 1290 when his uncle Edward I arranged a marriage for him with Beatrice, granddaughter of Duke Hugh IV of Burgundy.[12] There was a family connection, as Beatrice's grandmother the Duchess of Burgundy was the sister of Enrique I of Navarre, first husband of Thomas' mother Blanche of Artois, but in the end nothing came of the planned marriage as the girl died young in 1291. Edmund of Lancaster was overseas when his eldest son's future marriage was arranged.[13] By the end of 1292, Thomas had been betrothed instead to 11-year-old Alice de Lacy. She was set to inherit the earldom of Lincoln from her father Henry de Lacy and the earldom of Salisbury from her mother Margaret Longespee. On or around 28 October 1294, the young couple were married.[14] Thomas was probably 16, almost 17, and Alice not yet 13.

Edmund also arranged the future marriage of his second son: on 30 December 1291, his brother granted him the marriage rights of Maud Chaworth for Henry.[15] Maud was the heir of her father Patrick, who died in July 1283 when she was less than 18 months old, of her uncle Payn Chaworth, who died in 1279 and was one of Edmund's subordinates in Wales, and of her grandmother Hawise of London, mother of the Chaworth brothers.[16] Payn, Patrick and their brother-in-law Robert Tibetot were among the men who accompanied Edward and Edmund on crusade in 1270, so Edmund had known the family for many years.[17] The Chaworths owned extensive lands in southern England and Wales, and the lordships of Kidwelly and Carmarthen would pass to Henry and Maud.

Maud Chaworth was not quite 10 – she was born on or around 2 February 1282 – and Henry of Lancaster probably 10 or 11 when their future marriage was arranged. It is likely that Maud remained with her mother Isabella (née Beauchamp), now married to a baron named

Hugh Despenser the Elder and producing Maud's Despenser half-siblings, but probably she and Henry had opportunities to meet and get to know each other long before they married in about early 1297. The same applies to Thomas of Lancaster and Alice de Lacy. In 1290 Maud Chaworth was one of the noble companions of Thomas and Henry's cousin Edward of Caernarfon when she was 8 and Edward 6, and perhaps in other years as well. In typically not entirely romantic thirteenth-century fashion, the youngest Lancaster brother John was named as a substitute marriage partner for Maud in case Henry died, though otherwise Edmund of Lancaster is not known to have made any marriage arrangements for his third son. He did not arrange John's marriage to the woman John eventually did wed, the French noblewoman Alix Joinville, as she only married her first husband Jean d'Arcis-sur-Aube in 1300 and he lived until 1307, after the deaths of Edmund and Blanche of Artois. John of Lancaster and Alix were married by July 1312 when a grant by them to the abbey of Chapelle-aux-Planches is recorded.[18]

DEATHS OF TWO QUEENS

———⟨≈⟩———

Edmund of Lancaster was one of the great English magnates present at Amesbury Priory in Wiltshire, where his mother, the dowager queen, now lived, on 17 April 1290. Gilbert de Clare, Earl of Gloucester, was about to marry Edmund's niece Joan of Acre, the king and queen's second daughter, and swore an oath to the king that in the event of Edward I's death he would be loyal to his son Edward of Caernarfon. If the boy, born on 25 April 1284 and not quite 6 years old, died without heirs of his body, Gloucester would accept the king's eldest daughter Eleanor (b. 1269) as his liege lady. Edward I, having lost three of his four sons in childhood, was being forced to accept that the future of his dynasty hung on a little boy who might easily succumb to childhood illness as his three elder brothers had done, and that one day it might happen that his eldest daughter would reign as queen in her own right. It is interesting and revealing to see that the king preferred his daughter to reign as queen in case his own male line failed, rather than passing the line of succession to his younger brother Edmund of Lancaster and Edmund's three sons. Edmund surely attended the wedding of the Earl of Gloucester and Joan of Acre on 30 April 1290, and of his niece Margaret, the king's third daughter, to the future Duke John II of Brabant in early July.

Edmund's sister-in-law Queen Leonor died on 28 November 1290 at the age of 49, at Harby in Nottinghamshire, and was buried in Westminster Abbey on 17 December. The following day, his wife Blanche of Artois was given permission to go overseas after they had attended the funeral; she travelled with Alice, Prioress of Amesbury, to the convent in Wiltshire where her mother-in-law Eleanor of Provence and her niece-in-law Mary, the king's fourth daughter, lived.[1] Leonor's county of Ponthieu in northern France, which she had inherited from her mother the Dowager Queen of Castile in 1279, passed to 6-year-old Edward of Caernarfon, her only surviving son. Edward I and Leonor had been married for thirty-six years, and the king sent a poignant letter to the Abbot of Cluny a few weeks later, talking about his grief for the companion 'whom in death we cannot cease to love'.[2] For Leonor, Edward built the remarkable series of monuments known as the Eleanor Crosses, some of which still exist.

Edward and Edmund of Lancaster's mother Eleanor of Provence, the dowager queen, outlived her daughter-in-law by a few months and died at Amesbury Priory on 24 June 1291, in her late 60s. Edmund was one of the executors of the queen's will.[3] He and his brother the king, Eleanor's only surviving children, attended her funeral at Amesbury on 8 September, and as was usual with royal burials of the time, her heart was removed and buried separately in the church of the Franciscans in London.[4] This was where her daughter Beatrice had been buried in 1275 and where, in later decades, Eleanor's daughter-in-law Marguerite of France and granddaughter-in-law Isabella of France, queens of England, and great-granddaughter Joan of the Tower, Queen of Scotland, would also be buried. On 10 December 1291, Edmund of Lancaster was present in the church of Westminster Abbey with his brother, half-uncle William Valence and many others when his father Henry III's heart was delivered to the Abbess of Fontevrault near Chinon in France.[5] Henry had requested that his heart be buried at the abbey, with his mother Isabelle of Angoulême, uncle King Richard I ('Lionheart'), and grandparents Henry II and Eleanor of Aquitaine.

In November 1292, the ongoing competition for the throne of Scotland which followed the death of the little Margaret of Norway in September 1290 was finally decided, with Edward I of England adjudicating. As his fee for doing so, the English king demanded recognition of his right to feudal overlordship of Scotland, meaning that the kingdom would become a dependency of the kingdom of England and that the future

Scottish kings would owe him homage for it. (Edward did not, contrary to popular modern belief, claim the right to be King of Scotland himself.) The extinction of Alexander III's line with the death of his granddaughter Margaret in September 1290 meant that the 104 presiding auditors had to go several generations back to assess the numerous claims. The best candidates were John Balliol, grandson of the eldest daughter of David, Earl of Huntingdon, grandson of King David I; and Robert Bruce, son of Huntingdon's second daughter (and the grandfather of the Robert Bruce who eventually became king in 1306). Balliol was chosen, and crowned King of Scotland at Scone Abbey on 30 November 1292. Edmund of Lancaster was given a safe-conduct on 12 March 1291 to send goods and victuals to Scotland in anticipation of his arrival there and was staying in the castle of Jedburgh on 15 June 1291 supposedly until that Christmas, but the death of his mother the dowager queen took him home much earlier.[6]

The Lancaster brothers Thomas and Henry, but not their younger brother John, stayed with their cousin Edward of Caernarfon in the company of Edward's brother-in-law John of Brabant (the future Duke John II, who had married Edward's third sister Margaret in 1290) in February 1293 and again in June. On the latter occasion all three young men were accompanied by dozens of servants and horses, all of whom had to be fed and housed at Edward of Caernarfon's expense for six days, and the exasperation of the 9-year-old boy's clerk shone through as he wrote every day, probably through gritted teeth, 'they are still here'. His patience snapped on the sixth day, and he wrote 'here they are still. And this day is burdensome. For John of Brabant and Thomas and Henry the sons of Lord Edmund breakfasted at Kingston on their way to joust at Fulham, and caused great expense, because strangers joined them in large numbers.' In August 1293, the brothers visited Edward of Caernarfon again, and Henry stayed behind when Thomas left, because he was ill.[7] The brothers spent much of the period from November 1292 to May 1293 in the company of John of Brabant – his accounts roll happens to survive for this period – and attended many other jousting tournaments and went hunting with their cousin Edward. They had the typical preoccupations of their class and era, and Henry may have attended a tournament at Northampton in April 1342 and was present at one held in Leicester in November 1344 organised by his son to celebrate the wedding of his granddaughter. Half a century later, he had retained his interest in jousting. The account of 1292–93 reveals that Thomas of Lancaster had a servant called Hobekin and that the boys' armourer was called Gilkin.[8]

The Lancaster parents were also in England for part of 1292–93, though Edmund, who spent most of his adult life travelling regularly between England and France, was going abroad yet again in April 1292 and was outside England again that October.[9] In December 1292, Edmund arranged for his son Thomas to marry Alice de Lacy.[10] As well as arranging his second son Henry's future marriage to the heiress Maud Chaworth in December 1291, in August 1292 Edmund specified that his four castles in Wales (Skenfrith, White Castle, Grosmont and Monmouth), and the manors of Rodley and Minsterworth in Gloucestershire, would pass after his death to Henry and his heirs.[11] These lands would nicely complement the Chaworth lands in the same parts of the country that Henry and his future wife would hold, and Henry would become a landowner of some substance in Wales, Gloucestershire, Wiltshire and Hampshire. The Lacy lands which would come to Thomas via his marriage to Alice also bordered the Lancaster lands in many places, and Edmund's choices of brides for his two eldest sons were intelligent and well thought out ones. Thomas would inherit almost all their father's vast lands and his earldoms as well as the two earldoms of his future parents-in-law Henry de Lacy and Margaret Longespee, but Edmund was also taking care of his younger sons' futures. He planned for his third son, John of Lancaster, to inherit his and Blanche of Artois' lordships, including Beaufort, in her native France. Henry, the second son, was made John's heir to the French lordships if John had no children, as in the end he did not, and they duly passed to Henry; his son, the younger Henry; and his grandson-in-law John of Gaunt, who in the 1370s named his illegitimate children after the lordship of Beaufort. When and how Edmund and Blanche assigned the French lordships to John of Lancaster and made Henry his heir to them is not clear as the records of the grant do not seem to be extant, but probably Edmund was trying to split his large inheritance to benefit all his sons, and Thomas as the eldest would receive the bulk of it and hence had no real need of the lands in France.

Edmund and Blanche founded a religious house in London, the Minoresses without Aldgate, in June 1293.[12] The Minoresses, or Franciscan nuns, are often known as the Poor Clares, and the order was founded by St Clare of Assisi in 1212. A widow named Joan Coldcorn or Goldcorn granted Blanche of Artois her plot of land in the parish of St Botolph without Aldgate in or after November 1292, which Blanche's eldest son Thomas gave to his parents' foundation outright some years later, and Blanche brought some nuns from France to live at her new foundation. In November 1294, Edmund gave his and Blanche's foundation some tenements and plots of land he held in London.[13] Also in June 1293, Edmund was given permission by his brother to crenellate his house, called the 'Sauvey' or 'Sauveye', also in London.[14] This is better known as the Savoy Palace on the Strand, and had belonged to Edmund's great-uncle Peter of Savoy, Earl of Richmond; it would ultimately pass to Edmund's great-granddaughter Blanche of Lancaster and her husband John of Gaunt, and was left a smoking ruin after the Great Uprising of 1381. The famous Savoy Hotel now stands on the site.

Edmund's former mother-in-law Isabella Forz (née Redvers), Countess of Devon and mother of the late Aveline Forz, died on 9 November 1293. On her deathbed she gave the bulk of her inheritance to Edward I, probably with some coercion or manipulation, disinheriting her rather distant kinsman Hugh Courtenay and her daughter's five even more distant cousins, who had been named as Aveline's heirs in 1274.[15] Hugh Courtenay finally received the earldom of Devon from Edward I's grandson Edward III in 1335 when he was almost 60. As late as the 1380s, Aveline Forz's co-heir Sir John Plays, descendant of her distant cousin Ralph Plays, was still seeking some of her inheritance.[16] In May 1381, over a century after Aveline's death, a royal official in Buckinghamshire was ordered to inquire into her lands there.[17]

In 1293, Thomas of Lancaster was 15 or 16 and his brother Henry 12 or 13, and the boys must have been raised with a strong sense of their own importance and high birth: their father's brother was the King of England and their half-sister's husband was the King of France. Their mother Blanche was always called 'the Queen of Navarre' in English records of the era, and their father had been acknowledged as King of Sicily by the Pope, although it was only an empty title. Via their maternal grandmother Mathilde of Brabant, Countess of Artois and St Pol, Thomas and Henry were great-great-great-grandsons of the mighty German Emperor Frederick Barbarossa (d. 1190) and of the Byzantine Emperor Isaac Angelos (d. 1204), and they would certainly have been aware of their illustrious ancestors. Thomas spent all his adult life in England, and Henry most of his, but they almost certainly spent much time in France as children and were half-French. They were in England again in October 1294, when Thomas married Alice de Lacy, who was not yet 13; she was born on or around Christmas Day 1281. Alice was descended from Henry II (r. 1154–89) via the king's illegitimate son William Longespee, the Earl of Salisbury and a half-brother of King John. By now she was her parents' only surviving child and thus their heir, though she had an illegitimate half-brother called John de Lacy, who seems to have worked as a clerk in her household; he is mentioned in a petition she presented in the mid 1330s when he connived at his own half-sister's abduction and forced third marriage.[18]

Relations between the English and French royal families had been harmonious for decades, thanks in large part to Henry III and Louis IX marrying sisters and the kings' brothers Richard of Cornwall and Charles of Anjou marrying the other two Provence sisters. By 1293, however, the young King of France, Philip IV (Louis IX's grandson), was making war-like overtures towards England and demanding that Edward I appear before him in Paris to explain a quarrel between English and French sailors from Normandy which blew up into something quite serious when the English sailors sacked the port of La Rochelle.[19] Philip's letters to Edward were peremptory and rude, and not only failed to address him as King of England, but did not even acknowledge him as Duke of Aquitaine. Edward's answer was to ask his brother Edmund of Lancaster, who after all was the stepfather of Philip's wife, the first cousin of Philip's late father and an important and influential nobleman on both sides of the Channel, to soothe ruffled feathers and to talk things out with the French king. Edmund and his friend Henry de Lacy, Earl of Lincoln, were given protection in early May 1293 to go to France to discuss these matters with Philip IV, though in the end their journey was delayed by a few months.[20] Also in May 1293, Edward I sent out orders to the 'whole fleet of England' to cease their conflict with the sailors of Normandy, as, he said, 'God has given them victory over the malice of their enemies'.[21]

In early 1294, Edmund and his wife Blanche of Artois sat down with Blanche's daughter Jeanne of Navarre, Philip IV's queen, and Philip's step-mother Marie of Brabant, the Dowager Queen of France and widow of Philip III, and together they hammered out a sensible win–win solution for both sides. Part of the deal involved Edward I temporarily surrendering part of his French territories to Philip IV and receiving them back on new and better terms, and marrying Philip's half-sister Marguerite, daughter of Philip III and his second wife Marie of Brabant. Philip IV confiscated Gascony, on the understanding by Edward I, Edmund of Lancaster, Blanche of Artois, Marie of Brabant, and apparently even Philip's wife Jeanne, that the seizure would be temporary and little more than a gesture to assuage the French king's anger and his sense of offended dignity. Philip, however, had other plans and on 19 May 1294 confiscated the duchy outright and permanently. To his utter horror, Edmund of Lancaster had been cheated and played for a fool; his diplomacy had, thanks to Philip's dishonesty, failed catastrophically. One modern historian has described his and his fellow envoys' failure as 'among the most dismal episodes of English foreign policy' in all of history.[22] Two men close to the King of France were urging Philip to war and antagonism towards the English. One was the king's brother Charles, Count of Valois (b. 1270), ancestor of the Valois dynasty which was to rule France for centuries, who was said to have 'pursued the English with an inveterate hatred'.[23] The other was Robert, Count of Artois, Edmund of Lancaster's own brother-in-law but emphatically not his friend or ally.[24] And so Edward I found himself at war with France.

WAR WITH FRANCE

———⊶⟊⊷———

E dmund of Lancaster was appointed as the leader of the first and larger of his brother's two forces to Gascony, with Henry de Lacy of Lincoln as his deputy. The second royal force was to be led by Edmund and Edward's nephew John of Brittany (b. 1266), their late sister Beatrice's second son who spent most of his life in England. Edward I ordered the barons of the Cinque Ports and others to provide ships for Edmund to travel to Gascony on 3 September 1294.[1] The planned departure of both forces, however, was interrupted by an uprising which broke out across Wales, probably as a result of the overly harsh English administration of the principality. Edmund of Lancaster was at the Tower of London on 12 November 1294 when he began making preparations to go to Wales.[2] William Beauchamp, Earl of Warwick, and Gilbert de Clare, Earl of Gloucester and the king's son-in-law, played an important role in putting down the rebellion, and on 5 March 1295 the Earl of Warwick was responsible for a major victory at the Battle of Maes Moydog when he crippled the forces of the Welsh leader, Madog ap Llywelyn.

Edward I wrote to the Queens of France, Marie of Brabant and Jeanne of Navarre, on 12 August 1295 assuring them that recent events had not lessened his regard for them at all. On the same day he wrote to his aged aunt Marguerite of Provence, Louis IX's widow, Philip IV's grandmother, the eldest and last surviving of the four Provence sisters and yet another Queen of France, to enquire after her health.[3] Queen Marguerite did not have long to live, and died on 20 December 1295 at the age of about 74. She had outlived most of her children and lived long enough to see the birth of her great-granddaughter Isabella, sixth of the seven children of Philip IV and Jeanne of Navarre, who would marry Edmund of Lancaster's nephew Edward of Caernarfon in 1308 and become Queen of England. King Edward heard the news of her death on 2 January 1296, when he asked the two English archbishops to pray for her soul.[4]

Edmund of Lancaster and his force, meanwhile, intended to depart from England to Gascony shortly after 10 September 1295, a year late, but Edmund fell ill, and again his journey had to be postponed. Philip IV's brother Charles de Valois had invaded Gascony at Easter 1295, and by that summer most of the duchy, excepting the towns of Bayonne, Bourg and Blaye, was in French hands.[5] Edmund finally set out sometime between 26 December 1295 and mid January 1296, accompanied by some of the English magnates such as the young Earl of Arundel, who had initially refused to go and who had to be blackmailed by the king into doing so (he threatened to collect all the huge debts they owed to the Crown).[6] Edmund's wife Blanche of Artois had preceded him to Gascony, and on 17 November 1295 was given a safe conduct to return to England when it became clear that her husband's illness would prevent his departure. Edmund's faithful ally Henry de Lacy, Earl of Lincoln, went with him.[7] Sadly, Edmund's expedition achieved little, and he was never to see his homeland again.

On 5 June 1296, Edmund, Earl of Lancaster and Leicester, Steward of England, died in Bayonne in the far south-west of France, at the age of 51. The cause of Edmund's death is not known; perhaps he had never fully recovered from his illness of late 1295. Blanche of Artois was one of the executors of her husband's will (which is no longer extant).[8] Edmund's long Inquisition Post Mortem, unlike his will, still exists, though curiously it does not mention his sons and heirs. His and Blanche's eldest son Thomas, who was probably 18 in June 1296, received the bulk of the inheritance, including the earldoms of Lancaster and Leicester; Henry the lordships in Wales and Gloucestershire; and John the lands in France.[9]

At the time of Edmund of Lancaster's death, the Lanercost chronicler in the far north of England called him 'a valiant knight and noble, who was genial and merry, generous and pious'.[10] For many years he showed loyalty to his elder brother Edward I, loyalty which does him immense credit, and he was, like his father, a generous benefactor to the Church. Of his sons Thomas and Henry – virtually nothing is known of John – Henry resembled Edmund far more closely in personality than Thomas, and it would be Henry, and his son the younger Henry, first Duke of Lancaster, who took the Lancaster family to great heights. Edmund of Lancaster never did achieve his and his father's aim of gaining a kingdom for himself, but he married a queen, and founded a great dynasty, which was to become the most powerful and prestigious family in England in the fourteenth century. Although Edmund could not have known it, a little over a century after his death his great-great-grandson and heir Henry of Lancaster would become king, and ultimately a Lancaster would sit on the English throne.

PART II
1296–1330

DRAMATIS PERSONAE

Thomas of Lancaster (b. 1277/78): eldest son of Edmund of Lancaster and Blanche of Artois, second Earl of Lancaster, Earl of Leicester, Steward of England; nephew of Edward I of England and brother-in-law of Philip IV of France; from 1311, also Earl of Lincoln and Salisbury by right of his wife **Alice de Lacy** (b. 1281), daughter and heir of Henry de Lacy and Margaret Longespee

Henry of Lancaster (b. 1280/81): second son of Edmund and Blanche, Thomas' brother and heir; third Earl of Lancaster, Earl of Leicester; ancestor of all the later Lancasters and of much of the English nobility in the later fourteenth century and the fifteenth

John of Lancaster (b. before 1286): Thomas and Henry's obscure younger brother, and heir to their parents' French lands; married to Alix Joinville but dies childless in 1317; Henry is his heir

Maud Chaworth (b. 1282): heir to her father Patrick and uncle Payn Chaworth; marries Henry of Lancaster in or before early 1297

Edward II (b. 1284), often known as Edward of Caernarfon: fourth but only surviving son of Edward I and Leonor of Castile; becomes King of England in 1307; first cousin of the Lancaster brothers

Louis X, Philip V and Charles IV (b. between 1289–94): kings of France and Navarre; sons of Philip IV of France and Jeanne I of Navarre; grandchildren of Blanche of Artois; nephews of Thomas and Henry of Lancaster

Isabella of France (b. *c.* 1295): Queen of England; only daughter of Philip IV and Jeanne; marries Edward II in 1308; niece of Thomas and Henry of Lancaster

Marguerite of France (b. 1278/79): marries Edward I as his second wife in 1299; half-sister of Philip IV and aunt of Isabella of France; stepmother of Edward II and aunt-in-law of the Lancaster brothers

Thomas of Brotherton, Earl of Norfolk (b. 1300): elder son of Edward I and Marguerite; half-brother of Edward II; first cousin of Thomas and Henry of Lancaster

Edmund of Woodstock, Earl of Kent (b. 1301): younger son of Edward I and Marguerite; grandfather of King Richard II

Piers Gaveston (b. *c.* 1270s/early 1280s): Gascon nobleman, beloved of Edward II; marries the king's niece Margaret de Clare in 1307 and made Earl of Cornwall

Hugh Despenser the Younger, Lord of Glamorgan (b. *c.* 1288/9): younger half-brother of Maud Chaworth, brother-in-law of Henry of Lancaster and uncle of his children; marries Edward I's eldest grand-daughter Eleanor de Clare in 1306, chamberlain and over-mighty 'favourite' of his uncle-in-law Edward II in the late 1310s and 1320s

Roger Mortimer, Lord of Wigmore (b. 1287): enemy of Edward II and Hugh Despenser who escapes from the Tower in 1323; later the over-mighty 'favourite' of Edward's queen Isabella and self-appointed first Earl of March in 1328

Edward III (b. 1312), King of England from January 1327: eldest child of Edward II and Isabella of France; grandson of Philip IV and Jeanne of Navarre, and of Edward I and Leonor of Castile; great-nephew of Thomas and Henry of Lancaster

Henry of Grosmont (b. *c.* 1310–12): only son and heir of Henry of Lancaster and Maud Chaworth; nephew and ultimate heir of the childless Thomas of Lancaster; marries Isabella Beaumont in 1330; grandfather of King Henry IV

Blanche of Lancaster (b. *c.* 1302–05): eldest child of Henry of Lancaster and Maud Chaworth; marries Thomas, Lord Wake (b. 1298) in 1316; has no children

Isabella of Lancaster (b. *c.* 1305–08): second daughter of Henry and Maud; becomes a nun at Amesbury Priory, Wiltshire in 1327 and its prioress in 1343

Maud of Lancaster (b. *c.* 1310–12): third daughter of Henry and Maud; marries William de Burgh, Earl of Ulster (b. 1312), in 1327, and Ralph Ufford in 1343

Joan of Lancaster (b. *c.* 1313–15): fourth daughter of Henry and Maud; marries John, Lord Mowbray (b. 1310) in 1328

Eleanor of Lancaster (b. *c.* 1316–18): fifth daughter of Henry and Maud; marries John, Lord Beaumont (b. 1317) in 1330, and Richard Fitzalan, Earl of Arundel, in 1345

Mary of Lancaster (b. *c.* 1319–21): sixth and youngest daughter of Henry and Maud; marries Henry, Lord Percy (b. *c.* 1320/21) in 1334

Henry, Lord Beaumont (b. *c.* 1270 or 1280): son of Louis Brienne and Agnes Beaumont; French nobleman who spends most of his life in England; second cousin of Edward II; titular Earl of Buchan in Scotland

Alice Beaumont (née Comyn) (b. *c.* late 1290s); marries Henry in or before 1310; niece and co-heir of John Comyn, Earl of Buchan (d. 1308)

John, Lord Beaumont (b. 1317): son and heir of Henry and Alice; marries Eleanor of Lancaster in 1330

Isabella Beaumont (b. *c.* 1315/18): second daughter of Henry and Alice; marries Henry of Grosmont in 1330; grandmother of Henry IV

Robert Holland (b. 1270s/1280s): Knight of Lancashire; steward and close ally of Thomas, Earl of Lancaster; murdered in 1328 by Henry of Lancaster's men

Thomas, Lord Wake (b. 1298): marries Henry of Lancaster's eldest daughter Blanche in 1316; has no children

Margaret Wake, Countess of Kent (b. *c.* mid to late 1290s): Thomas' sister and heir; marries Sir John Comyn (d. 1314) and secondly Edward II's half-brother Edmund of Woodstock, Earl of Kent (b. 1301), in late 1325; grandmother of King Richard II

William de Burgh, Earl of Ulster (b. 1312): son and heir of Edward II's niece Elizabeth de Burgh (née de Clare) (b. 1295) and her first husband John de Burgh (d. 1313); heir to his grandfather Richard de Burgh, Earl of Ulster (*c.* 1259–1326); marries Maud of Lancaster in 1327

John, Lord Mowbray (b. 1310): son and heir of John, Lord Mowbray (1286–1322) and Alina de Braose; marries Joan of Lancaster in 1328

Henry, Lord Percy (b. *c.* 1320/21): son and heir of Henry, Lord Percy (1301–52) and Idonea Clifford; marries Mary of Lancaster in 1334

THE SECOND EARL OF LANCASTER

‐‐‐‐‐ ⟨∞⟩ ‐‐‐‐‐

Far away from Gascony, meanwhile, Edmund of Lancaster's brother Edward I had invaded Scotland after its king, John Balliol, renounced homage to him in March 1296. Balliol had been elected king in 1292 after winning the process to discover the rightful King of Scotland after the death of Alexander III, his children and his granddaughter Margaret of Norway. Edward was accompanied north by his Lancaster nephews Thomas and Henry, despite their youth (Henry was probably only 15). In June 1296, the month of his father's death, Henry of Lancaster's horse was stolen from a field outside Edinburgh.[1] The news of the Earl of Lancaster's death travelled north slowly: Edward I had prayers said for his brother's soul in Aberdeen on 15 July 1296 and had just heard about Edmund's demise almost six weeks later, though it was known in London on 3 July.[2] The grieving king talked of 'our only and dearest brother' who had always showed devotion and loyalty to him and to the affairs of his kingdom, and in whom many 'gifts of grace and virtue poured forth'.

The Scottish campaign was successful, the English Earl of Surrey defeated King John Balliol (his son-in-law) at the Battle of Dunbar, and Balliol was imprisoned then exiled. His son Edward Balliol, however – somewhat ironically named in honour of Edward I – came close to reclaiming Scotland decades later with the aid of Edward I's grandson Edward III. On his return to England, Edward I summoned Parliament to be held around the feast day of St Edmund, 20 November 1296, rather than at the feast of St Edward the Confessor on 13 October as was usual, and in the Suffolk town of Bury St Edmunds.[3] So did the king honour his faithful brother's memory.

The widowed Blanche of Artois returned to England in January 1297, perhaps just in time to attend the wedding of the king's fifth daughter Elizabeth to Count John I of Holland in Ipswich that month.[4] Edmund of Lancaster's remains were carried to England about six months after his death, and Blanche may have travelled with them. On 9 June 1297 in the chapel of the Archbishop of York's house near Westminster, Blanche swore fealty to her brother-in-law the king for her lands as well as an oath that she would not remarry without his permission (which was standard procedure). She received a third of her late husband's lands, as was usual, and the entire earldom of Derby formerly of Robert Ferrers.[5] Her second son, Henry of Lancaster, married Maud Chaworth, his fiancée since late 1291, on or before 2 March 1297, presumably with Blanche present. Maud, born on or around 2 February 1282, was 15 or almost when she married, and Henry was probably 16. He and Maud were the ancestors of all the later Lancasters, and of much of the English nobility in the late fourteenth and fifteenth centuries.

Henry was given possession of the lands held by his father in Wales and Gloucestershire on 20 March 1297 shortly after his marriage, although he was well underage, and by April 1299 also held the lands in Wales and southern England which his wife had inherited from her father Patrick and uncle Payn Chaworth, including the Welsh lordship of Kidwelly.[6] He was given permission to pay off all his late father-in-law's debts to the Exchequer in instalments of 20 marks a year, though by 1307 had failed to keep up the payments, and in 1329 had still not managed to clear the debt.[7] Sometime in or after 1307 Henry's younger brother John, who had been named as a substitute future husband for Maud Chaworth in 1291 but who seems rarely to have visited England, married Alix Joinville, whose father Jean came from a noble family of Champagne and was a great chronicler. Jean Joinville wrote the *Life of Saint Louis*, an account of Louis IX's Crusade of 1248 to 1254 which was commissioned by Jeanne, Queen of Navarre and France, the Lancaster brothers' older half-sister.

Henry of Lancaster was now married and a landowner and had already taken part in military action in Scotland, but in 1297 he was still only in his mid teens, and therefore had a guardian called John Ditton, appointed by the king to take care of his affairs until he was old enough to do so himself. Ditton acted as Henry's attorney that year when the young man went overseas with Edward I on another military campaign in Flanders.[8]

Even though Henry of Lancaster and Maud Chaworth were of an age to consummate their marriage in 1297, their first child, Blanche, was not born until 1302 at the earliest and perhaps 1305. Their only son and heir, Henry of Grosmont, was born around 1310 or 1312, and their youngest child, Mary, was born around 1320, more than two decades after their wedding and when they were close to 40. Five of Henry and Maud's seven children had children of their own, and in all cases there was a delay of a good few years between wedding and first pregnancy; none of the Lancasters were in an overwhelming hurry to reproduce. Henry's elder brother Thomas and his wife Alice de Lacy failed to produce any surviving offspring in almost thirty years of marriage. Thomas did have illegitimate sons, and there is a record of Alice being pregnant in 1307 or 1308 so she was not infertile either, but this pregnancy must have ended in miscarriage or stillbirth, or a child who died in infancy.[9]

Thomas' sister-in-law Maud Chaworth was said to be going overseas with her household and without her husband Henry on 23 August 1299, though the record does not state why or where.[10] Maud's father Patrick Chaworth had died in July 1283 when she was a baby, and in about 1286 her mother Isabella Beauchamp, daughter of the Earl of Warwick, married her second husband Hugh Despenser. He is usually known to history as Hugh Despenser the Elder to distinguish him from his son Hugh Despenser the Younger, Maud's half-brother, who was to become notorious in the 1320s as the chamberlain, favourite and perhaps lover of King Edward II. Maud Chaworth was the only child of her parents, though had six younger half-siblings from her mother's marriage to Despenser. Her half-brother Hugh was born around 1288 or 1289 and probably attended Maud and Henry's wedding, which might have been the first time Henry met the boy who in later decades would become the powerful and despotic royal favourite of his cousin Edward II and whose grotesque execution he would witness.

Edward I went on campaign against Philip IV of France in the summer of 1297, in alliance with the Count of Flanders. The king left his 13-year-old son Edward of Caernarfon as nominal regent of the kingdom with a council of much older and more experienced men to guide him, including

Maud Chaworth's grandfather the Earl of Warwick and stepfather Hugh Despenser the Elder. Shortly before he went, on 9 July 1297, the king ordered the tenants of Thomas of Lancaster's late father Edmund to do homage to Thomas, although he was still underage, almost certainly 19.[11] Thomas and Henry of Lancaster went on the campaign with their uncle, and the king's third daughter Margaret and fifth daughter Elizabeth also accompanied their father overseas and went to join their husbands, respectively Duke John II of Brabant and Count John I of Holland. Despite his young age this was already Henry of Lancaster's second military expedition, and his and his brother's military careers continued in the late 1290s as Edward I continued to try to assert his dominance over Scotland. In 1298 Thomas and Henry were again with the king in the northern kingdom, and each received a gift of a horse from him.[12] Both brothers had already been knighted, and both were summoned to Parliament in March 1299 and again in March 1300, even though Henry was probably only 18 in March 1299.[13] Henry's parliamentary career lasted for forty-five years: he was summoned for the last time in April 1344, the year before his death.[14] As for Edward I's war against Philip IV and France, it was finally resolved when he married Philip's half-sister Marguerite in September 1299, and his 15-year-old son and heir Edward of Caernarfon was betrothed to Philip and Jeanne of Navarre's only surviving daughter Isabella, who was barely 4 at the time.

Edmund of Lancaster, Earl of Lancaster and Leicester, was finally buried at Westminster Abbey on 20 March 1300, almost four years after his death – he had specified that his body should not be interred until all his debts had been paid – in the presence of his brother Edward I. Many English magnates and bishops also attended; Parliament was held in London from 6 to 20 March, and the funeral took place shortly after it ended. Presumably Edmund's widow Blanche and his sons Thomas, Henry and even the obscure John, who was in England for once in 1300, were there.[15] Edmund's embalmed body had remained in Bayonne for six months after his death, when it was carried to the convent of the Minoresses in London, which he and Blanche of Artois had founded in 1293.[16] On 20 March 1300, Edmund's 'bones' (the word used in the king's accounts) were taken from the Minoresses to Westminster Abbey via St Paul's Cathedral, and the king distributed alms to the poor on the way. Edward paid for 986 wax tapers for Edmund's exequies, and bought two horses from an Italian called Leo of Milan to be ridden before Edmund's body in the procession to

Westminster.[17] Edmund was buried north of the high altar with his first wife Aveline Forz, and their tombs still exist.

In July 1300, Edward I besieged the Scottish castle of Caerlaverock during his latest military campaign in Scotland, and the Lancaster brothers Thomas and Henry took part, as did their 16-year-old cousin Edward of Caernarfon. The English heralds wrote a glowing report (in French) of the siege and the English noblemen and knights who were there, describing Edward of Caernarfon as 'a well-proportioned and handsome person, of a courteous disposition, and intelligent, and desirous of finding an occasion to display his prowess. He managed his steed wonderfully well.' The Lancasters were called 'two brothers, cousins to the king's son, named Thomas and Henry, who were the sons of Lord Edmund [*Monsire Eymon*], the well-beloved'. The poet, perhaps revealingly, could find little to say about Thomas other than the rather obvious fact that 'Thomas was Earl of Lancaster' and that he used 'the royal arms of England with a label of France'. He wrote that Henry's 'whole daily study was to resemble his good father'.[18] A group of English barons sent a letter to Pope Boniface VIII a few months later, on 12 February 1301, promoting Edward I's claims to overlordship of Scotland and repudiating Boniface's own claims to such. Thomas, Earl of Lancaster, was named second on the list of barons, behind only the elderly Earl of Surrey (who died in 1304), and Henry of Lancaster, called *Henricus de Lancastre* and 'lord of Monmouth', was tenth overall, behind the seven earls who signed it and the only two noblemen who outranked him: his cousin Aymer de Valence, son of Henry III's half-brother William and later to become Earl of Pembroke, and the elderly William, Lord Leyburne (d. 1310). In their father's lifetime and occasionally afterwards, Thomas and Henry were usually referred to simply as 'the sons of Lord Edmund,' and after Edmund's death, Henry was generally called 'Sir Henry of Lancaster'. An early example of this came in June 1296, the month of his father's death.[19]

The Lancasters' mother Blanche of Artois spent the end of the 1290s and beginning of the 1300s in her native France, where her son-in-law and daughter ruled. She gave her dower lands, which had formerly belonged to Robert Ferrers, to her brother-in-law Edward I in April 1298.[20] Blanche, Dowager Queen of Navarre and Countess of Lancaster, died probably on 4 May 1302, three days after making her will in Paris, aged about 54 or 56. (The date of Blanche's death is almost always given by modern writers as

2 May, but her son Thomas kept her anniversary as the 4th.)[21] The executor of her will, or one of them, was her daughter Jeanne, Queen of France
and Navarre.[22] Blanche was buried at the Church of the Cordeliers, and
presumably her Lancaster sons and their wives Alice and Maud travelled
to Paris to attend her funeral. Queen Jeanne would be buried in the same
church three years later (she died in 1305 at the age of only 32 and was
succeeded in Navarre by 15-year-old Louis, eldest of her three sons). In
later years Thomas of Lancaster employed a chaplain to celebrate divine
service for his parents' souls and had daily Masses and yearly anniversaries
for them said in various churches, and was devoted to their memory. So
was Henry: he presented two clerks to Flaxley Abbey in Gloucestershire
on 8 August 1315 to pray for the souls of 'Edmund son of King Henry and
Blanche his wife, sometime queen of Navarre'. In December 1334, Henry
granted land to Canons Ashby Priory in Northamptonshire in return for a
Mass and requiem to be held every year on 5 June, the date of his father's
death almost forty years before. In March 1316 Thomas asked the Bishop of
Worcester to keep his father's anniversary on 4 June, but Edmund certainly
died on the 5th, so this is probably a scribal error (unless it was Thomas'
own error and he had forgotten the correct date). Henry requested prayers
for the souls of his father and his brother Thomas, by then dead for six
years, from Tupholme Abbey, Lincolnshire in 1328.[23] Blanche's only sibling Robert, Count of Artois, did not long outlive her: he was killed at
the Battle of Courtrai, also known as the Battle of the Golden Spurs, on
11 July 1302, when the army of Philip IV was heavily and humiliatingly
defeated by Flemish infantry. Numerous other French noblemen fell.
Count Robert's only son Philip had died in 1298, and so he was succeeded
in Artois by his daughter Mahaut, the Lancasters' first cousin, who became
countess in her own right in preference to her young nephew Robert,
Philip's son. The long and bitter struggle between Mahaut and Robert for
control of Artois was made famous in Maurice Druon's *The Accursed Kings*
novels many centuries later.

Edward I's campaigns in Scotland continued in the early 1300s, and
Thomas and Henry accompanied him there. At Christmas 1303, Thomas
and probably Henry, and Henry's wife's uncle Guy, Earl of Warwick and
her stepfather Hugh Despenser the Elder, dined with 19-year-old Edward
of Caernarfon, heir to the throne and another first cousin of the Lancasters.
On the Feast of the Purification, 2 February 1304, their cousin John of

Brittany, Earl of Richmond, joined them as well. He was a younger son of Edward I's late sister Beatrice, lived most of his life in England, and was known by the nickname 'Brito'.[24] Edward I generously rewarded his Lancaster nephews for their loyalty and good service in Scotland: he pardoned all Thomas' and his father Edmund's debts to the Exchequer, and exempted Henry and his wife Maud from having to pay the 'relief' (a kind of inheritance tax) due on the lands they had received from her uncle Payn and grandmother Hawise.[25] Thomas and Henry's uncle by marriage, Duke John II of Brittany, Brito's 66-year-old father and Beatrice's widower, died a peculiar death on 18 November 1305: a wall fell on him and crushed him as he led the horse of the recently elected Pope Clement V around Lyon. His eldest son Arthur II succeeded him as duke. Arthur had unwittingly created problems for his descendants by having a second family with his second wife Yolande de Dreux, widow of Alexander III of Scotland, in the 1290s; the competing claims of his granddaughter from his first marriage and his son with Yolande led to the War of the Breton Succession in the 1340s.

Thomas of Lancaster at least, and perhaps also Henry, seems to have been very close to their cousin Edward of Caernarfon before Edward's accession to the throne, although things were to go badly wrong later. Hundreds of Edward's letters from 1304–05 fortuitously survive, and he sent several to Thomas. One dated 22 September 1305 stated: 'Very dear cousin, we hold you well excused that you have not come to us, and your illness grieves us much, and if we can come to you we will do it willingly, to see and to comfort you.'[26] Another letter sent by Edward as king to Thomas' steward and close ally Sir Robert Holland on 20 November 1311 also says that Thomas had been very ill:

> We are very joyous and pleased about the good news we have heard concerning the improvement in our dear cousin and faithful subject Thomas, earl of Lancaster, and that soon he will be able to ride in comfort. And we send you word and dearly pray that as soon as he is comfortable and able to ride without hurt to his body, you should ask him … to hasten to us at our parliament.[27]

Thomas also told Edward in July 1317 that he could not attend a meeting of the royal council as he was 'in no condition to work'. This was in fact untrue, but evidently Thomas thought that claiming to be ill was a plausible excuse.[28] Perhaps Thomas suffered from some recurring illness or physical disability, and he spent most of the last few years of his life at his favourite castle of Pontefract in Yorkshire, rarely leaving except to go to York, 25 miles away.[29] His brother Henry was, according to the chronicler Jean le Bel, known as *Tort-Col* or 'Wryneck', either because of a physical disability – wryneck or torticollis is a painfully twisted and tilted neck – or because of the stiff-necked pride he displayed in his family and heritage.[30] It is not impossible that both Lancaster brothers suffered from a physical debility, though if so, it did not prevent Henry, at least, from doing anything: he took part in military campaigns from 1296 until 1333, and lived into his mid 60s. The metaphorical explanation of Henry of Lancaster's 'stiff-necked pride' is perhaps more likely than a physical condition, assuming he ever really was called 'Wryneck' and this is not simply the invention of one chronicler. On the other hand, Jean le Bel, who made this claim, did see Henry in person when he was in England in 1327, so was in a good position to know whether Henry suffered from wryneck or not.

Around 1302 to 1305, Henry and Maud Chaworth's first child was born, and named conventionally after Henry's mother, the Queen of Navarre and Countess of Lancaster; it was usual for the English nobility of the era to name their first daughter after her paternal grandmother. Blanche of Lancaster, eldest of Henry and Maud's seven children, was also the last of them to die: she lived until 1380, when she was in her mid or late 70s. Blanche was born in the reign of Edward I and lived into the reign of his great-great-grandson Richard II. Henry and Maud's second daughter Isabella, Prioress of Amesbury, was probably born about 1305 or 1308. She is often placed fourth on the list of Lancaster daughters with a date of birth estimated around 1317, but in fact was certainly the second.[31] Isabella of Lancaster went on pilgrimage with Edward II's sister Mary and niece Elizabeth de Burgh in 1317 so clearly cannot have been born that year, and she was named as the second of Henry's six daughters in his will of 1345, which listed the women in birth order. She bore the name of her maternal grandmother Isabella Beauchamp, which is further indirect evidence that she was the second daughter (conventionally the second daughter was named after the maternal grandmother). The middle three Lancaster children, Henry of Grosmont, Maud and Joan, were born around 1308 to 1315. Maud was the third daughter and married in 1327, Joan was the fourth and married in 1328, and Henry married in 1330. It is not clear where exactly Henry of Grosmont came in the birth order, though there was only one Lancaster son, born somewhere in the middle of six sisters; he was probably older than Joan the fourth sister, but may have been either older or younger than Maud, the third. The two youngest Lancaster siblings were Eleanor, born around 1316 to 1318, who married in 1330, and Mary, born around 1319 to 1321, who married in 1334.[32] The seven Lancaster children were widely spaced, born over a period of about sixteen or nineteen years, and there may have been others who died in infancy. Henry of Lancaster, like the good medieval noble father he was, arranged excellent marriages for five of his six daughters (except Isabella the nun). If Henry of Grosmont had not been born, or if he had died of a childhood illness as so many other medieval children did, the vast Lancastrian inheritance would have been divided among those five daughters on Henry of Lancaster's death in 1345.

The last great event of Edward I's reign was the knighting of his son Edward of Caernarfon and 266 other young men at Westminster on 22 May 1306. Henry of Lancaster's brother-in-law Hugh Despenser the Younger was one of the young men, and so was Roger Mortimer, Lord of Wigmore in Herefordshire, who would become Henry's greatest enemy in the late 1320s. Mere days after her son Hugh was knighted, Henry's mother-in-law Isabella Despenser (née Beauchamp), sister of the Earl of Warwick, died, and he and Maud received the dower lands Isabella had held from her first husband Patrick Chaworth, Maud's father. Thomas of Lancaster's mother-in-law Margaret Longespee, Countess of Salisbury, great-granddaughter and heir of Henry II's illegitimate son William Longespee, Earl of Salisbury, also died sometime around 1306 or 1308. Peculiarly, even an approximate date of death was not recorded and the year cannot be ascertained, but her widower Henry de Lacy, Earl of Lincoln, was married to his second wife Joan Martin by June 1310. Joan was at least forty years her husband's junior, and at least a decade younger than her stepdaughter Alice.[33] The Earl of Lincoln, as was the custom, kept his first wife Margaret Longespee's entire inheritance for the rest of his own life, when it would pass to their daughter Alice and her husband Thomas. It must have been a great relief to the couple that her father had no children with Joan Martin. Although Alice could not be displaced as her mother's heir, the birth of a son to her father and stepmother would have seen the entire Lacy inheritance snatched from her and Thomas' grasp after they must have grown accustomed to thinking of it as rightfully theirs for many years. A son took precedence over a daughter, even if he was decades younger, and would have become the Earl of Lincoln's sole heir from the moment of his birth, and any daughters born to Henry and Joan would have shared the inheritance equally with Alice. Joan Martin did have two children with her second husband Nicholas Audley, so Thomas and Alice – and Thomas' later Lancastrian heirs who benefited enormously from Henry and Alice de Lacy's lands and castles – were lucky.

Edward I's reign was to end with the king intending to lead another campaign to Scotland, this time against Robert Bruce, who had stabbed his great rival John 'the Red Comyn', Lord of Badenoch, to death in February 1306 and had himself crowned king shortly afterwards. Just four months before he died, Edward I pardoned his nephew Henry of Lancaster for helping a man called John Harper to escape from prison in Gloucestershire, and for subsequently receiving him.[34] The great king, now 68, died at Burgh-by-Sands near Carlisle in the far north-west of his kingdom on 7 July 1307, and the Lancaster brothers' 23-year-old first cousin Edward of Caernarfon succeeded as Edward II. Probably his first act was to recall his beloved Piers Gaveston, sent into exile in France by the old king a few weeks before, to England. Edward made Gaveston Earl of Cornwall and brought him into the royal family by marriage to his niece Margaret de Clare. The new king's favouritism towards Gaveston, whom he adored, soon earned him enemies.

Thomas, Earl of Lancaster, remained, however, firmly on his cousin's side at the start of the reign. He appears, judging by the evidence of charter witness lists, to have spent much of Edward II's first regnal year (July 1307 to July 1308) at court. He even witnessed charters in the company of Hugh Despenser the Elder (b. 1261), a close ally and friend of the young king but a man Thomas loathed.[35] The king rewarded Thomas' loyalty on 9 May 1308 by appointing him Steward of England, as his father had been, and Thomas and his younger brother and nephew held the position for many decades.[36] Around this time, sometime between Michaelmas (29 September) 1307 and Michaelmas 1308, Thomas' wife Alice de Lacy became pregnant. Alice, now 26, sent a messenger to the mayor and townspeople of Leicester, one of Thomas' towns, to inform them. They rewarded the messenger with a shilling.[37] This pregnancy must have ended in miscarriage or stillbirth, or perhaps the child died soon after birth, as there is no other record of any child born to Thomas and Alice, and they certainly had no surviving off-spring. Their marriage was an ill-fated one, and Alice left her husband a few years later; perhaps their childlessness, and the loss of the infant of 1307/08, was a factor in their unhappiness.

Edward II married the Lancaster brothers' niece Isabella of France, only surviving daughter of Philip IV and their late half-sister Queen Jeanne, on 25 January 1308, in the presence of their brother-in-law Philip and their eldest nephew Louis, King of Navarre. The marriage had been arranged almost ten years previously as a way of making peace between Edward I and Philip IV. Henry of Lancaster was one of the noblemen and women ordered to travel to Dover to greet his cousin and his niece when they arrived in England on 7 February 1308. With him were Mary, nun of Amesbury Priory, and Elizabeth, formerly Countess of Holland and now Countess of Hereford – the only two of Edward II's sisters still alive in England.[38] It is rather curious that neither of the Lancaster brothers travelled to France to attend the wedding of their niece and their cousin and to see their French relatives. Exactly a month after their wedding, Edward and his 12-year-old bride were crowned King and Queen of England at Westminster Abbey. Both Lancaster brothers played important roles in the coronation procession, but so did Piers Gaveston, the adored royal favourite, to the immense annoyance of everyone else.

CONFLICT WITH
THE KING

In or around late 1308, Edward II and Thomas, Earl of Lancaster, fell
out, though it is not at all clear what happened and why. Thomas was
at court and witnessed charters regularly until 15 November 1308, but
then left and did not return until March 1309.[1] There was no huge quarrel,
no sudden rift, which would have come to the attention of chroniclers, and
Thomas only gradually moved into opposition to his cousin, though would
maintain this position for the rest of his life.[2] Edward granted Thomas the
right to hold markets and fairs at two of his manors on 1 December 1308,
so seemingly all was still well then, but by late May 1309 Thomas demanded
a safe conduct to come and see his cousin.[3] In early 1310, Edward forbade Thomas from coming to Parliament 'with horses and arms'.[4] On
24 July 1309, however, Edward visited Thomas' Northamptonshire manor
of Higham Ferrers on his way to Parliament at Stamford and was at Thomas'
Yorkshire manor of Pontefract on 17 November 1309 and 9 August 1310.
On 10 August 1309, meanwhile, Thomas witnessed a grant by Anthony
Bek, Bishop of Durham and Patriarch of Jerusalem, to his cousin the king.[5]
Perhaps they were making some effort to reconcile and to put right whatever had gone wrong between them, and another man who witnessed
Bek's grant to Edward was Piers Gaveston, so apparently Thomas was
happy enough to be in the presence of his cousin's beloved companion and

perhaps lover. If Thomas and Edward did attempt a reconciliation, it failed, and the two men came to loathe each other. A group of barons and magnates headed by Thomas' father-in-law, the Earl of Lincoln, had successfully forced the king to send Piers Gaveston away from England in June 1308, his second exile, though at the last minute Edward appointed him Lord Lieutenant of Ireland and thus ensured he left the country in triumph, not disgrace. The infatuated king spent the next year manipulating his barons so that he could recall Gaveston, and it worked. The favourite returned in June 1309 and was restored to his earldom of Cornwall at the Parliament held in Stamford that August, but he and Edward carried on in the same way as they always had, and the goodwill and support the king had cleverly built up over the past year soon dissipated.

In March 1310, a group of English earls, barons and bishops formed themselves into a group called the Lords Ordainer and forced the king to consent to their reforms of his household and government. Both Lancaster brothers were among the Ordainers, as were eight of the eleven English earls alive in 1310, including Thomas' father-in-law Henry de Lacy of Lincoln – by far the oldest and most experienced of the English earls early in Edward II's reign – and the king's young nephew Gilbert de Clare of Gloucester.[6] Edward II did his best to obstruct the Ordainers and, accompanied by Queen Isabella, spent the period from September 1310 to September 1311 in the far north of England supposedly trying to defeat Robert Bruce, King of Scotland. This, predictably, failed completely.

While Edward was in the north in February 1311, Henry de Lacy, Earl of Lincoln died at the age of 60, and Thomas of Lancaster inherited his lands by right of his wife Alice. Thomas now became Earl of Lincoln and Salisbury to add to the earldoms he already held, and enjoyed a gross annual income of around £11,000, far greater than anyone in the kingdom except the king (the next richest man in the country was the young Earl of Gloucester, who earned about £7,000 a year). Thomas owed homage for his new lands – which included the castles of Pontefract, Pickering and Bolingbroke in Yorkshire and Lincolnshire – to Edward II, but refused to cross the River Tweed into Scotland to do so. Edward refused to return to England to accept the homage. Thomas threatened to take 100 knights to forcibly enter his lands, and once again, civil war loomed.[7] Eventually Edward caved in and agreed to meet his cousin at Haggerston, on the English side of the river. The two men 'saluted each other amicably and exchanged frequent kisses'; they were both well-versed in courtesy, manners and protocol, and each concealed his antipathy for the other in public. Edward also hid his annoyance that he had been forced to travel to meet Thomas when etiquette demanded that his subjects should come to him.

Sometime around 1310 or 1312, Henry of Lancaster and Maud Chaworth's only son Henry was born, presumably (given that he was sometimes called Henry of Grosmont) at Grosmont Castle in Wales. There is little evidence for Henry of Grosmont's age. He was knighted in 1330 and would have been at least 16 then, so it is almost certain that he was not born later than 1314.[8] The Inquisition Post Mortem (IPM) of his aunt-in-law Alice de Lacy taken in Lincolnshire in October 1348 says, with the typical vagueness of IPMs, that he was then 30, but this cannot be taken to mean that he was exactly 30 in 1348; jurors on IPMs often simply gave the nearest round number when estimating a person's age, and almost certainly this just means that Henry was older than 30 but not yet 40, hence born after 1308.[9] His father gave him lands for the first time in 1333, which might suggest that he had come of age, 21, that year, and hence was born in 1312. Henry of Lancaster was at his castle of Grosmont on 29 September 1312, which may give some indication as to his son's date of birth, though we cannot know for sure.[10] If Henry of Grosmont was born then, he was exactly the same age as his cousin Edward III, who was born on 13 November 1312, and his brother-in-law William de Burgh, Earl of Ulster, born on 17 September 1312. He first appears on record in 1323–24, when the townspeople of Leicester sent 'Sir Henry de Grosemound' 7 shillings' worth of oats.[11] According to his own later testimony, Henry of Grosmont was tall, slim and fair, and his daughter and heir Blanche, Duchess of Lancaster, was said to be tall and blonde by the poet Geoffrey Chaucer (her name means 'white' in French, and Chaucer commented on her appropriately pale skin and fairness). One fourteenth-century chronicle calls Henry of Grosmont's uncle Thomas, Earl of Lancaster, 'slender and of fair size', meaning tall.[12] This gives some indication of the Lancasters' appearance.

Edward II finally returned south to attend Parliament in September 1311 and was forced to consent to over forty wholesale reforms of his household called the Ordinances, and to the exile from England – for the third time – of Piers Gaveston. The latter left England in early November but returned two months later, perhaps only for the birth of his and Margaret de Clare's child Joan, but the king defiantly restored him to the earldom of

Cornwall and declared him 'good and loyal'. Thomas of Lancaster was one of the furious Ordainers who met in London to discuss Gaveston's fate, and pursued the king and his favourite north, holding jousting tournaments as a cover for assembling groups of armed men.[13] He arrived at Tynemouth on 4 May 1312 and, taking Edward and Gaveston completely by surprise, almost captured the favourite. Thomas did seize their baggage train and horses, which he restored to his cousin a few months later. The king and Gaveston fled by boat to Scarborough, where Gaveston was besieged in the castle there by the Earls of Pembroke and Surrey and Lords Percy and Clifford. He was forced to surrender after only nine days as the castle was not provisioned for a siege. Thomas of Lancaster sat with his army at his castle of Pickering 20 miles away as a further line of defence against the royal favourite.

While the Earl of Pembroke was taking Gaveston south to Parliament, where his fate would be debated and decided, Thomas' close ally Guy Beauchamp, Earl of Warwick, abducted Gaveston and took him to the dungeons of Warwick Castle. Thomas arrived some days later, in the company of Edward II's brother-in-law Humphrey de Bohun, Earl of Hereford, and the Earl of Surrey's brother-in-law Edmund Fitzalan, Earl of Arundel. The earls condemned Piers Gaveston to death, and on 19 June 1312 he was taken out to Blacklow Hill between the towns of Warwick and Kenilworth, on Thomas of Lancaster's lands. Here he was killed by being run through with a sword then beheaded. The *Vita Edwardi Secundi* (a life of Edward II written by one of Edward's clerks) makes the point that it was Thomas of Lancaster who specifically ordered Gaveston's death because he (Thomas) was 'of higher birth and more powerful than the rest'.[14]

Edward II was utterly devastated, and for a few months the country teetered on the brink of civil war as Thomas of Lancaster and the Earls of Warwick, Hereford and Arundel raised armies and took them to Hertfordshire just a few miles from London. Thomas' brother-in-law Philip IV of France (also the king's father-in-law) sent his half-brother the Count of Evreux and others to help the negotiations, and Gaveston's brother-in-law the young Earl of Gloucester also did his utmost to calm the situation. Matters were helped when Queen Isabella gave birth to her and the king's first child on 13 November 1312 at Windsor. It was a boy named Edward after his father and grandfather, and he immediately became heir to the throne. Two chroniclers state that the king's grief over Gaveston was much assuaged by his son's birth, but he never forgave his cousin Thomas of Lancaster for his role in the death of his beloved, and another chronicler comments on the 'mortal hatred, which endured forever' between them.[15] The king and his royal cousin had once been very close friends, but now were deadly enemies who each desired the other's destruction. Thomas and his allies had tried to improve the political situation by removing the hated royal favourite; as it would turn out some years later, they had made matters far worse.

11

END OF A MARRIAGE

⬦

Edward II officially pardoned Piers Gaveston's killers in October 1313, when Thomas of Lancaster, Guy Beauchamp, Earl of Warwick and Humphrey de Bohun, Earl of Hereford submitted to him 'with great humility, on their knees' in Westminster Hall.[1] Thomas' brother Henry was one of the hundreds of men granted an official pardon for all actions undertaken against Gaveston, though what role he had played is uncertain.[2] On 10 June 1312, nine days before Gaveston's murder, Henry had been at Kempsford in Gloucestershire with his wife Maud Chaworth (it was one of her own manors which she had inherited from her father). Although he could certainly have ridden the 50 miles to Warwick to be present with his brother Thomas at Gaveston's death, it seems that Henry rarely took part in the turbulent politics of these years and preferred to stay on his and Maud's lands with his family. He was at his castle of Grosmont in Wales on 29 September 1312, at a time when negotiations were taking place in London to try to reconcile the king and the men who had killed Gaveston, including Henry's brother. In the first half of March 1315, Henry briefly visited court at Westminster and witnessed a royal charter with his brother, but four days later was back at Kempsford.[3]

Henry of Lancaster did not witness a single one of Edward II's charters from the beginning of his reign in July 1307 until September 1314, not even in the first regnal year when his brother was often with the king, which indicates that he was rarely if ever at court.⁴ It is revealing that the first time Henry witnessed royal charters, in September 1314, came at a time when his brother Thomas was dominating the English government, and there is nothing to show that Edward and Henry of Lancaster were particularly friendly or close. Perhaps Henry preferred to stay away from court and leave politics to his brother, though things were to change in years to come when he succeeded as Earl of Lancaster. A few months before Edward officially pardoned him and his allies, in February 1313, Thomas had finally returned all the king's possessions he had seized at Tynemouth in May 1312 when Edward fled with Gaveston. These included some personal items given to the king by his mother and sisters, and dozens of horses. The day after his official pardon of the earls that October, Edward invited Thomas to dine with him. Given their mutual hostility, it was probably an awkward meal.

Edward II took a huge army north in June 1314 to fight Robert Bruce, King of Scotland. Only three of his earls – his nephew Gloucester, his brother-in-law Hereford and his cousin Pembroke – accompanied him. Thomas of Lancaster stayed at Pontefract and took his feudal obligation to send men to the king's wars very lightly indeed: he sent only four men-at-arms and four knights. He raised an army at Pontefract in case the king used a triumphant victory to strike against him on his return to England, but in the end he had nothing to fear, as Edward lost the battle. The king's nephew, the Earl of Gloucester, was the most important of the many Englishmen killed during the heavy defeat at the Battle of Bannockburn. Gloucester was only 23 and left no children; his heirs therefore were his three sisters: Eleanor Despenser, Margaret Gaveston and Elizabeth de Burgh. Thomas had been feuding with the young Earl of Gloucester, who was the second wealthiest nobleman in England after himself, in 1311: one anonymous letter-writer said he feared a riot when both men and their retinues arrived in London.⁵ Thomas seized the chance after Bannockburn to control his cousin the king, and at the York Parliament of September 1314 – when his brother Henry witnessed royal charters for the first time in the reign – he drastically reduced Edward II's household expenses and the king 'refused nothing' to him. Meanwhile in France, Thomas and Henry's 46-year-old brother-in-law Philip IV died on 29 November 1314 after a hunting accident, and was succeeded by their nephew Louis X, already King of Navarre as his inheritance from the Lancasters' half-sister Queen Jeanne.

Thomas of Lancaster lived like another king: he had an astonishing 708 people in his retinue, larger even than Edward II's (who had around 500 people in his household), and owned 400 horses. Thomas' gross annual income was about £11,000, which made him as rich as Croesus; most people in England at the time earned between 1 and 3*d* per day.[6] The *Vita Edwardi Secundi* stated of Thomas that 'as each parent was of royal birth he was clearly of nobler descent than the other earls. By the size of his patrimony you may assess his influence.'[7] Although he was richer than anyone in the country except his cousin the king and was a multi-millionaire, even a billionaire in modern terms, Thomas lived well beyond his means. Even by the standards of the time he was a despised, greedy and grasping landlord who seems to have oppressed his tenants with the aim of increasing his already vast income, and he borrowed money from the townspeople of Leicester on a few occasions.[8] Henry of Lancaster, although a far kinder, gentler and more generous individual than his brother, and certainly nowhere near as lavishly extravagant, also tended to throw his weight around whenever he could in later years after he became Earl of Lancaster.

Parliament opened in Lincoln, one of the towns of which Thomas of Lancaster was earl, on 27 January 1316, but Thomas arrived very late; he did not deign to come until 12 February. To the king's disgust, Thomas was made his chief counsellor, and Edward and his advisers were thereafter forced to consult with and seek the approval of the Earl of Lancaster as though he were another king. Famine was raging in northern Europe in the mid 1310s and the population of England suffered terribly, but little could be done to assuage their hunger, disease and suffering because the king and his mighty cousin loathed each other and refused to co-operate, and thus left the kingdom practically ungoverned. 'Whatever pleases the lord king the earl's servants try to upset; and whatever pleases the earl the king's servants call treachery.'[9] Rebellion broke out against corrupt and brutal royal officials in South Wales in early 1316, and Thomas' brother Henry, as Lord of Kidwelly, was one of the men sent by Edward II to suppress the uprising. Three of the others were Sir William Montacute, Sir Hugh Audley and Sir Roger Damory, the current influential court favourites, and perhaps infatuations, of the king.[10]

Edward II and Isabella of France's second son John was born at the Palace of Eltham in Kent on 15 August 1316, and the king, in Yorkshire, gave £100 to Isabella's servant who brought him news of the birth. Isabella asked her uncle Thomas of Lancaster to stand as John's sponsor, i.e. to be his godfather, but he failed to attend the baptism. This was an unforgivable insult. Thomas had, however, attended the christening of his ally the Earl of Warwick's son and heir Thomas Beauchamp in February 1314; the boy was named after him. Thomas gave his godson and namesake a gold casket containing a bone of St George.[11] Around the time of John of Eltham's birth, Thomas met the king in York and the two men had a furious row, apparently about Edward's ongoing unwillingness to abide by the Ordinances of 1311.[12] These were baronial reforms of the royal household and the king's power much promoted by Thomas, who saw himself as a successor in this respect to Simon de Montfort and his 1258 Provisions of Oxford. King and earl had taken to marching around the kingdom with large numbers of armed men, and refused to meet each other without protection. Edward was concerned enough about Thomas' hostility and military power to summon Queen Isabella to him in York with all speed, fearing for her safety. She travelled very fast, possibly because she also feared her uncle Thomas' intentions: on 22 September 1316 she was at Buntingford in Hertfordshire, 175 miles from York, and was reunited with Edward there on or soon after the 27th.[13] This was a remarkably fast journey for a woman who had only just given birth. Perhaps Edward took a malicious pleasure in the fact that he now had two healthy sons, while Thomas, in his late 30s, had no legitimate children. As the years wore on and Thomas and Alice de Lacy (who turned 35 at the end of 1316) produced no surviving offspring, his younger brother Henry must have grown used to the idea that one day he might inherit the Lancastrian estates and fortune.

Sometime before 9 October 1316, Henry of Lancaster and Maud Chaworth's eldest daughter Blanche married Thomas Wake, son and heir of the late John Wake, Lord of Liddell in Cumberland and an important landowner in Yorkshire and Lincolnshire. John died in April 1300 when Thomas was only 2 years old, which made him a ward of the king.[14] Thomas' sister Margaret had married the Scottish nobleman Sir John Comyn, who fell while fighting for Edward II at Bannockburn, and their little son Aymer Comyn died as a toddler shortly before 25 October 1316, not long after his uncle married Blanche of Lancaster.[15] Wake was 18 at the time of his wedding, Blanche between 11 and 14. Edward II had offered him the hand of Piers Gaveston's daughter and heir Joan, but Thomas refused her, and married Blanche of Lancaster instead without the king's permission. Wake's decision is perhaps a little puzzling. Joan Gaveston, though only 4 years old in 1316, was sole heir to her mother Margaret Gaveston (née de Clare) and Margaret's third of her late brother Gilbert's earldom of Gloucester, whereas Blanche of Lancaster had a brother and thus was not an heiress, and her father Henry of Lancaster was only the heir of his wealthy brother for as long as Thomas failed to produce legitimate children anyway. Perhaps Wake gambled that Margaret de Clare would marry again and have a son, which would instantly disinherit Joan, and ultimately his decision was vindicated when his father-in-law became Earl of Lancaster in 1327 and hugely influential. The unfortunate Joan Gaveston died in January 1325 around the time of her 13th birthday. Edward II, annoyed with Wake for 'refusing a suitable marriage which the king offered to him', fined him £1,000, but by 6 June 1317 had clearly forgiven him as he allowed him to take possession of his inheritance (although he was still two years underage), at Henry of Lancaster's request.[16] Thomas Wake and Blanche of Lancaster were married for thirty-three years but had no children, and Thomas' heir was his sister Margaret Comyn, who married her second husband, Edward II's half-brother Edmund, Earl of Kent, in late 1325.

In the spring of 1317, Henry of Lancaster and Maud Chaworth's second daughter Isabella went on pilgrimage to Canterbury with Edward II's sister Mary, nun of Amesbury Priory, and his niece Elizabeth de Burgh (née de Clare), one of the late Earl of Gloucester's three sisters and co-heirs. Isabella of Lancaster was only about 10 or 12 but already showing an interest in the religious life, and she later became a nun at Amesbury and in 1343 its prioress. She might already have been living at Amesbury by 1317, at least some of the time. Edward II paid all the expenses of the ladies' pilgrimage.[17] Elizabeth de Burgh had just married her uncle's latest infatuation, the Oxfordshire knight Sir Roger Damory, only a few weeks after she gave birth to her second husband Theobald de Verdon's posthumous daughter Isabella de Verdon. Elizabeth de Burgh and her older sisters Eleanor Despenser and Margaret Audley (formerly Gaveston) and their husbands became rich later in 1317 when the lands of their late brother the Earl of Gloucester were divided among them. In late April 1317, Margaret married Sir Hugh Audley, also a great favourite and perhaps lover of her uncle the king, who would be the only one of the royal favourites who survived the reign and who in later years became a staunch Lancastrian ally.

Thomas of Lancaster's marriage to Alice de Lacy had never been a happy one, and in May 1317 she left him for good. Various chroniclers say she was abducted by John de Warenne, Earl of Surrey, but it seems virtually certain that Alice wished to leave her husband and that Surrey merely helped her accomplish it, rather than taking her against her will. The *Anonimalle* and *Gesta Edwardi de Carnarvon* chronicles both say that Alice left Thomas voluntarily and that the Earl of Surrey took her under his protection.[18] Thomas feared the machinations of the current court favourites, Roger Damory, Hugh Audley and William Montacute, as well as the Earl of Surrey, and sent messengers to the king, claiming that 'he fears the deadly stratagems of certain persons who thrive under the protection of the royal court … they have already carried off the earl's wife to his disgrace and shame'. He asked Edward to remove them from court. Edward refused, and snapped, 'I will avenge the despite done to the earl when I can; I refuse to expel my household; for the abduction of his wife let him seek a remedy in law only.'[19]

Thomas and Alice de Lacy's separation proved significant for Henry of Lancaster, as they had no surviving children after twenty-three years of marriage and now certainly never would, and in the absence of any legitimate offspring, Henry was his brother's heir. Although it is often stated that Thomas and Alice's marriage was annulled in 1317, it was not, and they remained officially married for the remaining five years of Thomas' life. Perhaps he had given up any hope of fathering legitimate children, as he seemingly made no attempt to annul his failed marriage and wed another woman (he did father two illegitimate sons). This might also give weight to the notion that he had some recurring illness, or disability.

It is difficult to say very much about the personal relationship of the Lancaster brothers. Thomas' biographer has pointed out that none of Thomas' 750 surviving letters of 1318–19 were sent to his brother, which is perhaps revealing.[20] On the other hand, Henry was overseas for most of that period, which might explain the lack of correspondence. The brothers were together in York on 4 February 1319 when they both witnessed a charter of Edward II, and Henry witnessed more charters during his brother's period of political dominance in 1314–15 than at any other time during his cousin's reign.[21] Henry's close relationships with his children and their spouses reveal him to have been a man who loved his family, and in 1343 he asked the Pope for a dispensation for his nephew John of

Lancaster, one of Thomas' sons with a mistress, on the grounds of his illegitimacy. John later joined the household of Henry's son and heir Henry of Grosmont.[22] There is likely to have been much contact between the two Lancaster brothers which did not find its way onto extant record. In 1328, Henry protected the men who had killed Robert Holland, a close ally of Thomas' who betrayed him shortly before his execution in 1322. It is perhaps significant, however, that although Henry raised a cross to his brother's memory outside Leicester in about 1325 (according to one chronicler), he seems not to have made much, if any, effort to remember Thomas otherwise, and although his son Henry of Grosmont founded a chapel at the place where Thomas was executed in Yorkshire, Henry did not. Henry of Lancaster was not with his brother at the tournament of Dunstable in the spring of 1309 even though he loved jousting, which may reveal either that he was not particularly close to his brother or that he did not wish to act against his cousin the king, as this tournament was a cover for disgruntled nobles to meet and discuss their grievances against Edward II.[23] This is perhaps an example of how Henry stayed out of politics until he became Earl of Lancaster.

Thomas continued to demand that the royal favourites Damory, Audley and Montacute be expelled from court, and the lands Edward had granted them taken away. He sent the king a long letter in July 1317, stating that Edward kept men close to him who 'are in no wise fitting to be near you or in your service … but you have held them dearer than they were before'.[24] Of course, the three men had no intention of allowing Lancaster to diminish their vast influence over Edward. They selfishly counselled the king to remain hostile to his cousin and 'intrigued against the earl as best they could'.[5] It was in their interests to ensure that the king and the earl were not reconciled, and Edward, who detested his cousin anyway, was susceptible to their blandishments. Damory, Audley and Montacute may have had more sinister motives for their plots and schemes against Thomas of Lancaster: if they managed to engineer his downfall on the grounds of treason, his lands would be forfeit to the Crown, and it is possible that they hoped to persuade Edward to share them out amongst themselves.[26] Thomas therefore had good reason to fear the royal favourites and to distrust the king. Pope John XXII was trying to heal the breach between the king and his cousin in 1317 and 1318, begging Edward not to allow any 'backbiter or malicious flatterer' to bring about disunity between himself and his cousin, and to send away from court those men who offended the earl. The Pope asked Thomas to 'separate himself' from those who displeased Edward and to reject 'suggestions of whisperers and double-tongued men', and wrote to Henry of Lancaster exhorting him, as a near-relative of both Thomas and Edward and 'bound to pay them reverence and affection', to use his influence to reconcile them.[27]

Thomas of Lancaster's main response to his wife Alice's departure in May 1317 was to attack the Earl of Surrey's Yorkshire castles in revenge. He took a large group of armed men to besiege and capture Sandal, Conisbrough and Wakefield, and ejected Maud Nerford, Surrey's mistress and the mother of several of his illegitimate children, from her property. By the beginning of 1318, he had taken firm control over Surrey's Yorkshire lands.[28] And the powerful earl's lawlessness had not yet run its course. In early October 1317, Thomas seized Knaresborough Castle in Yorkshire, which his retainer John Lilburn did not surrender to the king until January 1318, and by the beginning of November had also forcibly gained possession of Alton Castle in Staffordshire.[29] Sir Roger Damory was the custodian of both, and Thomas saw Damory as his chief enemy at court and was determined to attack him.[30] Edward II ineffectually sent out orders to various sheriffs to retake the castles, and commanded Thomas to 'desist completely from these proceedings'.[31] Thomas' brother Henry finally restored the Earl of Surrey's Yorkshire castles and lands to him in March 1328.[32]

While this was going on, Edward II visited York, but could not go there by the most direct route as Thomas of Lancaster had blocked his way by placing armed guards on the roads and bridges south of York. Edward was furious that one of his subjects would dare to impede his progress through his own kingdom, and brought it up four and a half years later as one of the charges against Thomas at his trial.[33] When the king travelled south towards London after this visit to York, Thomas took his men to the battlements of Pontefract Castle to jeer at him as he rode past, a truly astonishing display of rudeness and *lèse-majesté*.[34] Edward, understandably furious, came close to allowing himself to be persuaded by his friends to attack Thomas, but the Earl of Pembroke fortunately talked him out of it.[35] This was sensible advice, as attacking Thomas would have caused civil war, but Edward never forgot or forgave.

FEUDING AND REBELLION

~∞∞~

S ometime before 13 June 1317, the obscure youngest Lancaster brother
John died in France and, as his marriage to Alix Joinville had remained
childless, Henry of Lancaster was heir to his lordships in Champagne
and Brie. On that date, Edward II asked Philip V of France – who was
his brother-in-law and the Lancasters' nephew, and the successor of his
late brother Louis X (d. June 1316) – to postpone Henry's homage for
the lands until after the next Feast of the Purification, 2 February 1318.
He needed Henry in England, Edward said, to take care of some 'arduous
business' relating to himself.[1] Henry duly went overseas in May 1318, and
on 28 September was said to be staying in France to claim his inheritance.[2]
He was back in England by early 1319 and was at court with the king
on 4 February – Henry's brother-in-law, Hugh Despenser the Younger,
and his brother Thomas' most hated enemy Roger Damory also witnessed
Edward's charters that day – and left again in May 1319, this time on his
cousin's service. Edward excused him from attending the siege of the
port of Berwick-upon-Tweed that September as he was 'on important
business' overseas.[3] Hugh Despenser the Elder, stepfather of Henry's wife
Maud, went overseas on the king's service at the same time and perhaps on
the same mission, and Despenser, at least, visited the Spanish kingdom of
Castile.[4] Henry of Lancaster was outside England and Wales for much of

the period from May 1318 to April 1322. On 21 August 1320 he was 'staying beyond the seas' until the following June, though returned for a while in November 1320, and he was out of England again on 30 January 1322 and expected to be so for another year. The dramatic and shocking events of that year, however, brought him home much earlier.[5] Maud Chaworth accompanied her husband overseas in 1320 and almost certainly on the other occasions as well. Their seventh and youngest child Mary may have been born abroad, or perhaps they returned to England in early 1319 or in November 1320 so that their latest child would be born there (though this is only speculation).

Edward II and Thomas of Lancaster finally came to terms in August 1318 and met in the Midlands village of Leake, where a treaty was signed stating, among much else, that Thomas would be pardoned for all his actions of the last few years and that Edward would keep the 1311 Ordinances. A group of magnates and bishops had been working hard for years to reconcile the two powerful men. The king gave Thomas the kiss of peace and a fine palfrey horse as a gift 'in recognition of his great love' for his cousin, and 'the lord king and the earl met and conversed long and intimately, with renewed friendship and mutual goodwill'.[6] Thomas once again demanded the removal from court of the three royal favourites he hated, Roger Damory, William Montacute and Hugh Audley, and even claimed that Damory and Montacute had tried to kill him. Surprisingly, Edward agreed.

Hugh Despenser the Younger, Maud Chaworth's younger half-brother, was elected as the king's chamberlain shortly before October 1318 at the request of the magnates, including Thomas of Lancaster. This would prove to be a catastrophic mistake. Despenser – who had been married to Edward's eldest niece Eleanor de Clare since 1306 but for many years was disliked and ignored by the king – parlayed his position close to Edward into immense influence. Edward became infatuated with him, perhaps as much as he ever had been with Piers Gaveston. Despenser was highly intelligent, manipulative, corrupt, greedy and ambitious almost beyond description, and before too long he was the most powerful man in England and a besotted king let him do whatever he wished. Whether or to what extent Henry of Lancaster and Maud maintained contact or any kind of relationship with her half-brother is impossible to say, though during the period of Hugh's absolute control over the English government in the

1320s there is not the slightest sign that he favoured his brother-in-law Henry in any way at all.

Robert Bruce had captured the port of Berwick-upon-Tweed in April 1318, and it was so important to retake it that even Thomas of Lancaster co-operated with Edward II for once. The Siege of Berwick in September 1319, however, proved an utter failure; the Lancasters' niece Queen Isabella came close to capture by a Scottish force, and Thomas was accused (probably wrongly) of aiding the Scots in exchange for a huge payment of £40,000. Edward still had not forgiven him for the death of Piers Gaveston and announced ominously, 'When this wretched business is over, we will turn our hands to other matters. For I have not yet forgotten the wrong that was done to my brother Piers.'[7] Both cousins had made an effort to spend time together and get along between the Treaty of Leake and the Siege of Berwick thirteen months later. Thomas witnessed thirty-nine of Edward's charters between August 1318 and September 1319 and was often at court, and on 5 June 1319 Edward confirmed their mutual grandmother Eleanor of Provence's 1286 grant of her rights in the county of Provence to Thomas and Henry.[8] But now it had all gone badly wrong again. The royal clerk who wrote the *Vita Edwardi Secundi* gave credence to the rumours about Thomas aiding the Scots, crying out, 'Oh! Earl of Lancaster, whose wealth is so great, why for such a sum of money have you lost your reputation and a name for constancy?' Rather bravely, Thomas approached Edward and made a dignified speech asserting his innocence and his willingness to face his accusers in due legal process.[9] Nothing more was heard of the matter, but in early 1322 Thomas and some of his allies certainly did commit treason by inviting a Scottish army to come to England and ride in arms with them against Edward.

Henry of Lancaster and Maud Chaworth were supposedly feuding in South Wales with their neighbour William Braose, Lord of the Gower Peninsula, around this time. Braose accused Henry and Maud sometime between 1317 and 1320 of entering his land of Gower and stated that they 'robbed, wounded and killed his people'. He further accused Maud specifically of putting a man called William Avenel and many others on the road to Carmarthen (Maud's lordship which she had inherited from her father) to kill his knights and ministers, and claimed that Henry and Maud had threatened his men 'with life and limb and the burning of their houses'.[10] This all sounds very melodramatic and unlikely. There is nothing in Henry of Lancaster's long career that even remotely suggests he was capable of such misdeeds or of threatening to do them, and he was away from England and Wales for most of this period anyway. William Braose was also feuding with Maud's half-brother Hugh Despenser the Younger, lord of nearby Glamorgan, in 1318, and before too long Hugh's ambitions to gain control of Gower would result in the Despenser War and, ultimately, the execution of Henry's brother Earl Thomas.

Henry and Maud's son-in-law Thomas, Lord Wake, was given permission to go overseas on pilgrimage on 24 April 1320, and set off for Santiago de Compostela in northern Spain with two attendants. At some point that year, their eldest daughter Blanche of Lancaster petitioned the king, calling herself 'Blanche Wake, cousin of our lord the king and consort of Lord Wake'. She stated that one of Wake's manors in Lincolnshire had been attacked and robbed and some of his and her own servants killed, and that she was frightened to go there. She asked for justices to sit on a commission of *oyer et terminer*, to 'hear and determine' what had happened. Rather poignantly, Blanche added that 'her father Sir Henry of Lancaster and her mother are overseas, and therefore she remains alone'.[11] Blanche was, after all, still only a teenager, perhaps 15 and no more than 18, and evidently she expected that her parents would have helped and protected her if they had been in the country. There is much evidence that Henry of Lancaster had a very close relationship with all his children, and this is perhaps another example. Although by this stage Blanche's uncle Hugh Despenser the Younger was high in the king's favour and powerful at court, her petition was rejected. Her husband was back in England from Santiago by 24 November 1320, when he settled two of his own manors in Yorkshire and Cumberland on himself and Blanche jointly. The attorney Thomas Wake used to carry out this settlement was Michael Meldon, a long-term Lancastrian adherent who served Edmund of Lancaster and his sons Thomas and Henry for decades.[12] Blanche's father Henry and almost certainly her mother Maud were also back in England by mid November 1320, at least for a while, and perhaps her youngest sister Mary of Lancaster was born around this time.[13]

Blanche Wake's uncle Hugh Despenser the Younger was pushing the Marcher lords, the men who owned lordships in Wales and along the English–Welsh border, into opposition to him, opposition which blossomed into open rebellion against the king and ended with the execution of twenty or so noblemen and knights including Blanche's other uncle, the

Earl of Lancaster. Among Despenser's rivals and enemies were Edward II's brother-in-law Humphrey de Bohun, Earl of Hereford, Roger Mortimer, Lord of Wigmore, Lords Clifford, Mowbray and Giffard, and Thomas of Lancaster, whom the others considered their leader. Henry of Lancaster owned the lordships of Kidwelly, Carmarthen and Monmouth in South Wales and was a neighbour and thus a potential enemy of his powerful brother-in-law, but luckily for him, he was overseas for almost all of 1320, 1321 and early 1322, which probably saved his life. His son-in-law Thomas Wake may have accompanied him abroad after his return from his pilgrimage to Santiago, or at least followed Henry's political lead, as he played no role in the 1321–22 baronial rebellion against Edward II and Hugh Despenser the Younger and thus also saved himself from execution, long imprisonment or exile.

In May 1321, the Marcher lords attacked Despenser's castles and manors in South Wales in a terrible orgy of vandalism, destruction and murder which spread to his and his father's English manors, and at a Parliament held in London that August they demanded the permanent exile and disinheritance of the two Hugh Despensers and their descendants. Hugh the Elder went overseas; Hugh the Younger became a pirate in the English Channel with Edward II's support and connivance. In late 1321 the king recalled the Despensers and set off on a military campaign against their baronial enemies, whom he took to calling the 'Contrariants'. Some of them, including Roger Mortimer of Wigmore and Lord Berkeley, submitted to the king in early 1322 and were imprisoned, and the rest fled towards Thomas of Lancaster in Yorkshire, their last remaining hope. These men included Roger Damory, former favourite of the king whom Thomas had once accused of trying to kill him; the rebellion had made strange bedfellows. Edward II wrote to Thomas on 8 February, claiming that he 'wished to continue and augment his affection to the earl' and ordering him not to adhere to the Contrariants, who, he said, 'have publicly boasted that they were going to the earl, and that they would draw him to them in the aforesaid excesses [burning towns and castles], and that they were sure of this'.[14]

Thomas and several other Contrariants including Roger Damory and Hugh Audley, another former favourite of the king and also married to one of his nieces, sent letters in late 1321 and early 1322 to Robert Bruce's men James Douglas and Thomas Randolph in Scotland. They asked them to come to England with an army and fight with them against their king. Thomas referred to himself in the letters by the conceited pseudonym 'King Arthur'.[15] This was clearly treason, and when the letters were found, Thomas had signed his own death warrant. His army was defeated at the Battle of Boroughbridge in Yorkshire on 16 March 1322; Edward II's brother-in-law Humphrey de Bohun, Earl of Hereford, was killed fighting for the Contrariants, and Thomas was captured and taken to his own castle at Pontefract. His brother Henry had the good fortune to be abroad, which spared him from having to make the terrible decision either to follow his brother into treason or to abandon him.[16] One man who did desert Thomas was his closest ally Sir Robert Holland, who would be murdered years later in revenge by Lancastrian adherents. Thomas supposedly groaned on hearing the news; 'How could he find it in his heart to betray me, when I loved him so much?'[17] Other former close adherents of Thomas abandoned him as well: his household knights Fulk Fitzwarin, William Latimer and John Lilburn all fought against him at Boroughbridge.[18]

According to the very pro-Lancastrian *Brut* chronicle, Thomas was forced to put on garments of the striped cloth that the squires of his household wore, an intentional humiliation of a man of royal birth and high rank. On the way from Boroughbridge to York, a crowd of people threw snowballs at him, called him a traitor, and shouted, 'Now shall you have the reward that long time you have deserved!'[19] Edward and the younger Hugh Despenser were waiting at Pontefract for Thomas when he arrived on about 21 March, and supposedly hurled malicious and contemptuous words in his face.[20] The author of the *Vita* says that Thomas had built a tower at Pontefract in which to imprison the king after he defeated Edward, but was locked up there himself instead (though he does say this was only a rumour which he could not confirm).[21] Also with the king were the Earls of Pembroke, Surrey, Arundel, Richmond and Kent, the Scottish Earls of Atholl and Angus, and Hugh Despenser the Elder. Thomas' niece Queen Isabella was perhaps also there; she was with her husband on 20 March two days before Thomas' trial when one of Edward's household squires told the Earl of Richmond that the king and queen were in good health, though no source specifically mentions her presence at Pontefract.[22] Of the men who condemned Thomas of Lancaster to death, four – Edward II and the Earls of Kent, Richmond and Pembroke – were his first cousins, and three, the Earls of Surrey, Atholl and Angus, had once served in his retinue.

Thomas' so-called trial was held in the great hall of his own castle. He was not allowed to speak in his own defence because he had not allowed Piers Gaveston to speak in 1312, nor the Despensers at the Parliament of August 1321 when they were exiled. The list of charges went back to 1312 when Thomas seized the king's goods at Tynemouth and included his jeering at Edward at Pontefract in 1317, and his crimes were deemed 'notorious', known to everybody. Not counting Piers Gaveston in 1312, no English earl had been executed since Waltheof in 1076, and Thomas was of the highest birth and the uncle of the King of France and the Queen of England. Surely everyone, including Thomas, believed that Edward would not and could not execute him, that his high royal birth would save him. It did not.

Thomas' judges sentenced him to death by hanging, drawing and quartering, though Edward II commuted the sentence to mere beheading, respiting the hanging and drawing out of love for Queen Isabella according to the *Brut*, and out of respect for Thomas' royal blood according to the *Vita* and the Sempringham annalist.[23] The parallels between the deaths of Gaveston and Thomas of Lancaster did not go unnoticed: 'he was neither drawn nor hanged, only beheaded in like manner as this same Earl Thomas had caused Piers de Gaveston to be beheaded,' says *Lanercost. Anonimalle* draws a similar comparison, and the *Brut* says 'the cursed Gascon' had brought Thomas to this predicament. The *Vita* agrees, saying, 'the earl of Lancaster once cut off Piers Gaveston's head, and now by the king's command the earl himself has lost his head. Thus, perhaps not unjustly, the earl received measure for measure, as it is written in Holy Scripture.' *Scalacronica* also makes the connection between the deaths of Thomas of Lancaster and Gaveston, and says that Thomas was executed 'for other offences which he had often and habitually committed against the king, and at the very place where he had once hooted, and made others hoot, at the king as he [Edward] was travelling to York'.[24]

Edward deliberately arranged Thomas' execution as a parody of Piers Gaveston's death. The earl could easily have been beheaded in the castle bailey, but Edward had him taken outside to a small hill, mirroring Gaveston's 1312 death on Blacklow Hill. Thomas of Lancaster was forced to ride 'some worthless mule' and 'an old chaplet, rent and torn, that was not worth a half-penny' was set on his head. A crowd of spectators again threw snowballs at him.[25] Presumably at the king's order, Thomas was forced to kneel facing towards Scotland, in a pointed reminder of his treasonous correspondence with Robert Bruce, and 'beheaded like any thief or vilest rascal' with two or three strokes of the axe.[26] And so died the greatest, wealthiest and most royal nobleman in England.

NOT THE THIRD EARL OF LANCASTER

⸺◦∞◦⸺

Thomas, Earl of Lancaster, was buried in the church of the priory of Pontefract.[1] On 5 June 1327 early in the reign of his great-nephew Edward III, when Thomas was being rehabilitated, the young king or his mother Queen Isabella ordered a chapel to be built on the hill where Thomas was beheaded.[2] A group of men were arrested in December 1327 after collecting alms 'for the pretended purpose of building a chapel' on the site of Thomas' execution.[3] Thomas' nephew Henry of Grosmont was said in 1355 to have begun to build another chapel at the place where he died, and he owned a ship called the *Thomas of Lancaster*.[4] Probably barely more than 10 years old at the time of his uncle's execution, Grosmont remembered and honoured him for many years. So did others: Edward II's nephew Humphrey de Bohun, Earl of Hereford (b. 1307), whose father of the same name was killed fighting with Thomas of Lancaster at the Battle of Boroughbridge, left 40 shillings in his will of 1361 for a 'good and loyal man' to travel to Pontefract and make an offering on his behalf at Thomas' tomb.[5]

Curiously, given that Thomas of Lancaster was one of the least righteous people imaginable, a movement to canonise him as a saint took strong hold in the fourteenth century, and for more than 200 years until the Reformation his hat and belt preserved at Pontefract were used as remedies in childbirth and for headaches.[6] The 14-year-old Edward III, or someone acting on his behalf, sent men to the Pope with a request for Thomas' canonisation on 28 February 1327, barely a month into his reign.[7] A Latin song written at the end of Edward II's reign or at the beginning of his son's laments 'the blessed martyr' and 'flower of knights', and adds 'the pouring out of prayers to Thomas restores the sick to health; the pious earl comes immediately to the aid of those who are feeble'.[8] Miracles were reported at the site of Thomas' execution as early as 1323: 2,000 people, some from as far away as Kent, gathered to pray at his tomb.[9] Edward II sent his clerk to Pontefract to investigate, his attitude towards the situation apparent from his description of the crowd as 'malefactors and apostates' and his comment that they were praying 'not to God but rather to idols'. The crowd made their feelings clear, too: the clerk was assaulted, and two of his servants killed.[10] The pro-Lancastrian *Brut* chronicle always calls the executed earl 'Saint Thomas of Lancaster', and includes a bizarre story in which Hugh Despenser the Younger, troubled and angered by the 'great heresy' of the alleged miracles being performed at Thomas' tomb, sent a messenger to Edward II to inform him about them. As the messenger passed through Pontefract, he 'made his ordure' at the place where Thomas had been beheaded – and later suffered punishment for this sacrilegious act when he 'shed all his bowels at his fundament'.[11]

Thomas left two known illegitimate sons, John and Thomas, who both eventually joined the Church. Interestingly, the mother of at least one of them, John of Lancaster, was Earl Thomas' second cousin or second cousin once removed: John was said in 1350 to be 'the son of a married man and a spinster related in the third degree of kindred'.[12] As all Thomas' legitimate second cousins (women with whom he shared a set of great-grandparents) were highly born and it is hard to see how he could have fathered a child with one out of wedlock without it coming to the attention of chroniclers, his mistress was presumably illegitimate or of an illegitimate line. Thomas and his unknown relative's child John of Lancaster, who had an MA in theology, was a clerk in the household of his first cousin Henry of Grosmont by 1355, and was a canon of Uttoxeter in Staffordshire, which was a Lancaster manor.[13] Earl Thomas' brother and heir Henry asked the Pope for a dispensation for his nephew John of Lancaster in 1343 because of his illegitimacy, and Edward III also acknowledged him as his kinsman in 1350. John died in or before 1361.[14] The earl's other illegitimate son Thomas of Lancaster was knighted by Edward III during his French campaign of 1346.[15] It was said in 1354 that this Thomas 'passed his youth at a university and other places, and afterwards in a war', and took part in an attack on the French town of Sens. Because he had killed and wounded men there, he 'wishes to change his life' and join the order of Franciscans, the Greyfriars. This Thomas was 'the son of a married man [Earl Thomas] and of a mother of whom it is doubted whether at the time he was begotten she was married or a spinster'.[16] As well as the rather intriguing questions of the identity of their mother or mothers, and why the younger Thomas did not know whether or not his mother was married to another man when she and his father conceived him, it is interesting to note that both of Thomas of Lancaster's illegitimate sons studied at university. There is no way to determine when Thomas' sons were born, though he must have had a reasonably long-term and serious relationship with their mother or mothers as he acknowledged the boys as his, and they were openly described as his sons in papal letters. Thomas' brother, nephew and great-nephew Edward III also acknowledged John of Lancaster as their kinsman.

Thomas, Earl of Lancaster's Inquisition Post Mortem was belatedly ordered on 5 February 1327, four days after the coronation of the new king Edward III. His brother and heir Henry was said, in the usual vague manner of fourteenth-century IPMs, to be aged 'thirty and more' or 'forty and more' (he was in fact about 46 then).[17] Henry of Lancaster was probably still abroad when his brother was executed, though for certain someone sent a messenger to inform him. He was back in England by 9 April 1322, eighteen days later.[18] Whatever the personal relationship between the two brothers may have been, he must have been profoundly shocked, and Henry's *annus horribilis* of 1322 continued when his wife Maud Chaworth died as well. They had been married for a quarter of a century, and Henry was only about 41, but never remarried though he outlived his wife by almost another quarter of a century. What little evidence we have suggests that their marriage had been a contented and devoted one and that they spent almost all their time together.

Maud was buried at Mottisfont Priory between Salisbury and Winchester in Hampshire, of which she and Henry were patrons, and Edward II sent cloth and jewels for her funeral in May 1322.[19] Rather oddly, there is a reference in the records of the borough of Leicester in 1327 to Sir Richard Rivers, one of Henry of Lancaster's retainers, 'coming on Saturday next before Michaelmas [26 September] with the body of the countess'.[20] Perhaps Henry intended to have his wife's remains reinterred in his own town, but in 1353 Henry of Grosmont told Pope Innocent VI that his mother was buried at Mottisfont.[21] Maud, because she died before Henry received the earldoms of Leicester and Lancaster, was never a countess anyway. Perhaps 'body' here means 'person' rather than a dead body, meaning that a live woman was being escorted to Leicester, but as Henry did not remarry he never had a countess, and the matter is unclear. Henry and Maud's eldest child Blanche was in her late teens or perhaps 20 when she lost her mother in 1322, and their youngest, Mary, was no more than a toddler and perhaps still a baby. For the only Lancaster boy, Henry of Grosmont, his uncle's execution was life-changing. Previously he had only been heir to his mother's Chaworth lands and his father's lordships in Wales, France and Gloucestershire. Now he was heir, after his father, to the vast Lancastrian inheritance – assuming his father would successfully be able to claim it. This was by no means clear.

In June and July 1322, Henry of Lancaster petitioned his cousin the king for the restoration of his inheritance as the son and heir of Edmund of Lancaster. Edward II pointed out sarcastically that 'Edmund had an older son, who was called Thomas', whom Henry had conveniently forgotten to mention. Henry had little choice but to drop the matter for now, but stated that he would return to it the following October.[22] Again on 6 May 1323, his attorneys Sir Thomas Blount and Sir Richard Rivers petitioned for the restoration to him of the earldoms of Lancaster and Leicester, though not the earldom of Derby, taken from Robert Ferrers by his father Edmund in 1269.[23] Finally on 29 March 1324, two years after Thomas' execution, the king granted Henry the earldom of Leicester, though not Lancaster, on the grounds of Thomas 'having gone the way of all flesh without heir of his body'. On 10 May at Westminster it was formally agreed by the royal council that Henry should be Earl of Leicester, and he received the lands of the earldom on 4 June and two months later was summoned to Parliament as Earl of Leicester.[24] Edward kept a large part of Henry's inheritance in his own hands, including the magnificent castle of Kenilworth, where he spent much time between 1324 and 1326. As well as the earldom of Leicester Henry had his lordships in France, Wales and Gloucestershire and his late wife Maud Chaworth's not inconsiderable inheritance which he had the right to keep for the rest of his life, so he was hardly poor, but this was surely small consolation for being deprived of a large part of his father's and brother's estates, and the earldom which gave him and his children their name.

Henry's brother-in-law Hugh Despenser the Younger was all-powerful in the government of the 1320s. Neither Henry nor his cousins, the king's much younger half-brothers the Earls of Norfolk and Kent, nor anyone else got much, if any, of a look in. When Edward went to war in the summer of 1324 against his brother-in-law, Henry's nephew Charles IV of France (who had succeeded his brother Philip V at the beginning of 1322), over Gascony, it was Hugh Despenser who directed the English war effort. Edward sent his half-brother Edmund of Woodstock, Earl of Kent, as one of his envoys to Charles IV. This made sense, as Kent was Charles' first cousin via his mother Queen Marguerite (Edward I's second wife and Philip IV's half-sister), but perhaps sending Henry of Lancaster would have been a wiser decision. Henry was the French king's uncle, twenty years Kent's senior and much more experienced, and very well acquainted with France and the French court. Edward, however, did not trust him. Neither did Hugh Despenser wish Henry to interfere in his control of the king and the government. For almost five years after his brother's execution, Henry was kept well away from any influence. It would have been far more prudent for Edward and Hugh to court Henry as an ally, and if they had they might well have averted their devastating downfall, but good sense was not a feature of the regime of the 1320s.

Despite his brother's execution, the withholding of much of his inheritance and the king's distrust, Henry's relations with the regime of his cousin and brother-in-law in and after 1322 seem not to have been entirely bad. It was, after all, in Henry's best interest to remain on as good terms as possible with the king and his powerful chamberlain, in the hope that one day, Edward might relent and restore the full inheritance to him. He went on the king's last campaign to Scotland in the late summer of 1322, which proved as unsuccessful and pointless as all the others and which almost ended in disaster for Henry's niece Queen Isabella when the Scots launched a counter-invasion of England and came close to capturing her at Tynemouth. A distressed and angry Isabella blamed Hugh Despenser the Younger, probably unfairly, for her predicament. In and after 1322 the queen rarely appears on any record and her political influence came to an abrupt end, though she continued to spend time with her husband and frequently sent him letters when they were apart, and gave him a gift at New Year 1325 as was customary.[25] Despenser had come between the royal couple, and when Edward confiscated his wife's lands in September 1324 on the rather implausible grounds that her brother Charles IV might land on them if he invaded England, Isabella blamed Despenser for that too. It was one of the factors which was to push her into opposition to her husband.

Henry of Lancaster slipped up in 1324–25 and came close to disaster. He adopted his late brother's arms, which were of course also his father's arms and thus he had a perfect right to use them, and built a cross outside his town of Leicester in Thomas' memory. It was hardly unreasonable for him to remember and honour his own brother or to use his father's coat of arms, but Edward II's regime in the 1320s was precarious and unstable, and these actions brought the king's wrath down on Henry's head. Henry compounded these grievances by sending a supportive letter to the Bishop of Hereford, Adam Orleton, whom the king accused of aiding the Contrariant Roger Mortimer of Wigmore against himself in 1321–22 and whom he was persecuting. Orleton asked Henry to intervene on his behalf with the king, and Henry advised him to remain patient and to hope that God would mitigate Edward's wrath.[26] His kindness, and his wish to remember his brother, led to his cousin accusing him of treason and of insulting him, the king, personally. Henry was summoned to Edward to explain himself and did so by confirming that he had taken his father's arms, 'which pertained to him by hereditary right', and had erected a cross for his brother to 'excite the spiritual devotion of the faithful for his brother's soul'. Indeed, he added, 'prayer ought certainly to be allowed for the faithful, since Holy Church frequently prays for Jews and heretics'.[27]

Henry's eloquent defence did not save him, and he was summoned to Westminster in June 1325 to answer the charges. No official record exists of this Parliament, so it is impossible to confirm the *Vita*'s narrative, but the chronicler says that in the end the charges were never heard because events were overtaken by the pressing question of whether, when and how Edward II should go to France to swear homage to Charles IV for his lands of Gascony and Ponthieu. The chronicler says Henry was let off 'perhaps because he was of better blood than the others, [and] his presence was considered necessary to the lord king's son who would be in charge of the realm while his father was abroad'.[28] In fact, Henry was given protection in

September 1325 to accompany the king to France when Edward II went to pay homage to Henry's nephew Charles.[29] This was probably a case of Edward's wish to have Henry nearby where he could keep an eye on him rather than out of any desire for his company. In the end, after weeks of changing his mind on an almost daily basis, Edward II decided to stay in his realm and to send his son to pay homage in his place after Hugh Despenser begged him not to leave him and his father alone in England. The 12-year-old Edward of Windsor sailed for France on 12 September 1325 and was reunited with his mother Isabella at the French court, where she had gone six months earlier to negotiate peace between her brother and husband.

With her son under her control and under her brother's protection, Isabella felt confident enough to issue an ultimatum to her husband, that he must send Hugh Despenser away from him or she and her son would not return. Edward, dependent on Despenser in some way, refused, and left Isabella with no alternative but to make good on her threat and stay in France. She began an alliance with the remnant of the Contrariant faction who had fled from England in and after 1322, including Roger Mortimer of Wigmore, who had escaped from the Tower of London in 1323 and who was the leader of the English exiles on the continent. These men wished for nothing more than to destroy Hugh Despenser and his regime, and to return home. They found plenty of allies, including Edward II's half-brother the Earl of Kent, who joined them in Paris and who married Margaret Comyn (née Wake) in late 1325. She was a first cousin of Roger Mortimer, and the sister of Henry of Lancaster's son-in-law Thomas Wake.

Edward and Hugh Despenser spent the period from 26 February to 7 March 1326 in Henry's town of Leicester, and he joined them at court on 28 February and perhaps on other days as well. He was also at court in Merevale on 10 March, when he witnessed another royal charter (his brother-in-law Despenser witnessed both as well).[30] One of the few important commissions Henry received from his cousin came on 28 February 1326 – the day he was at court with Edward – when he was appointed as a justice of *oyer et terminer* to investigate the murder of Sir Roger Belers, a chief baron of the Exchequer, in Leicestershire on 19 January 1326.[31] Belers was a former adherent of Thomas of Lancaster who, like many others, pragmatically switched his allegiance to the Despensers in and after 1322. At the time of his murder, Belers was supposedly on his way to dine with Henry of Lancaster, and was certainly

riding in the direction of the town of Leicester.[32] Henry's son-in-law
Thomas Wake was with the king at Kenilworth – which Wake must surely
have believed rightfully belonged to his father-in-law – on 20 April 1326.
It is surely no coincidence that on that day Henry of Lancaster was given
permission to give one of his manors to his attorney William Blount, and
it seems highly probable that Wake asked the king to grant this favour to
his father-in-law.[33] Other than these brief mentions and the allegations
in the *Vita Edwardi Secundi* that he came close to disaster in 1325, little is
known of Henry of Lancaster during the years of Despenser dominance.
At some point between July 1325 and July 1326 he was at his manor of
Monmouth, a small town in Wales, so perhaps he was keeping well out
of the way.[34] He did, however, witness seven of Edward II's twenty-one
charters issued between July 1324 and July 1325, the king's eighteenth
regnal year, so clearly did visit court sometimes.[35]

Henry's niece Queen Isabella spent the summer of 1326 looking for
allies on the Continent to help her invade her husband's kingdom and
bring down the hated Hugh Despenser, and betrothed her son, Edward
of Windsor, to Philippa, daughter of the Count of Hainault, in exchange
for his aid and support. The queen's invasion force landed in Suffolk on
24 September 1326. Henry was in his town of Leicester when they arrived,
and sent letters to both Edward II and Isabella, still hedging his bets for
the time being. His kinswoman Elizabeth de Burgh, the king's niece and
Hugh Despenser the Younger's sister-in-law, did the same thing.[36] Henry
openly joined his niece on 3 October, nine days after her landing; possibly
he had wrestled with his conscience for a time before doing so. She represented the best hope for him to regain the bulk of his inheritance. Whether
Henry or Isabella or anyone else desired the downfall of Edward II himself
rather than merely that of Hugh Despenser and his father is uncertain – it
seems that Isabella at least did not – but within just a few weeks it became
apparent that Edward's support had collapsed and that he could no longer
continue as king. Henry brought the northern lords with him as well as
his influential son-in-law Wake, while another important ally of the queen
in 1326 was John Stratford, Bishop of Winchester and future Archbishop
of Canterbury, a friend and ally of Henry. Edward did not confiscate his
cousin's lands until 10 October, and then only the Welsh ones.[37] Henry, for
his part, seized a large sum of money taken to Leicester Abbey by retainers
of Hugh Despenser the Elder, Earl of Winchester. Around midnight on

4 October, men Henry had placed in the streets to 'watch for evil-doers' saw a large group of strangers arrive on horseback, followed them to the abbey on realising they were Winchester's men and besieged them overnight.[38] The king, the Despensers and their ally the Earl of Arundel, meanwhile, left London on 3 October and made their west towards South Wales, pursued at a distance by the queen, who according to the *Anonimalle* chronicle wished to re-join her husband and to force him to abandon the Despensers.[39]

On 26 October at Bristol, Edward II and Isabella's son Edward of Windsor was made keeper of the realm under the fiction that his father had left the country, and Henry was styled 'Earl of Lancaster and Leicester' for the first time.[40] The mayor of Henry's town of Leicester, curious to know what was going on, sent two men to Bristol 'to find out what the magnates were doing'.[41] Thomas Wake was also there with his father-in-law, and they were among those who witnessed the execution of 65-year-old Hugh Despenser the Elder, Earl of Winchester and stepfather of Henry's late wife Maud, at Bristol on 27 October.[42] Henry was one of the men subsequently sent into South Wales to find the king and the younger Despenser. Edward had left £6,000 in Neath Castle, and Henry found and took possession of it; it was still in his custody in March 1329.[43] He and his allies also found the chancery rolls in Swansea Castle, and a further £29,000 and more government records were found in Caerphilly Castle, Despenser's great stronghold, when it finally surrendered in March 1327.

The king, Hugh Despenser the Younger and a handful of others were captured near Llantrisant on 16 November 1326. The following day their ally Edmund Fitzalan, Earl of Arundel, and two men with him were beheaded in Hereford on the orders of Roger Mortimer, without a trial. Despenser was led slowly to Hereford and treated with all possible indignities; Edward II was given into Henry of Lancaster's care and treated with much more respect. Henry took his cousin to Kenilworth in Warwickshire via his castle of Monmouth, though he was also one of the judges who condemned his brother-in-law Despenser to a grotesque death in Hereford on 24 November, so perhaps Edward was also in Hereford when his beloved chamberlain was hanged, drawn and quartered. The charges against Despenser, which he was not allowed to answer because Thomas of Lancaster had not been allowed to answer the charges against him in March 1322, frequently mentioned Thomas, and absurdly held Despenser and his father solely responsible for his execution.

When Henry arrived at the great castle of Kenilworth in Warwickshire with his cousin the king on or a little before 5 December 1326, it was the first time he had seen it since he – still unofficially for now – became its owner.[44] It was sixty years to the month since his grandfather Henry III had given Kenilworth to his father Edmund. Edward II spent a sad Christmas at the castle, while Henry, Isabella, Roger Mortimer, Edward's half-brothers, the Earls of Norfolk and Kent, and others discussed his fate at Wallingford. At the Parliament which sat in London in January 1327, it was decided that the king must be made to abdicate his throne to his 14-year-old son, and Henry was one of the delegates sent from London back to Kenilworth to break the news to Edward. For the first time in English history a king had been deposed, and Henry of Lancaster, in alliance with his niece the queen, had made it possible.

The Palace of Westminster, now the Houses of Parliament since the original medieval palace burned down in 1834, probably the location of Edmund of Lancaster's birth in January 1245.

Kenilworth Castle, Warwickshire, which was granted to Edmund of Lancaster in 1266 and remained in his family for generations. His second son Henry spent a lot of time here in the 1330s and 1340s, and his nephew Edward II was forced to abdicate his throne here in January 1327.

A painting of Pontefract Castle, Yorkshire, from the early seventeenth century: it was the favourite residence of Thomas of Lancaster in the 1310s and early 1320s, and he was executed here in March 1322. The first Lancastrian king Henry IV had his cousin Richard II killed here in February 1400.

The ruins of Bolingbroke Castle, Lincolnshire, which passed from Alice de Lacy, Countess of Lincoln, to her husband Thomas of Lancaster and his descendants, and was the birthplace of Henry of Lancaster, later King Henry IV, in April 1367.

Lancaster Castle, given to Edmund in 1267 and partially rebuilt by his great-great-grandson Henry IV after his accession to the throne in 1399.

Tutbury Castle, Staffordshire, which passed from Robert Ferrers, Earl of Derby, to Edmund of Lancaster in 1269. Edmund's granddaughter Mary of Lancaster married Henry Percy here in 1334, and his great-granddaughter and heir Blanche of Lancaster died here in 1368.

Windsor Castle, Berkshire, where Edmund grew up with his siblings in the 1240s and 1250s, and where Edward I's grandson Edward III was born in November 1312.

Grosmont Castle, Monmouthshire, Wales, almost certainly the birthplace of Henry of Grosmont, first Duke of Lancaster, in about 1310 or 1312.

Westminster Abbey, where Edmund of Lancaster married Aveline Forz in 1269 and where they are both buried. His father Henry III, brother Edward I and sister-in-law Leonor of Castile are also buried here, as his great-great-great-grandson Henry V, second of the Lancastrian kings of England.

The motte of Fotheringhay Castle, Northamptonshire, which was the chief residence of Edmund of Langley, first Duke of York and his son Edward the second Duke, and which may have been the latter's birthplace. (Courtesy of Iain Simpson under Creative Commons)

An engraving of a farm building in the early nineteenth century, said to incorporate a small part of the palace at Kings Langley, Hertfordshire – Edmund of Langley's birthplace in 1341.

Surviving building of Kings Langley Priory, founded by Edward II in 1308 next to the palace; his grandson Edmund of Langley and Edmund's wife Isabel of Castile, and their daughter-in-law Anne Mortimer (mother of Richard, third Duke of York) were buried at the priory.

Canterbury Cathedral, Kent, burial place of Richard II's father Edward of Woodstock in 1376, and of Edward of Woodstock's nephew Henry IV in 1413 and Henry's second wife Juana of Navarre in 1437.

City walls and minster of York, seat of the dukedom given to Edmund of Langley by his nephew Richard II in 1385.

St Paul's Cathedral, the newer cathedral which has stood on the site of the older church since the early 1700s. Old St Paul's was the burial place of Blanche of Lancaster (d. 1368) and her husband John of Gaunt (d. 1399), but burned down in 1666.

THE LANCASTER FAMILY

—⊶⊷—

The coronation of the young king Edward III was arranged and held quickly, and took place at Westminster Abbey on 1 February 1327. Henry of Lancaster took part in the ceremony and knighted the boy personally. One chronicle says that Roger Mortimer got carried away with himself and dressed his sons as earls, though sadly there is no more information on how earls dressed in the early fourteenth century and how they looked different from other magnates. Numerous favours came Henry's way in the weeks and months after the coronation. The sentence of treason on his brother Thomas was revoked and Henry was restored to the full Lancastrian inheritance, minus the Lincoln title and some estates of his sister-in-law Alice de Lacy, who was still alive (and lived until 1348). Henry and his son and grandson-in-law gained control of them piecemeal over the decades. On the day of her son's coronation, Queen Isabella granted herself the castles and lands of Pontefract, Clitheroe and other estates which had belonged to Thomas of Lancaster as part of Alice de Lacy's inheritance and which now belonged by right to Henry, not to his niece.

In February 1327, Henry of Lancaster was granted the marriages of two important young noblemen.[1] One was John Mowbray (b. 1310), son and heir of John, Lord Mowbray who had been executed in March 1322 after the Contrariant rebellion, and a fierce young man. Making his feelings about Edward II and Hugh Despenser perfectly clear – they had imprisoned him in the Tower of London in February 1322 with his mother Alina even though he was only 11 – the 15-year-old John besieged the royal castle of Tickhill in Yorkshire on or before March 1326. He and his associates managed to capture it.[2] Via his mother Alina, John Mowbray was the grandson and co-heir of William Braose (d. 1326), Lord of the Gower Peninsula, who had melodramatically accused Henry of Lancaster and his wife Maud of trying to kill his ministers in the late 1310s. Henry's brother Thomas, Earl of Lancaster, had given 20 shillings to the messenger who brought him news of Mowbray's birth in Hovingham, Yorkshire on 29 November 1310.[3] The other young nobleman was William de Burgh (b. 1312), whose grandfather died in 1326 making him Earl of Ulster in Ireland. William was also the heir of his mother Elizabeth de Burgh (née de Clare), Edward II's niece, and to her third of the earldom of Gloucester – though he never inherited it as he died many years before Elizabeth. Henry married the young men to two of his daughters: William wed the third Lancaster daughter Maud between 1 May and 16 November 1327 when he was 14 or 15 and she the same age or a little older, and John Mowbray wed the fourth, Joan, before 4 June 1328 when he was 17 and she perhaps 13 or 15.[4]

The year 1327 saw a flurry of activity in the Lancaster household, after matters had been left on hold for five years after Thomas' execution. As well as the marriages, Henry's second daughter Isabella was professed as a nun at Amesbury Priory in Wiltshire on Ascension Day, 21 May, with no fewer than thirty-five other girls and women entering the priory with her.[5] Edward II's sister Mary and niece Joan Monthermer were also nuns at Amesbury and Henry's grandmother the Dowager Queen Eleanor of Provence was buried there, and it lay only 17 miles from Mottisfont Priory, where the Lancasters' mother Maud Chaworth had been buried five years before. Isabella of Lancaster was probably already 20 or so in 1327, an unusually late age for a woman of her class to be either unmarried or not yet veiled as a nun, so it may be that she had been living at Amesbury since about 1317, the year she went on pilgrimage with the royal nun, Mary.

Henry of Lancaster related to his children as individuals, not merely as pawns to use in the noble marriage market. He allowed his second daughter to become a nun; the children of the medieval nobility often went into the Church, but it was far more usual for a younger daughter or son to do so, not a second daughter, who would almost always be expected to marry. This suggests that Isabella had a vocation which her father accepted and encouraged, and in 1343 she became prioress of Amesbury. Henry married his third daughter Maud to William de Burgh, who was born in September 1312, and his fourth daughter Joan to John Mowbray, who was born in November 1310. In short, he may have matched the couples by personality, rather than merely assigning the third daughter to the elder of his two wards and the fourth daughter to the younger. Perhaps he thought that Maud, who had a stronger and more outgoing personality than her quiet younger sister Joan, was better equipped to handle leaving England for Ireland and to deal with the conflicts and troubles faced by the Anglo-Irish nobility there. All the husbands he found for his daughters were close to them in age, and of high noble birth.

Henry was a loving, generous and indulgent father. By 1334 all the Lancaster siblings except the nun Isabella were married, yet they and their spouses spent most of their time living with Henry, even Blanche, who had married as early as 1316.[6] Mary, the youngest, stayed with her father until she married in 1334 and probably for some years afterwards as well. Isabella of Lancaster spent considerable time away from Amesbury Priory visiting her family long after she was professed as a nun: during one year in the early 1330s, she stayed with them for a total of ninety-six days at Kenilworth, and the next year visited her father at Tutbury and Kenilworth for a few weeks. She stayed with him on yet another occasion in 1334, accompanied by 'the ladies of her chamber'. On the way back to Amesbury after one visit, the eldest sister Blanche travelled with Isabella and ended up staying at the priory with her for at least six months (she paid some of her own expenses), and in 1336 Isabella travelled from York to Leicester with the fifth sister, Eleanor. Earl Henry sent letters to his daughter at Amesbury, and Isabella reciprocated. She also wrote to her namesake aunt Isabella, Lady Hastings, Maud Chaworth's half-sister and full sister of the late Hugh Despenser the Younger, and went to stay with her. Lady Hastings lent her niece a palfrey horse to ride on her return journey to Amesbury.[7]

The middle Lancaster sisters, Maud and Joan, lived with their father most of the time even after their marriages, and Henry of Grosmont, the only brother, and his young wife Isabella Beaumont also spent much time with his father, sisters and brothers-in-law. Grosmont was at Leicester with his father, sisters Blanche and Eleanor and his wife Isabella in June and September 1330, with his father at Kenilworth in September 1333 and June 1338, and with him again on numerous other occasions. The Lancaster siblings attended a famous jousting tournament at Cheapside in London in September 1331 together, and in April 1348 Blanche Wake and her niece Elizabeth de Burgh, Maud's daughter, watched Henry of Grosmont compete in a tournament at Lichfield.[8] William de Burgh, Earl Henry's son-in-law and the young Earl of Ulster, sometimes lived in Ireland, but on other occasions with the Lancasters, and Henry's other sons-in-law would also have lived with him at least sometimes, certainly when they were underage. William de Burgh visited a jousting tournament with his brother-in-law Grosmont in February 1328, and was still with the Lancasters in June that year.[9] Henry, Earl of Lancaster paid the expenses of his fifth daughter Eleanor and her new husband John Beaumont, and John's sister Isabella who was married to Henry of Grosmont, at Kenilworth from 6 November 1330 until at least 2 February 1331.[10]

The Lancaster siblings also often visited, wrote to and demonstrated their affection for each other. In February 1332, Henry of Grosmont and Eleanor of Lancaster stayed with their sister Blanche at Deeping in Lincolnshire, and Blanche's husband Thomas Wake was one of the men who accompanied Grosmont to Spain in 1343. Wake, on excellent terms with his father-in-law Earl Henry for many years and a member of his council, visited Henry in Leicester in July 1339 and gave him one of his manors in Yorkshire.[11] Wake fled from England in early 1330 after taking part in a conspiracy with his brother-in-law the Earl of Kent, and returned in November; Blanche spent the period with her father and siblings and attended the weddings of Henry of Grosmont and Eleanor to the Beaumont siblings that year. The two youngest Lancaster sisters Eleanor and Mary sent letters to Isabella at Amesbury Priory in 1334 and in the same year Isabella sent gifts for Mary's wedding. Isabella wrote to Blanche at Wakes Colne in Essex, and Eleanor stayed in Melton Mowbray, Leicestershire with the fourth sister Joan and her husband John Mowbray in September 1343.[12] Blanche and Isabella, the two eldest siblings, seem to have been particularly close. In the early 1330s they visited Salisbury, Winchester and King's Somborne in Hampshire – a manor which had belonged to their late mother, now held by their father – together as well as spending at least half a year in each other's company at Amesbury Priory.[13] Maud of Lancaster visited the papal court at Avignon in 1343 and made requests of the Pope on behalf of her father the earl and her sister Eleanor.[14]

Henry of Grosmont talked in 1344 of his 'sincere affection' for his 'dearly beloved sister' Isabella when granting a favour to Amesbury Priory, and he and his household officials helped the third sister Maud look after her affairs when she was widowed for a second time in 1346. In 1337, Grosmont gave Blanche and Thomas Wake one of his manors, to pass after their deaths to Thomas' foundation of Haltemprice Priory in Yorkshire, and in 1361 appointed Blanche as one of the executors of his will, a sign of his trust in her.[15] Of his six sisters, Grosmont seems to have spent the most time with Eleanor, perhaps because they were married to the siblings Isabella and John Beaumont, and because her second husband the Earl of Arundel was a close associate of his.[16] Eleanor's son Henry Beaumont had joined the household of his uncle Grosmont by 1355, Mary's son Henry Percy also spent most of his youth in his uncle's household, and Joan's son John Mowbray was also often with his uncle and witnessed his charters.[17] According to the Alnwick chronicle, Henry Percy – later the first Earl of Northumberland – was 'greatly beloved' by his uncle Grosmont.[18] This all gives an extremely pleasant impression of a close-knit and loving family who for many years thoroughly enjoyed spending time together and who looked after each other. Henry, Earl of Lancaster's father Edmund had grown up in the affectionate family atmosphere created by his parents King Henry III and Eleanor of Provence, and although almost nothing is known of Henry of Lancaster's childhood, he created the same environment for his own children. They in turn carried it on to the next generation.

The Lancaster sisters and their sister-in-law Isabella Beaumont all married in their early to mid teens but did not become pregnant until they were at least 20. Eleanor was born around 1316–18, married in 1330, and had her first child in 1339; Mary was born around 1319–21, married in 1334, and had her first child in 1341; Joan married in 1328 and gave birth to her only son in 1340 when she was at least 25, though her two daughters may have been older; Maud married in 1327 at about 15 and had her first child in 1332; Isabella Beaumont married Henry of Grosmont in 1330 when she was about 12 or 15, and their first surviving child was born in 1340, though another is mentioned in 1338/39 who must have died in infancy. The young couples were not thrown into bed together as soon as they reached puberty, but were given plenty of time to get to know each other, under Henry of Lancaster's care and protection. Henry and Maud Chaworth had been married for at least five years and perhaps eight when

they had their first child, and seemingly he encouraged his children and
their spouses not to rush into parenthood either. Others were not so sensible or considerate. Henry's adherent Henry, Lord Ferrers of Groby married
his much younger wife Isabella de Verdon, half-sister of William de Burgh,
Earl of Ulster, probably in the late 1320s. Isabella was born in March 1317
and gave birth to her first child by Ferrers in February 1331, before she was
even 14. Perhaps not surprisingly, the child did not survive.[19]

Earl Henry supplied his children with plenty of money, and in 1332 paid
over £666 for his son and heir Grosmont's expenses, although the king had
granted the young man an income of 500 marks annually by then.[20] Henry
gave his third daughter Maud his manor of Melbourne near Derby in 1338
when she was a widow, and in 1326 was involved in a deal where Thomas
Wake settled three of his own manors on himself and Henry's eldest daughter Blanche jointly.[21] Even after she was cloistered at Amesbury Henry gave
his second daughter Isabella two manors in Wiltshire and Berkshire for her
lifetime, officially held on her behalf by his attorneys, though she admin-
istered her property herself. They had both belonged to her mother Maud
Chaworth, and would revert to her brother Grosmont after her death.[22]
Henry was also willing to use his considerable influence to protect his
children: in September 1332, for example, Blanche Wake took three deer in
the forest of Pickering without a licence, and Henry ordered the justices
of the forest to 'stay all further proceedings' against his daughter.[23] As late
as 1341 when all his children were well into adulthood and the youngest
five were parents, Henry still made loans of money to them when they
needed it. An extant record of that year reveals that Henry lent his daughter
Maud £30, his son-in-law John Beaumont 50 marks, and his son Henry of
Grosmont a staggering £1,129. The earl still had a surplus of over £1,500
in his wardrobe at the end of that fiscal year, so although generous was not
extravagant as his elder brother Thomas had been.[24]

THINGS GO WRONG AGAIN

⸺⟡⸺

On 6 April 1327, most of Thomas of Lancaster's lands were given to Henry, minus a few to which his niece the Dowager Queen Isabella had helped herself.[1] Henry remained in charge of his cousin, the deposed king, now simply called Sir Edward of Caernarfon. He was also appointed as head of the regency council which would rule during the 14-year-old Edward III's minority, and as the official guardian of his great-nephew. Finally, after the years of Despenser dominance, Henry was granted roles that were rightfully his and could look forward to wielding real influence. Yet it was all soon to go badly wrong again. Isabella and Sir Roger Mortimer, although not elected to the regency council, had no intention of giving up power to anyone, and Isabella ruled via her personal relationship with her son, with Mortimer as her chief ally and counsellor. Once again, Henry of Lancaster was edged out of his rightful position while an unelected royal favourite wielded illegitimate power.[2]

For some months, Edward of Caernarfon lived at Kenilworth with Henry and his family. There is little information about his life there, though by all accounts Henry treated his cousin with respect and courtesy. By contrast, his elder brother Thomas had supposedly built a tower at Pontefract in which to imprison Edward once Thomas had defeated him and had the king at his mercy. When Henry had the king at his mercy after Edward's sudden fall from grace, he treated him kindly, honourably and deferentially, which demonstrates the difference between the two Lancaster brothers. The *Vita Edwardi Secundi* stated that Henry 'was kind and sympathetic to those in trouble', and chronicler Jean le Bel that he was 'one of the finest, worthiest knights alive' and 'a most worthy man'.[3]

A group of Edward of Caernarfon's supporters, led by brothers called Thomas (a Dominican friar) and Stephen Dunheved, were making strenuous efforts throughout 1327 to free him from captivity; one of them, that summer, was temporarily successful. The gang's ongoing attempts to free Edward may have been a pretext to remove him from Henry's custody and put him under Roger Mortimer's control.[4] On 3 April 1327, Edward of Caernarfon was removed from Kenilworth Castle and given into the custody of Mortimer's son-in-law Thomas, Lord Berkeley of Berkeley Castle in Gloucestershire, and Berkeley's brother-in-law Sir John Maltravers. The later Leicester chronicler Henry Knighton thought that Earl Henry willingly gave up custody of his cousin, supposedly being concerned about security at Kenilworth during his many absences, but it seems unlikely that he would voluntarily deliver such a powerful political weapon into the hands of Roger Mortimer and his faction.[5] On the other hand, Henry was given most of his late brother's lands on 6 April, three days after Edward was removed from his custody, so it is not impossible that this was intended as some of kind of quid pro quo. The annalist of St Paul's Cathedral claimed that some of the English magnates were involved in the plots to free Edward of Caernarfon in 1327 but does not name them, and although this may or may not be true, Henry of Lancaster may have had connections to the Dunheved gang.[6] In 1330, he stood as guarantor for a man called Gregory Foriz, who was accused of murder before King's Bench. William Aylmer, a former Despenser adherent and certainly one of the men attempting to free Edward of Caernarfon with the Dunheveds in 1327, was also named as a guarantor of Foriz.[7] Events of 1327 are so murky it is impossible to tell what was really happening.

On 21 September 1327, the former king Edward II reportedly died at Berkeley Castle. Whether he really was dead or not remains a matter for debate – many influential people of the time believed he was alive for years afterwards – but his funeral took place at St Peter's Abbey in Gloucester on 20 December 1327. Presumably Henry of Lancaster attended his cousin's interment, though little is known about the former king's funeral, or who was present. Edward's half-brother Edmund, Earl of Kent, certainly was, and so were his widow Isabella, his son Edward III, and his niece Elizabeth de Burgh, who was now connected to Henry of Lancaster via the marriage of their children William and Maud. It is also possible that some of the older Lancaster children attended the funeral of their father's cousin, including Henry of Grosmont, who was now about 15 or 17 and around the same age as the young king.

A royal wedding followed hard on the heels of a royal funeral when Edward III married Philippa of Hainault in York on 25 January 1328. The greed of the Dowager Queen Isabella, however, was rapidly emptying her son's coffers. She granted herself the largest income that anyone in England (excepting the kings) received in the entire Middle Ages, at least 20 per cent higher than the income her uncle Thomas of Lancaster had received from his five earldoms: 20,000 marks or £13,333. Neither did she allow her daughter-in-law Philippa of Hainault to be crowned as queen until February 1330, when she was already five months pregnant with the royal couple's first child. On 3 March 1328 Henry of Lancaster asked for the annulment of the 1322 judgement against Thomas to be confirmed, and on the same day the judgement of treason was again officially annulled.[8] This suggests that Henry felt insecure about his niece's behaviour and was concerned that he might again be deprived of his inheritance.

Matters were made even worse for Henry and his allies on 17 March 1328 when the Treaty of Edinburgh between England and Scotland was signed, and the English government officially recognised Robert Bruce as king. Four months later Bruce's 4-year-old son and heir David married Joan of the Tower, Edward II and Isabella's 7-year-old daughter, against the wishes of Joan's brother Edward III, but the young king was powerless to prevent it. Three close allies of Henry of Lancaster – his son-in-law Thomas Wake and Lords Beaumont and Percy, both of whom had children who would marry three of Henry's – were furious, as they had claims to lands and titles in Scotland which they would have to give up. That July, at the royal children's wedding, the Scottish government made a special concession to return the three men's lands.[9] If this was intended to reconcile Henry of Lancaster, it failed. At a meeting of the royal council held in Worcester held in mid June 1328, Henry publicly emerged as the leader of the opposition to the regime, and when another meeting was held at York on 31 July, he refused to attend. When he and his armed retinue encountered Edward III at Barlings in Lincolnshire soon afterwards, the young king demanded that he attend the Parliament summoned to Salisbury in October. Henry had no intention of doing so, at least not without a large armed retinue to protect himself.

He stated that 'those who are around our lord the king' did not wish him to attend Parliament and made a series of criticisms of the bad governance to which England was being subjected.[10] It was a direct attack on the regency of his niece Isabella and Roger Mortimer. When Parliament opened at Salisbury in October 1328, Henry conveyed his excuses and went instead to Winchester, staying there from 30 October to 3 November. Jurors ordered to inquire into his conduct there declared, rather defiantly, that he and his followers (including Thomas Wake and Hugh Audley) stayed peacefully in the city 'and did no harm to anybody'.[11] Meanwhile in Salisbury, Roger Mortimer swore an oath on the Archbishop of Canterbury's cross that he meant Henry no harm, but during this Parliament appointed himself Earl of March, an unprecedentedly grand title meaning Earl of all the English–Welsh borderlands. This was a massive provocation to Henry and others, including Edward III's uncles the Earls of Norfolk and Kent; even the last over-mighty royal favourite Hugh Despenser the Younger had not awarded himself a grandiose earldom. By 1330, Mortimer had taken to walking ahead of the king and remaining seated in his presence, and such discourteous, arrogant swagger by a man who had never been chosen to rule for, advise or even to stay near the king infuriated contemporaries. Isabella and Roger Mortimer, it seemed, had learned nothing from the mistakes of the regime they had overthrown and were now emulating it.

In the middle of all the discord between Henry of Lancaster and the ruling regime, Sir Robert Holland was murdered. Holland, a Knight of Lancashire, had been a close ally and friend of Earl Thomas of Lancaster, who granted him manors and favours and arranged his marriage to an heiress, but Holland abandoned the earl and went over to Edward II before the Battle of Boroughbridge in March 1322. Even so, the king committed him to prison for the rest of his reign. Restored to royal grace in the new reign, Edward III (or rather, someone in his name) ordered Holland's lands to be given back to him in 1327. Earl Henry petitioned Parliament protesting against this.[12] On 15 October 1328, a group of Lancastrian knights and men-at-arms encountered Robert Holland at Borehamwood in Essex, quarrelled with him, and cut off his head. They sent it to Henry of Lancaster at Waltham Abbey before fleeing to High Wycombe in Buckinghamshire. It is not impossible that Henry ordered Holland's execution – he was only 15 miles away at Waltham when it happened – though it is perhaps more probable that the death occurred during an angry and violent row with Lancastrians furious at Holland's betrayal of Earl Thomas and that they had not planned to kill him. Still, there seems little doubt that Henry protected and sheltered the killers, and the macabre gift of Holland's head sent to him suggests the knights knew he would be pleased at the death of the man who had abandoned his brother. Jurors appointed to inquire into the murder claimed rather suspiciously and implausibly not to know anything whatsoever about the circumstances of it or who had promoted it – pointing a finger at the wealthy, powerful and royal Earl of Lancaster was surely deemed unwise – and Henry was certainly an accessory after the fact, if not before.[13]

Those with Henry in his protest against the regime in late 1328 and early 1329 included close members of his affinity. Hugh Audley, a former favourite of Edward II who was imprisoned for years after the Contrariant rebellion of 1321–22, seems the odd one out, but was growing closer to the Lancaster circle: in the early 1330s, he and Henry's second daughter Isabella the nun frequently sent each other gifts and letters and exchanged greyhounds, and in 1344 Audley's grandson married Henry's granddaughter.[14] Thomas Roscelyn and William Trussell had been on the continent with Roger Mortimer in and before 1326, and Trussell had pronounced the death sentence on both Hugh Despensers, but both had grown sick of Mortimer's regime. The lands of Henry and his followers including Audley, Roscelyn, Trussell and Thomas Wake were seized on 16 January 1239.[15]

Edward II's half-brothers Norfolk and Kent abandoned Henry at the last moment, and Roger Mortimer took an army to Henry's lands and ravaged Leicester and the countryside around it.[16] With his main allies gone and his power base sacked, Henry was forced to come to terms with his niece and her hated favourite. At Bedford, he knelt in submission to Isabella and Edward III, and soon afterwards was forced to recognise liability for a staggeringly huge debt of £30,000 – 'by reason of the riding with horses and arms' – and made to swear a humiliating oath of future good behaviour. Hugh Audley was forced to recognise liability for £10,000, Thomas Wake 15,000 marks, David, Earl of Atholl £5,000, Henry Ferrers 2,000 marks, and several dozen other men smaller amounts. Henry Beaumont,

Thomas Roscelyn, William Trussell and Thomas Wyther were excluded from the pardon, and fled abroad after their arrest was ordered on 18 January 1329. Roscelyn was in Paris by 19 May when he acknowledged receipt of a loan of 100 marks (£66) from Henry, and Henry continued to pay the fee he owed Roscelyn, as his retainer, from his French estates.[17] On 12 December 1330 after Edward III took over his own realm, the debts were cancelled, and soon afterwards he pardoned all the rebels.[18] Henry's brief rebellion against Isabella and Mortimer's regime had failed, yet he kept his head on his shoulders and died peacefully in his bed many years later, unlike his brother Thomas and unlike his cousin Kent, who would be judicially murdered by Mortimer fourteen months later – and unlike Mortimer himself, who had under two years left to live.

The rather later chroniclers Geoffrey Baker and Henry Knighton both state that Henry of Lancaster went blind around 1329/30.[19] Henry is often depicted by modern writers as elderly, infirm and frail at the time of his rebellion and shortly afterwards, but he was only 47 or 48 in late 1328, and lived for another seventeen years.[20] Edward III sent Henry as an envoy to France in February 1331 and summoned him on a military campaign to Scotland in 1333, which he would hardly have done if Henry were a near-invalid and blind, or if the torticollis he perhaps suffered from was a major issue. Henry was still being appointed as a keeper of the peace and com-missioner of *oyer et terminer* in 1340, and was called to Parliament for the last time in April 1344. As late as 1 July 1345, Henry was appointed as a member of the advisory council to aid the Keeper of the Realm while Edward III went overseas.[21] He still travelled extensively around his estates in the last few years of his life, even in 1345, the year he died (his favourites residences were Kenilworth, Leicester, Higham Ferrers, Tutbury and Kempsford).[22] It is possible that Henry did go blind or lose part of his vision, but perhaps some years later than Geoffrey Baker and Knighton claim, and there is no evidence that he was ever weak or senile even near the end of his life. Henry was still lucid and aware enough on 15 July 1345, ten weeks before his death in his mid 60s, to make an indenture with a servant of his called John Popham.[23]

Henry's lands were restored to him on 6 February 1329, and the order in the chancery rolls reveals that he owned lands in thirty English coun-ties.[24] After the failure of his brief rebellion, Henry retreated to his own lands. On 9 and 10 February 1329, he was at Kempsford in Gloucestershire,

85 miles away from the king, then in London.[25] Kempsford was part of his late wife Maud Chaworth's inheritance and he had often spent time there with her, so perhaps his withdrawal there of all places reveals something about his state of mind. For the remaining twenty months of his niece's regency, Henry rarely visited court. The Earl of Lancaster, however, was far too influential for Isabella and Mortimer to be able to ignore completely. His rights and liberties in his earldom of Leicester were inspected and confirmed on 9 May 1329 by Edward III, or rather by his mother Isabella or whoever was acting in the name of the 16-year-old king at the time.[26] This perhaps represents an attempt at an olive branch. On 12 September 1329 Henry received letters of protection to go overseas, and left England that month for France with a large retinue. He and the Bishop of Norwich were instructed to discuss issues relating to the unsatisfactory homage Edward III had made to the new French King Philip VI for his French lands on 6 June 1329 (Henry's son Henry of Grosmont may have travelled to France with Edward), and he expected to be in France until Easter 1330. Henry and his fellow envoys also negotiated a future double marriage between England and France: Philip VI's eldest son the future King John II (b. 1319) and Edward III's sister Eleanor of Woodstock (b. 1318), and between Edward's brother John of Eltham, Earl of Cornwall (b. 1316), and Philip's daughter Marie (b. 1326).[27] Neither marriage ever took place.

Henry of Lancaster briefly returned to England in early 1330 and founded a hospital in Leicester on 20 January, and three days later gave his daughter Isabella the nun of Amesbury a manor in Wiltshire. He then went back to France to resume the negotiations.[28] Henry gave 4 acres of land in Leicester to his hospital, which would take care of fifty poor and infirm people and have a warden, four chaplains, two clerks and five women, presumably looking after the sick. None of the patients were to 'frequent taverns', walk alone at night, provoke quarrels, or seek out the company of women.[29] One might speculate that Henry founded a hospital in 1330 to mark his fiftieth year or, if the story is true, perhaps his worsening vision had made him more sympathetic to the plight of the handicapped and afflicted. The ease with which Henry travelled between England and France in 1329/30 and again in 1331, however – as his father Edmund had so often done – argues against the notion that he had already gone completely blind. He would later be buried in the chapel of his Leicester hospital, and his son extended his foundation into a college called the Newarke, meaning 'new work'. It was already called that in 1332/33.[30]

Henry was probably still overseas when his cousin Edmund of Woodstock, Earl of Kent, was suddenly and dramatically arrested in Winchester on 13 March 1330. Kent confessed that he had been trying to free his supposedly dead half-brother Edward II from captivity, and was beheaded in Winchester only six days after his arrest. He was 28. Whether Henry of Lancaster shared his belief in Edward's survival is hard to say, though he sent a letter to London on 5 November 1328, telling the mayor and aldermen he had heard news from Kent that he could not write down but which his messenger would tell them orally.[31] This may (or may not) relate to the former king's survival. Henry's son-in-law, Thomas Wake, whose heavily pregnant sister Margaret was the Earl of Kent's wife, was one of the many men who fled overseas after Kent's execution, and joined Henry Beaumont and Thomas Roscelyn.[32] His wife Blanche of Lancaster stayed in England with her family and attended the weddings of two of her siblings that year. Inquisitions were held throughout England and Wales to discover Kent's adherents, many of whom were imprisoned and their lands and goods confiscated. People were arrested for saying that Edward II was still alive, and the Archbishop of York appeared before King's Bench on a charge of treason: he had informed Edward's friend the Scottish Earl of Mar that Edward was alive, and Mar promised to bring an army to England to release the supposedly dead king. At least seventeen other men besides Thomas Wake fled the country, including the teenage Richard, son and heir of the Earl of Arundel executed in 1326, who fifteen years later would marry Henry of Lancaster's widowed fifth daughter Eleanor.

There was some good news in 1330 at least: Queen Philippa gave birth to a son at the Palace of Woodstock near Oxford on 15 June, and called him Edward after his father, grandfather and great-grandfather. A sergeant-at-arms called Peter Eketon brought news of Edward of Woodstock's birth to Henry of Lancaster, who rewarded him with an income of 10 marks annually for life.[33] Indeed, the earl must have been delighted that the young king, still only 17, had secured the succession to his throne, and the boy was Henry's great-great-nephew, the great-grandchild of his late half-sister Jeanne, Queen of France and Navarre (d. 1305). Henry had made one of his rare visits to court a week before: he was at Woodstock on 8 June, probably in anticipation of Queen Philippa shortly giving birth.[34] He and Edward III would be on cordial terms for the rest of Henry's life, so they must have reconciled at some point after Henry's rebellion, which Edward surely knew was aimed at his mother and her favourite, not at him personally.

Sometime before 24 June 1330 when he was about 18 or 20, Henry's only son and heir Henry of Grosmont married Isabella, daughter of Henry, Lord Beaumont, titular Earl of Buchan. Henry Beaumont was a French nobleman and a second cousin of Edward II, though he and two of his siblings (Louis, elected Bishop of Durham in 1317, and Isabella, Lady Vescy) spent most of their lives in England. They took the name of their mother Agnes, Viscountess of Beaumont-au-Maine, rather than their father Louis Brienne's. Louis Brienne is also sometimes called Louis of Acre, and his father John Brienne (d. 1237) was King of Jerusalem, Latin Emperor of Constantinople and claimant to the throne of Armenia. Louis' mother Berenguela of Leon, the Beaumont siblings' paternal grandmother, was the daughter of the King of Leon and the Queen of Castile.[35] Despite his high birth and impressive family connections, Henry Beaumont's early life is obscure and he was entirely dependent on the patronage of Edward I; Edward's queen Leonor, who was Beaumont's close relative; and their son Edward II. In August 1305, two years before his accession, the latter wrote, 'we are much obliged to our dear cousin Sir Henry Beaumont, and we greatly desire his advancement', and Beaumont was Edward II's loyal ally for most of his reign, but they fell out when the king made a thirteen-year peace settlement with Scotland in 1323.[36] Beaumont's uncle John Brienne had ruled the county of Champagne for Henry of Lancaster's father Edmund in the late 1270s and 1280s during Edmund's absences in England, so the connections between their families went back decades. Henry's older brother Thomas of Lancaster, however, had long been hostile to Henry Beaumont, and at the height of his political power in 1314 had demanded Beaumont's removal from court.[37]

Edward II arranged Henry Beaumont's marriage in or shortly before 1310 to Alice Comyn, niece and co-heir of John Comyn, Earl of Buchan in Scotland. Alice was many years Henry Beaumont's junior and was born around 1297/98 – she was underage in July 1310 and had reached her majority, age 14, by December 1312 – so she is unlikely to have begun bearing children before about 1313. Katherine was the first Beaumont child and married Henry of Lancaster's ally David Strathbogie, Earl of Atholl, in or after January 1327, with either Isabella or her brother John the second. John was born in December 1317.[38] Isabella Beaumont was thus born sometime between 1315 and 1320, and although she was the great-granddaughter of an Emperor of Constantinople and rather distantly related to the royal houses of England and Spain, she was not an heiress or even her father's eldest daughter. She was therefore hardly a great marital catch for the most eligible bachelor in England, but her marriage to Henry of Grosmont was a product of the tense political situation in England at the time. Henry Beaumont was one of the men who joined Henry of Lancaster's rebellion against Queen Isabella and Roger Mortimer, and fled from England in early 1329. Edward III pardoned Beaumont after he overthrew his mother and Mortimer and began ruling in his own right, and Beaumont returned to England in or soon after late November 1330. He received £500 from Edward III 'in recompense for his losses during the time he was banished from the realm', but missed the weddings of two of his children to two of Earl Henry of Lancaster's that year.[39] Sometime between 1 September and 6 November 1330, and probably before 19 October as Henry of Lancaster was extremely busy after that date, his fifth daughter Eleanor of Lancaster married John Beaumont, son and heir of Henry Beaumont and Alice (née Comyn).[40] John was born on or around Christmas Day 1317, so was 12 going on 13 at marriage, and Eleanor was about the same age.[41] John lived with the Lancasters after his wedding until at least February 1331, though he and Eleanor were still too young to consummate their marriage, and their son – inevitably called Henry – was not born until late 1339.

At the time of Eleanor and John's wedding, the regime of Queen Isabella and Roger Mortimer was about to topple. In July and August 1330, John's father Henry Beaumont, Thomas Roscelyn and other allies of Henry of Lancaster on the continent plotted an invasion of England with the aid of the Scottish Earl of Mar, which caused panic. The queen and her favourite arrayed knights, squires and men-at-arms, and ordered the coast to be defended.[42] One of the Lancastrians accused of the murder of Sir Robert Holland in October 1328 was John, son of Robert Tebbe, who was imprisoned for the murder but escaped.[43] In July 1330 at exactly the time when the Earl of Kent's adherents were being searched for and investigated and Henry Beaumont was planning an invasion of England, an order to arrest 'the sons of Robert Tebbe' and several others 'charged with unlawful assembly and breaches of the peace' was issued.[44] One of the others to be arrested was Walter Comyn, an adherent of Henry Beaumont and presumably a relative of Beaumont's wife Alice Comyn.[45] This may be an indication that Henry of Lancaster was in some way involved in the plot of the Earl of Kent to free the supposedly dead former king, and in the planned invasion of England. In the end, the invasion did not take place, perhaps because Queen Isabella's enemies did not want to be seen to be acting against the young king himself, but it was becoming clear that the dowager queen and her favourite could not be allowed to stay in power much longer. Not only had they judicially murdered the king's uncle Kent, they had bankrupted the kingdom while enriching themselves on a scale not even dreamed of by Hugh Despenser the Younger, and by the early autumn of 1330 they had alienated almost everyone.

Parliament was held at Nottingham in October 1330. According to the rather later and sometimes unreliable chronicler Geoffrey le Baker, Roger Mortimer refused to allow Henry of Lancaster to stay in the town as he was an enemy of Queen Isabella, and forced him to take lodgings a league away from Nottingham. This was a grave insult to one of royal birth.[46] On 19 October, Edward III, still not quite 18 years old, and twenty or so young knights burst into the chamber where Isabella and Mortimer were meeting their few remaining allies, and arrested Mortimer. Charter witness lists reveal that Henry of Lancaster was rarely at court or close to Edward III in 1329–30 after his rebellion, but that, perhaps significantly, he witnessed a royal charter on 16 October 1330, three days before Mortimer's arrest.[47] Various historians have speculated that Henry's involvement in the young king's coup was deeper than might appear from existing records, and he was also briefly with his great-nephew at Nottingham on and around 10 September, so perhaps they were indeed plotting Mortimer's downfall.[48] Surely Edward knew that Henry supported him and his young knights against the detested Mortimer, and Henry was present in Nottingham with plenty of manpower to help afterwards. Whether Edward could or would have carried out the coup against the mighty royal favourite without Lancastrian support is unlikely.[49]

Edward III apparently wanted to executed Mortimer on the spot, but Henry persuaded him to give the loathed favourite a trial before Parliament. Significantly, Mortimer was taken to London, where he was walled up at the Tower, via Henry's town of Leicester, which Mortimer had ravaged in early 1329. Henry of Lancaster led the procession, and they spent four days in Leicester.[50] Parliament began at Westminster on 26 November, and Edward III's fury at his mother's favourite and his appropriation of royal power is apparent; the king called himself 'like a man living in custody' owing to Mortimer placing spies in his own household. Two of the fourteen charges against Mortimer (the third and the fourth) mention Henry of Lancaster by name: that Mortimer had compelled the king to ride in force and arms against Henry in 1328 and constrained the earl and his allies to pay heavy fines to recover royal favour, and that he had kept Henry away from his rightful position as the king's adviser. Edward III further accused Mortimer of 'sedition and enmity' against Edward II, himself, Queen Philippa and their son Edward of Woodstock, and 'against certain magnates of the royal family', a reference to Henry of Lancaster and his cousin, the judicially murdered Earl of Kent.[51] Mortimer was hanged at Tyburn on 29 November 1330. Henry and all his followers were deemed 'guiltless' of everything, restored to their lands and goods and pardoned the huge fines they had been forced to acknowledge, and those forced to flee from England such as Henry Beaumont and Thomas Wake were invited home.[52] The governance of England finally lay in the hands of a just and competent ruler again, and the future of the House of Lancaster looked brighter than it had for many years.

PART III
1330–62

DRAMATIS PERSONAE

Henry of Lancaster, third Earl of Lancaster, Earl of Leicester, Steward of England (b. 1280/81): second son and heir of Edmund of Lancaster (d. 1296) and Blanche of Artois (d. 1302); grandson of Henry III, great-uncle of Edward III; widower of Maud Chaworth (d. 1322)

Henry of Grosmont, Earl and later Duke of Lancaster (b. *c.* 1310–12): only son and heir of Henry; marries Isabella Beaumont in 1330; Earl of Derby 1337, Earl of Lancaster and Leicester 1345, Earl of Lincoln 1349, first Duke of Lancaster 1351, also Lord of Bergerac and Beaufort and Steward of England; grandfather of Henry IV

Blanche Wake, Isabella of Lancaster, Maud de Burgh, Joan Mowbray, Eleanor Beaumont and Mary Percy: daughters of Henry, Earl of Lancaster, sisters of Henry of Grosmont

Thomas, Lord Wake; William de Burgh, Earl of Ulster; John, Lord Mowbray; John, Lord Beaumont; Henry, later Lord Percy: sons-in-law of Henry, Earl of Lancaster

Alice de Lacy, Countess of Lincoln in her own right (b. 1281): widow of Henry of Lancaster's elder brother Thomas of Lancaster (d. 1322); married secondly to Sir Eble Lestrange; has no children, and her heir is Henry of Grosmont

Isabella Beaumont, Countess and later Duchess of Lancaster, Countess of Derby, Leicester and Lincoln (b. *c.* 1315–20): second daughter of Henry, Lord Beaumont (d. 1340) and Alice Comyn (d. 1349), and sister of John, Lord Beaumont (b. 1317); marries Henry of Grosmont in 1330; mother of Maud and Blanche of Lancaster, grandmother of Henry IV

Edward III, King of England from January 1327 (b. 1312): son of Edward II and Isabella of France

Philippa of Hainault, Queen of England (b. *c.* 1314): daughter of Willem, Count of Hainault and Holland, and niece of Philip VI of France; marries Edward III in 1328

Isabella of France, Dowager Queen of England (b. *c.* 1295): widow of Edward II and mother of Edward III; niece of Henry, Earl of Lancaster and Leicester

Philip VI, King of France (b. 1293): first Valois King of France; first cousin of Queen Isabella and uncle of Queen Philippa

Edward of Woodstock, Prince of Wales and Aquitaine, Duke of Cornwall, Earl of Chester (b. 1330): eldest son of Edward III and Queen Philippa, heir to the English throne; marries Joan of Kent in 1361

Joan of Kent (b. 1326/27): daughter and ultimate heir of Edmund of Woodstock, Earl of Kent (d. 1330), and granddaughter of Edward I; niece and heir of Thomas, Lord Wake; marries Edward of Woodstock as her third husband; has four children with Sir Thomas Holland (d. 1360), second son of Sir Robert Holland (d. 1328)

Margaret of Norfolk, sometimes called Margaret Marshal (b. *c.* 1322): daughter and heir of Thomas of Brotherton, Earl of Norfolk (d. 1338), and granddaughter of Edward I; Countess and later Duchess of Norfolk in her own right; marries John, Lord Segrave and secondly Walter, Lord Manny

Elizabeth de Burgh, Duchess of Clarence, Countess of Ulster (b. 1332): only child and heir of William de Burgh, Earl of Ulster, and Maud of Lancaster; Henry, Earl of Lancaster's eldest grandchild; also heir to her paternal grandmother Elizabeth de Burgh (née de Clare) (b. 1295)

Lionel of Antwerp, Duke of Clarence, Earl of Ulster (b. 1338): second surviving son of Edward III and Philippa of Hainault; marries Elizabeth de Burgh in 1342; made first Duke of Clarence in 1362

John of Gaunt, second Duke of Lancaster, Earl of Richmond, Leicester, Lincoln and Derby (b. 1340): third son of Edward III and Queen Philippa; marries Henry of Grosmont's daughter and co-heir Blanche of Lancaster in 1359 as the first of his three wives

Edmund of Langley, Earl of Cambridge, later first Duke of York (b. 1341): fourth son of Edward III and Queen Philippa; marries Isabel of Castile, younger daughter of King Pedro 'the Cruel' in 1372, and secondly Joan Holland in 1393; founder of the House of York

Thomas of Woodstock, later Earl of Buckingham and first Duke of Gloucester (b. 1355): fifth and youngest son of Edward III and Queen Philippa

Maud of Lancaster, Countess of Leicester (b. 1340): duchess of Lower Bavaria; Countess of Leicester, Hainault and Holland; marries Ralph Stafford (b. *c.* late 1330s) in 1344 and secondly Wilhelm (b. 1330), Duke of Lower Bavaria and Count of Hainault and Holland, in 1352

Blanche of Lancaster, Duchess of Lancaster, Countess of Richmond, Leicester, Lincoln and Derby (b. 1342/44): younger daughter and ultimately the sole heir of Henry of Grosmont and to the entire Lancastrian inheritance when her elder sister Maud dies childless in 1362; marries John of Gaunt in 1359; mother of Henry IV

Philippa of Lancaster (b. 1360): eldest child of John of Gaunt and Blanche of Lancaster; later Queen of Portugal; granddaughter of Edward III, also granddaughter of Henry of Grosmont

Elizabeth of Lancaster (b. 1363): younger daughter of John and Blanche; later Countess of Pembroke and Huntingdon and Duchess of Exeter

Henry of Lancaster (b. 1367): only surviving son of John and Blanche, and the Lancastrian heir; sometimes called Henry of Bolingbroke after his birthplace in Lincolnshire; later Earl of Derby, then first Duke of Hereford and third Duke of Lancaster; becomes King Henry IV in 1399

Richard Fitzalan (b. *c.* 1313), Earl of Arundel: son and heir of Edmund, Earl of Arundel (1285–1326); also heir of his uncle **John de Warenne**, Earl of Surrey (1286–1347); marries Isabella Despenser in 1321 and the widowed Eleanor of Lancaster, Lady Beaumont, in 1345

Richard Fitzalan (b. 1346/47), Earl of Arundel: eldest son and heir of Richard and Eleanor of Lancaster; marries Elizabeth de Bohun, sister of the Earl of Hereford, in 1359

Joan de Bohun (née **Fitzalan**) (b. 1345/46), Countess of Hereford: elder daughter of Richard Fitzalan and Eleanor of Lancaster; marries Humphrey de Bohun, Earl of Hereford (b. 1342), great-grandson of Edward I, in 1359; grandmother of King Henry V

Alice Holland (née **Fitzalan**) (b. 1348–50), Countess of Kent: younger daughter of Richard and Eleanor; marries Thomas Holland, Earl of Kent (b. 1350/51), half-brother of Richard II; mother of the Duchess of York, the Countess of March and others

John Arundel (b. *c.*1350), Admiral of England: second son of Richard and Eleanor; marries Eleanor Maltravers in 1357; his son and heir is **John** (b. 1364)

Thomas Arundel (b. 1352/53), Archbishop of York, then of Canterbury; third son of Richard and Eleanor

Henry, Lord Beaumont (b. 1339): only child of Eleanor of Lancaster and her first husband John, Lord Beaumont (1317–42); stepson of the Earl of Arundel (b. *c.* 1313); his son and heir is **John** (b. 1361)

John, Lord Mowbray (b. 1340): son and heir of John Mowbray (b. 1310) and Joan of Lancaster (b. *c.* 1313–15), fourth daughter of Henry, Earl of Lancaster and Leicester

Elizabeth Mowbray (née **Segrave**) (b. 1338): daughter and heir of Margaret, Countess of Norfolk (b. *c.* 1322), and John, Lord Segrave (1315–53); great-granddaughter of Edward I; marries John Mowbray (b. 1340) in 1349

Philippa of Clarence, Countess of March and Ulster (b. 1355): only child and heir of Lionel of Antwerp (b. 1338) and Elizabeth de Burgh (b. 1332); granddaughter of Edward III and Philippa of Hainault; also granddaughter of Maud of Lancaster, Countess of Ulster (b. *c.* 1310/12)

Edmund Mortimer, third Earl of March, Earl of Ulster (b. 1352): son of Roger Mortimer, second Earl of March (1328–60), and Philippa Montacute; marries Philippa of Clarence in 1358

Humphrey de Bohun, Earl of Hereford, Essex and Northampton (b. 1342): great-grandson of Edward I; half-brother of Roger Mortimer, second Earl of March; marries Joan Fitzalan in 1359; grandfather of King Henry V; his sister **Elizabeth** marries Joan's brother Richard Fitzalan, Earl of Arundel (b. 1346/47)

Henry Percy (b. 1341): first son of Henry, Lord Percy (b. *c.* 1320/21) and Mary of Lancaster (b. *c.* 1319–21); made first Earl of Northumberland in 1377; marries Margaret Neville in 1358; his son and heir is **Henry 'Hotspur' Percy** (b. 1364)

Thomas Percy (b. 1343/44): second son of Henry Percy and Mary of Lancaster; made Earl of Worcester in 1397; never marries

THE RISE AND RISE
OF THE LANCASTERS

⊶∞⊷

Firmly back in his great-nephew's favour after the king's *coup d'état* at Nottingham in October 1330, Henry, Earl of Lancaster was one of the men sent to Paris to negotiate on Edward III's behalf with envoys of Philip VI in February 1331. With him went the Bishops of Worcester and Norwich, and Henry's allies Hugh Audley and Henry Percy. The men were to 'treat of the mutual debts of the two kings' and to 'treat of all matters in dispute'.[1] Henry of Lancaster and his retinue were paid by the king from 21 January 1331 and should have sailed across the Channel to Wissant a week later, but were delayed at Dover for twelve days because of contrary winds (it was the depths of winter, when travel across the Channel was often very difficult). He finally arrived in Paris on 23 February, and Philip VI arrived in his capital on the 24th.[2] Henry and his fellow envoys signed a treaty with Philip VI's men on 9 March 1331, and the following month the two kings met in person at Pont-Sainte-Maxence. Edward III left England secretly and disguised as a merchant on 4 April with only a small retinue, who included Henry's son Henry of Grosmont. Curiously, Henry of Lancaster was never officially named as one of the king's envoys to France in February and March 1331, and his name appears nowhere in the extant records of the envoys' appointment in January and the treaty they made with the King of France a few weeks later. He certainly went to

Paris, however, as a membrane of his and his retinue's expenses and itinerary still exists and reveals that his return journey from London to Paris cost the king £320; perhaps his presence was meant to be kept secret for some reason. Henry returned from Paris to the port of Wissant and sailed from there to Dover on 17 March, and waited at Dover for the arrival of his son and the king on 3 April before Edward III himself travelled to France to meet Philip VI.[3] This was probably Henry of Lancaster's last visit to France, his mother Blanche of Artois' homeland, where he had spent so much time over the decades. On 3 April, the day the king arrived at Dover and met his great-uncle Henry, Edward III wrote to Pope John XXII and fourteen cardinals urging the canonisation of the late Thomas of Lancaster, which is a sign of his favour towards Henry and his son Grosmont.[4]

In March 1332, Edward III talked of his 'special affection' for Henry of Grosmont – they were first cousins once removed and much the same age – and granted him an income of 500 marks a year 'because his father Henry Earl of Lancaster has not yet made such provision for him as becomes his estate'.[5] In 1333, Earl Henry handed over the castles and lands of Kidwelly, Grosmont, Skenfrith, Ogmore and others to his son, which perhaps indicates that Grosmont turned 21 that year and had thus come of age.[6] Edward III and Queen Philippa's first daughter Isabella was born at the royal palace of Woodstock near Oxford in about June 1332, and Henry of Grosmont was present at the palace with the royal couple.[7] He may have been Isabella's godfather.

All the way back in 1296, Edward I had removed John Balliol from the throne of Scotland, and Balliol had gone into exile on the Continent with his son Edward Balliol. Edward III was forced to recognise Robert Bruce as King of Scotland in 1328 and to see his sister Joan married to Bruce's son and heir David, and when Bruce died in 1329, the 5-year-old David and his 8-year-old wife succeeded as King and Queen of Scotland. In 1328 Henry of Lancaster's son-in-law Thomas Wake and friends Henry Beaumont and Henry Percy were promised the restoration of their lands in Scotland, but this never came about, and Anglo-Scottish relations quickly deteriorated. Beaumont, Wake and the others began to call themselves 'the Disinherited', and when Edward Balliol decided to try to take the Scottish throne in the summer of 1332, Henry Beaumont went with him. On 11 August 1332 at the Battle of Dupplin Moor, John Balliol and Beaumont defeated the Scottish forces led by the Regent of Scotland, Donald, Earl of Mar. (Mar was a former close friend of Edward II and Henry Beaumont's ally in his planned invasion of England two years before.) Donald of Mar was killed, as were the Earls of Moray and Menteith and one of the late Robert Bruce's illegitimate sons. It was a remarkable victory for the Disinherited. Edward Balliol was crowned king soon afterwards, but was humiliatingly expelled from Scotland a few months later after a surprise attack at Annan when he and his supporters were in bed. Balliol barely escaped with his life. Henry, Earl of Lancaster was summoned by Edward III on 21 March 1333 to come to him with men and arms at Newcastle a few weeks later to 'set out thence with the king against the Scots'. His sons-in-law Thomas Wake and John Mowbray were also among the men summoned.[8] This, coupled with Henry's (apparently secret) journey to Paris two years before, would argue against the notion that he had already gone blind, though after the early 1330s he appears to have played a smaller role in public life than previously. During the 1333 campaign, Edward III recaptured the important port of Berwick as his father had singularly failed to do in 1319, and comprehensively defeated a Scottish force at the Battle of Halidon Hill.[9]

Henry of Lancaster's first grandchild, or at least his first legitimate grandchild – as it is not impossible that Henry of Grosmont had fathered one or several of the illegitimate kind – was born on 6 July 1332.[10] She was the only surviving child of Maud of Lancaster and William de Burgh, Earl of Ulster, and was named Elizabeth after William's mother. Elizabeth de Burgh was a great heiress, set to inherit her father's earldom and her paternal grandmother Elizabeth's third of the earldom of Gloucester. Eleven months after her birth, on 6 June 1333, the Earl of Ulster was murdered near Carrickfergus in Ireland; he was only 20 years old and therefore still underage and officially Edward III's ward. His widow Maud fled back to England with their baby daughter, to the safety of her father. Edward III granted Maud an income of 100 marks a year 'for her proper and honourable maintenance', and to support her daughter; the king may already have had it in mind that the tiny heiress would one day make an excellent wife for a son of his. He soon increased Maud's allowance to 150 marks a year, then 200, and allowed her daughter to remain in her custody.[11] The king was now Elizabeth de Burgh's legal guardian, and in December 1334 appointed a man called John Gernoun to look after her interests in Ireland. Gernoun was also Maud of Lancaster's attorney there.

There are two references on the Patent Roll to at least one and perhaps two more daughters of William de Burgh and Maud of Lancaster. On 16 July 1338, mention is made of 'Isabella, daughter and heir of William, late Earl of Ulster'.[12] It is not impossible that this is in fact a reference to Elizabeth, as the names Elizabeth and Isabella were sometimes interchangeable in the Middle Ages, though by this stage of the fourteenth century they seem to have been considered separate names, and all other references to the girl name her Elizabeth, not Isabella.[13] And on 6 April 1340 there is a reference to 'Margaret, daughter and heir of William de Burgh, Earl of Ulster', when Edward III granted her marriage to his sister Eleanor of Woodstock's husband Reynald, Duke of Guelders, for Eleanor and Reynald's second son Eduard (b. 1336).[14] Unless this is a scribal error and Elizabeth was meant, it would seem that Maud of Lancaster was pregnant with twins in 1333 when her husband was killed and she fled back to England, but Margaret and Isabella de Burgh must have died young in or after 1340 as there are no other references to them. William's Inquisition Post Mortem of July/August 1333 names only his daughter Elizabeth as his heir, so Margaret and Isabella (assuming they did exist) cannot have been born yet, or they would have been William's joint heirs with Elizabeth and would have remained so had they lived.[15]

Maud of Lancaster visited her mother-in-law Elizabeth de Burgh the elder in the summer of 1334 before returning to her father's castle of Tutbury in Staffordshire for her youngest sister Mary's wedding, and some years later received a gift of two spaniels from Elizabeth. The women sent each other letters, and evidently were on good terms. Maud's father Henry, Earl of Lancaster also visited Elizabeth de Burgh and hunted in her chases, and she visited him at Higham Ferrers in Northamptonshire in 1344, the year before his death.[16] Whether with good reason or not, Maud of Lancaster believed herself to be in danger from her husband's enemies even after her return to England: in August 1334, she claimed that 'she is laid in wait for and threatened by certain of her rivals in Ireland who killed the said earl [of Ulster], and who will destroy the countess if they can take her'.[17] In 1337 Maud accused Richard Mandeville and his wife Gylle of complicity in her husband's murder, and offered a reward of 100 marks to anyone who took them, dead or alive.[18] Gylle was the sister of Walter de Burgh, a cousin of the Earl of Ulster, whom William had starved to death in February 1332. William's murder was Gylle's revenge.

Around mid August to early September 1334, the sixth and youngest Lancaster daughter, Mary, married Henry Percy at Tutbury Castle, one of her father's many homes.[19] Percy was born around 1320 or 1321, so was Mary's age, and was heir to his father Henry, Lord Percy (b. 1301), probably the greatest nobleman in the north of England and a friend of Henry of Lancaster.[20] Mary's sister Isabella, the nun of Amesbury, gave her a valuable cup and ewer as wedding gifts – she had sent a servant to London to purchase them – and had previously sent another cup and ewer, a cameo and a brooch with emeralds for her sister when the Pope granted a dispensation for Mary and Henry to marry.[21] The first Percy child was not born until November 1341, so as was the case with her older sisters, Mary probably remained with her father for some years and did not rush into parenthood; she and her husband were at the beginning of their teens when they married and 20 or 21 when they had their first child. She was marrying into a large family: her husband had five younger brothers, including a future Bishop of Norwich, and four sisters. Mary and her husband succeeded as Lord and Lady Percy on the death of her father-in-law in 1352; Henry Senior left Mary an enamelled bowl in his will.[22]

In early December 1334, the Lancasters' aunt Isabella, Lady Hastings, one of the Despenser half-siblings of the late Maud Chaworth, died. Henry of Grosmont was given custody of her dower lands.[23] Henry, Earl of Lancaster spent Christmas 1334 at his castle of Leicester, and the townspeople sent him gifts of 'Cretan wine', a swan and a heron, and between Christmas and Easter 1335 further gifts of twelve partridges and some lampreys. On other occasions they sent him bread, wine, twelve capons, twelve 'fat geese', cloves and a popular dessert made from honey called *sucre de plate*, and gave his son Henry of Grosmont bread, wine, geese and chickens. Earl Henry stabled his horses at St Mary's Abbey in the town, and the records of Leicester Borough reveal that he had a Fool named Ricard and that his barber was called Adinet. A rather curious entry in the Leicester records of 1335–36 talks of 'the Earl of Lancaster and the countess'. Henry was a widower, and none of his daughters or his daughter-in-law had married an earl by 1335/36 so the reference cannot mean them (his son Grosmont was made Earl of Derby in 1337, and his fifth daughter Eleanor wed the Earl of Arundel in 1345). In 1327 there is also a reference in the Leicester accounts to the 'countess' being brought to the town by one of Henry's knights.[24] Perhaps Henry had a mistress, who was delicately and diplomatically referred to as his 'countess'. As he had lost his wife as far back as 1322 it would hardly be surprising, though if Henry had out-of-wedlock children there is no known record of them. He owned a house at the New Temple in London, which had previously belonged to his brother Thomas and was given to Henry's brother-in-law Hugh Despenser in 1324; it was one of the many properties Henry retrieved in and after 1327. He kept some treasure hidden there in the garden, buried under a pear tree, but in June or July 1335 it was stolen during the night.[25]

Henry's sister-in-law Alice de Lacy, Countess of Lincoln in her own right and Thomas of Lancaster's widow, had married her second husband Sir Eble or Ebolo Lestrange in 1324, and enjoyed a seemingly very happy and loving marriage with him. Eble never used the title 'Earl of Lincoln' as he was entitled to do by right of his wife, indicating that he had married Alice for herself and not for her titles and wealth, and later in life Alice called herself 'widow of Eble Lestrange' but never 'widow of Thomas of Lancaster', despite the latter's far higher rank and status.[26] Lestrange died in September 1335, and within months of his death, in late 1335 or in the first few weeks of 1336, Alice was abducted from her own home of Bolingbroke Castle in Lincolnshire by an obscure knight called Sir Hugh de Frene (or Freyne or Frayn) and a number of armed men. Frene took her the 30 miles to Somerton Castle and married her against her will, even though she had taken a vow of chastity after Eble Lestrange's death.[27] Born in December 1281, Alice was now in her mid 50s, and Frene must have been much younger, as he was knighted in early 1327 which implies that he was born well after 1300.[28] Edward III heard of the abduction sometime before 20 February 1336, on which date he ordered three men to arrest Frene and his victim as well, and to take Alice's lands into the king's hands. Alice was said to have already escaped from Somerton, as had Frene, who had also been imprisoned there on the king's orders after Edward learned what he had done.[29]

Alice described her ordeal in a subsequent petition to the king – who had ordered her arrest so was hardly disposed to be sympathetic towards her – and it makes uncomfortable reading. Although she did not describe it as such, there is no doubt that what happened to her was kidnap and rape, and after she escaped from Somerton and Edward III ordered her to be arrested, Hugh de Frene took her to the Tower of London. She remained there 'in such confinement that none of her friends or well-wishers could go near her or talk to her', only Frene's adherents and members of his retinue.

She appears to have still been incarcerated in the Tower against her will when she dictated her petition, as she asked Edward III to remedy her situation as quickly as possible so that she might again be 'at liberty among her friends'. What must have made Alice's nightmare even worse was her knowledge that Frene had kidnapped her in her own home thanks to the 'treachery' or 'betrayal' of her own brother John de Lacy — who must have been an illegitimate son of Henry de Lacy, Earl of Lincoln (d. 1311) — and some of her servants.[30] She pointed out twice in her petition that what had happened to her was *contre son gree*, 'against her station (in life)' and against her vow of chastity. Other than the temporary imprisonment at Somerton Castle, Edward III did not punish Hugh de Frene in any way, and to add insult to injury, in July 1338 Pope Benedict XII ordered the Bishop of Lincoln to 'warn and compel' Alice 'by spiritual penalties' to keep the vow of chastity she had taken, as though she was in any way responsible for having failed to do so.[31] Benedict claimed that Alice had 'consented to live with [Frene] in matrimony until his death', but as she had absolutely no way to stop being married to Frene after he kidnapped her and forced her to go through a wedding ceremony with him, her alleged consent was meaningless.

Perhaps the only meagre consolation for Alice was that Hugh de Frene was sent on campaign to Scotland not too long after their wedding and died there in December 1336 or January 1337, only a few months after his abduction and rape of her; they cannot have lived together very long, and Frene gained very little benefit from his abduction of her.[32] Her own lands were restored to her in late February and early March 1337 after Frene's death, though her run of ill luck was not yet over. Sometime before early May 1337, Countess Alice was attacked again at her castle of Bolingbroke by her late husband's brother or nephew Roger Lestrange, John de Lacy (presumably the man of this name who was her illegitimate half-brother and who had connived at her abduction by Frene the year before), and more than thirty other men including the Abbot of Rocester in Staffordshire and one of his canons.[33] They stole twenty of her horses, worth £200, and other goods, imprisoned Alice within the castle temporarily, and assaulted her servants. It must have been heartbreaking for the countess to be attacked and robbed by her own half-brother and her beloved Eble's kinsman. Still, a born survivor, she finally came out the other side of all the hardship and lived until October 1348; she outlived her brother-in-law Henry of Lancaster by three years.

ON THE CONTINENT

———⊗⊗⊗———

King Edward III suffered a bereavement in September 1336 when his younger brother John of Eltham, Earl of Cornwall, died in Scotland, aged only 20. John was unmarried and childless, and his mother Queen Isabella outlived him by more than twenty years; she also outlived her elder daughter Eleanor, Duchess of Guelders, who died in April 1355 at the age of 36. In 1336, the king turned a blind eye to another abduction and forced marriage of a noblewoman which took place in England that year. This one involved his cousin Margaret Audley, only child and heir of Margaret de Clare and Hugh Audley, who was taken from her home in Thaxted, Essex by Sir Ralph Stafford, and probably the king took no action to punish Stafford because the latter was a close friend of his who had helped him arrest Roger Mortimer at Nottingham in October 1330. Margaret Stafford (*née* Audley) was probably only 13 or 14 at the time, and Stafford was twenty years her senior. Edward did perhaps try to mollify Margaret's father Hugh Audley by making him Earl of Gloucester in March 1337, though he also made the abductor Ralph Stafford the first Earl of Stafford some years later. Also in 1337, Henry of Grosmont was made Earl of Derby, the title his grandfather Edmund of Lancaster had taken from Robert Ferrers almost sixty years earlier.[1] Other friends of the king were rewarded with earldoms: his first cousin William de Bohun (son of Edward II's sister Elizabeth) became Earl of Northampton, Robert Ufford became Earl of Suffolk, and William Clinton Earl of Huntingdon. The king's son and heir Edward of Woodstock was made the first duke in English history in 1337 (excepting that the kings of England had long been dukes of Aquitaine in France) when his father made him Duke of Cornwall, although he had to wait until 1343 before receiving the title of Prince of Wales.

Edward III officially claimed the throne of France in 1337. His mother Isabella was the fourth and youngest child of Philip IV, and her brothers Louis X, Philip V and Charles IV had all reigned as kings of France and died in their 20s and early 30s. All three men left daughters but no surviving sons, and so in 1328 the throne of France passed to their cousin Philip VI, born Philip de Valois, son of Philip IV's brother Charles, Count of Valois (who had urged Philip IV to war against England in 1294 when Edmund of Lancaster's diplomacy failed badly). Philip VI was the uncle of Edward's queen Philippa of Hainault and the first cousin of Edward's mother Isabella, so it was a family affair. Edward III, claiming that a grandson had a better claim to a throne than a nephew, opened hostilities, and spent the entire period from mid July 1338 until late February 1340 outside England, in Flanders, Brabant and Germany.[2] He met the German Emperor Ludwig of Bavaria – whose wife Margareta was Queen Philippa's sister – in Koblenz in early September 1338 and persuaded him to ally with him against France. This was a great diplomatic coup, though in the end the alliance did not last long. Philippa accompanied her husband to the continent and gave birth to their third, but second surviving, son at the Abbey of St Michael in Antwerp on 29 November 1338. They gave him the Arthurian name of Lionel.[3] Lionel of Antwerp was the ancestor of the fifteenth-century Yorkists; although they took their name from Lionel's younger brother Edmund, Duke of York, also their ancestor, their descent from the second son of Edward III in the female line gave the dynasty its claim to the English throne.

King Edward and Queen Philippa specifically asked Eleanor of Lancaster and her husband John Beaumont to accompany them abroad, and Edward later rewarded Eleanor with an income of £100 a year for her 'charges and labours' while attending the queen. John also received a gift for his 'great labours in the king's service'.[4] The king and queen greatly enjoyed the young couple's company. Eleanor's sister Joan and brother-in-law John,

Lord Mowbray were also on the Continent with the king.[5] Their father
Henry, Earl of Lancaster and Leicester, meanwhile, spent Christmas 1338
in his town of Leicester, and received a tun of wine and two swans as a
gift from the townspeople. The earl held a feast in the town to celebrate
the Feast of the Assumption in 1339, 15 August, and provided numerous
minstrels to enliven the proceedings. His daughter-in-law Isabella (née
Beaumont), Countess of Derby, attended the feast, and had recently become
pregnant; she must have been with her husband Henry of Grosmont, the
king and her sisters-in-law Joan and Eleanor on the Continent, but had
returned to England. Her father Henry, Lord Beaumont visited Henry of
Lancaster at his castle of Tutbury in early October 1338, and her brother-
in-law Thomas, Lord Wake also visited his father-in-law at Leicester in
July 1339 and gave him a manor in Yorkshire for life.[6]

Sometime in the early months of 1339, Eleanor of Lancaster also became
pregnant, and her first child Henry Beaumont the younger was born in
the duchy of Brabant before mid January 1340, probably in late 1339.[7] He
would be Eleanor and John's only child. In case their son's birth outside
England and outside the lands ruled by the King of England caused the boy
legal problems in the future – as in fact it did – Edward III announced in
December 1340 that 'the king's kinsfolk John de Bello Monte [Beaumont]
and Eleanor de Lancastre' had accompanied him and the queen overseas at
his command and had intended to return to England for the birth of their
child, but Edward and Philippa persuaded them to stay with them because
their company was 'very desirable'.

In a fourteenth-century example of inappropriate oversharing, the king
further stated, 'taking into consideration that the said John and Eleanor at
the time of the conception and birth of the said Henry were cohabiting
continually in Brabant in his [the king's] company in marital intercourse,
[he] reputes Henry to be their true and legitimate son'.[8] John and Eleanor
had married in 1330 when he was not yet 13 and she about the same age,
and now in the late 1330s they were in their early 20s and evidently thoroughly enjoying married life together. John Beaumont may have been
named after his father's grandfather John Brienne, King of Jerusalem and
Emperor of Constantinople, and he and Eleanor named their son after both
their fathers. (Their son Henry in turn named his son John after his father,
and the Beaumonts would alternate the names John and Henry for their
eldest sons for many generations.) Despite Edward III's statement, when

John Beaumont's mother Alice Comyn died in July 1349 – John was already dead by then – her heir was returned as John's younger brother Thomas rather than John's son Henry, as should have been the case, because John had died 'without an heir of his body born within the realm of England or the allegiance of the king of England'.[9] The Parliament of February 1351, however, declared that Henry Beaumont and all other Englishmen 'born beyond the sea' should have the full right to their inheritances, and Henry duly inherited his father and grandmother's lands.[10]

On 4 April 1340, Henry of Grosmont and Isabella Beaumont's first child who survived infancy was born. It was a girl, named Maud after Henry's late mother Maud Chaworth, and she was the first cousin on both sides of the family of the young Henry Beaumont, born in Brabant some months before; they had all four grandparents in common. A few weeks earlier on 10 March, Isabella's father, the influential Henry, Lord Beaumont, had passed away. He was probably aged between 60 and 70 when he died, and his son and heir John Beaumont received his lands remarkably quickly on 13 March.[11]

Henry of Grosmont and Isabella Beaumont's second daughter Blanche of Lancaster, named after Henry's grandmother Blanche of Artois, was perhaps born on 25 March 1342, though there is some doubt as to the correct date. The only real source for the two Lancaster daughters' dates of birth is Henry of Grosmont's Inquisition Post Mortem, when the estimated ages of the two women in 1361 range from 16 to 26. Only the Derbyshire and Staffordshire jurors assigned Maud and Blanche precise dates of birth, and both sets of jurors agreed exactly on the dates: 4 April 1340 and 25 March 1342. As Henry of Grosmont was Earl of Derby at the time of his daughters' births, it is perhaps important that the Derbyshire jurors gave specific ages for them, as they would have been in a good position to know. The jurors of Maud of Lancaster's own IPM in 1362, however, estimated the age of her sister and heir Blanche as anywhere between 16 and 24 that year, and none of the jurors gave Blanche a precise date of birth. Even the Staffordshire jurors who had given Blanche an exact date of birth in 1361 said unhelpfully a year later only that she was 'twenty-one and more', and thus contradicted themselves. The jurors of Leicestershire, heartland of the Lancastrian patrimony, said that Blanche was 'nineteen years and more' in April 1361 and 'twenty-two years and more' in April 1362.[12] The evidence of Inquisitions Post Mortem can be vexingly vague and contradictory.

One possible problem with assigning a birthdate of March 1342 to Blanche is that Henry of Grosmont spent most of 1340 and 1341 in prison, or least in a kind of prison, in Flanders because of debts owed by Edward III, and was still there on 3 September 1341. He was back in England by 24 September 1341.[13] On the other hand, Henry was a highly born and partly royal nobleman and would not have been thrown into a dismal dungeon, and may have been allowed conjugal visits. His wife Isabella Beaumont did travel to the Low Countries in 1341.[14] Another issue is that a date of birth in March 1342 for Blanche would make her 17 when she married John of Gaunt in May 1359. This seems implausibly old by the standards of her family. Her sister Maud married her first husband when she was only 4 years old and her second when she was not yet 12, and Blanche herself was first betrothed in 1347. Her first cousin Elizabeth de Burgh married Lionel of Antwerp when they were 9 and 3, her first cousin John Mowbray married Elizabeth Segrave before he was 9, and yet another first cousin, Maud Ufford, married Thomas de Vere when she was 4. It seems a little odd that Henry of Grosmont would have waited until she was 17 before getting Blanche married, as he had no sons and it was in his interest to have his daughters producing their own sons as quickly as possible. By age 17, Blanche would already have been fertile for some years.

At any rate, Henry of Grosmont's heirs were his two daughters Maud and Blanche of Lancaster, born in the first half of the 1340s during the lifetime of their grandfather Earl Henry – who died in 1345 knowing that his only son had not yet fathered a son and who surely must have been worried about the future of the dynasty. The names 'Blanche' and 'Maud' were, thanks to Blanche of Artois and Maud Chaworth, hugely popular in the Lancaster family in the fourteenth century, while many of Edward III's granddaughters were called Philippa after the queen. The name Blanche in the fourteenth century was often written 'Blaunche' or 'Blaunch', which gives a clue as to how they pronounced it, and Maud was sometimes spelled Mahaud, Mahud, Mahaut or Maude. Philippa was spelled Phelip, Phelipe or Philippe, confusingly, as this is now the male form of the name Philip in modern French, and Henry was sometimes spelled Henre. The contemporary form of the name Eleanor was Alianore or Alienore, Joan was Johane or Johanne, and Isabella was spelled in many different ways including Isabele and Yzabel. In Henry of Lancaster's 1345 will, his youngest daughter Mary's name appeared as Marie.

The records of the Borough of Leicester indicate that Henry of Grosmont and Isabella Beaumont had another daughter called Isabella, who was older than their surviving daughters Maud and Blanche. The Mayor of Leicester's account of September 1338 to September 1339 includes the following entry: 'Sent to the countess of Derby and the lady Isabella daughter of the lady countess, two gallons of white wine.'[15] The Countess of Derby in 1338–39 was certainly Isabella Beaumont; Henry of Grosmont was made Earl of Derby in 1337. This daughter must have died young, as there is no other known record of her. The couple may also have had two sons who died in childhood. John Leland (1506–52) visited the Newarke in Leicester not long before it was dissolved in Edward VI's reign (1547–53) and said that he saw the graves of two boys buried there with Henry of Grosmont's father Earl Henry, 'under the arche nexte to his hedde'.[16] As it is impossible that Henry of Grosmont or his descendants would have buried children who were not members of their family next to Grosmont's father, it is certain that these boys were Lancasters. Perhaps they were sons of Grosmont and Isabella Beaumont who died in infancy, or perhaps they were Earl Henry's sons and Grosmont's brothers, moved from wherever they had originally been interred and reburied after Henry of Lancaster founded the Newarke in 1330. Earl Henry and Maud Chaworth had six daughters but only one son, so there may have been other sons who died in childhood. A Gloucestershire antiquarian in 1712 narrated a local tale he had heard that Henry of Grosmont had a young son who drowned at his manor of Kempsford, but as this was 350 years after Henry's death and is unsupported by other evidence, we cannot place too much credence in it.[17] The likeliest scenario is that the two boys whose graves were seen in the middle of the sixteenth century were Henry of Grosmont's grandsons, children of his younger daughter Blanche and her husband John of Gaunt, who died in infancy. King Henry IV, son and heir of Blanche and John, had prayers said in June 1404 for his wife Mary de Bohun, stepmother Constanza of Castile, and 'the king's brothers', who were all buried at the Newarke.[18]

Overall, it seems that Henry of Grosmont and Isabella Beaumont's marriage was not a particularly happy or fulfilling one. Henry openly admitted in his famous work *The Book of Holy Medicines* in 1354 to enjoying women and to having kissed many (the Anglo-Norman word he used, *beiser*, in modern French can either mean 'kiss' or what is often rendered as 'the f-word'). He admitted that he would prefer a poor and ugly but lascivious

prostitute to a good woman of high status, however beautiful she was; and
that the more a woman loved and served God, the less it pleased him to
kiss her. He liked women to admire him and deliberately stretched out
his legs in his stirrups at jousting tournaments so that the watching ladies
would notice his fine calves, and danced elegantly for the same purpose.
Henry also admitted that he had 'a great desire to be prized, then loved,
then lost'.[19] Considering that Isabella Beaumont was the first duchess in
English history, and the grandmother of a king of England and a queen
consort of Portugal (Henry IV and Philippa of Lancaster), she is oddly
obscure, and even the date of her death is, most unusually, not known for
certain. She played little, if any, role in Henry's public life, and was perhaps
a shy and retiring personality. Even though for years she was the second
lady in England after Queen Philippa – Edward of Woodstock, the Prince
of Wales, did not marry until 1361 – no chronicler even mentioned her.
Henry of Grosmont had such a larger-than-life personality that he simply
overshadowed his wife entirely.

JOHN OF GAUNT AND EDMUND OF LANGLEY

————— ❦ —————

On 6 March 1340, just a month before Henry of Grosmont's daughter Maud was born, his future son-in-law John of Gaunt arrived into the world. John was born in Ghent in modern-day Belgium, the fourth, but third surviving, son of Edward III and Queen Philippa. The king had already returned to England some weeks before, but the queen was too advanced in pregnancy to be able to accompany him, and Edward did not see his latest child until about 10 July when he returned to Ghent. Edward III had officially been proclaimed King of France in Ghent on 26 January 1340, a few weeks before John was born.[1] The king gave the large sum of £200 to be shared among the three women who brought him news of his son's birth: Amice of Gloucester, Alice Betyngfield and Margery St Maur, Queen Philippa's damsels.[2] John's first nurse was the same Margery St Maur, who by February 1346 had been replaced by Isolda Newman, and his wet-nurse was Margery Tilsthorpe. He arrived in England in November 1340 with his older brother Lionel of Antwerp, and in addition to his nurse and 'rocker' (the girl or woman who rocked his cradle) he had three female attendants, two male squires of the body and six male chamber servants. John had bright green and red bedding, and was dressed in silken robes.[3] In his own lifetime the boy was, like his siblings, named after his birthplace – in documents it was usually Latinised as 'John de Gandavo' – and thanks to the immortal first line of William Shakespeare's play about John's nephew Richard II, he will forever more be thought of as 'Old John of Gaunt, time-honour'd Lancaster'.

The fourth Lancaster sister Joan also gave birth in 1340, probably around 24 or 25 June, to her only son. He was inevitably named John Mowbray after his father.[4] On 25 March 1349, the Pope issued a dispensation for the younger John Mowbray, not yet 9, to marry Elizabeth Segrave, daughter and ultimately the co-heir of Edward I's granddaughter Margaret, Countess of Norfolk, and the heir of her father John, Lord Segrave. This was done at the request of Henry of Grosmont, because he wished 'to make peace between the lords John Mowbray and John Segrave and their successors, between whom, they being near neighbours, quarrels and scandals may arise'.[5] Elizabeth Segrave was twenty months older than her husband, born in Croxton Abbey in Leicestershire on 25 October 1338, a few weeks after the death of her maternal grandfather Thomas of Brotherton, Earl of Norfolk and son of Edward I, who was only 38 when he died.[6] Young though she was, Elizabeth had her own chamberlain by 1351.[7] Her marriage to John would result in the Mowbrays becoming dukes of Norfolk at the end of the fourteenth century.

Joan of Lancaster and John Mowbray (b. 1310) had two daughters as well, Eleanor and Blanche Mowbray. Blanche first appears on record on 13 March 1342, when her parents arranged a future marriage for her with Edward Montacute, nephew of the Earl of Salisbury. The marriage never took place, though Blanche Mowbray's marital career was an interesting one: she had no fewer than five husbands, though no surviving children. Eleanor Mowbray first appeared on record in 1343, and may have been Joan of Lancaster's eldest child: she married a man born in 1326, Roger de la Warre, in or before 1358.[8] Warre was, via his mother Margaret, a grandson of Robert Holland killed by Lancastrians in 1328. John Mowbray gave his 'dearest wife' (*treschere compaigne*) Joan of Lancaster the Yorkshire manors of Thirsk and Hovingham – the latter was his birthplace in November 1310 – for the expenses of her chamber on 30 December 1341. They were worth £100 a year.[9] Little is known about Joan and John Mowbray's personal relationship, though this grant may indicate that they were happy enough together, and it was dated at Epworth in the Isle of Axholme in Lincolnshire, one of Mowbray's main seats and where they probably spent much of their time.

On 5 June 1341 or a little earlier, perhaps in May, the founder of the House of York was born, and like the founder of the House of Lancaster was named Edmund.[10] This Edmund was the fourth surviving son of Edward III and Queen Philippa, and was born at the manor of Langley in Hertfordshire (now called Kings Langley) and named, presumably, after Edward III's late uncle Edmund of Woodstock, Earl of Kent. The middle three sons of the king were very close in age: Lionel of Antwerp, born 29 November 1338, John of Gaunt, born 6 March 1340, and now Edmund of Langley, barely fifteen months younger than John. The royal children Isabella (b. 1332), Joan (b. 1334), Lionel, John and Edmund were looked after by a noblewoman called Isabella de la Mote and on other occasions by Marie de St Pol, Dowager Countess of Pembroke, and on 20 November 1342 the king officially gave custody of them to their mother Queen Philippa.[11] Edmund of Langley's nurse was Joan of Oxford and the rocker of his cradle was Maud Plumpton, and they had both previously cared for his eldest brother, Edward of Woodstock. Later, Joan was replaced by Agnes Markaunt.[12] His godfathers included the elderly (b. 1286) Earl of Surrey, John de Warenne, and Surrey's nephew and heir Richard Fitzalan, Earl of Arundel.[13] Surrey died in June 1347 when Edmund was 6, and left his godson, calling him *Sire Esmon de Langele* or 'Sir Edmund of Langley', a crystal goblet ornamented with silver-gilt and a tripod.[14] Edmund remained in his mother Queen Philippa's custody until the end of September 1354 when he was 13, when he 'withdrew from her keeping'.[15] The same year, he petitioned his father regarding some lands in Yorkshire, calling himself 'his little son Edmund' (*son petit fuiz Esmon*).[16] Edmund of Langley's remains were examined in 1877, and his skeleton measured about 5 feet 6 or 7 inches. He was therefore several inches shorter than his father, whose life-size effigy measured 5 feet 10½ inches, and much shorter than his great-grandfather Edward I, who stood 6 feet 2 inches.[17] Richard II, Edward of Woodstock's son and Edmund of Langley's nephew, was 6 feet tall.

In 1340–41, Edward III quarrelled with John Stratford, formerly Bishop of Winchester and now Archbishop of Canterbury, and a long-term friend and ally of Henry, Earl of Lancaster. Edward besieged the town of Tournai in August and September 1340 and received no money at all from England throughout, and exclaimed afterwards, 'I believe that the archbishop wished me, by lack of money, to be betrayed and killed'.[18] The long and emotional instructions to the envoys Edward sent to the Pope on 18 November 1340, in which he accused Archbishop Stratford of wishing him dead, also included the remarkable statement that Stratford 'spoke apart [i.e. separately] of me to my wife, and apart of my wife to me, in order that, if he were listened to, he might provoke us to such anger as to divide us forever'.[19] Edward and Queen Philippa, then pregnant with Edmund of Langley, had a famously strong and close marriage, so it is curious that the king believed that the archbishop was trying to drive them apart. Edward's biographer Ian Mortimer has pointed out that Edmund must have been born prematurely, as the king did not return to his wife at Ghent after the two-month Siege of Tournai until 28 September 1340 (he had left Ghent on 16 July 1340). That is a short pregnancy for a child born on 5 June and perhaps even in late May 1341. It is possible, though only possible, that Stratford had made some accusation of adultery on Queen Philippa's part. If he did, it did not cause a permanent rift between king and queen, and their next child Blanche (who died young) was born in March 1342 remarkably soon after Edmund.[20] The king certainly never disavowed his son.

It does seem to be the case, however, that Edward III showed more favour to his three eldest sons than to his youngest two, Edmund of Langley and Thomas of Woodstock (who was not born until 1355). Edward of Woodstock, the eldest son, was made Earl of Chester in March 1333 when he was not yet 3, John of Gaunt was made Earl of Richmond in January 1342 before he turned 2, and Lionel's marriage to the heiress Elizabeth de Burgh was arranged in May 1341 when he was 2½. Edmund did not gain a title until November 1362 when he was 21 – the only one of the five royal brothers not to marry an heiress – and Thomas was not given a title until 1377 when he was 22, and even then, it was granted by his nephew Richard II, not his father (although Edward III did arrange Thomas' marriage to a wealthy heiress in 1376 or before).[21]

In October 1341 Henry of Grosmont went to Scotland as the king's lieutenant and was there until April 1342, so if his younger daughter Blanche was indeed born on 25 March 1342, he missed the birth.[22] Henry's youngest sister Mary of Lancaster, future Lady Percy (her father-in-law lived until 1352), gave birth to her first child on 10 November 1341. This was Henry Percy, the latest in an almost absurdly long family line of Henry Percys which stretched back to the thirteenth century and far into the future. This Henry Percy became the first Earl of Northumberland in

1377, and the ninth earl, who died in 1632, was also called Henry Percy. Mary of Lancaster had a younger son who happily was not called Henry but Thomas, who was born in 1343 or 1344 and would be made Earl of Worcester by Richard II in 1397. All the Lancaster children except Blanche Wake the eldest and Isabella the nun were now parents.

The great heiress Elizabeth de Burgh, daughter of Maud of Lancaster, Dowager Countess of Ulster, was betrothed to the king's second son Lionel of Antwerp on 5 May 1341. She was 8 going on 9 and he not yet 2½ – they were born on 9 July 1332 and 29 November 1338 respectively – and Edward III held a great tournament at Dunstable in Bedfordshire in February 1342 to mark the event.[23] Incredibly young though they were, Elizabeth and Lionel's wedding took place in the Tower of London on 15 August 1342, and Edward III held a great banquet to celebrate.[24] Edward had stated in May 1341 that Lionel would marry Elizabeth 'when he is old enough', and apparently 3 years and 7½ months was deemed 'old enough'. Perhaps the 1336 abduction of Elizabeth de Burgh's cousin Margaret Audley, also a great heiress, persuaded the king that it was in his, his son's and his daughter-in-law's best interests to get the children married as soon as possible before anyone else took it into their heads to abduct and marry Elizabeth instead. Elizabeth lived thereafter in the official custody of her mother-in-law Queen Philippa rather than her mother Maud of Lancaster's, with her little husband and his siblings Isabella, Joan, John and Edmund. The queen was granted custody in May 1346 of all the Irish lands of Elizabeth's late father William, Earl of Ulster, until Elizabeth came of age, i.e. 14 (which in fact occurred in July 1346, so this was not a long-term gift).[25] A marriage was also on the cards for the little John of Gaunt in June 1345, when Edward III wrote to Maria of Portugal, Queen of Castile, suggesting a marital alliance between John and her sister.[26] This presumably means Maria's youngest sister Leonor of Portugal, who was born in 1328 and was therefore a dozen years John's senior, was later also put forward as a possible bride for his eldest brother Edward of Woodstock, a boy much closer to her own age. Matters advanced so far in 1347 that English envoys to Portugal were instructed to arrange a time and place for Leonor's arrival in England and for her wedding to Edward, but their journey there was so delayed that they arrived too late and found that Leonor had just married the King of Aragon.

According to the royal clerk and chronicler Adam Murimuth, the fifth Lancaster sister Eleanor's husband John, Lord Beaumont was killed at a jousting tournament in Northampton on 14 April 1342.[27] However, there is an entry on the Patent Roll dated 10 May 1342, which gave John Beaumont royal permission to settle three of his own manors on himself and his wife Eleanor jointly. Either this permission was only recorded by royal clerks a few weeks after John was already dead, or the date of his death given by Adam Murimuth is wrong.[28] Jean le Bel says that Beaumont took part in a great tournament in London in August 1342, though does not mention that he was killed there. The tournament, he says, was held in the presence of King Edward III, Queen Philippa, possibly Eleanor's father the Earl of Lancaster and brother Grosmont, and numerous English and continental noblemen and women, including ten other earls. Supposedly 800 knights took part and 500 ladies watched, and the jousting, feasting and dancing lasted for fifteen days.[29] Le Bel is also wrong about John Beaumont, however: John was certainly dead by 26 June 1342 when his Inquisition Post Mortem was ordered. His lands were taken into the king's hand on 1 July, and an entry on the Close Roll of 10 August calls Eleanor 'late his wife'. She was one of his executors.[30] Remarkably, Edward III assigned to Eleanor all the lands which had belonged to John as her dower.[31] Widows always received dower of one-third of their late husband's lands, so this was a sign of the highest favour, though John never held his full inheritance as his mother Alice (née Comyn) outlived him. Eleanor and her second husband, the Earl of Arundel, later owned a house near London Bridge called Beaumont's Inn, which presumably, given the name, had belonged to John Beaumont and his family and was bequeathed to her.[32] She lived as a widow for more than two and a half years after John's early death, going to stay with her sister Joan Mowbray in Melton Mowbray, Leicestershire in the late summer of 1343 and no doubt visiting other family members as well, and probably began an affair with her second husband Arundel before she married him and while he was still married to her first cousin, Isabella Despenser.

Eleanor of Lancaster was also made official custodian of the lands in England of Fécamp Abbey and the lands of the late Sir John Botetourt and the marriage rights of his heir, in part payment of the debts Edward III owed to her late husband. The king gave her and her second husband Arundel the rights to her son Henry Beaumont's marriage in October 1345; Henry was barely 2½ when his 24-year-old father died.[33] Henry Beaumont joined the household of his mother's brother Henry of Grosmont, and proudly styled himself 'nephew and *donsel* of the duke of Lancaster'.[34] Grosmont's sisters often called themselves or were called by others by their maiden name 'of Lancaster' or 'daughter of Henry, Earl of Lancaster', even after they were married and even long after their father's death. This is unusual and demonstrates their immense pride in their natal family and prestige of the Lancaster name. Eleanor also sometimes called herself 'Eleanor Beaumont' during her second marriage, which surely reveals her great affection for John Beaumont, and her second husband called her 'Alianore de Lancastre' in his will of late 1375; the Lancastrian name had lost none of its cachet.

Eleanor frequently interceded with Edward III, and he was enormously fond of her and did her numerous favours, including giving her all the lands her late husband had held as her dower. In July 1337, for example, he gave her and her husband John joint custody of the Somerset manor of Somerton, but specifically stated his wish that the income from the manor went to Eleanor only. Four years later he pardoned Eleanor for all hunting offences and gave her a licence to have 'one course with her greyhounds' in any royal park or forest in England, whenever she passed through.[35] Eleanor and her older sisters Blanche Wake; Isabella, the nun of Amesbury; and Maud de Burgh, Countess of Ulster, were all forceful, capable and energetic women, willing and able to use their influence on behalf of themselves, their families and their retinues, and they were close to their cousin the king. Maud, for example, received custody of the English lands of the abbesses of Fontevrault and Caen in France (Fontevrault was the mother house of Amesbury, where their sister Isabella became prioress in 1343) from Edward III.[36] Edward gave Isabella three tuns of wine every year, and six beech trees and twelve oaks from royal forests for her firewood at Amesbury Priory, also annually.[37] He bought a book of romance from her in 1335 so they clearly kept in touch.[38] In the 1350s Edward III interceded with the Bishop of Ely on behalf of the eldest Lancaster sister Blanche Wake, who was involved in an extremely acrimonious and occasionally violent dispute with the bishop over lands, and even contravened one of his own statutes to help her.[39] Like her sisters Maud and Eleanor, Blanche often interceded with the king and petitioned the Pope.[40] The fourth and sixth Lancaster sisters Joan Mowbray and Mary Percy had more introverted personalities and were not nearly as close to Edward III as the others, and rarely put themselves forward. It is perhaps revealing that on the one known occasion when Edward granted a favour to someone at Joan's request, she was called 'the king's kinswoman, the wife of John Mowbray'. The king courteously acknowledged their familial relationship, but did not use her given name.[41] As for Mary Percy, she hardly ever appears on record at all, though the little evidence we have suggests that she and Henry Percy had a contented marriage, and after her death he named his daughter with his second wife after her.

19

SHABBY TREATMENT

———◦∞◦———

The infant John of Gaunt, not yet 2 years old, was made Earl of Richmond on 21 January 1342, a title which had belonged to Duke John III of Brittany (a great-grandson of Henry III of England) since the death of the duke's uncle 'Brito' in 1334. Gaunt was officially confirmed as earl on 20 September 1342.[1] Duke John III's childless death in April 1341 led to the War of the Breton Succession between his niece Jeanne de Penthièvre and his half-brother John de Montfort, son of Duke Arthur II and his second wife Yolande de Dreux, once briefly married to Alexander III of Scotland (d. 1286). Edward III took de Montfort's side, and Philip VI of France Jeanne de Penthièvre's; her husband Charles of Blois was his nephew. The de Montfort side eventually won the struggle. Henry of Grosmont went on campaign in Brittany in 1343, then set off to the south of Spain to 'fight against the enemies of God and Christianity', meaning the Muslim rulers of Granada and Algeciras.[2] Alfonso XI of Castile was besieging Algeciras, and it fell to the Christians in 1344 after a two-year siege. Grosmont and William Montacute, Earl of Salisbury, took part in the siege 'for the salvation of their souls' and to meet and befriend the Spanish king.[3]

Henry's brother-in-law Thomas Wake was another man who accompanied him, and Spanish chroniclers made much of the English lords' courage.[4] Grosmont and Richard Fitzalan, Earl of Arundel, who was also soon to become Grosmont's brother-in-law, were appointed royal lieutenants in Aquitaine and empowered to negotiate alliances with Portugal, Castile and Aragon, the two biggest Spanish kingdoms. When Henry of Grosmont returned to Leicester after his visit to Spain, the townspeople, evidently proud of their young lord and future earl, gave him a generous gift of £20. Unaware of geography, they declared that he had just returned from 'the Holy Land'. Grosmont went hunting near Leicester in August 1344, while his father, surely past the age to hunt and perhaps blind, gave the town some wasteland on which to build 'a privy for the ease of all the community'.[5] The Earl of Lancaster and Leicester, now over 60, took part in a ceremony at Lincoln Cathedral sometime in 1343, when he was admitted into the confraternity of the cathedral with his great-great-nephews Edward of Woodstock (aged 13), Lionel of Antwerp and John of Gaunt.[6]

The earl's third daughter Maud of Lancaster, widowed from the Earl of Ulster for a decade, married her second husband Sir Ralph Ufford sometime before 8 August 1343.[7] He was the younger brother of Robert Ufford, Earl of Suffolk, and was appointed justiciar of Ireland in February 1344.[8] Maud, who was devout even by the standards of the age, visited the papal court at Avignon in person in 1343, and asked for favours for members of her retinue and for her father the earl and her sister Eleanor. In or before 1343 Maud made a vow to go on pilgrimage to Santiago de Compostela in northern Spain with her damsels Petronilla Pagham and Agnes Waleys, but was released from it on condition of founding a chapel dedicated to St James or 'making a subsidy for the Christians against the Turks'.[9] Her elder sister Isabella of Lancaster, meanwhile, was appointed prioress of Amesbury before 20 August 1343.[10] Isabella's accounts only survive for a short period in the 1330s, but it would be reasonable to assume that in the 1340s she was still often visiting her family and sending them letters and gifts, and despite taking a vow of poverty, the prioress had a taste for expensive things, including the book of romance she sold to her cousin Edward III for the remarkable sum of 100 marks (or £66). As kind and generous as her father the earl, she often gave lavish gifts to family and friends. Isabella of Lancaster was unwilling to give up the number one hobby of the medieval nobility, hunting, and kept four greyhounds for the purpose. She and Hugh Audley, one of her father's allies during his rebellion of the late 1320s and made Earl of Gloucester in 1337, exchanged greyhounds, and he also sent Isabella letters and a gift of lampreys on two occasions.[11]

Hugh Audley's grandson and heir Ralph Stafford married Isabella's 4-year-old niece Maud of Lancaster, elder daughter and co-heir of Henry of Grosmont, at Leicester on 30 November 1344. Maud's grandfather Henry, Earl of Lancaster and Leicester, was surely present, and his son held a jousting tournament in the town to mark the occasion.[12] Like his new wife, Ralph Stafford was a child; he cannot have been born earlier than late 1336 and was probably younger than that. His mother Margaret Audley was a great-niece of Edward II and sole heir to her mother Margaret de Clare's one-third of the earldom of Gloucester, and such a rich marital prize that Sir Ralph Stafford abducted her from her father's home in Essex in February 1336 and forcibly married her. It was arranged on 10 October 1344 that Henry of Grosmont 'will have the custody and upbringing' of both his daughter Maud and young Ralph, but the marriage of the two children did not last long. Ralph Stafford was already dead when his maternal grandfather Hugh Audley, Earl of Gloucester, died in November 1347, and his parents' heir was his younger brother Hugh Stafford, who succeeded their father in 1372 as Earl of Stafford.[13] Even though Maud of Lancaster was still only 7 years old in late 1347, the little widow inherited various lands and rents which had been settled on her and Ralph Stafford jointly by Audley, and the king took her fealty for them before 3 December 1347.[14] In February 1344, Henry of Grosmont had acted as steward at a great jousting tournament held at Windsor, in his father's absence – the old earl may have been ill, though was still travelling around his lands in 1344 and 1345. Chronicler Jean le Bel's powers of description failed him when it came to the Windsor tournament: 'It was modelled upon the Round Table, but I can't describe it in any more detail so I'll leave it at that.'[15]

Eleanor of Lancaster, the widowed Lady Beaumont, married for the second time on 5 February 1345, at Ditton in Buckinghamshire in the presence of Edward III and Queen Philippa. She had spent much time with the queen on the Continent from 1338 to 1340, and the king thought very highly of her, so it is not surprising that they came to her wedding. The groom was Richard Fitzalan, Earl of Arundel and heir to his elderly childless uncle, the Earl of Surrey, and Eleanor was almost certainly already having a relationship with him.[16] Eleanor was granted a safe conduct to go on pilgrimage to Santiago in Spain in March 1344, two days after her brother Henry of Grosmont and future husband Arundel were empowered to travel to the Iberian kingdoms of Castile, Aragon and Portugal and negotiate

alliances there, which is hardly likely to be a coincidence.[17] Arundel had
married Isabella, eldest daughter of Hugh Despenser the Younger and a
great-niece of Edward II, in February 1321 when he was 7 and she 8. After
the executions of her father and grandfather in 1326, Isabella Despenser
was of little use to Arundel as a wife, and now that Eleanor was widowed he
saw an opportunity to ally himself with the wealthy Lancasters, 'England's
most powerful and prestigious family'.[18] He petitioned the Pope in 1344
saying that he and Isabella had renounced their marriage vows taken as
children when they came to puberty, but were forced to consummate
their marriage, and he and Eleanor of Lancaster claimed that he had an
'illegitimate son' with Isabella Despenser. This was Edmund, Arundel and
Isabella's only child, conceived and born probably in 1326 when they were
at the beginning of their teens and were supposedly 'compelled by fear and
blows to cohabit'.[19] Edmund was married to Sybil, one of the daughters of
Edward III's close friend William Montacute, Earl of Salisbury, who was,
conveniently for the Earl of Arundel, killed jousting on 30 January 1344.
This was the main reason why Arundel finally took steps to annul his
marriage to Isabella Despenser this year; to maintain his daughter's position
and status, Salisbury would have strongly opposed and fought against his
son-in-law being made illegitimate. The Earl of Salisbury's son and heir,
William the younger, was only 15 and in no position to protect his sister,
her husband and her mother-in-law from the machinations of Arundel and
his powerful Lancaster in-laws.[20] King Edward III wrote to the Pope on
22 February 1345, asking him to confirm the dissolution of Arundel and
Isabella Despenser's marriage and to grant a dispensation for his marriage
to Eleanor of Lancaster.[21]

   The Earl of Arundel and Eleanor of Lancaster stated that they 'feared
certain dangers' if they did not marry hastily and clandestinely, though
failed to explain what these might be. They also stated, whether truth-
fully or not, that they married 'at the instance' of the king and queen,
and cheerfully admitted to the Pope that they had immediately consummated their marriage.[22] The situation was complicated regarding papal
dispensations because Eleanor and Isabella Despenser were first cousins,
but Pope Clement VI obligingly annulled Arundel and Isabella's marriage on 4 December 1344 and left him free to wed Eleanor. This made
Arundel and Isabella's unfortunate son Edmund illegitimate.[23] Edmund
petitioned the Pope in 1347 protesting against his treatment. It is apparent

from Clement VI's response to his petition that Arundel and Eleanor had tried to disguise Eleanor's real identity to evade the problem of their own consanguinity (they were third cousins but claimed implausibly not to have known this until months after their marriage) and Eleanor's close family relationship to Isabella Despenser. They pretended that Eleanor was called 'Joan Beaumont' until after they were safely married, when they could openly refer to her as 'Eleanor, daughter of Henry, Earl of Lancaster'. They lied about the relationship of 'Joan Beaumont' to Isabella Despenser in another attempt to conceal Eleanor's identity, stating that 'Joan' was related to Isabella on her father's side rather than on her mother's. They hid the fact that Eleanor and Isabella Despenser were second cousins once removed via common descent from Henry III and Eleanor of Provence, as well as being first cousins. Finally, they lied about the date of their wedding, telling the Pope that they married on the last Saturday in Lent when in fact they married eleven days before the start of Lent (as they correctly told him on another occasion, forgetting the earlier fabrication).[24]

Nastily, the Earl of Arundel was to refer to his own child in later years as 'that certain Edmund who claims himself to be my son', and before his death set aside 5,000 marks for his heirs with Eleanor of Lancaster to fight any claim Edmund might make to his earldom.[25] In or around late 1376, after his father's death, Edmund and a group of followers attacked five manors in Essex now in the hands of his much younger half-brother, Eleanor's son.[26] The Earl of Arundel and Eleanor of Lancaster's first child, Joan, future countess of Hereford, was born in late 1345 or early 1346. Eleanor may already have been pregnant with her in July 1345 when the couple asked for 'the legitimation of their offspring present and future'.[27] They were also to have a younger daughter and three sons: the Countess of Kent, the Earl of Arundel, the Archbishop of Canterbury and the Marshal of England. The tomb and effigies which still exist in Chichester Cathedral and inspired Philip Larkin's famous poem 'An Arundel Tomb' may represent Richard Fitzalan, Earl of Arundel, and Eleanor of Lancaster. No doubt they were happily married, and no doubt Richard enjoyed Eleanor's excellent family connections while she enjoyed his endless riches, but the deceitful circumstances of their marriage and their callous treatment of a young man who had done nothing wrong leave a nasty taste in the mouth.

Eleanor's father Earl Henry possibly was too elderly and infirm to attend the wedding, though she and Arundel visited him not long before it took place: they were at Henry's castle of Leicester on 16 January 1345. Edward III's friend William Clinton, Earl of Huntingdon, was also visiting Henry then.[28] The old Earl of Lancaster was still travelling around his estates as late as the summer of 1345, however; Henry was at Kenilworth on 1 May and 15 July and at Leicester again by 8 September. On 1 July 1345, the earl was appointed as an adviser of the king's 6-year-old son Lionel of Antwerp, his grandson-in-law and great-great-nephew, official (though of course only nominal) regent of the kingdom while Edward III went to Flanders.[29] This would be the last appointment of a political and military career which lasted for half a century. Henry of Lancaster made his will on 8 September 1345, appointing his son Grosmont as one of his six executors, and asked to be buried in the choir before the high altar in the church of the hospital he had founded in Leicester in 1330. The earl left bequests to his daughters 'Blanche Wake, Isabella, Maud, Johane, Alianore Countess of Arundel, and Marie Percy', as well as charitable bequests and gifts to servants.[30] Probably the earl heard of his son's great victory over the French at the Battle of Bergerac on or around 24 August 1345, before he passed away.

At Leicester on Thursday, 22 September 1345 two weeks after making his will, Henry, Earl of Lancaster and Leicester, Steward of England, and the last surviving grandchild of Henry III and Eleanor of Provence, died aged about 65. His niece Queen Isabella, great-nephew Edward III, and Queen Philippa attended his funeral in Leicester on 15 January 1346, and the king and his wife bought black cloth for themselves and their households.[31] A large number of magnates and prelates also attended the funeral of this greatest of English noblemen. Most of the earl's six daughters were surely also there (probably not Maud, who was pregnant and in Ireland), and Henry of Lancaster was luckier than most medieval parents, being outlived by all his children. A few years later Henry of Grosmont had his body moved to the collegiate church of the Annunciation of Our Lady of the Newarke in Leicester, his extension of his father's 1330 foundation. Grosmont told the Pope in 1349 that his father chose to be buried at Leicester, 'leaving the royal burial place' – by which he meant Westminster Abbey where Earl Henry's father Edmund, uncle Edward I and grandfather Henry III were buried. Grosmont added that he himself had already decided that one day he would be buried in Leicester as well.[32]

Earl Henry is in many ways the forgotten Lancaster, overshadowed by his older brother Thomas and his deadly quarrels with Edward II, his son

Henry the younger, the great warrior and flamboyant epitome of four-teenth-century chivalry, and his grandson-in-law John of Gaunt, by far the most famous Lancaster even though he was not born into the dynasty. Yet it was Henry who saved the house of Lancaster after Thomas did his utmost to throw away their birthright in the early 1320s, who patiently and pains-takingly rebuilt the inheritance and made the Lancasters the most eminent and admired family in England, and who survived the turbulent years of Edward II's reign and its aftermath to die peacefully in his bed where many other nobles did not.

THE FOURTH EARL OF LANCASTER

―∞∞―

I t was the beginning of a new era. Henry of Grosmont, in his early or mid 30s, at last came into his full inheritance, and was now Earl of Lancaster and Leicester as well as Derby, and Steward of England. His 1345–46 campaign in France was, like everything he did, brilliantly successful, and the French chronicle *Chronique des quatre premiers Valois* called him 'one of the best warriors in the world'.[1] Jean le Bel wrote of Henry, 'this young man was to perform so many acts of prowess in so many places that he deserved to be deemed exceedingly valiant.' In 1340, he called Henry 'the worthiest knight in the world'.[2] Henry of Grosmont landed at Bordeaux on 9 August 1345, and as well as his great victory at Bergerac around 24 August, defeated a French force at Auberoche on 21 October, a month after his father's death. With the ransoms he earned from French noblemen taken prisoner, something in the region of £50,000 or hundreds of millions in modern money, Henry rebuilt the Savoy Palace in London on a magnificent scale, and he was acknowledged as Lord of Bergerac by 1 June 1347 and used the title for the rest of his life.[3] On 6 May 1346, Edward III talked of 'the glorious success of the Earl of Lancaster in parts beyond sea', and asked for prayers for Henry and for the continued success of his mission. One of the men in Gascony with Henry was John Tebbe, who had been imprisoned for his role in the murder of Sir Robert Holland in 1328, but escaped.[4] Henry took Tebbe to Gascony with him before the latter was pardoned for the murder, his escape and any subsequent outlawries, which hardly suggests that he shed any tears over the death of the man who betrayed his uncle Thomas in 1322. Henry of Grosmont missed his father's funeral in January 1346 as he was still overseas, but when he returned to his town of Leicester later in 1346, the proud townspeople gave him gifts of wine, bread, eels, pike, lampreys and a dozen salmon, which was his favourite dish. The fish were kept in two fish-locks in the River Soar until Henry's arrival.[5]

Meanwhile, his fifth sister Eleanor of Lancaster's first child from her second marriage, Joan, future countess of Hereford, was born in late 1345 or 1346, perhaps around the time of her grandfather the Earl of Lancaster's funeral. Joan married Humphrey de Bohun, earl of Hereford, and gave birth to her daughters in 1366 and c. 1369; her first grandchild was born in April 1382. Eleanor of Lancaster and the Earl of Arundel's second child was Richard, his father's successor as Earl of Arundel, who was born by 1 March 1347 and married the earl of Hereford's sister Elizabeth de Bohun in 1359. The second daughter and third child was Alice, Countess of Kent, who gave birth to her large family between about 1371/73 and 1387/88, and the second son and fourth child was John, Marshal and Admiral of England, who was betrothed or married to the heiress Eleanor Maltravers by 4 August 1357 when he was little more than 7 and she a few years older. John's own first child was born in November 1364 and he was a very young father, only 14 or so. Thomas the third son was the baby of the family: born in the last four months of 1352 or in 1353, he was elected Bishop of Ely in August 1373 when he was 20.[6] He was the youngest grandchild of Henry, Earl of Lancaster, and Maud Chaworth (d. 1322). Alice Fitzalan was named after her father's mother Alice de Warenne, sister of the Earl of Surrey; Alice's sister Joan may have been named after their aunt Joan of Lancaster, Lady Mowbray, who died in July 1349. The Arundel/Lancaster children, and their own children, married and had offspring when they were very young. Eleanor of Lancaster's son Henry Beaumont from her first marriage (b. late 1339) married Margaret de Vere, daughter and sister of earls of Oxford, and had two children, and Eleanor became a grandmother in March 1361 when his son John Beaumont was born (the same month as her brother Henry of Grosmont died). Henry Beaumont seemingly was on good terms with his stepfather Richard, Earl of Arundel: when he went overseas in 1363 and again in 1364, he appointed Arundel as one of his attorneys to look after his affairs while he was away.[7]

Just months after losing her father, Earl Henry of Lancaster's third daughter Maud of Lancaster, Dowager Countess of Ulster, lost her second husband Ralph Ufford, the justiciar of Ireland, as well. She was pregnant in November 1345 and had a daughter she named Maud after herself – who grew up to become the mother of Richard II's notorious 'favourite' of the 1380s, Robert de Vere – but Ralph Ufford died on 9 April 1346.[8] There has been some debate in modern books and on websites as to Maud Ufford's correct parentage, owing to her heir in 1413 being returned as a rather obscure cousin called Robert Willoughby and her mother wrongly called 'Elizabeth', and because the jurors on her father Ralph Ufford's IPM in England in July 1346 did not know who his heir was, because he died outside England and had no heir of his body born there.[9] It has sometimes been assumed that Maud Ufford's mother was not Maud of Lancaster but Ralph Ufford's first wife, whoever she was and assuming he even had one. However, an entry on the Patent Roll of October 1347 talks of Maud of Lancaster's two daughters, 'Elizabeth de Burgh and Maud de Ufford'. Edward III called Maud Ufford 'the king's kinswoman' in July 1374, and if she were not Maud of Lancaster's child, her relationship to Edward III would have been too distant for him to acknowledge.[10] Her mother Maud of Lancaster fled to England after Ralph Ufford's death as she had after the murder of William de Burgh in 1333, possibly the only woman in history to flee from Ireland to England twice with a baby daughter both times, and was back in England by 14 June 1346.[11] According to the derisive Dublin annalist, Maud had 'gloriously entered' the city with 'regal pomp' some years before, but now 'slipped away furtively … to avoid the jeers of the crowd'. With malicious sarcasm, the same annalist referred to her husband Ralph Ufford's body as 'this treasure, scarcely to be reckoned among saintly relics'.[12]

Maud had Ufford's remains transferred from Ireland to the Augustinian priory of Campsea Ashe in Suffolk, and herself became a canoness there in or before April 1348.[13] By August 1347 Maud had already decided 'to enter religion and take the habit of a regular', and that October her brother Henry of Grosmont requested that she be allowed to create a perpetual chantry at Campsea to pray for the souls of her husbands William de Burgh and Ralph Ufford and for herself and her daughters Elizabeth de Burgh and Maud Ufford after death, because of her 'pious resolve to devote herself forever to divine obsequies so far as human weakness will allow'.[14] This sentence may indicate that she was suffering from a grief-related illness after Ralph Ufford's death, and Henry of Grosmont and some of his officials helped Maud take care of her affairs between 1346 and 1348, which may indicate that she was unable to do so herself (Maud had always been thoroughly capable of looking after her own affairs before).[15] Either Maud of Lancaster herself before she entered religion or, more probably, her 15-year-old daughter Elizabeth de Burgh, attended a famous jousting tournament held at Lichfield, Staffordshire on 9 April 1348 with Maud's eldest sister Blanche Wake, the king's eldest daughter Isabella of Woodstock who was exactly Elizabeth de Burgh's age, and his first cousin Margaret of Norfolk, Lady Segrave. Maud's brother Henry of Grosmont was one of the knights taking part, as did the king himself, and the dress code was a blue robe with white hood which the ladies themselves also wore, with masks and visors.[16]

Maud of Lancaster's perpetual chantry at Campsea Ashe was moved 8 miles away to the village of Bruisyard in August 1354 because 'the way is too distant from the priory, and the priests ... repute it too great a burden in winter or rainy season to go so great a distance to celebrate the divine offices'. As well as moaning about the rain and cold, the priests maintained that they would prefer to 'say service where there is no conversation of women ... it happens at times that they mutually impede one another by the noise of voices'.[17] Maud of Lancaster's son-in-law Lionel of Antwerp founded a monastery of Minoresses or Poor Clares at Bruisyard for her in April 1364, and Maud moved there. John II, the King of France then captive in England, supported her petition to the Pope to do so. Supposedly joining the Minoresses had been a wish of hers since childhood, perhaps because her grandparents Edmund of Lancaster and Blanche of Artois had founded a house of Minoresses in London. Maud decided in 1364 that she could not 'stay with peace of her soul' at Campsea any longer, and desired to 'escape the number of nobles coming to Campsea'.[18] Anything a Lancaster did immediately became fashionable and desirable to many others, and evidently a stream of noble ladies followed Maud into the contemplative life at Campsea, to her displeasure; one of them was her husband's niece and her daughter's first cousin and namesake Maud Ufford, daughter of the Earl of Suffolk. In April 1364 and again in July 1366, Maud of Lancaster's sister

Eleanor, Countess of Arundel, received permission from Pope Urban V to stay for three days (though not nights) in a Minoress establishment with her sons, daughters and other relatives, which surely means that she and her children were visiting their aunt at Bruisyard. Urban specified that Eleanor and her party must don 'decent dress'.[19] Maud's daughters Elizabeth, Duchess of Clarence, and Maud, Countess of Oxford, would both be buried at Bruisyard, in 1363 and 1413 respectively, and in 1381 her grandson-in-law Edmund Mortimer, Earl of March, left the house 40 marks.[20] Maud of Lancaster herself was buried at Campsea Ashe, next to her second husband, Ralph Ufford.

Edward III continued to press his claim to the throne of France, and on 26 August 1346 won a great victory at the Battle of Crécy, where his 16-year-old son Edward of Woodstock, Prince of Wales, commanded the vanguard. Henry Percy, Mary of Lancaster's husband, was one of the many English noblemen who fought at Crécy, and he campaigned with his brother-in-law Grosmont in Gascony in 1347 and 1349. Another nobleman at Crécy was Eleanor of Lancaster's husband, the Earl of Arundel, and Eleanor's cousin, Thomas of Lancaster, one of the illegitimate sons of the late Thomas, Earl of Lancaster (d. 1322), was knighted by Edward III during the 1346 campaign.[21] The king knighted his son the Prince of Wales during this campaign as well. Among the French magnates killed at Crécy were the Duke of Lorraine and the Counts of Blois and Alençon (the latter was Philip VI's brother and Queen Philippa's uncle Charles), and so was John 'the Blind', King of Bohemia, whose granddaughter Anne would marry Edward III's grandson Richard II many years later. During the king and his eldest son's long absence abroad from early July 1346 until October 1347, Edward's second son Lionel of Antwerp, Maud of Lancaster's son-in-law, was appointed official keeper of the realm for the second time, although he was still only 8 years old.

Henry of Grosmont was back in England by early 1347, and on 3 May that year contracted a future marriage between his younger daughter Blanche of Lancaster, now 3 or 5 years old, and John Segrave, son and heir of John, Lord Segrave (b. 1315) and Edward I's granddaughter Margaret, Countess of Norfolk (b. *c.* 1322).[22] Two years later, the younger John's sister Elizabeth Segrave (b. 1338) married Blanche of Lancaster's cousin John Mowbray (b. 1340), but Blanche and John Segrave's wedding never took place as he died as a child, leaving his sister Elizabeth as their parents' heir.

Their father John, Lord Segrave died on 1 April 1353, only in his late 30s.[23] His marriage to Margaret of Norfolk had never been a happy one, and Margaret tried to have it annulled; she left England for the papal court in Avignon without her cousin Edward III's permission. She subsequently married the Hainaulter knight Sir Walter Manny or Mauny, who had come to England in the retinue of Queen Philippa, also without royal permission. Edward III ordered Margaret's arrest on 26 July 1354 and she was imprisoned for a time in Somerton Castle in Lincolnshire, but was pardoned by the king in late 1355. It was not an arduous confinement: Margaret's household accompanied her, and Walter Manny was allowed to visit his wife whenever he wished and even to stay with her.[24] Their daughter Anne Manny, later Countess of Pembroke, was born on 24 July 1354, two days before the king ordered Margaret's arrest.[25] As well as his daughter and heir Anne, Walter Manny also had two illegitimate daughters who were both nuns and to whom he left money in his will, the rather intriguingly named Mailosel and Malplesant, and he had a cousin with the equally peculiar name of Cishbert.[26] Margaret of Norfolk was the daughter and heir of Edward I's son Thomas of Brotherton, Earl of Norfolk and Earl Marshal of England (d. 1338). From her father and grandfather, she inherited a gold cross containing part of the True Cross, which she gave to Thomas Beauchamp, Earl of Warwick (b. 1314), godson of Thomas, Earl of Lancaster.[27]

John de Warenne, Earl of Surrey, died at the end of June 1347, the day before his 61st birthday. His heir was his nephew Richard Fitzalan, Earl of Arundel, and he left items in his will to his many illegitimate children and to his mistress Isabella Holland, daughter of the Robert Holland killed by Henry of Lancaster's men in 1328. Surrey called Isabella his *compaigne* or 'wife' in his will, though in fact had been unhappily married to Edward II's niece Jeanne de Bar for more than forty years and had unsuccessfully tried to annul the marriage on several occasions, once by claiming implausibly to having had an affair with her late aunt Mary (d. 1332), a nun of Amesbury Priory. Edward III used Surrey's Yorkshire lands to benefit his fourth son Edmund of Langley, now 6 years old and Surrey's godson, to be held for him while he was underage by his mother, Queen Philippa.[28] In the summer of 1348, Edward III instituted a new chivalric order, the Knights of the Garter. His 18-year-old son, the Prince of Wales, was the first member, and Henry of Grosmont the second. Even more titles and lands came Grosmont's way after 2 October 1348 when his aunt-in-law Alice de Lacy, widow of Thomas of Lancaster and Countess of Lincoln in her own right, died at the age of almost 67. Alice's lands were delivered to Henry, and on 20 August 1349 he was officially made Earl of Lincoln.[29]

The Black Death struck Europe with a terrible vengeance in 1348 and 1349, killing a huge percentage of the population. One of its victims was Edward III and Queen Philippa's 14-year-old second daughter Joan, on her way to Spain to marry Pedro, heir to the throne of Castile. In the terrible year of 1349, several members of the English nobility died (perhaps of the plague or perhaps not; cause of death is unknown). They included the Lancaster siblings' first cousin Hugh Despenser, Lord of Glamorgan and eldest son of the notorious Hugh Despenser the Younger; Isabella Ferrers (née Verdon), half-sister of the late William de Burgh, Earl of Ulster; Eleanor of Lancaster's former mother-in-law Alice Beaumont (née Comyn); Thomas Wake, husband of the eldest Lancaster sister Blanche, after thirty-three years of marriage; and Wake's sister Margaret, widow of Edward II's half-brother Edmund and Dowager Countess of Kent. Two of the six Lancaster sisters also died in 1348–49. Isabella, Prioress of Amesbury, was still alive on 30 January 1348 but died before 4 February 1349, and Joan the fourth sister, Lady Mowbray, died on 7 July 1349, not long after her only son John was married or betrothed to Elizabeth Segrave.[30]

By early March 1351 Joan of Lancaster's widower John Mowbray had married his much younger second wife Elizabeth, daughter of John de Vere, Earl of Oxford.[31] Mowbray, born in November 1310, was now 40, the same age as his wife's parents, and despite his second marriage he remained firmly within the Lancaster sphere of influence. His wife's sister Margaret married Henry Beaumont, son of the fifth Lancaster sister Eleanor, and her brother Thomas, who succeeded their father John as Earl of Oxford, married Maud Ufford, daughter of the third Lancaster sister Maud. Thomas de Vere and Maud Ufford were already married or betrothed by 10 June 1350, when Maud was only 4 years old (her mother entered a religious house in 1347 or 1348 when Maud was just a toddler, so she may have grown up in the de Vere household) and Thomas about 14.[32] That same year, Maud Ufford and her much older half-sister Elizabeth de Burgh, Countess of Ulster and the king's daughter-in-law, visited Elizabeth's paternal grandmother the elder Elizabeth de Burgh at Clare in Suffolk.[33]

In early May 1351 Elizabeth Mowbray (née de Vere) was pregnant, though she and John Mowbray did not have any surviving children.[34] After Mowbray's death in 1361 Elizabeth married Sir William Cosynton, and the couple surrendered themselves to debtors' prison after Elizabeth's stepson, the younger John Mowbray, Joan of Lancaster's son, sued her for wasting his estates given to her in dower. The elder John Mowbray was perpetually in serious debt, and in 1359 acknowledged that he owed his brother-in-law Henry of Grosmont a staggering £10,000. Henry promised to forgive the debt if John settled all his lands north of the River Trent on him for life, to revert to the younger John (Henry's nephew) after Henry's death. As Henry died just over two years later, this was not a bad deal for John Mowbray.[35] Henry of Grosmont was a witness to grants made to his nephew John Mowbray and John's wife Elizabeth Segrave in August 1349 (John was then only 9 years old, Elizabeth 11), and in April 1355 both John Mowbrays witnessed the statutes of Henry's collegiate foundation of the Newarke in Leicester.[36] In and before 1353 the older Mowbray was feuding with his father-in-law the Earl of Oxford, and Grosmont managed to bring them together and settle the dispute on 26 April 1353. Rather startlingly, John Mowbray was claiming that he did not need to provide food, drink or clothing for his wife Elizabeth or her attendants, or any children the couple might have.[37] In 1341 he had given his first wife Joan of Lancaster two of his manors to provide her with £100 annually for the expenses of her chamber, so it seems that his first marriage was far more harmonious than his second.

The marriage of Joan of Kent (b. 1326/27) and William Montacute (b. 1328), Earl of Salisbury, was annulled in 1349 on the (possibly spurious and invented) grounds that she had previously been married to Sir Thomas Holland. Joan resumed or began her marriage to Holland, and their first surviving son Thomas the younger, who would marry Eleanor of Lancaster's daughter Alice Fitzalan, was born in 1350 or 1351. Joan of Kent and Thomas Holland's younger son John Holland also married a Lancaster bride; by the late fourteenth century it was nearly impossible not to. Joan was the daughter of Edward II's half-brother Edmund of Woodstock, Earl of Kent, and became his heir and Countess of Kent in her own right when her younger brother John died in December 1352; she also inherited the lands of her childless maternal uncle Thomas, Lord Wake. Her younger brother John, Earl of Kent, born in 1330 as the posthumous son of Edmund

of Woodstock, married Queen Philippa's niece Elisabeth of Jülich, but they
had no children and he died at the age of 22. Elisabeth outlived John by
almost sixty years; she wrote her will on 20 April 1411 and died on 6 June
that year, and was buried in the Greyfriars' church in Winchester with her
long-dead husband.[38] Joan of Kent's husband Sir Thomas Holland was the
second son of Sir Robert Holland, murdered in 1328. Blanche Wake was
perhaps not thrilled by her niece's marriage to the son of the man who
had betrayed her uncle Thomas of Lancaster, but there was nothing she
could do about it, and two of her other nieces (Eleanor Mowbray and Alice
Fitzalan) married two of Robert Holland's grandsons.

John of Gaunt, still only 10 years old, witnessed military action for the
first time on 29 August 1350 when his father and his eldest brother the
Prince of Wales fought the sea battle usually called the Battle of Winchelsea
or, more colourfully, *Les Espagnols sur Mer* or 'the Spaniards on the Sea'. The
boy did not watch the engagement safely from the shore, but was with
his brother on his ship, right in the thick of fighting. Don Carlos de la
Cerda, a Spanish and partly French nobleman and from a cadet branch of
the Castilian royal family, and a soldier of fortune, had captured a number
of English trading ships, robbed them and threw their crews overboard.
Edward III and his eldest son lay in wait for him and his fleet on his way
back to Spain from Flanders, and sank many of the Spanish ships, though
not without great losses to their own vessels. John's future father-in-law
Henry of Grosmont also took part in the sea battle, which lasted for many
hours, and saved the lives of the Prince of Wales and John of Gaunt just as
their ship was about to sink.[39] John was probably a member of his brother
the prince's household between 1350 and 1355, while his younger brother
Edmund of Langley remained in the custody of their mother the queen,
and Edward bought clothes, saddles and other items for John and two of
his attendants. Rather intriguingly, there were two 'Saracen' (i.e. Muslim
or Arab) children in John's company at this time, called Sigo and Nakok.[40]

Edward III demonstrated his huge affection for and trust in his kinsman
Henry of Grosmont on 6 March 1351, six months after Henry saved the
lives of two of his sons on the sea, when he upgraded Henry's title to Duke
of Lancaster rather than merely earl.[41] Henry was only the second duke in
English history, following the king's eldest son, the Prince of Wales, who
had been made Duke of Cornwall in 1337. In late 1351, the new Duke of
Lancaster decided to join the Teutonic Knights in Prussia and to go on

a crusade in Lithuania to fight against the few non-Christians still left in Europe. The Baltic *reyse* was the crusade of choice for all discerning European noblemen in the second half of the fourteenth century, until Lithuania completed its process of Christianisation and thus brought the exciting experience of killing pagans to an end. Edward III once said of Henry of Grosmont that he 'delights in acts of war', though he would have been virtually unique among medieval noblemen if he had not.[42] Henry's grandson and heir Henry of Lancaster, the future King Henry IV – also grandson of Edward III – followed in his footsteps some decades later. One historian has pointed out that the *reyse* was basically a 'knightly package tour', carefully organised and with plenty of feasting and hunting provided as side attractions.[43] Not a man willing to do without his luxurious possessions, Henry of Grosmont took them with him: his baggage train took a full two days to pass a single point in Silesia. He was accompanied by Robert Ufford the Earl of Suffolk, elder brother of Henry's late brother-in-law Ralph Ufford, and William Montacute the young Earl of Salisbury, perhaps still smarting from the humiliation of his partly royal wife Joan of Kent preferring to be married to a mere knight than to him.[44] Salisbury's father had accompanied Henry of Grosmont to Spain in 1343, and in 1375 Henry's son-in-law John of Gaunt was to call the younger Salisbury 'our very dear and beloved companion'.[45] Grosmont's brother-in-law Henry Percy, husband of the youngest Lancaster sister Mary, also went with him, and succeeded as Lord Percy while in Poland on the death of his father in February 1352.

On this occasion, however, Henry for once proved less than successful. Not long after he landed on the continent, he and his retinue were imprisoned in northern Germany and forced to pay a large ransom, and soon afterwards he was ambushed and robbed by a gang of Westphalian knights. He got as far as Stettin when he heard that a truce had been concluded between Christians and pagans and therefore returned to Cologne, though one French chronicle claims that Henry reached Estonia and did battle with pagans and kings of Estonia and Poland alike. This seems unlikely, as he was back in Cologne by 11 April 1352, surely not enough time for him to have achieved all the derring-do attributed to him by admirers. In Cologne Cathedral in the presence of the princes of Mark and Jülich and many citizens of the city, Henry accused the German nobleman Otto, Duke of Brunswick of being involved in the ambush on him by Westphalian knights with the knowledge of King John II of France. (Presumably he spoke in French, not German.) He challenged Otto to a duel.[46] Otto responded immediately and made his feelings on the matter clear by declaring that Henry had spoken 'maliciously, shabbily and dishonestly', and accepted the challenge.[47]

Edward III gave Henry permission on 23 August 1352 'to excuse himself in respect of things wickedly laid to his charge by the duke of Brunswyk', and to travel to France with a retinue of sixty knights and an earl.[48] Henry duly headed for Paris and was honourably received by King John II at the Louvre, and a duel was arranged at the Pré-aux-Clercs. The king's sons conducted Otto of Brunswick into the lists, and King Carlos II of Navarre, John II's son-in-law, and his brother Felipe conducted Henry. The combatants prepared for battle, but John intervened and settled the quarrel by declaring that Henry's words in Cologne Cathedral had been misreported to Otto. After this anti-climactic though no doubt wise announcement, John held a banquet for the two dukes, and allowed Henry a choice of many valuable presents afterwards; the pious Henry selected a thorn from the precious relic the Crown of Thorns in Sainte-Chapelle. He returned to England and spent Christmas 1352 with Edward III.[49]

Early in 1352, though the date is not precisely recorded, Duke Henry's elder daughter and co-heir Maud of Lancaster, widow of the young Ralph Stafford, married her second husband Wilhelm of Bavaria in the royal chapel of Westminster in the presence of the king and queen. Maud was not quite 12 and Wilhelm was 21, and had been invited to England by Edward III on 12 November 1351.[50] He was a nephew of Queen Philippa, the second son of her eldest sister Margareta and the Holy Roman Emperor Ludwig of Bavaria, and became Duke of Lower Bavaria and Count of Hainault and Holland. That Maud of Lancaster was deemed a suitable wife for the son of an emperor reveals how highly thought of the Lancasters were, though the match would not be a happy one. Chronicler Jean le Bel says of Wilhelm that he was 'tall, strong, swarthy and agile, more fleet and dexterous than any man in his land ... but he was curiously distant and inscrutable: he wouldn't welcome or acknowledge people ... and took no pleasure in the company of ladies and damsels'.[51] Duke Henry could not attend his daughter's wedding as he was on his way to Stettin, and whether the bride's mother, the obscure Isabella Beaumont, was present is not recorded. Despite her youth, and despite the inauspicious lack of interest her new husband took in the company of ladies, Maud left England to reside with her husband and (presumably) his family. She saw her father only once again, in the Low Countries at Christmas 1353, and bore a daughter in 1356 when she was 16, who died not long after birth and who would be her only child.[52] In about 1357, the unfortunate Wilhelm began showing signs of insanity and in 1358 had to be confined, 'bound hand and foot' as Jean le Bel puts it. Although he lived until 1389, poor Maud, still only in her teens, became a widow in all but name. She was, however, as capable and resilient as almost all the Lancasters, and despite her youth, 'the two lands of Hainault and Holland were governed by the lady his [Wilhelm's] wife'.[53]

HOLY MEDICINES

⚬⚬⚬

In 1354, Henry of Grosmont wrote his long and remarkable *Book of Holy Medicines*, or *Livre de Seyntz Medicines* in Anglo-Norman, the language of the text (and the first language of the English nobility in this period). It is an extended treatise on the seven deadly sins, with Christ and the Virgin Mary offering healing cures for the wounds of the body and soul inflicted by them. Quite a lot of Henry as a person is revealed in the text: his aforementioned preference for having sex with low-born women (though he admitted noblewomen smelled better); his love of fine cloth, the rings on his fingers, dancing, the smell of flowers, hunting, eating salmon and getting drunk on wine to the point where his legs would not carry him; his fondness for taking 'too much delight in frivolous books' and in gossip; being vain and fishing for compliments, and enjoying being admired by ladies; his frequent failures to get out of bed early enough in the morning to hear Mass and telling himself he would hear it twice tomorrow instead; his frank admissions that he recoiled from the smell of the poor and sick and begrudged the leftovers from his feasts being given to them. He also stated that he behaved in a covetous manner because of his fear of becoming poor, and although this might simply have been a conventionally penitential comment, perhaps the uncertainties of the years after his uncle Thomas of Lancaster's execution in 1322 affected him as he was growing up.[1] Henry claimed that he had come to learning late in life, which might be true, and that as he was English he had not had much experience with French, which is but a mere literary conceit; the French of the text is not only fluent but cultured and witty.

The text of *Holy Medicines* reveals Henry of Grosmont to have been an intelligent and thoughtful man, a man conventionally dedicated to the usual pursuits of his class and his era such as jousting and hunting (as his father Earl Henry had been), but also a man unusually capable of self-insight and self-criticism. It is hard to think of any other fourteenth-century English nobleman who would have been able to conceive of and produce such a long, complex, intelligent and informed text, and Grosmont wrote it while he was busy with numerous other matters both military and political. In 1394, forty years after he wrote it, Mary Ros (née Percy), Lady Ros and Oreby, much younger half-sister of Grosmont's nephews Henry and Thomas Percy, left a 'French book of the duke of Lancaster' to her kinswoman Isabella Percy in her will.[2] This must have been the *Book of Holy Medicines*, and its fame had clearly spread among the English nobility (Mary Ros was not even born until 1368, fourteen years after Henry wrote it).

Despite his admission that he recoiled from the smell of the sick, Henry extended his father's 1330 foundation of a hospital in Leicester called the Newarke into a college with a dean and canons, and his collegiate foundation was officially witnessed on 1 April 1355. Among the many witnesses were John Mowbray, widower of Henry's sister Joan of Lancaster, and Henry's nephew the younger John, aged 14. The hospital was extended so that it could care for a hundred poor and sick men rather than fifty as before, although 'evil livers and able-bodied paupers shall be dismissed'. They would all live in one house with a chapel with Mass said at dawn, and the dean, canons and vicars were expressly forbidden to say Mass for the dead except for Henry's family. Henry asked the Pope to grant an indulgence to penitents who visited the collegiate church on ten feast days and who said an 'Our Father' and a 'Hail Mary' for the souls of his parents Earl Henry and Maud Chaworth.[3]

Henry of Grosmont's great-niece and Edward III's eldest legitimate grandchild Philippa was born at the royal palace of Eltham in Kent on 16 August 1355 (Edward of Woodstock had already provided at least one grandchild of the illegitimate kind), and was named after her paternal grandmother the queen.[4] Philippa was born thirty-seven weeks after her father Lionel of Antwerp turned 16 on 29 November 1354, and perhaps he and his wife Elizabeth de Burgh, six and a half years his senior, had finally consummated their marriage because at 16 he was deemed old enough to do so. Philippa became known as Philippa of Clarence when her father was made Duke of Clarence in November 1362. On 5 March 1356 when she was a few months old, Edward III sent Philippa to live at the priory of Campsea Ashe in Suffolk, where she would join her maternal grandmother Maud of Lancaster, Dowager Countess of Ulster and now a canoness there.[5] Philippa married Edmund Mortimer, heir to the earldom of March, in or before December 1358 when she was 3 and he 6.[6] Edmund was the great-grandson and heir of the Roger Mortimer the king had executed in 1330; never a man to visit the sins of the father on the son, Edward III had now brought the Mortimers into his own family, and this marriage was to give the Mortimer family a strong claim to the throne later in the century as well as giving them the earldom of Ulster and the third of the earldom of Gloucester which Elizabeth de Burgh inherited from her grandmother. As his son Lionel was still only 20 years old when his daughter Philippa married in late 1358, however, Edward III must have expected him and his wife Elizabeth de Burgh to produce more children, and did not anticipate that Philippa would be her parents' only child and thus their heir. Edward III gave a marriage portion of 5,000 marks with his granddaughter, which indicates he believed at the time that she would not inherit her parents' lands and titles. That she did, and that the Mortimers received the enormous sum of 5,000 marks as well, was a massive stroke of luck for the family.[7] Philippa and Edmund Mortimer were the ancestors of the fifteenth-century Yorkists, and had four children: their son and heir Roger was Richard II's heir general in the 1380s and 1390s, and a great-grandfather of Edward IV and Richard III.[8]

Edward III and Queen Philippa's youngest child Thomas of Woodstock was born at the beginning of 1355 – he was thirteen and a half years younger than his nearest surviving sibling Edmund of Langley and only seven months older than his niece Philippa – and when barely 6 months old, on 1 July 1355, was appointed official guardian of the realm when his father and elder brothers left the country on another military campaign to France.[9] Eleanor of Lancaster's husband Richard, Earl of Arundel and both English archbishops were among the men appointed as the real rulers of the kingdom in the king's absence, and her brother Grosmont went with the king.

Little Thomas of Woodstock's eldest brother Edward of Woodstock, Prince of Wales, who was a quarter of a century his senior, won a great victory over the French at the Battle of Poitiers on 19 September 1356. Edward captured the King of France himself, John II, and brought him to England as a captive, albeit a captive treated with the utmost respect and deference and allowed a sizeable retinue. Edward's elderly grandmother Isabella of France, the dowager queen and widow of Edward II, was one of the many people who attended the victory parade in London. Queen Isabella did not have much longer to live: she died at Hertford Castle on 22 August 1358, aged 62 or 63. She was buried at the Greyfriars Church in London, where her aunt Marguerite of France had been buried in 1318, on 27 November. Henry of Grosmont had dined with the dowager queen, who was his first cousin – they were both grandchildren of Blanche of Artois, Queen of Navarre and Countess of Lancaster – in the months before her death.

A royal wedding took place in Reading on 19 May 1359 when Henry of Grosmont's younger daughter and co-heir Blanche of Lancaster married Edward III's third son John of Gaunt, Earl of Richmond, in a ceremony performed by a clerk of the queen's chapel called Thomas Chynham.[10] A dispensation for consanguinity had been issued by Pope Innocent VI on 6 January 1359.[11] John was 19 when he wed; Blanche, according to the evidence of her father's Inquisition Post Mortem two years later, was 17, or perhaps more realistically, about 15. They must have known each other all their lives. John's parents Edward III and Philippa of Hainault attended the wedding, as did, presumably, Duke Henry and his wife Isabella Beaumont. The king's sister Joan of the Tower (b. 1321), Queen of Scotland, whose husband David II had until recently been a prisoner in England, was also there. Blanche and her father had visited Henry's town of Leicester before the wedding, and 3 shillings and 8 pence were spent on minstrels who performed at their arrival. The townspeople gave Blanche and her lady attendants a generous gift of £25.[12] Edward III paid £30 for two silver buckles for his eldest daughter Isabella of Woodstock to give to her new sister-in-law, and a membrane still exists in the National Archives detailing gifts given to the bride (called *dame Blaunch*, 'Lady Blanche') by her new husband, father-in-law, aunt-in-law Joan of the Tower, brothers-in-law Lionel, Edmund and 4-year-old Thomas, sisters-in-law Isabella of Woodstock, Margaret and Mary, and Lionel's wife Elizabeth de Burgh, Countess of Ulster. Edward of Woodstock is a rather curious omission from the list. John bought his new wife a gold brooch with a balas ruby and pearls and a gold and diamond ring, and Elizabeth de Burgh gave her first cousin Blanche a silver cup and a ruby ring.[13] The king and his sons Edward, Lionel, John and Edmund appeared at a jousting tournament held in Blanche's honour, at Smithfield in London from 27 to 29 May, dressed as the mayor and aldermen of London.

Poet Geoffrey Chaucer wrote a detailed description of Blanche of Lancaster which makes it apparent that she absolutely personified her society's standards of beauty. She was pale-skinned and blonde-haired, long of body and limb, 'fattish and fleshy' (a sign of wealth and privilege in fourteenth-century England when many people did not have enough to eat, and hence admired as a marker of beauty), and had round breasts and broad hips. The chronicler Jean Froissart admired Blanche's personality: she was 'light-hearted, happy, fresh, amusing, sweet, guileless, of humble manner', and he jocularly requested a plaster to be placed over his heart at the memory of her many years later.[14] Combined with the vast wealth and influence she would bring John as her inheritance from her father, it must have been very easy for him to fall in love with her, and both Blanche and her father inspired immense affection and admiration.

In late May 1359 shortly after Blanche's wedding, it seems likely that her mother Isabella Beaumont, Duchess of Lancaster, was dying. The Pope granted Duke Henry, regarding an indult previously granted that his chaplains should give him and Isabella plenary remission at the time of their death, an extension 'to another wife, if he takes one after the death of Isabella'.[15] The statutes of the Newarke in the mid 1350s indicate that Henry, then in his early or mid 40s, still hoped for a son, perhaps with another woman: ' … after the duke's death to his heir, if he be a male; otherwise, if the inheritance of the said duke happens to be divided among females …'.[16] The date of Duchess Isabella's death is, rather sadly and unusually, not known. She was certainly dead by July 1361 when her late husband's lands were divided between their two daughters, and there is no reference to any dower, which would have been considerable, being assigned to Henry of Grosmont's widow. An earlier assumption by historians that Duchess Isabella outlived Henry is based on a misunderstanding that the reference in his will to 'my lady, Lady Isabella' (in the original French, *madame dame Isabell*) being invited to his funeral meant his wife. In fact, it meant Edward III's eldest daughter, Isabella of Woodstock. Fourteenth-century noblemen referred to their wives as *ma compaigne*, not as *madame*, 'my lady'. It is unfortunate that we do not know the date when the first English duchess in history died, but Isabella Beaumont's death is as obscure as her life.

Blanche of Lancaster became pregnant just weeks after she married John of Gaunt. Edward III demonstrated his anxiety for his pregnant daughter-in-law on 9 January 1360 by commenting that 'because of the concern that we feel for her condition' he wished her to stay with Queen Philippa for the last month or two before her delivery.[17] Perhaps Blanche's mother died while she was expecting her first child, increasing the king's concern for her well-being, and if she had lost her mother this might explain why Edward wished his wife, a woman with strong maternal feelings, to look after her. John of Gaunt was out of England from late October 1359 until 10 May 1360, so missed the last few months of his wife's first pregnancy and the birth. Edward III had extended a truce with France until 14 June 1359, then demanded greater territorial concessions from his foes, which they, not surprisingly, rejected. The king therefore set off on yet another military campaign in France in October 1359, accompanied by his sons Edward, Lionel, John and Edmund, and John's father-in-law Henry of Grosmont. Grosmont's 20-year-old nephew Henry Beaumont, Eleanor of Lancaster's eldest son, also went on the campaign, and was given a personal gift of £100 by the king to help defray his costs.[18] Presumably Beaumont must have been back in England by June 1360 as his son John Beaumont, Eleanor's first grandchild, was born in about March 1361. King John II of France was still captive in England, and died at the Savoy Palace – which by then belonged to John of Gaunt and Blanche – in April 1364, and his kingdom was ruled in his absence by his eldest son, the future Charles V.

On 31 March 1360, ten months and twelve days after her parents' wedding, John of Gaunt and Blanche's first child Philippa of Lancaster was born, and named, inevitably, after her paternal grandmother, the queen. She was Duke Henry's second grandchild, after Maud and Wilhelm of Bavaria's daughter who died soon after her birth in 1356. Perhaps the duke was disappointed; he had failed to father any sons and now another grandchild was female, and Henry did not live long enough to see any of his other grandchildren, Blanche and John's younger children. As his other son-in-law Wilhelm of Bavaria was incarcerated, he could expect no heirs from that quarter. Perhaps John of Gaunt was also disappointed that his first legitimate child was a girl, but of course he was still only 20 and Blanche some years younger, so they had plenty of time to build a larger family. A few weeks after Philippa of Lancaster's birth, Edward III gave John Hertford Castle and three other manors in Hertfordshire formerly belonging to John's grandmother Queen Isabella, because 'he has not yet castles, houses or other buildings wherein he can lodge as befits his estate'. John's 19-year-old brother Edmund of Langley was hiring carpenters, masons, tilers, roofers and others to repair his castles in Yorkshire in 1360, and in 1361 was inducted into the Order of the Garter.[19]

DEATH OF A DUKE

⟨⟨⟩⟩

The elder Elizabeth de Burgh, granddaughter of Edward I and mother of the late William de Burgh, Earl of Ulster, died on 4 November 1360 at the age of 65. Her heir was her granddaughter, the younger Elizabeth de Burgh, Countess of Ulster, Maud of Lancaster's daughter. Elizabeth wrote in her very long will, 'I bequeath to Lady Elizabeth, my [grand]daughter, countess of Ulster, all the debts my son her father owed me on the day of his death', which she probably intended to be less caustically sarcastic than it sounds, and left items to her only surviving child Elizabeth Bardolf (*née* Damory) and to several of her many grandchildren. She also left a 'little psalter' and a cross containing a piece of the True Cross to the Duke of Lancaster; but the great Henry of Grosmont was also dying.[1] He wrote his will on 15 March 1361 and appointed his 'very dear' eldest sister Blanche, Lady Wake and his 'very dear' cousin-in-law Eleanor Walkington (not, as usually stated, her husband Sir William) as two of his ten executors.[2] He called himself 'Henry, duke of Lancaster, earl of Derby, Lincoln and Leicester, steward of England, lord of Bergerac and Beaufort', and asked to be buried on the opposite side of the high altar in the church of the Newarke as his father but not until 'three weeks after the departure of the soul'. He invited the king and queen, the Prince of Wales and his younger brothers, the king's eldest daughter Isabella of Woodstock who was perhaps his goddaughter, his surviving sisters Blanche, Maud, Eleanor and Mary and his 'brothers[in-law], their lords' (meaning their husbands, though Eleanor and Mary were now the only married Lancaster sisters), and *les autres grauntz de nostre saunk*, 'the other great people of our blood', to attend his funeral.

Duke Henry of Lancaster died in Leicester in the morning of Tuesday, 23 March 1361 at the age of about 48 or 50, and was buried at the Newarke on 14 April three weeks after death, as he had requested.[3] It has sometimes been assumed that Henry died of bubonic plague, which came to England again in 1361. He was, however, already ill at the beginning of March, and his making his will eight days before death also argues against his dying of plague, as does the statement in it 'if we die at Leicester' (which suggests that he was not yet ill enough that moving to another location seemed impossible).[4] Henry was still lucid enough on 20 March, three days before death, to appoint an under-sheriff of Lancashire.[5] His son-in-law John of Gaunt was assigned temporary custody of all his lands and their issues on 25 March, two days after Henry's death, by letters of secret seal. Henry had held lands in no fewer than thirty-four of the thirty-nine English counties; it would have been far easier for the king's clerks to list the counties where he did not own lands than those where he did.[6] His lands were officially divided between his two daughters on 16 July 1361: Maud received the lands south of the River Trent and Blanche those in the north, where John of Gaunt was already Earl of Richmond.[7] Maud of Lancaster had returned to England by mid July 1361 and performed homage to the king in person – her husband Wilhelm would normally have done so but the unfortunate man was unable to – while John did the same for his and Blanche's lands. Duke Henry also left an illegitimate daughter called Juliane, who of course was not one of his heirs. The identity of her mother is not known, nor the year (or even the decade) of her birth. Juliane married William Dannet of Leicester in or before 1380 and had descendants, and was still alive in 1407 in the reign of her nephew Henry IV, Blanche of Lancaster's son.[8] Henry of Grosmont fathered at least four daughters – Maud and Blanche his heirs, Juliane, and another legitimate daughter called Isabella mentioned on record in 1338/39 who must have died young – but no sons, or at least none who survived infancy and found their way onto record (excepting a claim by an antiquarian in 1712 that Grosmont had a son who drowned at Kempsford in Gloucestershire). His father Henry of Lancaster had six daughters and only one son.

John Mowbray, Duke Henry's brother-in-law, soon followed him to the grave and died at the age of 50 on 4 October 1361, months after his and Joan of Lancaster's son John had come of age (i.e. 21). The younger John Mowbray (b. 1340) and Elizabeth Segrave (b. 1338) had a daughter Eleanor born in March 1364; a son John born around 1 August 1365; and another son Thomas, their youngest child and ultimate heir, and ancestor of the Dukes of Norfolk, probably born in March 1367.[9] Thomas Mowbray features as a character in Shakespeare's play about Richard II, as Henry of Bolingbroke's adversary in the famous duel of 1398.

Maud de Vere (née Ufford), younger daughter of Henry of Grosmont's third sister Maud, the Dowager Countess of Ulster and now a canoness, had become Countess of Oxford in early 1360 when her father-in-law John de Vere was killed fighting in one of Edward III's campaigns in France, and her husband Thomas succeeded him as earl. She gave birth to her and Thomas' only child on 16 January 1362 when she was 16 or almost; he was Robert de Vere, later to become notorious as the great favourite and perhaps lover of Richard II in the 1380s.[10] Maud de Vere's cousin, the younger Maud of Lancaster, Duchess of Lower Bavaria and Henry of Grosmont's elder daughter and co-heir, had returned to England in 1361 for the first time, as far as is known, since 1352. Despite the serious illness and confinement of her husband Wilhelm in Le Quesnoy, Maud continued living with him or somewhere near him, with the result that the jurors of several counties at Duke Henry's Inquisition Post Mortem in 1361 did not even remember her name, or did not know whether she was still alive or had children.[11]

The unfortunate Maud did not long outlive her father, and died on 9 or 10 April 1362, just days after her 22nd birthday, leaving no surviving children.[12] It is unclear what killed a previously healthy young woman at such a young age; perhaps the bubonic plague, or a sudden infection. Maud was born into limitless wealth and privilege but lost her first husband when she was still only 7 years old or younger, left her homeland before she was even 12, only ever saw her father once again after her second marriage and her mother probably never, married a man who became insane and had to be confined for his own safety and hers, lost her only child when she was 16, and now was dead at 22. It was a sad end to a sad life. The vast Lancastrian inheritance, worth around £12,000 a year, thus passed entirely to Maud's younger sister Blanche and John of Gaunt, a windfall neither they nor their fathers the king and Henry of Grosmont can have expected.

A silly rumour that John had poisoned his sister-in-law was reported by the Leicester chronicler Henry Knighton, but there is no reason at all to believe that Maud's death was anything but natural; John of Gaunt's sisters Margaret and Mary died in late 1361, both still in their teens, and perhaps the two young women were also victims of plague or another very serious illness then going around.[13] Maud's husband Duke Wilhelm continued to live in confinement until he finally died in 1389 when he was almost 60, but her aunt Mary of Lancaster, Lady Percy, slipped away almost unnoticed on 1 September 1362, in her early 40s. Mary was the youngest and quietest of the six Lancaster sisters, and almost never appears on record. Her sons Henry and Thomas Percy, 20 and 17 or 18 at her death, both became earls later in the century. Edward III's sister Joan of the Tower, Queen of Scotland, outlived her cousin Mary Percy by six days, and was almost exactly the same age. Joan had been living in her native England for the previous few years, after the breakdown of her unhappy and childless marriage to David II, and was buried with her mother Queen Isabella at the Greyfriars' church in London.

The Prince of Wales, the king's eldest son and probably the most eligible bachelor in Europe, had finally married. In the spring or early summer of 1361, he wed Joan of Kent, granddaughter of Edward I and thus his first cousin once removed, and the widow of Sir Thomas Holland. For Blanche, Lady Wake this marriage had potential advantages, as Joan was heir to the dower lands Blanche held from her late husband Thomas Wake, Joan's uncle, and now Joan had married the second most important man in the country. The king, however, was less than happy about the marriage of his son and his first cousin, though he did eventually accept it. Joan had supposedly been married to Thomas Holland and to William Montacute, Earl of Salisbury, at the same time, keeping her Holland marriage secret for years. This rather less than ideal situation was to cause her son Richard II problems in the future when his enemies used his mother's colourful marital history against him and claimed he was not his father's true son, and there were also issues with the dispensation granted by the Pope for Joan and Edward's consanguinity and it had to be reformulated and reissued later. Joan's eldest son Thomas Holland the younger, born in 1350 or 1351, married Eleanor of Lancaster's second daughter Alice Fitzalan (or Arundel) between August 1363 and September 1367, and they began building their large family in the early 1370s. Thomas, aged 16 or 17, was knighted by his stepfather the Prince of Wales in Spain in April 1367.[14] Decades previously, Alice's grandfather Henry, Earl of Lancaster, had received the severed head of her husband's grandfather Sir Robert Holland at Waltham Abbey.

King Edward III began negotiating a marriage for his fourth son Edmund of Langley in early 1362, with Margaret, daughter and heir of the Count of Flanders, and already widow of the young Duke of Burgundy even though she was not yet 12 (Edmund, born in May or early June 1341, was now 20).[15] Margaret of Flanders and her late husband the duke were both great-grandchildren of Philip V of France (r. 1316–22), and Margaret had a reasonable claim to the throne of France. Edward III celebrated his 50th birthday on 13 November 1362 by raising his three middle sons to titles: Lionel of Antwerp became first Duke of Clarence, John of Gaunt became second Duke of Lancaster, and Edmund of Langley became Earl of Cambridge.[16] The king's eldest son and heir the Prince of Wales was created Duke of Aquitaine in July 1362 and went there to rule, accompanied by his wife Joan of Kent; their two sons would be born in the duchy. Lionel of Antwerp, the king's second son, was appointed Lieutenant of Ireland.[17]

John of Gaunt was now officially Lancaster, and today is the most famous member of the dynasty even though he was not born into it. In the 1360s there were even plans for him to succeed the childless King David II of Scotland, widower of John's aunt Joan of the Tower. This had first been put forward as a possibility in 1350/51 when John was only 10, and in November 1363 it was discussed again when David met his brother-in-law Edward III at Westminster. The idea that the King of England himself would succeed David after the latter's death was mooted, and John of Gaunt was chosen as the best candidate of the five royal sons to succeed his father in turn. He was already Duke of Lancaster with vast estates in the north of England, and thus had a vested interest in maintaining peace and cordial relations with Scotland on the other side of the border. In the end the Scottish Parliament rejected the idea and upheld the rights of David II's half-nephew Robert the Steward or Stewart, who would become King Robert II in 1371 on David's death (and the first of the many Stewart or Stuart monarchs of Scotland). John of Gaunt never did become King of Scotland, but in the 1370s he would claim a throne in distant Spain, and at the end of the century his son would become the first Lancastrian King of England.

PART IV
1362–1400

DRAMATIS PERSONAE

John of Gaunt, second Duke of Lancaster, Earl of Richmond, Lincoln, Leicester and Derby, titular King of Castile (b. 1340): third son of Edward III and Philippa of Hainault; marries 1) Blanche of Lancaster in 1359, 2) Constanza of Castile in 1371, and 3) Katherine Swynford in 1396

Philippa of Lancaster, Queen of Portugal (b. 1360): John's eldest child with Blanche of Lancaster; marries João I, King of Portugal, in 1387 and the mother of the Illustrious Generation

Elizabeth of Lancaster, Duchess of Exeter, Countess of Huntingdon (b. 1363): John and Blanche's younger daughter; marries 1) John Hastings, heir to the earldom of Pembroke (b. 1372; marriage annulled before consummation) in 1380, and 2) John Holland, Richard II's half-brother, in 1386

Henry of Lancaster (sometimes called Henry of Bolingbroke), third Duke of Lancaster, first Duke of Hereford, Earl of Derby (b. 1367): only surviving son of John and Blanche, and the Lancastrian heir; first cousin of King Richard II; marries his second cousin Mary de Bohun, co-heir of her father the Earl of Hereford, in 1381; becomes King Henry IV in 1399

Catalina (Katherine) of Lancaster, Queen of Castile (b. 1372/73): only child of John of Gaunt and his second wife Constanza of Castile, and her mother's heir; half-sister of Philippa, Elizabeth and Henry; marries her cousin Enrique III of Castile (b. 1379) in 1387

Edmund of Langley, first Duke of York, founder of the House of York (b. 1341): fourth son of Edward III and Philippa of Hainault; marries 1) Isabel of Castile in 1372, and 2) Joan Holland in 1393

Constanza of Castile, Duchess of Lancaster (*c.* 1354–94), and her sister **Isabel of Castile**, Duchess of York (*c.* 1355–92): daughters of Pedro 'the Cruel', King of Castile (1334–69); Constanza is her father's heir

Edward of York (sometimes wrongly called Edward of Norwich),
second Duke of York, Duke of Albemarle, Earl of Rutland (b. 1373/74):
elder son and heir of Edmund of Langley, Duke of York, and Isabel of
Castile; grandson of Edward III, first cousin of Richard II and of the
Lancaster siblings; marries Philippa Mohun in the late 1390s but is childless

Constance of York, Lady Despenser (b. 1374/6): only daughter of
Edmund of Langley and Isabel of Castile; marries Thomas, Lord Despenser
(b. 1373) in 1379; grandmother of Anne Neville (née Beauchamp)
(d. 1492), Countess of Warwick and mother-in-law of Richard III

Richard of Conisbrough (b. *c.* 1375 or more probably 1385): second
son of Edmund and Isabel; later Earl of Cambridge; marries Anne
Mortimer (b. 1390), daughter of Roger, Earl of March; grandfather of
Edward IV and Richard III

Lionel of Antwerp, first Duke of Clarence (b. 1338): second son of
Edward III; marries the heiress Elizabeth de Burgh (b. 1332); their heir is
their daughter Philippa, Countess of March and Ulster (b. 1355); ancestor
of the fifteenth-century Yorkists

Eleanor de Bohun (b. 1366): elder daughter and co-heir of Humphrey
de Bohun, Earl of Hereford, and Joan Fitzalan; granddaughter of Eleanor
of Lancaster, Countess of Arundel; marries Edward III's fifth and youngest son **Thomas of Woodstock**, first Duke of Gloucester (b. 1355)

Humphrey of Gloucester (b. 1382) and **Anne of Gloucester**,
Countess of Stafford (b. 1383): children of Eleanor de Bohun and Thomas
of Woodstock; grandchildren of Edward III; Humphrey dies young and
unmarried, and Anne is their parents' heir

Mary de Bohun (b. *c.* 1369): younger daughter and co-heir of
Humphrey de Bohun; granddaughter of Eleanor of Lancaster; marries
Henry of Lancaster (b. 1367) in 1381

Henry of Monmouth (b. 1386): eldest son of Henry of Lancaster and Mary de Bohun; heir of the Lancasters; later King Henry V

Thomas, John and Humphrey of Lancaster (b. 1387–90): younger sons of Henry of Lancaster and Mary; later Dukes of Clarence, Bedford and Gloucester

Blanche and Philippa of Lancaster (b. 1392 and 1394): daughters of Henry of Lancaster and Mary de Bohun; later Electress Palatine of the Rhine and Queen of Denmark respectively

Richard II, King of England (b. 1367): second but only surviving son of Edward III's eldest son **Edward of Woodstock**, Prince of Wales and Aquitaine, and Joan of Kent; marries 1) Anne of Bohemia (b. 1366) in 1382, and 2) Isabelle of France (b. 1389) in 1396

John, Thomas, Henry and Joan Beaufort (b. *c.* 1372–79): children of John of Gaunt and his mistress Katherine Swynford, later legitimised after John marries Katherine as his third wife in 1396; half-siblings of Henry of Lancaster, later Henry IV; John is the great-grandfather of Henry VII, Joan the grandmother of Edward IV and Richard III

Maud de Vere (née **Ufford)**, Countess of Oxford (b. 1345/46): daughter of Maud of Lancaster, Countess of Ulster (b. *c.* 1310–12) and her second husband Ralph Ufford (d. 1346); half-sister of Elizabeth de Burgh, Duchess of Clarence (1332–63); married to Thomas de Vere, Earl of Oxford (*c.* 1336–71)

Robert de Vere, Earl of Oxford, Marquis of Dublin and Duke of Ireland (b. 1362): only child of Maud Ufford and Thomas de Vere; beloved of Richard II in the 1380s; married to Richard's first cousin Philippa Coucy, daughter of Edward III's eldest daughter Isabella of Woodstock (1332–79)

Thomas Holland, Earl of Kent (b. 1350/51): eldest son and heir of Joan of Kent, and half-brother of King Richard II; great-grandson of Edward I; marries **Alice Fitzalan**, younger daughter of Eleanor of Lancaster and Richard, Earl of Arundel

Thomas Holland, Earl of Kent, Duke of Surrey (b. *c.* 1371–4): elder son and heir of Thomas and Alice; half-nephew of Richard II; his heir is his brother **Edmund Holland** (b. 1383)

John Holland, Earl of Huntingdon, Duke of Exeter (b. *c.* 1352–5): Richard II's other half-brother; marries John of Gaunt's second daughter Elizabeth of Lancaster (b. 1363) in 1386; their son and heir John the younger is born in 1395

Thomas Mowbray, Earl of Nottingham, first Duke of Norfolk (b. 1367): second son and heir of John Mowbray (b. 1340) and Elizabeth Segrave (b. 1338); grandson and heir of Margaret, Countess and later Duchess of Norfolk; grandson of Joan of Lancaster; his elder brother **John** (b. 1365) dies in 1383

Elizabeth Mowbray (née **Fitzalan**), Countess of Nottingham, Duchess of Norfolk (b. *c.* 1366–68): eldest daughter of Richard Fitzalan the younger, Earl of Arundel (b. 1346/47), and Elizabeth de Bohun; granddaughter of Eleanor of Lancaster; marries Thomas Mowbray in 1384

Thomas Mowbray, Earl of Norfolk (b. 1385): first son of Thomas and Elizabeth; executed in 1405; marries Elizabeth of Lancaster's daughter Constance Holland but has no children

John Mowbray, Duke of Norfolk (b. 1390): second son and ultimate heir of Thomas (b. 1367) and Elizabeth; marries Katherine Neville in 1412; ancestor of the later Mowbrays

Roger Mortimer, Earl of March and Ulster (b. 1374): son and heir of Edmund, Earl of March (b. 1352) and Philippa of Clarence (b. 1355); grandson and heir of Lionel of Antwerp; great-grandson of Edward III; also great-grandson of Maud of Lancaster, Countess of Ulster (b. *c.* 1310–12)

Alianore Holland, Countess of March and Ulster (b. *c.* 1373): marries Roger Mortimer in 1388; eldest daughter of Thomas Holland, Earl of Kent, and Alice Fitzalan; granddaughter of Eleanor of Lancaster

Anne Mortimer (b. 1390): eldest child of Roger and Alianore; marries Edmund of Langley's younger son Richard of Conisbrough, Earl of Cambridge; mother of Richard, third Duke of York, and grandmother of Edward IV and Richard III

Edmund Mortimer, Earl of March and Ulster (b. 1391): son and heir of Roger and Alianore; marries Anne Stafford, but childless

Richard, third Duke of York (b. 1411): only son of Richard of Conisbrough, Earl of Cambridge, and Anne Mortimer; heir to his childless uncles Edward, second Duke of York, and Edmund Mortimer, Earl of March and Ulster; marries **Cecily Neville** (b. 1415) and father of Edward IV and Richard III

Ralph Neville, first Earl of Westmorland (b. *c.* 1364): marries John of Gaunt's daughter Joan Beaufort as his second wife; father of, among many others, Katherine Mowbray, Duchess of Norfolk, Cecily, Duchess of York, and Eleanor Percy, Countess of Northumberland; grandfather of Edward IV and Richard III

John Montacute, Earl of Salisbury (b. *c.* 1350): nephew and heir of William Montacute, Earl of Salisbury (1328-97); his son and heir is **Thomas Montacute**, Earl of Salisbury (b. 1388), who marries **Eleanor Holland**, half-niece of Richard II, granddaughter of Eleanor of Lancaster

Henry Percy, first Earl of Northumberland (b. 1341): elder son of Henry Percy (d. 1368) and Mary of Lancaster (d. 1362); marries Margaret Neville in 1358

Thomas Percy, first Earl of Worcester (b. 1343/44): younger brother of Northumberland, above; never marries

Henry 'Hotspur' Percy (b. 1364): eldest son and heir of Henry Percy
(b. 1341), first Earl of Northumberland; grandson of Mary of Lancaster;
marries **Elizabeth Mortimer** (b. 1371), sister of Roger Mortimer, Earl
of March (b. 1374) and eldest great-grandchild of Edward III

Philippa Mortimer, Countess of Pembroke and Arundel (b. 1375):
younger daughter of Philippa of Clarence (b. 1355); sister of Roger, Earl
of March (b. 1374) and Elizabeth (b. 1371); marries John Hastings, Earl
of Pembroke (1372–89) and secondly Richard Fitzalan, Earl of Arundel
(b. 1346/47), son of Eleanor of Lancaster

Joan Holland, Duchess of York (b. *c.* 1375–80) second daughter of
Thomas Holland the elder and Alice Fitzalan; granddaughter of Eleanor
of Lancaster; marries the widowed Edmund of Langley, Duke of York
(b. 1341) in 1393; subsequently marries another three husbands

Margaret Holland, Countess of Somerset (b. *c.* early 1380s): third daughter of Thomas Holland the elder and Alice Fitzalan; marries John of
Gaunt's son John Beaufort (b. *c.* 1372) in 1397; mother of Joan Beaufort,
queen consort of Scotland, and great-grandmother of Henry VII

Thomas Despenser, Earl of Gloucester (b. 1373): son and heir of
Edward, Lord Despenser (1336–75), and a descendant of Edward I;
marries Edmund of Langley's daughter Constance of York in 1379; great-
grandfather of Richard III's queen Anne Neville

Juana of Navarre, Duchess of Brittany, Queen of England (b. *c.* 1370):
daughter of Carlos II 'the Bad', King of Navarre, and granddaughter of
John II of France; marries Duke John IV of Brittany (d. 1399) in 1386,
and King Henry IV of England in 1403

BIRTH OF AN HEIR

⟨ornament⟩

John of Gaunt and Blanche of Lancaster's second surviving child was born in February 1363, and it was another girl, rather surprisingly named Elizabeth instead of the usual Maud or Blanche. Perhaps they named their daughter in honour of John's sister-in-law, the Duchess of Clarence and Countess of Ulster, Elizabeth de Burgh. Duchess Elizabeth died on 10 December 1363 at the age of 31, leaving her 8-year-old daughter Philippa of Clarence (already married to Edmund Mortimer) as her heir, her widower Lionel, still only 25, and her mother Maud of Lancaster, the Canoness of Bruisyard. John of Gaunt's father the king had by now probably already begun his long-term extra-marital relationship with a woman called Alice Perrers, who was to become notorious as a greedy, flaunting royal mistress. In around 1364, Alice bore Edward a son called John de Southeray, much younger half-brother of Lionel of Antwerp, John of Gaunt and Edmund of Langley; Alice and Edward had two daughters together as well. In early 1377 John de Southeray married Mary Percy (b. 1368), younger half-sister of Mary of Lancaster's children Henry and Thomas Percy, when they were both still underage. The marriage was annulled some years later after the death of Southeray's father, on the grounds that Mary 'in no way wishes to have the said John, who is not noble but plebeian', as her husband.[1] John Arundel, second son of Eleanor of Lancaster and her second husband the

Earl of Arundel, became a father at a young age in November 1364 – he cannot have been more than about 14 – when his wife Eleanor Maltravers gave birth to their son, also John. The younger John grew up in the household of the Prince of Wales' second son Richard of Bordeaux, the future King Richard II, who was two years and two months his junior.[2]

In or before November 1365, John of Gaunt was sent to negotiate his brother Edmund of Langley's marriage to Margaret, Dowager Duchess of Burgundy and heir to the county of Flanders. The marriage, under discussion since early 1362, had been 'arranged in Dover Castle' on 19 October 1364.[3] Under pressure from France, however, the Pope refused to issue a dispensation for the two to marry – they were both descended from Philip IV of France (d. 1314) and thus were related – and in 1369 Margaret married Philip 'the Bold', youngest son of John II of France and brother of Charles V. Charles had succeeded John II as King of France when John died at John of Gaunt's London palace of the Savoy in April 1364. Charles was a very different man to his father, and was determined to restore French fortunes during the endless wars with England begun when Edward III claimed the throne of France in the 1330s. As for John of Gaunt, in the 1360s he was the eldest son of the king resident in England, as his eldest brother Edward was away ruling Gascony for most of that decade and his second brother Lionel was in Ireland and spent most of his time there, dealing with the governance of the lands he held in that country. John himself left England in November 1366, travelled through Brittany, and was reunited with his brother Edward of Woodstock at Dax, the first time they had seen each other for years.[4] He left his wife Blanche of Lancaster in England, about four months pregnant.

The future King Richard II of England was born in Bordeaux on 6 January 1367 as the second son of Edward of Woodstock and Joan of Kent, who was 40 or close to it when she gave birth to her youngest child. When his elder brother Edward of Angoulême died in late 1370 or early 1371 at the age of 5 or 6, Richard of Bordeaux became heir to the English throne behind his father. Just three months after his birth, probably on 15 April (Maundy Thursday) 1367, Richard of Bordeaux's first cousin and nemesis was born: Henry of Lancaster, only surviving son of John of Gaunt and Blanche, and the Lancastrian heir from the moment of his birth. John and Blanche probably had two or even three older sons, John, perhaps a second John, and Edward, who all died as infants.[5] Henry was born at Bolingbroke Castle in Lincolnshire, which had once belonged to Thomas of Lancaster's wife Alice de Lacy (d. 1348), and was named Henry after his maternal grandfather; he is often known to history as Henry of Bolingbroke, the name Shakespeare called him. Henry of Lancaster's other grandfather the king gave £5 to Ingelram Falconer, Duchess Blanche's messenger, who brought him news of the birth. This in fact was none too generous given that a few months before, Edward III had paid 40 marks, or £26 13s 4d, to the messenger who brought him news of a son born to the Duke and Duchess of Berry, brother and sister-in-law of Charles V.[6]

John of Gaunt missed the birth of his son and heir as he was in Spain with his brother the Prince of Wales and Aquitaine, helping King Pedro 'the Cruel' of Castile defeat his half-brother and enemy Enrique of Trastamara at the Battle of Najera on 3 April. The vanquished Enrique, however, soon returned to Castile with the support of Charles V of France, killed his half-brother, and made himself king. John of Gaunt would marry Pedro's elder daughter and heir Constanza in September 1371, three years after he had been widowed from Blanche, and the following year his brother Edmund of Langley would marry Pedro's younger daughter Isabel. John returned to England in early October 1367 and saw his son and heir Henry for the first time. Unlike his two, or perhaps even three, older brothers who died in infancy or shortly after birth, Henry of Lancaster was a sturdy, healthy little boy, and from the moment of his birth he was heir to all the Lancastrian lands. Henry never had the chance to know his larger-than-life maternal grandfather Henry of Grosmont, who died six years before his birth, but he must have been told plenty of stories about him.

Mary of Lancaster's widower and Henry of Grosmont's brother-in-law Henry, Lord Percy died on 17 May 1368, and their first son the younger Henry Percy, born in November 1341 and then 26, came into his large inheritance in the north of England. The elder Henry (b. c. 1320/21) married a second and decades-younger wife, Joan Oreby, some years after Mary of Lancaster died in 1362. Percy and Joan had a daughter born at his Northumberland castle of Warkworth on 12 March 1368, just three months before Percy died.[7] They called her Mary in honour of Percy's late Lancastrian wife, and the little girl was the heir of her mother Joan and Joan's mother Margaret Oreby. Rather sadly, the two women died within three weeks of each other in 1369, so not only was little Mary Percy left an orphan by the time she was a few months old but she had lost her grandmother too.[8] Mary Percy was four years younger than her half-nephew, the younger Henry's first son, who was born in May 1364 and inevitably and confusingly named Henry, and who was Mary of Lancaster's eldest grandchild and is known to history as 'Hotspur'. Mary of Lancaster's younger son Sir Thomas Percy, born in 1343 or 1344 and sent to France to act as seneschal of Poitou and the island of Oléron in the 1370s, was described by chronicler Jean Froissart and others as a gentle, loyal and valiant knight, and there was much of his grandfather Henry, Earl of Lancaster (d. 1345), about him.[9] Peculiarly for a medieval nobleman, Thomas never married. His much younger half-sister Mary Percy left valuable items in her will of 1394 to an 'Isabella Percy' whose identity is unclear; it is not impossible that she was an illegitimate daughter of Thomas, or of his older brother Henry.[10]

Mary of Lancaster's 28-year-old nephew John, Lord Mowbray, Joan of Lancaster's only son, died either on 17 June, 24 June, 8 September, 21 September or 9 October 1368. (As he died overseas, the jurors of his IPM were not at all sure.)[11] John was killed near Constantinople, modern Istanbul, fighting the 'Saracens' on his way to Crusade in the Holy Land. His heir was his elder son John, then 3, and he left three daughters and a 1-year-old younger son Thomas, his ultimate heir and ancestor of the later Mowbrays. The two Mowbray brothers were given into the custody of their great-aunt Blanche Wake on 18 April 1372, as their mother Elizabeth (née Segrave) had also died.[12] Somewhat mysteriously, Blanche presented a petition in or after 1372 asking for her expenses looking after her ward 'Leo son of Sir John Mowbray' to be paid; the identity of 'Leo' is unclear.[13] It seems unfortunate that Blanche Wake had no children of her own as she was evidently a maternal type, and in the late 1360s and early 1370s also looked after Philippa, Elizabeth and Henry of Lancaster, the grandchildren of her brother Grosmont, for a while. In October 1371, the children travelled between two of Blanche's manors, Ware in Hertfordshire and Deeping in Lincolnshire, though did not remain with her much longer as their father returned to England from southern France soon afterwards. John of Gaunt called Blanche Wake his 'very dear and beloved aunt'.[14]

John's older brother Lionel of Antwerp, Duke of Clarence, married his second wife Violante Visconti in Milan in June 1368, in a lavish ceremony attended by his father-in-law Galeazzo Visconti, Lord of Milan, and his brother-in-law Gian Galeazzo, later the first Duke of Milan. Lionel died in

Alba on 17 October 1368, not quite 30 years old; rumour had it that he was poisoned by his Visconti in-laws, though illness or infection seems far more probable. He wrote his will on 3 October two weeks before his death, and as people only made their wills when they thought they might be dying, it seems highly unlikely that he was poisoned. Lionel left his wife Violante his clothes and gold coronets and appointed her as one of his executors, which also argues against the notion that he suspected her family of having had him murdered. To two of his knights, Lionel left coursers (horses) called Gerfacon and Maugeneleyn.[15] Lionel was buried at the church of Saint Peter in the Sky of Gold in Pavia though his body was later returned to England, and his heir was his only child Philippa of Clarence, Countess of March, aged 13 in 1368. Edward III's friend and close ally Robert Ufford, Earl of Suffolk – one of the young knights who arrested Roger Mortimer with the king at Nottingham in 1330 – was also dying, and made his will on 29 June 1368. He left 20 marks to Maud of Lancaster, Dowager Countess of Ulster and the widow of his brother Ralph, for her and her son-in-law Lionel of Antwerp's priory at Bruisyard, and gave her a gold ring which had belonged to her brother Henry of Grosmont.[16]

The year 1368 proved a terrible one for the English nobility. Blanche, Duchess of Lancaster, also died on 12 September 1368, a month before her brother-in-law Lionel died in Italy and around the same time as her first cousin John Mowbray died in faraway Constantinople. She was only 24 or 26 and left her children: 8-year-old Philippa, 5-year-old Elizabeth and 1-year-old Henry. Blanche's elder sister Maud, Duchess of Lower Bavaria and Countess of Leicester, Hainault and Holland, had died at age 22; Henry of Grosmont's daughters lived sadly short lives. It is possible that Blanche's death was related to pregnancy or childbirth, and she gave birth to several children who died young, one or two sons called John and one called Edward, and perhaps a daughter, Isabella.[17] If this is indeed the case, Blanche was pregnant at least five and perhaps seven times between her wedding in May 1359 and her death in September 1368. She was buried at St Paul's Cathedral in London, and more than thirty years later John of Gaunt would be buried next to her, though their tombs were lost during the Great Fire of London in 1666. John marked the anniversary of Blanche's death every year by having Masses sung for her soul, and paid £486 for her tomb and an altar besides it where two chaplains would 'sing for her soul'. The altar was made by Master Robert, joiner of

London.[18] Blanche's heir was her only surviving son Henry, who was not even 18 months old at her death and cannot have had any memories of her, though thanks to the custom called the 'courtesy of England' John of Gaunt was entitled to keep her entire enormous inheritance for the rest of his own life. The poet Geoffrey Chaucer wrote his first great work about Blanche, *The Book of the Duchess*, which was most probably commissioned by John not long after his wife's death.

Less than a year later, on 15 August 1369, Blanche's mother-in-law Queen Philippa passed away at Windsor, in her mid 50s. She had been married to Edward III for more than forty years, and their marriage had been a most happy and close one, at least until the king met his ambitious mistress Alice Perrers in the early 1360s. The queen was buried at Westminster Abbey on 9 January 1370 and outlived seven of her twelve children, including all but one of her daughters (Isabella of Woodstock, the eldest). Philippa's eldest son Edward of Woodstock, with his wife Joan of Kent and their 4-year-old son Richard of Bordeaux, returned to England in early 1371. Edward and Joan's elder son Edward of Angoulême had died in Aquitaine and was buried there, though his brother Richard later had his body moved to England and reinterred at Langley Priory in Hertfordshire. The Prince of Wales, who picked up a serious and recurrent illness while campaigning in Spain in 1367, was now little more than an invalid, and the journey back from the south of France exhausted him.

Maud of Lancaster, Dowager Countess of Ulster, became a great-grandmother on 12 February 1371 when she was about 60 years old: her granddaughter Philippa of Clarence, Countess of March, gave birth to her first child Elizabeth Mortimer. Philippa was 15½ at the time, and was to have three younger children: Roger, born in 1374 and heir to the earldoms of March and Ulster, Philippa, who was a countess twice over and enormously wealthy but who died in her 20s, and Edmund. As was the case with almost all her family, Elizabeth Mortimer was to marry young. In 1380 when she was 9, Elizabeth wed Henry 'Hotspur' Percy, then 16, grandson of Mary of Lancaster and heir to the earldom of Northumberland.

Maud of Lancaster's son-in-law Thomas de Vere, Earl of Oxford, died on 18 September 1371 in his mid 30s, leaving his 9-year-old son and heir Robert and his widow Maud (née Ufford), Maud of Lancaster's younger daughter. Maud de Vere, still only 25 when she was widowed, became seriously ill presumably from the shock of bereavement: on 18 November 1371 two months after her husband's death, she was said to be 'too feeble to travel'. The Bishop of London therefore travelled to her at her home in Earls Colne, Essex on or before 10 December to take her fealty to the king and her oath (always taken by the widows of tenants in chief) not to remarry without royal licence.[19] Maud had been married or at least betrothed to Thomas de Vere since she was 4 years old, and had probably grown up with him and his family after her mother entered a religious house when she was only a toddler; she must have known her husband all her life. Whatever the illness was, Maud survived, and outlived Thomas de Vere by forty-two years and her son Robert de Vere, his successor as earl, by twenty-one. In his will, Oxford left her all his reliquaries, all the furniture in his chapel, and his 'cross made of the very wood of Christ's cross'.[20] Despite her youth when she was left a widow, Maud never remarried, though in July 1374 her kinsman Edward III took her under his protection as 'certain persons … purpose to ravish and carry off the countess against her will'.[21] This was an intended abduction of a wealthy noblewoman and subsequent forced marriage, which was sadly all too common in medieval England.

THE NEW DUCHESS OF LANCASTER

⸻∞∞⸻

Johohn of Gaunt brought his new bride Constanza of Castile to England
in November 1371, and her new family gave her splendid wedding gifts.
She received a gold crown with emeralds, rubies and pearls from her
father-in-law the king, and a gold circlet with diamonds, rubies, pearls,
emeralds and sapphires, and two gold brooches with precious stones, one in
the shape of a stag and one with an image of St George, from her brother-
in-law the Prince of Wales. John himself piled Constanza with presents:
among much else, a gold mirror with sapphires, rubies, pearls and diamonds; a gold tablet with an image of Our Lady; a necklace or collar with
more precious stones; almost 500 pearls for a 'fret' (a headdress of interlaced
wire); cloth of gold; and a gold brooch with rubies, sapphires, diamonds and
pearls with a matching necklace.[1] The writer of the *Anonimalle* chronicle
was much taken with Constanza of Castile, calling her a 'beautiful young
lady' in 1371 and a few years later 'a woman of great beauty'.[2] Constanza
was probably 17 when she married John, and was the elder daughter and
heir of the late King Pedro 'the Cruel', King of Castile, who was stabbed to
death by his half-brother Enrique of Trastamara in 1369. Her younger sister
Isabel also moved to England, where she married Gaunt's brother Edmund
of Langley and became an ancestor of the Yorkists. Constanza, who was
always referred to as a queen in English records as she was considered the

rightful occupant of the Castilian throne now held by her illegitimate half-uncle Enrique of Trastamara, made a formal entry into London on 9 February 1372. John of Gaunt began calling himself 'king of Castile, Leon and Toledo', and after his marriage to Constanza was known as *Monseigneur d'Espaigne*, 'my lord of Spain' (which in fourteenth-century usage meant the kingdom of Castile rather than the entire country).

For all his generosity to his new wife and his talk of his 'very dear and beloved consort', however, John had recently begun what is probably one of the most famous relationships of the English Middle Ages with his long-term mistress Katherine Swynford. John and Constanza of Castile had a daughter called Katherine or Catalina of Lancaster, born probably in 1372, but around the same time he and Katherine Swynford had an illegitimate son called John Beaufort. Beaufort was one of the lordships in France John had inherited from Blanche of Lancaster and ultimately from her great-grandmother Blanche of Artois, and he surely chose the name not because his children were born there but to make it apparent that they were not his legitimate children and had no claim to his inheritance.

On 6 June 1372, John told his receiver in Leicestershire to send 'the wise woman' (*la sage femme*) Ilote to his wife Constanza at Hertford Castle as quickly as he possibly could. This suggests that Constanza was close to giving birth, or that she was having a difficult first pregnancy. If Constanza did give birth on or shortly after 6 June 1372, this was only thirty-seven weeks after her wedding to John on 21 September 1371, which implies that she became pregnant on her wedding night or very soon afterwards. Ilote the wise woman had previously served Blanche of Lancaster, and is presumably to be identified as the *Elyot la middewyf de Leycestre* or 'Elyot the midwife of Leicester' mentioned by John in 1375.[3] The Duchess of Lancaster sent Katherine Swynford to Edward III to give him the news of her daughter Catalina's birth in the full knowledge that the king would reward Katherine financially, and a payment of 20 marks to Swynford was recorded on 31 March 1373, a considerable increase on the £5 Edward had given for news of Catalina's half-brother Henry of Lancaster's birth in 1367. This hardly indicates hostility between the two women, and Duchess Constanza may even have named her daughter after her husband's mistress, unless she intended to honour St Katherine. John of Gaunt confirmed an annual grant of 20 marks to Swynford on 15 May 1372 'for the good and pleasant service which she gives and has given' to his wife, 'and for the very great affection which our said consort [Constanza] has towards the said Katherine'.[4] John also gave Katherine Swynford £10 *del doune monseignur*, 'of my lord's gift', on 1 May 1372. This may have been his reaction to news of her pregnancy with their first child John Beaufort or in anticipation of the birth, as the reason for the gift was not stated in his register as one might normally expect it to be.[5] It is possible that John of Gaunt's daughter Catalina and his son John Beaufort were born at almost the same time.

John carried on his relationship with Katherine Swynford for much or most of his marriage to Constanza and had three more children with her throughout the 1370s, Henry, Thomas and Joan Beaufort. Katherine's huge influence over and closeness to him is apparent from the large number of references to her in his extant registers and from, for example, an entry in the records of Leicester (one of John's towns) sometime between September 1377 and September 1378. The mayor gave Katherine a horse 'for expediting the business touching the tenement in Stretton, and for other business which a certain lord besought the aforesaid Katherine with good effect for the said business and besought so successfully that the town was pardoned the lending of silver to the king in that year'. A couple of years earlier, the town had paid 16 shillings for wine to send to 'Lady Katherine of the duke of Lancaster' (a word is obviously missing between 'Katherine' and 'of', probably deliberately).[6] If anyone wished a favour from John of Gaunt, approaching Katherine Swynford and asking her to use her influence with him was an effective strategy.

Whether John's long, intense and fruitful relationship with Katherine Swynford bothered his wife is unclear, though Constanza herself had been born to her father's mistress Maria Padilla while his wife and the rightful Queen of Castile, the French noblewoman Blanche de Bourbon, languished in prison. Constanza and her younger sister Isabel were only legitimised after the unfortunate Blanche, imprisoned by her husband for eight years, died in 1361. Although we cannot know how he behaved towards his royal wife in private, John of Gaunt's references to Constanza in letters and grants were always respectful, warm and courteous. In July 1373, for example, he spoke of the 'sincere love and affection which we have for our very dear and beloved consort the queen [of Castile], Lady Constanza'.[7] Constanza has been written of in modern times as little more than a smelly religious fanatic, a faceless, characterless impediment to John and Katherine's glorious love affair who finally does the decent thing by dying and thus allows them to fulfil their wildly romantic destiny of marrying, but she had a personality and interests of her own. She had a Welsh jester in her household called Yevan, and some years later hired a 'wild knight' for her and her attendants' entertainment.[8] It is probably true, though, that Constanza tended to be rather quiet, retiring and serious, in contrast to her younger sister Isabel, whom the chronicler Thomas Walsingham called 'a pampered and voluptuous lady'.[9]

For New Year 1372, John bought lavish gifts for friends and family including Constanza and Isabel, described respectively as 'our very dear and beloved consort' and 'our very dear and beloved sister, Lady Isabelle, younger daughter of the king Don Petre [Pedro], whom God absolve'. John also bought a gift of two silver flasks for his father the king, given to Edward in Constanza's name, and a decorative greyhound of white gold with eight sapphires for 'our very honoured and beloved sister[-in-law] the princess of Aquitaine and Wales', i.e. Joan of Kent. He also bought rich cloth and other coverings for the altar where chaplains said Masses and prayers for the soul of 'our very dear and beloved consort [Blanche], late duchess of Lancaster, whom God absolve'.

Some weeks later, John bought over 1,800 pearls 'of the largest kind' and 2,000 smaller ones, a gold circlet with emeralds and rubies, a fillet (headband) also of gold with four rubies and twenty-one large pearls, and other precious items, for 'our beloved consort the queen [of Castile]'.[10] John sent a letter in late 1374 about the four 'young ladies of Spain' who were staying in Nuneaton, Warwickshire at his expense but did not wish to remain there any longer, and hired one to look after 'our very dear and beloved daughter Kateryne', i.e. Catalina of Lancaster. By early 1375 Catalina and her household were living at Melbourne near Derby, a manor given by Henry, Earl of Lancaster (d. 1345) to his daughter Maud, Countess of Ulster in 1338, which Maud must have returned to her brother Henry of Grosmont some years later when she joined a religious house and which passed to Grosmont's daughter Blanche and son-in-law John. Catalina's nurse was Agnes Bonsergeant, and another of her servants was called Simon Templar. John of Gaunt granted Agnes 5 marks a year for life from the issues of the Hampshire manor of King's Somborne, part of the inheritance of Maud Chaworth (d. 1322) which he now held, for her good service to his daughter. Some years later, Lady Mohun – (née Burghersh), mother-in-law of William Montacute, Earl of Salisbury – was put in charge of

Catalina's household.[11] Catalina's mother Constanza got on well with her young stepson Henry of Lancaster, Catalina's half-brother, who was only 4 years old when Constanza married his father in 1371. Henry and his older sisters Philippa and Elizabeth lived with their stepmother at Tutbury most of the time, and for many years Constanza and John gave Henry material for clothes, lent him their servants and craftsmen when necessary, and paid for his alms and gifts.[12] Constanza's stepdaughter Elizabeth of Lancaster (b. 1363) in particular was obviously extremely fond of her: Elizabeth named two of her four daughters Constance in her stepmother's honour, Constance Holland from her second marriage to Sir John Holland and Constance Cornwall from her third to Sir John Cornwall. Constance Cornwall was born in the early 1400s a few years after Duchess Constanza died, so Elizabeth must have remembered her stepmother with fondness, and she may have asked Constanza to act as godmother to Constance Holland, who was born in about 1387.

Eleanor of Lancaster, Countess of Arundel and formerly Lady Beaumont, died at Arundel Castle in Sussex on 11 January 1372. She was about 54 years old, and a grandmother many times over. She was buried at Lewes Priory also in Sussex, and the heir to the dower lands she held from her long-dead first husband John was her grandson John Beaumont the younger, who was 10 when she died.[13] Eleanor was the fifth daughter of Henry, Earl of Lancaster, and the fifth of his seven children to die; she was outlived by her older sisters Blanche Wake and Maud, Dowager Countess of Ulster. Four of her five children with the Earl of Arundel had descendants, and although Eleanor outlived her eldest child Henry Beaumont, his son John and grandson Henry (b. 1379) continued the Beaumont line. Walter Manny, a Hainaulter lord who was made one of the Knights of the Garter and married Edward III's first cousin Margaret, Countess of Norfolk, died four days after Eleanor, on 15 January 1372. His only legitimate child, 17-year-old Anne, was his heir, and was married to John Hastings, Earl of Pembroke; she gave birth to her only child John Hastings the younger on 11 November 1372, ten months after her father's death.[14] John of Gaunt paid for 500 'masses to be sung for the soul of our very dear companion Sir Wauter de Manny', and kept the first anniversary of his aunt-in-law Eleanor of Lancaster's death in January 1373.[15]

Edmund of Langley, Earl of Cambridge and founder of the House of York, married Constanza of Castile's younger sister Isabel at Wallingford on 11 July 1372. He was already 31 and she probably 16 or 17. Edmund's four brothers all married heiresses, but Edmund himself gained no advantage from his marriage, no lands or income or powerful in-laws, and the couple seem to have been mismatched on a personal level. It says a great deal about Edmund's character and outlook that he accepted a marriage which strengthened English ties to the deposed royal line of Castile but which brought him personally no benefits whatsoever, something his four more spirited brothers would not have done, and he also consented (willingly or otherwise) to give up any claim to the Castilian throne on his wife's behalf. Then again, Edward III had attempted for years to marry his fourth son to the great heiress Margaret of Flanders, which would have given Edmund control of the counties of Flanders, Rethel, Nevers and Artois when Margaret's father Louis died in 1384, but was foiled by France and the papacy. Isabel of Castile apparently found her husband staid and boring, and may have had an affair with John Holland, the second son of Edmund's sister-in-law Joan of Kent and (from 1386) the husband of his niece Elizabeth of Lancaster.

Chronicler Jean Froissart called Edmund of Langley 'indolent, guileless and peaceable', and it is hard to disagree.[16] He had little ambition or energy, and throughout his long life rarely demonstrated much if any political acumen, though in fairness his lack of landed wealth severely hampered the exercise of any abilities he might otherwise have demonstrated. His nephew Richard II (or rather, the boy-king's council) granted Edmund an income of £500 a year in November 1377, but by February 1380 this had still not been paid. Not only had Edmund not received any of the £500 or any lands which would provide this amount, he had had to sue the Exchequer at 'great expense' to himself for the income he had been promised.[17] This seems sadly all too typical of the way Edmund was often overlooked and had to fight to receive even the crumbs from the royal table.

Edmund of Langley and Isabel of Castile's first child, named Edward after his paternal grandfather the king, was born in 1373 or 1374, a year or two after their wedding. Correctly, he is called Edward of York after the dukedom his father received in 1385, or Edward of Rutland, the earldom given to him in 1390. He is sometimes wrongly called Edward of Norwich, which seems to be a modern confusion of Everwyk, the name for York in medieval Anglo-Norman, misread as 'Norwyk' or Norwich. There seems no reason to suppose that Edward was born in Norwich.[18]

Edward was followed by a sister named Constance after her Castilian aunt the Duchess of Lancaster (perhaps also her godmother) in about 1374 to 1376, and a younger son Richard of Conisbrough, who may not have been born until *c.* 1385. Edward of York was childless and the fifteenth-century House of York was descended from his younger brother Richard, who was the paternal grandfather of Edward IV and Richard III, while their sister Constance of York was the great-grandmother of Richard III's queen Anne Neville. There was and is some speculation that Richard of Conisbrough's real father was Richard II's half-brother John Holland, not Edmund of Langley – Edmund did not mention his younger son in his will and did precious little for him in his lifetime – but Edmund certainly never disavowed Richard of Conisbrough and was his legal father. Unless DNA evidence ever proves the contrary, it is safest to assume that Edmund was also Richard's biological father, and in fairness, he did not leave bequests in his will to his other two children either.

Between April 1372 and May 1373 John of Gaunt was thinking of getting his eldest child, 12-year-old Philippa of Lancaster, married, though the potential groom, if he had one in mind, was not mentioned; he simply asked several of his officials to prepare for it financially.[19] In the early 1380s he tried to arrange a match for her with Wilhelm of Hainault, son and heir of Duke Albrecht of Bavaria, though nothing came of it.[20] Curiously, Philippa did not marry until February 1387 when she was almost 27 – an unusually advanced age for a royal lady of the fourteenth century – though made an excellent match with the King of Portugal and bore nine children, the last when she was 42, of whom six survived infancy and are known as the Illustrious Generation. Philippa's aunt Isabella of Woodstock, John of Gaunt's eldest sister, married even later, when she was 33, but this was extremely rare, and most women of their family married in childhood or adolescence.

English politics in the 1370s descended into factionalism and discontent in the absence of any real leadership from the king, who was growing more and more senile. Edward of Woodstock was ill much of the time, with the result that John of Gaunt became powerful as the eldest son of the king still capable of leadership. Edward III left his kingdom under the nominal command of his 5-year-old grandson Richard of Bordeaux in August 1372, when he and his three younger surviving sons, John, Edmund and 17-year-old Thomas, led his last expedition to France, a response to increasing

French and Castilian hostilities in the Bay of Biscay. John Hastings, the young Earl of Pembroke, formerly the king's son-in-law and now married to his cousin Anne Manny, was captured and subjected to harsh imprison-ment, and died in April 1375 aged only 27. The king was now almost 60, and the expedition achieved absolutely nothing and was soon called off. He did manage to sign a treaty of 'permanent peace' with King Fernando of Portugal on 16 June 1373, which was sealed a few years later by the mar-riage of his granddaughter Philippa of Lancaster to Fernando's son.

John of Gaunt ordered some presents for his family, friends and serv-ants for New Year 1373.[21] He sent his brother the Prince of Wales a gold goblet and a gold belt, 'to our beloved sister[-in-law] the princess', i.e. Joan of Kent, another gold goblet, and to his wife Constanza a gold ornament in the shape of a wild boar with gemstones, and a gold eagle enamelled with white. Their daughter Catalina was not mentioned, perhaps consid-ered too young to be given anything (assuming she had even been born yet), but his three children with Blanche of Lancaster, Philippa, Elizabeth and Henry, all received gifts. Philippa and Elizabeth got ten gold buttons each, and 'our beloved son Henry' (*nostre tres ame filz Henre*) a gilded silver cup. John's brother Edmund of Langley, whom John's clerk accidentally and rather amusingly called 'the king of Cambridge' instead of 'earl', received a gilded silver goblet and matching ewer, and his wife Isabel of Castile a gold and enamelled tablet. John's youngest brother the teenaged Thomas of Woodstock was not mentioned, and had perhaps rather reveal-ingly not been sent a gift the year before either. Presents went, however, to Edward III's first cousin Margaret of Norfolk, still called Lady Segrave twenty years after the death of her first husband; John's niece Philippa of Clarence, Countess of March; and Eleanor, Lady Warre and Blanche, Lady Poynings, who were the two daughters of Joan of Lancaster (d. 1349) and John Mowbray (1310–61). Katherine Swynford received 'a pair of paternosters with a gold fastening', as did the woman in charge of Duchess Constanza's household; Katherine was not referred to by name, but as 'the governess of our dear children'. John also bought a palfrey horse for his daughter Philippa, now almost 15, in early 1375, and on another occasion sent his 'very dear cousin' Blanche Poynings a tun of Gascon wine.

Eleanor of Lancaster and the Earl of Arundel's elder daughter Joan Fitzalan had married Humphrey de Bohun, Earl of Hereford, Essex and Northampton and a great-grandson of Edward I, in 1359 when she was about 13. Joan de Bohun (née Fitzalan) had two daughters, Eleanor, born on or before 8 May 1366, and Mary, born in *c*. 1369, and her husband died on 16 January 1373 leaving her a widow in her mid 20s.[22] Eleanor and Mary de Bohun were great heiresses, and in or before August 1376 Edward III snapped up Eleanor for his youngest son Thomas of Woodstock.[23] John of Gaunt was equally keen to secure Mary for his son Henry, which was to cause some friction between the two royal brothers.

Eleanor of Lancaster's widower Richard Fitzalan, Earl of Arundel and Surrey, died on 24 January 1376, almost exactly four years after his wife's death and three years after his son-in-law Humphrey de Bohun's. Arundel's will of 5 December 1375 showed a marked partiality for the children of his and Eleanor's second son John (b. *c*. 1350): he left 1,000 marks to John's eldest daughter (whom the will did not name), and smaller sums of money to John's younger sons Henry, Edward and William. John's eldest son John, then 11, was not mentioned, and neither were any of Arundel's many other grandchildren, who included the great heiresses Eleanor and Mary de Bohun. The earl left his eldest son and heir Richard his best coronet, while the second-best went to his elder daughter Joan and the third to his younger daughter Alice; the two women were countesses, hence were entitled to wear them. He ended his will by asking his executors to 'be good to my children', among whom he did not include the son from his first marriage, Edmund, cast off in 1344.[24] Arundel asked to be buried without any pomp at the priory of Lewes in Sussex next to his 'beloved wife Alianore de Lancastre', and the couple's effigies probably still exist in Chichester Cathedral, where they were taken after Lewes was closed in 1537 during the Dissolution. Arundel's heir to his two earldoms was his son the younger Richard, now 30, and he left the staggering sum of just over £60,000 in cash (equivalent to several hundred million pounds today).[25]

Edward of Woodstock, Prince of Wales and Aquitaine and Duke of Cornwall, had been ill ever since his Spanish campaign of 1367, and it cannot have been much of a surprise when he died on 8 June 1376, a week before his 46 birthday. He was buried at Canterbury Cathedral, and the heir to the English throne was now his 9-year-old son Richard of Bordeaux, acknowledged as such by Edward III and made Prince of Wales. The question of the succession after Richard, however, was pressing. In October 1376, not long after his son's funeral, Edward III made an entail declaring Richard his heir, but excluding his granddaughter Philippa of

Clarence, only child of his late second son Lionel of Antwerp, from the succession. He stated that his third son John of Gaunt and his male heirs came after Richard in the succession, followed by Edmund of Langley and his male heirs, then Thomas of Woodstock and his. There was no doubt that the king considered his grandson Richard, son of his eldest son, as his successor, though English history had a precedent whereby John of Gaunt might be considered the rightful successor to the throne instead. On the death of Richard Lionheart in 1199, Richard's youngest brother John had become king instead of their nephew Arthur of Brittany, son of John's dead older brother Geoffrey. Edward of Woodstock had died before becoming king, and therefore Richard of Bordeaux was, like Arthur of Brittany, not the son of a king, whereas his uncles John, Edmund and Thomas, like King John, were. They also had the advantage of being adults, whereas it was perfectly clear that Edward III could not live much longer and that the next King of England would be a child. The King of Navarre, Carlos II 'the Bad', told the Count of Flanders sometime between 1372 and 1376 that he had heard John of Gaunt wished to declare his nephew Richard illegitimate and rule in his place, though when Richard did become king, John supported him faithfully for the rest of his life.

England was now ruled by a man in decline, with a young boy waiting to succeed him. The most powerful man in England was John of Gaunt, Duke of Lancaster; he was also the most loathed.

THE CHILD KING

Richard of Bordeaux, his uncle Thomas of Woodstock and his cousin Henry of Lancaster were knighted on 23 April 1377 during the annual festivities to mark the feast of St George. Both Richard and Henry were 10, and Henry began to be known as Earl of Derby around this time. Also knighted were the king's illegitimate son, John de Southeray, and the sons of the Earls of Stafford and Salisbury; Eleanor of Lancaster's grandsons John Beaumont and John Arundel; Joan of Lancaster's 11-year-old grandson John Mowbray; Mary of Lancaster's three Percy grandsons Henry 'Hotspur', Thomas and Ralph; and Maud of Lancaster's grandson, the 15-year-old heir to the earldom of Oxford and Richard of Bordeaux's future great favourite, Robert de Vere. It is interesting to note that of the thirteen boys and young men knighted in April 1377, no fewer than eight were great-grandsons of Henry, Earl of Lancaster (d. 1345). Richard of Bordeaux and his cousin Henry of Lancaster were also made Knights of the Garter in April 1377, although for some reason Edward III did not induct his youngest son Thomas of Woodstock into the order, and it was left to Richard to do so in 1380. Maud of Lancaster, Dowager Countess of Ulster and a canoness for the previous thirty years, died on 5 May 1377 not long after the knighting of her grandson Robert de Vere, in her mid 60s or so; she had lived long enough to see the births of her great-grandchildren

Elizabeth, Roger, Philippa and Edmund Mortimer, children of Philippa of Clarence. Her death left her eldest sister Blanche Wake as the only surviving child of Henry, Earl of Lancaster and Maud Chaworth.

Maud's cousin Edward III outlived her by a few weeks, dying at the royal palace of Sheen west of London on 21 June 1377, aged 64, after a reign of fifty years and six months. He was buried at Westminster Abbey on 5 July, and the coronation of his 10-year-old grandson Richard II took place also at Westminster Abbey on 16 July 1377. The English nobility jostled for position and favours and to be allowed to perform ritual duties during the ceremony and at the magnificent banquet afterwards. John of Gaunt carried the Sword of Mercy, Curtana, during the procession, and at the banquet Henry of Lancaster stood in front of Richard holding Curtana. Eleanor of Lancaster's son the Earl of Arundel acted as butler, Maud of Lancaster's grandson Robert de Vere acted as chamberlain, served the king with water and removed his basins and towels, and Mary of Lancaster's son Henry Percy acted as marshal, 'appeasing debates in the king's house, assigning lodgings and guarding the door of the king's chamber'. Percy, now 35, was made Earl of Northumberland on the day of the coronation, and Joan of Lancaster's grandson John Mowbray, born in 1365 and not quite 12, became Earl of Nottingham (the *Anonimalle* chronicler called him 'the son of Mowbray').[1] Edward III's youngest son Thomas of Woodstock finally gained a title and became Earl of Buckingham, and Richard II knighted several young noblemen including his cousin Edward of York, son of Edmund of Langley and Isabel of Castile, who was only 3 or 4 years old. The *Anonimalle* chronicle claims that Edward was made Earl of Colchester, but there is no other evidence of this and it appears to be an error or misunderstanding. A few months after the coronation, Richard II, or someone acting in his name, gave his uncle John of Gaunt a 'new inn lately built by Alice Perrers, near the Thames', and all the houses adjoining 'the great gate of the said inn'. Perrers had been Edward III's mistress and for a few years enjoyed considerable favour and expensive gifts, which came to an abrupt end on the day the old king died. The following year, John gave her inn and houses to his brother Edmund of Langley.[2]

The early years of the reign of England's child-king were mostly quiet, though French forces landed in England in June 1377 only days after the death of Edward III and the end of a two-year truce signed in June 1375 and attacked the Isle of Wight and burnt the town of Rye. No regent was appointed, though a council took care of business in the young king's name, and Richard's royal uncles and his mother Joan of Kent were active and influential. Edmund of Langley was appointed Constable of Dover Castle and Warden of the Cinque Ports.[3] The king's relationships with John of Gaunt and Thomas of Woodstock fluctuated dramatically throughout his reign; at one point, Richard was told that John intended to kill him and ordered John's execution in a fit of rage, though fortunately he soon calmed down. The two men were sometimes at loggerheads, though when John left England for three years in the late 1380s, Richard missed his calming influence, and after his return was on good terms with him for the rest of his uncle's life. As for Thomas, uncle and nephew came to loathe each other, and Richard would order Thomas' death. Edmund of Langley, a calm and peaceful man, enjoyed cordial relations with his nephew throughout the reign, and in and after the mid 1390s rose high in his favour. This says something about Edmund's excellent interpersonal skills, as the highly emotional Richard was often a very difficult man to get on with, and Edmund's managing to stay on his good side for more than twenty years was a real achievement not often acknowledged.

Europe saw the beginning of the Great Schism in 1378 when two Popes, Urban VI and Clement VII, were elected in strict opposition to each other. England supported the Rome Pope Urban, France the Avignon Pope Clement, and the rest of Europe split on pre-existing political lines in their support. The Schism was to bring Richard II a bride: the young King of Germany and Bohemia, Václav, also favoured the Rome Pope, and offered his half-sister Anne of Bohemia as Richard's wife. Richard's counsellors had been contemplating a match for him with the wealthy and powerful Visconti rulers of Milan – his uncle Lionel of Antwerp had married into the family in 1368 – but negotiations were overtaken by the Schism, and it was not to be.

In late 1379 Richard, or rather his counsellors, sent Eleanor of Lancaster's son Sir John Arundel, Admiral of England, to aid Richard's brother-in-law Duke John IV of Brittany against his internal enemies. Arundel set off, but was caught up in a terrible storm and drowned off the coast of Ireland on 15 December 1379. Three chroniclers give the unpleasant story that John Arundel allowed his men to rob the poor and to rape women on their way to the coast, and that they abducted a group of nuns and subsequently threw them overboard to lighten the load on their ships during the nine-day storm. To what extent any of this is true is not completely clear, but it seems to have been a widely told story in the late fourteenth century. John's heir was his 15-year-old son John, eldest of his seven children, who had been knighted in 1377 with Richard of Bordeaux and Henry of Lancaster, Earl of Derby. Custody of the younger John was given to his uncle Richard, who had been Earl of Arundel since the death of his father of the same name in 1376.[4]

On 3, 9 or 10 July 1380, Blanche, Lady Wake, finally passed away. She was at least in her mid 70s and perhaps older, had married as far back as 1316, and had been a widow for thirty-one years. Born in the reign of her great-uncle Edward I, she lived into the reign of his great-great-grandson Richard II. Blanche asked to be buried not next to her husband Thomas at his foundation of Haltemprice Priory in Yorkshire but at the Franciscan church in Stamford, Lincolnshire, which might reveal that their marriage had not been a particularly happy one (though it was not that uncommon for women to choose not to be buried next to their husbands). Blanche called herself 'Blanche of Lancaster, Lady Wake' in her will, and appointed her niece Joan, Countess of Hereford, as one of the will's supervisors. The heir to Blanche's dower lands was Thomas Wake's niece Joan of Kent, the king's mother – who would be buried at the same church as Blanche some years later, next to her husband Thomas Holland – and Blanche's other heir was Henry of Lancaster, Earl of Derby, grandson of her only brother Grosmont.[5] Richard II's first cousin Philippa of Clarence and her husband Edmund Mortimer, Earl of March, also both died at the beginning of the 1380s, both still only in their 20s, leaving their 7-year-old son Roger Mortimer as their heir and their three other children Elizabeth, Philippa and Edmund.

Henry of Lancaster's elder sister Elizabeth married in the summer of 1380: the groom was John Hastings, heir to the earldom of Pembroke and grandson and co-heir of Margaret, Countess of Norfolk. It was an unlikely match, as Elizabeth (b. February 1363) was a decade older than John (b. November 1372), and it ended in annulment some years later before it was ever consummated. John of Gaunt referred to Elizabeth after her wedding as 'our daughter of Pembroke', and continued to pay £100 annually for her expenses.[6] Sometime before 4 May 1381 John paid £50 for pearls to be given to his eldest daughter Philippa of Lancaster, not yet married, and to his mistress Katherine Swynford.[7] By the end of the 1370s, John and Katherine had four children together: John, Henry, Thomas and Joan Beaufort. John of Gaunt also sent gifts for the wedding of his niece, Constance of York, and Thomas Despenser, son and heir of the late Lord Despenser and a descendant of Edward I, who married in or before November 1379. Edmund of Langley had been granted Thomas' marriage, 'for the purpose of marrying the said heir to his daughter', on 16 April 1378.[8] It was yet another marriage of children: Thomas, born in September 1373, was only 6 when he wed, and Constance no more than 5 and perhaps only 3. Richard II granted his cousin Constance an income of 80 marks a year for her sustenance in January 1384, during her husband's minority (Thomas Despenser, who lost his father when he was 2, would not come of age until September 1394).[9] Constance was made a Lady of the Garter in 1386, when she was no more than 12 and probably younger.

Henry of Lancaster, Earl of Derby, married his second cousin Mary de Bohun, younger daughter and co-heir of the late Earl of Hereford, on 5 February 1381; Henry's cousin the king and their uncle Edmund of Langley both sent minstrels to perform for the couple, and Edmund was probably present in person. Henry's sisters Philippa and Elizabeth of Lancaster also attended, and each gave their new sister-in-law a goblet and ewer.[10] Richard II had granted Mary's marriage to John of Gaunt on 27 July 1380 in exchange for 5,000 marks, which John did not have to pay as a larger sum was owed to him for his war wages.[11] As a result of his marriage, Henry not only had the vast Lancastrian inheritance, including the earldoms of Leicester, Lincoln, Richmond and Derby and the dukedom of Lancaster, to look forward to one day, but he and Mary would also hold half the earldoms of Hereford, Essex and Northampton. Henry was not yet 14 when he married and Mary 11 or 12, and she remained with her mother Joan (née Fitzalan) for the time being. Mary's elder sister Eleanor was married to Henry's uncle Thomas of Woodstock, Earl of Buckingham, and supposedly the couple had wished Mary to take vows as a nun so that they could enjoy the entire de Bohun inheritance. Chronicler Jean Froissart claimed that John of Gaunt abducted Mary de Bohun from Thomas' Essex manor of Pleshey, and whether that is true or not, the wedding took place at Rochford, also in Essex, one of Mary's mother Joan's manors.

Joan played an important role in arranging her daughter's marriage to the greatest heir in the country, and was as formidable a character as her late mother, Eleanor of Lancaster. Richard II paid the countess £40 annually for her daughter's upkeep, and on 31 January 1382 John of Gaunt gave 100 marks annually to 'our very dear and very well-beloved cousin Lady Johanne de Boun [Bohun]' for her expenses looking after his daughter-in-law until Mary reached the age of 14.[12] The son assigned to Henry of Lancaster and Mary de Bohun by some modern historians, supposedly born in April 1382 when Mary was still a child herself, was in fact her nephew Humphrey of Gloucester, first child of her elder sister Eleanor and Thomas of Woodstock.[13] Henry and Mary's first child Henry of Monmouth, the future Henry V, was born in September 1386 when his father was 19 and his mother 16 or 17. Henry of Lancaster's mother and mother-in-law were first cousins, and his children were descended from Henry, Earl of Lancaster (d. 1345) and the earl's uncle Edward I (d. 1307) several times over. His wife's sister was married to his uncle, meaning that the children of Eleanor de Bohun and Thomas of Woodstock were both his first cousins and his nephews and nieces.

In June 1381, England erupted into chaos during the Great Uprising, or Peasants' Revolt as it used to be known, when large groups of people descended on London in a fury at the imposition of an unfair poll tax and at their less than ideal social circumstances. Richard II, just 14, bravely faced the rebels in person, though his departure from the Tower of London was the cue for an invasion of the fortification, and the chancellor and treasurer of England were dragged out and summarily beheaded. Henry of Lancaster, also just 14 and inside the Tower, was saved from the mob by a man called John Ferrour; perhaps he hid Henry or beat off the rebels trying to seize him. We do not know how he saved the boy's life, but Henry never forgot it. His father's great palace of the Savoy, rebuilt in grand style by Duke Henry in the 1350s, was razed to the ground by the rebels and left a smoking ruin; John's clothes, jewels, gold and silver vessels and countless other precious possessions were thrown into the Thames, and by the time the rebels were finished scarcely one stone of the building stood on top of another.[14] Fortunately for John, he had recently been appointed to extend the truce between England and Scotland and left London before the rebellion began, or he would certainly have ended up murdered and his head paraded around on a spike. Even in distant Yorkshire, however, Duchess Constanza was not safe: John's constable at Pontefract Castle refused to allow her to enter, and she and her household were forced to travel on to Knaresborough.[15] According to his Register,

John was at Knaresborough Castle on 28 June 1381, Bamburgh on 14 July
and Pontefract on 22 July.[16]

John and his late wife Blanche's first cousin, Henry Percy, Earl of
Northumberland, had a furious row in the summer and autumn of 1381
over Northumberland's alleged refusal to shelter John during the uprising.
Several chroniclers wrote extensively about it, claiming that the quarrel between the two powerful noblemen threatened to destroy England,
and Northumberland refused to climb down; he and John almost came
to blows during a feast at Westminster, and subsequently both brought
large armed retinues to London. In the end, however, Northumberland
was forced to make a grovelling apology to John on his knees in
November 1381. Addressing him as *Monseigneur d'Espaigne* or 'my lord of
Spain', Northumberland stated:

> In the presence of my very dread lord the king, in my ignorance
> I answered you in another way than I should have done, my lord, who are
> son of my very dread liege lord the king, whom God absolve, and uncle
> of my very dread liege lord the present king, and of such high person and
> of such very noble and royal blood as you are, my lord.

He went on in similar vein, stating that God knew it was never his wish to
be disobedient to the greatest man in the realm after the king, and he submitted himself to John's good lordship, which he desired with all his heart.[17]
The two men had previously been close allies, even friends, and there seems
little doubt that John was deeply hurt by what he saw as a personal betrayal
by a man he had thought he could rely on. The Westminster chronicler
talked of 'hearts warped by passion' and 'intensified ill-feeling between the
estranged nobles'.[18] John and Northumberland had been close, and in 1377
were enjoying a lunch of oysters when they were interrupted by a mob and
forced to flee together across the Thames.[19]

Edmund of Langley, Earl of Cambridge, was away from England at the
time of the uprising: he had travelled to Portugal, an ally of England, in
May 1381 to aid the kingdom against the frequent raids by the kingdom
of Castile, formerly England's ally and now France's. It was arranged that
Edmund's son Edward of York would marry King Fernando of Portugal's
only surviving child Beatriz, and the two youngsters, who were both born
in 1373 or 1374, were duly married or betrothed. This would have made

them joint rulers of Portugal one day, but the marriage was annulled in 1382 and Beatriz never became queen; her father was succeeded in 1383 by his illegitimate half-brother João I, later the husband of Philippa of Lancaster. Beatriz instead married Juan I of Castile, son of the usurper Enrique of Trastamara, but was not the mother of his heir Enrique III, and died in obscurity in about 1420. Edmund of Langley's campaign ended ignominiously, his troops went out of control, and Fernando went behind his back and made peace with Castile. Edmund and his retinue, who included a Gascon knight called Soldan Delatran, returned to England in late 1382.[20]

Richard II married Anne of Bohemia on 20 January 1382, two weeks after his 15th birthday. Anne, who was eight months his senior, was the daughter of the Holy Roman Emperor Karl IV (d. 1378), half-sister of the King of Germany and Bohemia and full sister of the King of Hungary and Croatia and future Holy Roman Emperor Zikmund, and on her mother's side was descended from kings of Poland and dukes of Lithuania and Pomerania. The royal marriage was to prove a very happy and close one, though in their twelve and a half years together the couple had no children, though possibly Anne had a miscarriage or several. As Richard had no children, no surviving full siblings and no nieces and nephews, the result was many years of uncertainty over the succession and, decades later, war between the houses of Lancaster and York as they battled over the throne. Throughout Richard's reign, it was never entirely clear who his rightful successor was: his uncle John of Gaunt, third son of Edward III, followed by John's son Henry of Lancaster; or Roger Mortimer, Earl of March (b. 1374), grandson of Edward's late second son Lionel of Antwerp and heir of his mother Philippa of Clarence, who died in 1381. The question of whether the descendants of Edward III's second son in the female line or Edward III's third son in the male line had precedence continued to vex England throughout the fifteenth century.

THE FIRST DUKE OF YORK

———⊗⊗⊗———

J oan of Lancaster's grandson John Mowbray, Earl of Nottingham, died on 8 February 1383 at the age of 17½, leaving his younger brother Thomas as his heir.[1] Thomas was created Earl of Nottingham four days later, on 12 February, despite his youth (he was probably not yet 16), and on 30 June 1385 was made Earl Marshal of England for life, a title once held by his great-grandfather Thomas of Brotherton, Earl of Norfolk. Richard II commented on his wish to do 'further honour' to Thomas Mowbray 'according to his merits and illustrious birth'.[2] Probably sometime in 1384, without the king's permission, Mowbray married Elizabeth Fitzalan, eldest daughter of the earl of Arundel and granddaughter of Eleanor of Lancaster. The two teenagers, young as they were, had both been married before: Thomas to the daughter and heir of Lord Lestrange of Blackmere, and Elizabeth to the Earl of Salisbury's only son William Montacute, who had tragically been killed jousting in August 1382 by his own father. Thomas and Elizabeth were both great-grandchildren of Henry, Earl of Lancaster and Maud Chaworth, and hence second cousins. Their first son Thomas Mowbray the younger was born in September 1385, and their second son and ultimate heir John, ancestor of the Dukes of Norfolk, in June 1390.

Richard II's youngest uncle Thomas of Woodstock, Earl of Buckingham, was raising a family with his young wife Eleanor de Bohun, daughter of the late Earl of Hereford and another granddaughter of Eleanor of Lancaster. Their son Humphrey of Gloucester was born in April 1382 when Eleanor de Bohun was 16 or almost, and their eldest daughter Anne, future Countess of Stafford and ancestor of the Dukes of Buckingham and the Earls of Essex, was born on or a little before 6 May 1383 when her uncle John of Gaunt sent gifts for her baptism at Pleshey in Essex. He also gave generous gifts of cash to his little niece's attendants, including 13 shillings to her 'rocker' sent 'in the name of our son of Derby', i.e. Henry of Lancaster. John referred to Thomas of Woodstock simply as 'our brother of Buckingham', not 'our very dear brother' as would have been customary, which, in combination with his failure to send Thomas presents on two occasions in the early 1370s when he sent them to the rest of his family, perhaps reveals something about his relationship with his much younger brother. John had recently been visited by a German knight called 'Sir Poto' who presented him with a destrier (an expensive war-horse) on his departure.[3]

In the summer of 1385, Richard II upgraded the titles of his youngest uncles, Edmund of Langley and Thomas of Woodstock, making them Duke of York and Duke of Gloucester respectively. He also made Edmund Justice of Chester for life. The king gave Edmund an income of £500 a year to aid 'the support of his family becomingly', but this was a sum Edmund had been promised as far back as November 1377 and had struggled ever to obtain, and besides, the amount was not much for a royal duke and the son of a king. The amount was upgraded to £1,000 a year, though one wonders if Edmund ever managed to obtain it.[4] By way of comparison, Edmund's brother John of Gaunt enjoyed an annual income of about £12,000. And although promoting two sons of a king to the same title as their older brothers was entirely expected and uncontroversial, Richard also gave Maud of Lancaster's grandson Robert de Vere, Earl of Oxford, who was his closest friend and perhaps his lover, the title of Marquis of Dublin, which gave de Vere precedence over all the English earls. The following year, Richard made de Vere Duke of Ireland as well. Previously the only English dukes had been Edward III's sons, i.e. Richard's father and uncles, and the royal cousin Henry of Grosmont. Robert de Vere was a nobleman of ancient and impeccable lineage and married to the king's cousin Philippa Coucy (daughter of Edward III's eldest daughter, Isabella of Woodstock), but was not of royal birth, and his elevation caused a scandal.

Another man prominent at court, and despised, was Richard's former tutor Sir Simon Burley, on whom Richard may have wished to bestow the earldom of Huntingdon when it fell vacant in 1380, but could not, owing to Burley's unpopularity. In 1387 a group of five noblemen formed themselves into a group called the Lords Appellant, because they intended to appeal the king's allies and supporters, especially Robert de Vere and Simon Burley, for treason. The three eldest noblemen were Richard Fitzalan, Earl of Arundel, Eleanor of Lancaster's son; Thomas Beauchamp, Earl of Warwick; and the king's uncle Thomas of Woodstock, Duke of Gloucester. Joining them, surprisingly, were Richard's cousin Henry of Lancaster, Earl of Derby, and Henry's second cousin Thomas Mowbray, Earl of Nottingham. Thomas was Arundel's son-in-law, which might explain his change of allegiance; he was usually an ally and friend of the king.

Henry of Lancaster caught Robert de Vere unawares at Radcot Bridge in December 1387, when de Vere was bringing an army south to Richard. De Vere escaped and fled abroad; Richard would never see him again, and de Vere died in exile in 1392 at the age of only 30. His mother Maud (née Ufford), was pardoned in 1391 for going to visit her son in Brabant and taking him gifts.[5] The Lords Appellant held a long Parliament in London in 1388 that was notorious for its vindictiveness and brutality, and became known as the Merciless Parliament. Many of Richard II's supporters were executed, including his friend and former tutor Sir Simon Burley. Richard was helpless to protect them – both his queen Anne of Bohemia and his uncle Edmund of Langley pleaded with the Appellants to spare Burley, to no avail – but kept his rage and grief inside him, and a decade later was to take revenge on the Appellants. The Appellants also expelled some ladies from court, including Joan of Lancaster's much-married daughter Blanche, Lady Poynings, a favourite of the king who spent much time at court and often received presents from Richard (her relationship with him was, given the large age difference of more than a quarter of a century, presumably maternal rather than romantic).

In 1385, Richard's half-brother John Holland killed the king's good friend Ralph Stafford, heir to the earldom of Stafford, in a violent rage. Ralph's father Hugh, Earl of Stafford, went on pilgrimage soon afterwards to the church of the Holy Sepulchre in Jerusalem and died on the island of Rhodes during the journey. Richard II, utterly furious with his half-brother, refused at first to pardon him, even when their dying mother Joan of Kent pleaded with him to do so. The Dowager Princess of Wales and Aquitaine died in August 1385 in her late 50s, and was buried at Stamford in Lincolnshire with her husband Thomas Holland and near her aunt-in-law Blanche of Lancaster, Lady Wake. John of Gaunt left England for Castile in June 1386, taking his daughters Philippa, Elizabeth and Catalina with him; his son and heir Henry remained in England, and joined the Appellants. Elizabeth of Lancaster married John Holland shortly before their departure, and apparently was already pregnant by him. Her unconsummated marriage to John Hastings, heir to the earldom of Pembroke, who was still only 13 in the summer of 1386 to Elizabeth's 23, had to be hastily annulled. While John of Gaunt was in Spain, his son and heir Henry began to build a family with Mary de Bohun, who was pregnant with their eldest son Henry of Monmouth when John sailed from England. Monmouth was born that September. Their second son Thomas of Lancaster was born in about August 1387, their third, John, on 20 June 1389, and their fourth, Humphrey, probably in September 1390 after John's return to England.[6]

John of Gaunt had hoped to claim the kingdom of Castile for himself and his wife Constanza at last, but it was not to be; he would never be anything more than a king in name only. Like his first wife Blanche's great-grandfather Edmund, the first Lancaster, he yearned for a crown but never wore one. Perhaps the marriages of his daughters provided some small consolation. In February 1387, Philippa of Lancaster, almost 27, married the King of Portugal, João I, and a few months later her 15-year-old half-sister Catalina married her 9-year-old cousin, the future King Enrique III, grandson of Enrique of Trastamara who had usurped the throne of Catalina's grandfather Pedro the Cruel. The two rival Castilian royal lines were now united. Edmund of Langley and his wife Isabel, Pedro's younger daughter, were not compensated for giving up any claims to the Castilian throne, or apparently even consulted about their wishes on the matter.

Both Philippa and Catalina of Lancaster had children, and John of Gaunt was the grandfather of two Iberian kings, Duarte I of Portugal and Juan II of Castile. Catalina of Lancaster was the grandmother of the great Spanish queen Isabel 'the Catholic' of Castile, and the great-grandmother of Katherine of Aragon, who married Henry VIII of England and who was presumably named after Catalina. Philippa of Lancaster's children, the Illustrious Generation, included Henrique or Henry the Navigator, one of the great early explorers, Isabel, Duchess of Burgundy, and Fernando, the Holy Prince. Philippa named her eldest child, who died in infancy, after her mother Blanche of Lancaster, and her eldest son Duarte after her grandfather Edward III.

Back in England, Richard II finally declared himself of age and able to rule in his own right in May 1389, when he was 22. Later in the year, he ordered his uncle John of Gaunt to come home to England from Spain and treated him with conspicuous favour; time and distance had dulled the king's occasional hostility to John, and he came to appreciate John's support, unending loyalty and sound advice. The 17-year-old heir to the earldom of Pembroke and former husband of John's daughter Elizabeth of Lancaster, John Hastings, was killed during the Christmas jousting at the palace of Woodstock in 1389. Hastings' widow Philippa (née Mortimer), still only 14 but in possession of a small fortune as her Pembroke dower, married her second husband in August 1390: he was Richard Fitzalan, Earl of Arundel, thirty years her senior and a widower since the death of the Earl of Hereford's sister Elizabeth de Bohun in 1385. Philippa and Arundel were first cousins twice removed, as he was the son of Eleanor of Lancaster, and she was the great-granddaughter of Eleanor's elder sister Maud of Lancaster, Countess of Ulster. They married without Richard II's permission and without a proper papal dispensation for consanguinity, and paid a fine of 400 marks for failing to marry without a royal licence in November 1391, a few weeks after the Pope declared their marriage legal.[7] Despite the huge age difference, the marriage was a happy one, and by March 1392 Arundel had renamed his castle at Shrawardine 'Castle Philippa' in his wife's honour.[8]

Henry of Lancaster set off on crusade to Lithuania in the summer of 1390, following in his grandfather Henry of Grosmont's footsteps almost four decades before, and thus missed the birth of his fourth son, Humphrey of Lancaster, and a great jousting tournament held by Richard II at Smithfield in October 1390. While travelling around Europe, Henry met Queen Anne's half-brother Václav, King of Germany and Bohemia, and her full brother Zikmund, King of Hungary and Croatia and a future Holy Roman Emperor, whom his son would make a Knight of the Garter many years later. In 1392–93, Henry also undertook a pilgrimage to Jerusalem, after a second voyage to Lithuania. He was still only 23 in 1390, but had four sons with Mary de Bohun, and in 1392 and 1394 they were to have daughters as well, named Blanche after Henry's mother and Philippa after his late grandmother Philippa of Hainault. His fertility contrasted sharply with his cousin the king's: after almost a decade of marriage, Richard II and Anne of Bohemia had no children, and were never to have any. If they had had a son or sons who lived, England would almost certainly have avoided the Wars of the Roses.

The exiled Robert de Vere, Earl of Oxford, defeated by Henry of Lancaster at Radcot Bridge in December 1387, died in Louvain in 1392, aged 30. His body was returned to England and buried at Earl's Colne in Essex with the rest of the de Veres, and both the king and de Vere's mother Maud (née Ufford) attended the funeral. Countess Maud, who was something of a troublemaker, was accused a few years later of having the prior of Earl's Colne assaulted and imprisoned by her men, and of dragging him around Essex 'shamefully clad'. Maud launched a counter-accusation that the brothers of Earl's Colne Priory besieged her in her mansion in the village and 'threatened her with arson and other evils so that for a long time she dared not leave it'.[9]

Richard II never took another favourite after Robert de Vere, though later in the 1390s showed great favour to his cousin Edward of York, and in February 1393 retained John Beaumont (b. 1361), Eleanor of Lancaster's grandson from her first marriage, as one of his household knights and also showed him much favour.[10] The two men had been knighted together in 1377. In 1395 Beaumont founded a chantry to celebrate divine service for himself, the king, John of Gaunt, and Beaumont's half-uncle Thomas Arundel, Eleanor of Lancaster's youngest son and Archbishop of York since 1388 (and to be made Archbishop of Canterbury in 1396).[11] Like his half-uncle John Arundel, Beaumont was an admiral, and was Warden of the Cinque Ports and Dover Castle and appointed Warden of the Scottish March with his kinsman Henry 'Hotspur' Percy, Mary of Lancaster's grandson.[12]

Isabel of Castile, Duchess of York, died on 23 December 1392 aged only about 37, leaving her three children Edward of York, Constance Despenser and Richard of Conisbrough. Isabel asked Richard II to look after her youngest child Richard, his godson, and the king did show much generosity to his cousin. Isabel left a crown to her son Edward, a fret of pearls to her daughter Constance, a tablet of jasper given to her a few years before by King Levon of Armenia (who visited England in late 1385) to her brother-in-law John of Gaunt, and a gold tablet to her sister-in-law Eleanor (née de Bohun), Duchess of Gloucester. She left nothing to her husband.[13]

He buried her at Langley Priory in Hertfordshire, his birthplace, and where his nephew Richard II had recently buried his elder brother Edward of Angoulême (he had the body brought from the south of France where it had originally been interred). A few months later, in about November 1393, Edmund of Langley married his second wife Joan Holland. She was the second of the five daughters of Richard II's half-brother Thomas, Earl of Kent, and Alice Fitzalan. Joan's elder sister Alianore – or Eleanor in modern spelling – was the Countess of March and Ulster, having married Roger Mortimer in or before 1388, and they had three younger sisters, Margaret, a second Eleanor and Elizabeth, and two brothers, Thomas and Edmund. (Alice Holland (née Fitzalan) named two of her five daughters after her mother Eleanor of Lancaster.) Joan Holland's date of birth is usually estimated as about 1380, but as she was the second Holland daughter and Alianore the eldest was born *c.* 1373, Joan may have been some years older, perhaps born in 1375/76.[14] At any rate, the new Duchess of York was decades younger than Edmund, and a teenager when she married her 52-year-old husband. Her stepson Edward of York was older than she, and perhaps her stepdaughter Constance Despenser as well.

At the Parliament of January 1394, John of Gaunt petitioned for his son Henry to be recognised as the king's heir, and allegedly raised a story that his first wife Blanche's great-grandfather Edmund of Lancaster, or Edmund 'Crouchback', had been the elder son of Henry III but was set aside in favour of his brother Edward I on the grounds of his physical deformity. He did so in a row with the young Roger Mortimer, Earl of March – his great-nephew – over the rightful succession to the throne. Richard II interceded and told both men to be quiet.[15] As it seems that John of Gaunt did not himself invent the legend but was merely repeating it, the question arises of precisely when, how and by whom the story of Edmund of Lancaster's deformity was first told. This is a difficult question to answer, but it seems clear that the tale does not date to Edmund of Lancaster's own lifetime – he died in 1296 – but to sometime in the fourteenth century. Whatever John's interests in promoting his son's claims to the throne, it is hard to understand why he would publicly push the story. If nothing else, it would make his own father Edward III a usurper on the throne, and would therefore make his own high rank and status as a king's son open to question.

John supposedly 'said that King Henry III had two sons, Edmund the firstborn and Edward. But Edmund had a crooked back and judged himself unworthy for the crown; whence their father arranged it that Edward should reign and after him the heirs of Edmund'.[16] Edward I, according to this version of events, was rightful King of England by the choice of his father, but Edward should have been succeeded by his nephew Thomas of Lancaster on his death in 1307 and subsequently by Thomas' younger brother Henry and Henry's descendants, not his son Edward II and then his grandson Edward III. The story was, as John himself and everyone else knew, utter nonsense: Edward I (b. June 1239) was five and a half years older than his brother Edmund (b. January 1245).

Joan Holland, the teenaged Duchess of York, became the second lady in England after Queen Anne when Constanza of Castile, Duchess of Lancaster, died on 24 March 1394 at the age of about 40. Whether Constanza's marriage to John of Gaunt and her life in England had been happy or satisfactory is impossible to say, and her only child Catalina was far away in Constanza's native Castile when her mother died. John buried his duchess at the Newarke in Leicester, the hospital founded by his first wife's grandfather Henry, Earl of Lancaster in 1330 and considerably extended into a collegiate church by Henry's son Grosmont, John's father-in-law. One historian states that John buried Constanza 'in relative obscurity' at Leicester, but that hardly seems fair to John (or to Constanza), as the Newarke was the mausoleum of the Lancasters and the foundation and burial place of two of the most esteemed English noblemen of the entire fourteenth century.[17] John's son Henry IV was to state ten years later that his brothers, presumably meaning John's sons with Blanche of Lancaster who died young, were buried at the Newarke, and Henry's wife Mary was buried there too. John was honouring Constanza, not burying her somewhere obscure and forgotten.

As well as his stepmother Constanza, Henry of Lancaster, Earl of Derby, lost his wife Mary de Bohun in 1394. Barely even 25, she died in June after giving birth to her sixth child and second daughter, Philippa of Lancaster. Duchess Constanza's funeral took place at the Newarke on 5 July, and the following day Mary was buried there as well. In 1400 after he had become King of England, Henry of Lancaster sent twenty-four masons, carpenters and others to work on the still uncompleted Newarke. Their eldest child Henry of Monmouth was not yet 8 when he lost his mother, and after he succeeded his father as king in 1413 had an effigy of his mother made and placed on her tomb.[18] And the king also became a widower when

Queen Anne died at the Palace of Sheen on 7 June 1394, the third death in what was a truly horrible year for the women of the English royal family. Anne was buried at Westminster Abbey two months later. Richard II's awful grief was visible in April 1395 when he ordered the Palace of Sheen, where he had spent much time with his wife, to be pulled down to the ground, and he assaulted the Earl of Arundel during her funeral when Arundel arrived late and tactlessly asked for permission to leave early, and imprisoned him in the Tower. Richard was now 27 years old and had no immediate prospect of fathering children. The question of the succession to the throne remained as urgent as ever.

A SECOND SOLOMON

⊸∞∞∞⊸

E dmund of Langley's elder son Edward of York began to play an important role in politics in the mid 1390s, now in his early 20s. He had been made Earl of Rutland on 25 February 1390, by 1392 was a member of the royal council and was made Constable of the Tower of London for life after Richard's half-brother the Earl of Kent died, was appointed Admiral of England, and in 1395 accompanied the king to Ireland. One early grant made to Edward, in March 1388 when he was only about 14 – custody of the lands of one Thomas Bekering, who was reported to be dead – had to be revoked when it transpired that Bekering was still alive and appeared before chancery to prove it.[1] It is possible that Edward had been seriously ill in October 1391: he arranged for his debts to be paid 'in case he die before his father'.[2] As Edward was only 17 or 18 then and his father 50, it seems odd that he was preparing for the eventuality of debt settlement after his own death and in Edmund's lifetime unless there was something badly wrong with him, but if so, he recovered. Edward of York was often at court with his cousin in the 1390s, as revealed by the numerous grants, favours and pardons made at his request: the words 'at the supplication of the king's cousin the Earl of Rutland' appear frequently in the chancery rolls. He and Thomas Arundel, Archbishop of York and Eleanor of Lancaster's fourth and youngest son, were appointed custodians of the lands, castles and goods of the late Queen Anne.[3] Edward was made Constable of England as well as Admiral, and in the late 1390s was addressed as 'Earl of Cork' in Ireland as well as Earl of Rutland; his fond cousin the king piled him with honours and appointments.

On or shortly after 14 January 1396, the twice-widowed John of Gaunt took the remarkable step of marrying his long-term mistress Katherine Swynford. This decision did not meet, to put it mildly, with univer-sal approval. John's brother Thomas of Woodstock, Duke of Gloucester, declared that he would never acknowledge Katherine as his sister, and their great-niece Philippa Fitzalan (née Mortimer), Countess of Pembroke and Arundel, and Thomas' wife Eleanor (née de Bohun) led the group of court ladies who refused to give the new duchess and first lady of England precedence. Richard II was friendly towards his new aunt, however, and the year after the wedding, John and Katherine's children, John, Henry, Thomas and Joan Beaufort, were legitimised. The eldest, John, was made Earl of Somerset. Before 28 September 1397, John Beaufort married Richard II's half-niece Margaret Holland, third daughter of the recently deceased Earl of Kent, sister of the Duchess of York and the Countess of March, and one of Eleanor of Lancaster's numerous granddaughters.[4] Margaret and John Beaufort's half-dozen children, born in the early 1400s, included Joan, queen consort of Scotland as the wife of King James I, and Edmund, Duke of Somerset, who was killed at the Battle of St Albans in 1455. Their grand-daughter Margaret Beaufort, only legitimate child of their second son John, was the mother of Henry VII.

Richard's uncles John of Gaunt and Thomas of Woodstock and their wives and children, and his kinsmen Edward of York and Thomas Mowbray, accompanied him to France when he married his second wife Isabelle, eldest daughter of Charles VI, in early November 1396. Edmund of Langley was left behind in England as regent, as he had been the year before when the king visited Ireland. Isabelle of France was still a child; she turned 7 five days after her wedding, and her dolls and toys accompanied her to England. Richard had made it clear to his advisers that he would accept only a king's daughter as his bride, and the choice of Isabelle sealed a peace settlement with France intended to last until 1426 (hardly surprisingly, it did not), but the new Queen of England would not be able to give her husband children for at least eight years, when Richard would be close to 40. As the question of the succession was still so urgent, marrying a child was hardly the most sensible step he could have taken. The English and French also discussed the possibility that two of Charles VI's younger daughters could marry Richard's cousin Edward of York and his cousin Henry of Lancaster's eldest son Henry of Monmouth, though ultimately nothing came of it (Henry of Monmouth did ultimately marry Charles' youngest daughter Katherine in 1420 when he was king, but she was not born until 1401). Little Queen Isabelle was crowned Queen of England on 7 January 1397, the day after her husband's 30th birthday.

Richard II showed conspicuous favour to his uncle Edmund of Langley and cousin Edward of York in the 1390s, and the greatest honour of all came in early 1397, when the king began referring to Edward as his 'brother'.[5] Although it has been suggested that Richard only did this because Edward's future marriage to the sister of the king's second wife Isabelle was under negotiation, it is probable that there was far more to it than that, and that Richard perhaps had it in mind to make his York relatives his heirs to the throne. Richard himself said as much to the courtier William Bagot in 1398: 'he said moreover that if he were to renounce it [the throne], the most able, wise and powerful man to whom to renounce it would be the duke of Aumale', i.e. Edward of York (who became Duke of Albemarle in 1397).[6] As any brother of the king born legitimately to his late father the Prince of Wales would automatically have been heir to the throne, it is hardly likely that Richard was unaware of what he was doing when he named Edward as his brother. Richard probably harboured ambitions of being elected Holy Roman Emperor as his wife Anne of Bohemia's father Karl IV had been, and perhaps imagined resigning his throne to his cousin. The king was a fearful man in the late 1390s and presided over a highly factional court where alliances were made and broken almost daily and no man could be sure where he stood, however firmly ensconced he seemed to be in the king's favour. Edward of York managed skilfully to navigate the stormy waters and remain close to his paranoid and frightened cousin, and later in life was called 'a second Solomon' by a chronicler.[7]

Richard's half-brother Thomas Holland, Earl of Kent, died on 25 April 1397, and left a will in English which thanked his wife Alice, Eleanor of Lancaster's younger daughter, for the 'love and trust that hath been between us'.[8] This is a nice example of how marriages arranged when the partners were children could work out successfully (sometimes, of course, they did not). Holland was succeeded as earl by his elder son Thomas and later by his second son Edmund, but as both men were childless, on Edmund's death in 1408 the

Holland heirs were Edmund's four surviving sisters Joan, Margaret, Eleanor and Elizabeth, and the son of the eldest sister Alianore. The elderly William Montacute, Earl of Salisbury, who decades before had been married to the king's mother Joan of Kent, died in June 1397, close to 70 years old. He left his nephew John Montacute as his heir, and John's son and heir Thomas, born in 1388, later married yet another Holland bride, Eleanor, fourth of the five daughters of Thomas Holland and Alice Fitzalan.

In 1397, the king finally took his revenge on the three senior Lords Appellant, the men who had executed and exiled many of his supporters almost a decade before, with the support of his cousin Edward of York, half-brother John Holland and others. Thomas Beauchamp, the elderly Earl of Warwick (he was almost 60), was sent to prison on the Isle of Man. Richard Fitzalan, Earl of Arundel, Eleanor of Lancaster's son, was condemned to death before Parliament on 21 September 1397 and immediately taken out to Tower Hill and beheaded. He was accompanied to his execution by his nephew Thomas Holland, the new Earl of Kent – also the king's nephew – and his son-in-law Thomas Mowbray, Earl of Nottingham. Mowbray tied a cloth over the eyes of the man who was his children's grandfather before the axe fell. Arundel's brother Thomas Arundel, youngest son of Eleanor of Lancaster and Archbishop of Canterbury since 1396, was exiled from England, a vindictive move on the king's part. Richard II's own uncle Thomas of Woodstock, Duke of Gloucester, was, shockingly, smothered to death in Calais at Richard's command, an order carried out by Thomas Mowbray, or rather by one of Mowbray's men.

Richard rewarded his followers by upgrading their titles at the Parliament of September 1397. The elderly Margaret of Norfolk (she was about 75), Thomas Mowbray's maternal grandmother and Edward I's only surviving grandchild, was made Duchess of Norfolk, the first Englishwoman in history to be made a duchess in her own right. Mowbray himself became Duke of Norfolk. Thomas Holland, Earl of Kent, became Duke of Surrey, his uncle John Holland Duke of Exeter, and Thomas Despenser Earl of Gloucester. Thomas Percy, younger brother of the Earl of Northumberland and grandson of Henry, Earl of Lancaster (d. 1345), was made Earl of Worcester. Richard's cousin Edward of York was made Duke of Albemarle, his other cousin Henry of Lancaster Duke of Hereford, and Henry of Lancaster's half-brother John Beaufort Marquis of Dorset. Contemporaries derisively referred to them as *duketti* or 'little dukes'.

One important nobleman whose title was conspicuously not upgraded was Roger Mortimer, Earl of March and Ulster. Although a great-grandson of Edward III and heir of Edward's second son Lionel of Antwerp, March had always been something of an outsider in English politics, and on 20 July 1398 he was killed in Ireland. He was 24 years old and his son and heir Edmund only 7, and March's death put paid to any notion that one day a Mortimer might sit on the English throne. Richard II gave custody of the lands in England which had belonged to the late Roger to his first cousin Edward of York on 11 August 1398, calling him 'the king's brother'. The king's half-brother John Holland, now Duke of Exeter, received all March's lands in South Wales, and his ally William Scrope, Earl of Wiltshire, those in North Wales.[9] Edmund Mortimer was to have no children, but passed on the Mortimer claim to the throne to his sister Anne's son Richard, Duke of York, the heir of both himself and Edward of York. As well as the rich earldoms of March and Ulster Richard of York inherited from his mother via her brother and father, she bequeathed him descent from Edward III's second son, a crucial point in York's claim to the English throne in the middle of the fifteenth century.

Edward of York, Earl of Rutland and now Duke of Albemarle, married sometime in the late 1390s, and his choice of bride was a rather peculiar one: Philippa Mohun, who was the widow of two rather obscure knights called Walter FitzWalter and John Golafre (Golafre was a knight of Richard II's household who died in November 1396). She was many years Edward's senior, perhaps as many as twenty. Her sister Katherine, who was her full sister and not a much older half-sister, married William Montacute, Earl of Salisbury, who was born in 1328 and had a son old enough to be killed jousting in 1382.[10] Philippa had no children by either of her first two husbands, and may have been past childbearing age when she wed Edward. She was not wealthy or powerful or well connected and had little to bring to the marriage, which, coupled with the probable fact that she would not be able to give Edward children and heirs, strongly suggests that their marriage was a genuine love-match and that Edward married her for herself. He was one of the greatest noblemen in Europe and the grandson of two kings (Edward III of England and Pedro the Cruel of Castile), and could have married the daughter of the King of France, but instead made his own unconventional choice and opted for Philippa Mohun. It seems doubtful that Edward's father Edmund of Langley approved of or was thrilled about his son's marriage.

If Edward had no children, the heir to the dukedom of York after him would be his younger brother Richard of Conisbrough, the son Edmund seems to have thought little of and done little for. The York family had minimal wealth or landed power and Edward's marriage would do nothing to increase it.

The two remaining Lords Appellant of 1388 were Henry of Lancaster and Thomas Mowbray. Not only had they not been punished by the king, he had made them dukes, but they trusted each other and Richard II not an inch, and when Henry went before Richard accusing Mowbray of treason and plotting against the king, Richard commanded them to settle their quarrel by a duel in Coventry in the autumn of 1398. In a scene made famous 200 years later by Shakespeare, the king dramatically stopped the joust before it had even begun and sentenced his cousin Henry to ten years' exile, which he may have reduced to six. For Mowbray, Richard's kinsman and staunch ally for the last decade, came a harsher sentence: perpetual exile from England. Henry went to Paris where he was greeted warmly and treated with considerable honour by the French royal family, while Mowbray went to Venice, intending a pilgrimage to the Holy Land. His exile did not last long: he was dead within a year of leaving England. Henry left most of his children behind in England, though took his second son Thomas of Lancaster, supposedly his favourite child, with him. His father John suggested either that he go to Paris or visit his sisters Philippa and Catalina in Portugal and Spain respectively.[11] He chose the former.

For all his loyalty to and support of his nephew for so many years, 'old John of Gaunt, time-honour'd Lancaster' was unable to prevent the exile of his son and heir, and he died on 3 February 1399 without ever seeing Henry again. He was not quite 59. John wrote a long will in French on the day he died, and asked not to be embalmed or buried until forty days after death; there had been premature reports of his demise, and it may be that he feared being buried alive.[12] His funeral took place at St Paul's Cathedral a few weeks later and he was buried next to Blanche of Lancaster, whom he had outlived by thirty years. John left his 'second best gold stag' and a gold goblet to his eldest daughter Philippa, Queen of Portugal, another gold goblet to his third daughter Catalina, Queen of Castile, and a brooch and a white silk bed to his second daughter Elizabeth, Duchess of Exeter. His son Henry of Lancaster and his Beaufort children John, Henry, Thomas and Joan were all left bequests, as were his third wife Katherine Swynford and his grandsons Henry of Monmouth and John of Lancaster, the first and third sons of his son Henry of Lancaster, though John left nothing to any of his numerous other grandchildren (he ultimately had over forty of them, though only about seventeen had been born by 1399). Henry Beaufort had by this time been elected Bishop of Lincoln, though was only in his 20s, and John called him 'the reverent father in God and my beloved son the bishop of Lincoln'. John asked for prayers to be said on the anniversary of his own death and on those of his two late wives, Blanche and Constanza. He left numerous bequests to charity and to religious houses, including £100 of silver to the Minoresses near the Tower of London, the foundation of his first wife's great-grandparents Edmund of Lancaster and Blanche of Artois in 1293, and a red vestment embroidered with suns to her father and grandfather's foundation of the Newarke in Leicester. Other items John owned which he mentioned in his will included a gold table in his chapel which he had bought at Amiens in France and called 'Domesday', and a tapestry given to him by the Duke of Burgundy at Calais. One of John's executors was Thomas Percy, Earl of Worcester and Steward of the king's household, a first cousin of Blanche of Lancaster.[13]

The death of his mighty and wealthy uncle left Richard II with a dilemma. John had been loyal to him for decades, but his son Henry was a different proposition. The entire enormous Lancastrian inheritance was now Henry's by right, and by the custom called the 'courtesy of England', Henry held his late wife Mary de Bohun's large inheritance for the rest of his life too. Richard faced the same prospect as his great-grandfather Edward II had in the 1310s and early 1320s: a Lancastrian first cousin he neither liked nor trusted, whose vast wealth gave him the potential to become almost a second king in England. Just two days after John of Gaunt's funeral, on 18 March 1399, Richard II made the astonishing decision to seize Henry of Lancaster's inheritance and to sentence him to permanent exile. (Another great windfall came into the king's hands when his elderly kinswoman Margaret, Duchess of Norfolk, finally died on 24 March 1399 in her mid to late 70s, and as her grandson and heir Thomas Mowbray was in exile, the king seized all her large estates as well.) Although the king did not officially confiscate Henry's lands, the seizure of them would lead to Richard's downfall and death mere months later; Henry of Lancaster was not a man to stand by and allow his birthright and his homeland to be taken from him, and many English noblemen agreed. The second deposition of a King of England in the fourteenth century was about to happen.

ANOTHER DEPOSITION

＊＊＊

Richard II set off for Ireland in June 1399, a decision which with hindsight at least seems foolish, leaving his uncle Edmund of Langley, Duke of York, as regent of England in his absence, as he usually did. His cousin Edward of York, Duke of Albemarle, half-brother John Holland, Duke of Exeter, Thomas Despenser, Earl of Gloucester, and John Montacute, Earl of Salisbury, were among those who sailed with him. Henry of Lancaster, with the exiled Thomas Arundel, Archbishop of Canterbury – his mother's first cousin – in his company, returned in early July and landed in Yorkshire with a small force of men. Another of Blanche of Lancaster's first cousins, Henry Percy, Earl of Northumberland, and his son Henry 'Hotspur' immediately joined Henry of Lancaster, as did Ralph Neville, Earl of Westmorland, Lancaster's brother-in-law (the husband of his half-sister Joan Beaufort). Henry made remarkably rapid progress, and the number of his followers swelled to the point where he had to send men home as he was unable to feed them. Edmund of Langley, the regent, made little if any effort to prevent Henry's advance; Henry was, after all, as much his nephew as Richard was, and he surely sympathised with him over his disinheritance. By late July 1399 Henry, with his uncle Edmund at his side, had reached Bristol, and summarily executed some of Richard's followers there.

Richard returned to Milford Haven in Wales around 24 July. He had Henry of Lancaster's eldest son Henry of Monmouth (b. September 1386) with him, presumably as a hostage, though he did nothing to harm the boy, and on or before 5 March 1399 had granted him a generous income of £500 a year.[1] The king made the remarkable decision to send his army away from him, and travelled through Wales to Conwy Castle and then on to Flint disguised as a friar with a small company including his half-brother John Holland and nephew Thomas Holland, and Thomas Despenser. Edward of York and John Montacute were sent to raise troops; Montacute met Richard at Conwy with the dire news that most of his army had deserted or gone to join Henry of Lancaster. Edward of York, meanwhile, also joined Henry at some point. Henry sent Henry Percy, Earl of Northumberland, to Flint Castle to negotiate with Richard on his behalf. Whether knowingly or not, Northumberland led the king into a trap, and Richard gave himself up to his cousin on 20 August, which, as the St Albans chronicler Thomas Walsingham correctly pointed out, was only the forty-sixth or forty-seventh day after Henry's return to England. Richard was taken captive and forcibly separated from his friends and allies. He was led south, having lost his kingdom with hardly a blow struck.

Richard was taken through London on 1 September by the two young men whom Henry of Lancaster had deputed to guard him: his 17-year-old cousin Humphrey of Gloucester, whose father Thomas of Woodstock he had had murdered two years before, and Thomas Fitzalan, 18-year-old son and heir of the Earl of Arundel executed by Richard at the same time. The king was incarcerated at the Tower of London. His uncle Edmund of Langley and cousin Edward of York visited him there and tried to persuade him to give up his throne to Henry, and he hurled abuse at them and rudely addressed them with 'thou'.[2] Although it would be easy to condemn the two men for cowardice and for disloyalty to their king, they were astute enough to see which way the wind was blowing, and allying themselves with Henry of Lancaster saved the House of York from the fate of Richard II and his allies. Richard himself perhaps expected that he would be placed in temporary captivity and deprived of his executive powers, but that he would eventually be restored to full capacity when he would be able to avenge himself on his enemies. In fact, events overtook him and he was never to wield power again. The intense factionalism he had created

and allowed to flourish at his court, and his riding roughshod over the laws
of his kingdom, was to bring him down.

Henry of Lancaster, meanwhile, was treated like a conquering hero, and
went into St Paul's Cathedral to pray at the tomb of his father; he had not
been able to attend John's funeral a few months before, and cried very
much. His and Richard's teenage cousin Humphrey of Gloucester died on
2 September 1399, the day after leading the defeated and captured King
Richard through London. Humphrey's mother Eleanor (née de Bohun)
followed him to the grave a month later, though she had probably been
seriously ill since 9 August when she made her will. Written mostly in
French but with the occasional sentence in English creeping in, her will
reveals that she owned many books, including a history of France in French
and a poem with the rather intriguing title 'Story of the Knight and the
Swan', also in French. She left 10 marks to the Lancastrian foundation the
Minoresses' house in London, a pair of coral paternosters to her mother
Joan (née Fitzalan), and, among other things, two beds with all hangings,
a coat of mail which had belonged to Edward III, and a gold cross with
four pearls which she described as her favourite possession to her only son
Humphrey. Eleanor did not update her will in the month after Humphrey's
death, perhaps being too ill or grief-stricken. One of her executors was her
kinsman Thomas Percy, Earl of Worcester.[3] She was still only 33 years old
when she died, and her mother Joan outlived her by twenty years.

Whether Henry of Lancaster had had it in mind to take the throne when
he sailed to England, or whether he had merely wanted to claim his rightful
inheritance, the almost delirious joy with which much of the population
greeted him and their fury towards Richard II persuaded him and many
others that he should take the throne and that Richard should be deposed.
Richard II was therefore persuaded to abdicate in favour of his cousin. The
notion that Edmund of Lancaster, Henry's great-great-grandfather, was a
hunchback who had been set aside in favour of his supposedly younger
brother Edward I because of his disability, was used to promote his claim to
the throne. Henry knew perfectly well this was not true and would mean
that his grandfather Edward III, great-grandfather Edward II and great-
great-grandfather Edward I had all been usurpers, but it was considered
the best option. Claiming the throne by right of conquest would mean
that no king would be able to sit securely on his throne in the future, and
it would make men insecure about their property and their right to hold

it, if someone else could claim their lands also 'by conquest'. The story of Edmund of Lancaster's disability had allegedly been raised by John of Gaunt some years before.

Meanwhile, far to the south, the exiled Duke of Norfolk Thomas Mowbray died in Venice on 22 September 1399, still only in his early 30s. His heir was his elder son Thomas, aged 14 at his death, who was destined to be beheaded before he was even 20, and Mowbray had only outlived his elderly grandmother Margaret, Duchess of Norfolk by six months. His widow Elizabeth, eldest daughter of the Earl of Arundel executed in 1397, married Sir Robert Goushill, third of her four husbands, in or before August 1401 without royal permission. King Henry had previously granted her £1,000 to pay her late husband's debts.[4] Mowbray died without knowing that the man who exiled him permanently from his homeland had lost his throne.

A document known as the 'Manner of King Richard's Renunciation' was issued at the Tower of London between 28 and 30 September 1399. In it, Richard II admitted that he had been 'entirely inadequate and unequal to the task of ruling', and Henry of Lancaster declared in English that he was the rightful heir of Henry III (d. 1272) and that God had sent him to recover the realm of England 'which realm was on the point of being undone by default of governance and the undoing of the good laws'.[5] Like his great-grandfather Edward II in 1327, Richard II was not allowed to speak in his own defence. Chronicler Adam Usk saw Richard in the Tower on 21 September, and heard him make a long and doleful speech about the manifold cruel fates of his ancestors, the kings of England, which 200 years later inspired Shakespeare's famous 'For God's sake let us sit upon the ground, and tell sad stories of the death of kings' soliloquy he has Richard speak in his play about him.

Henry of Lancaster's reign as Henry IV officially began on 30 September 1399, and he was crowned at Westminster on 13 October, the feast day of St Edward the Confessor (like Thomas Becket, a hugely popular saint among the fourteenth-century English royal family, and particularly venerated by Richard II). Henry IV was the first of three Lancastrian kings who ruled England from 1399 to 1461. He knighted his three younger sons Thomas, John and Humphrey of Lancaster at the time of his coronation, and made his eldest son Henry of Monmouth, now 13, Prince of Wales, Duke of Cornwall and Earl of Chester.[6] Not long after, Henry of Monmouth was made Duke of Lancaster and Aquitaine as well. Thomas of Lancaster, barely 12 years old, was made Steward of England, and a little later also Lieutenant of Ireland.[7] John of Lancaster, the third son, and Philippa of Lancaster, the king's second daughter, were living at Berkhamsted Castle by 1402, in the company of Edmund Mortimer, the 11-year-old heir to the earldom of March, and his younger brother Roger.[8] John had previously lived in the household of the elderly Margaret of Norfolk, Duchess of Norfolk (d. 1399), at Framlingham in Suffolk, and until their grandfather John of Gaunt's death the same year, their eldest brother Henry of Monmouth lived with him at least part of the time.[9] Henry IV himself, who could read and write in English, French and Latin, was something of a bookworm, and he gave his children an excellent education – his daughters as well as his sons. Henry of Monmouth received seven books of Latin grammar in one volume in the autumn of 1395 when he was 9, John of Lancaster received another Latin grammar in February 1398 when he was 8, and Blanche and Philippa were bought 'two books of ABC' in February 1397 when they were still only 4 and 2 years old. Later in life when he was Duke of Bedford and regent of France, John of Lancaster bought a remarkable 800 books for his library; he had certainly inherited his father's love of reading.[10]

The *duketti* created by Richard II were downgraded to their previous titles in late 1399: Thomas Holland to Earl of Kent, John Holland to Earl of Huntingdon, John Beaufort (Henry IV's half-brother but somewhat tainted at the start of the reign by his previous loyalty to Richard) to Earl of Somerset. Thomas Despenser lost his earldom of Gloucester, and even Henry's first cousin Edward of York lost his dukedom of Albemarle and was once again merely Earl of Rutland. The former king, now Sir Richard of Bordeaux, was imprisoned first in the Tower of London, then sent to distant Pontefract Castle in Yorkshire. Pontefract was where Thomas of Lancaster, brother of Henry IV's great-grandfather Earl Henry, had been executed in 1322 by Edward II, the great-grandfather with whom Richard II had long been fascinated and whose canonisation he had promoted for years.[11] Sending Richard to Pontefract of all places was, therefore, a deliberate and pointed decision by Henry, and a reminder that unlike his great-great-uncle Thomas, he had won this second struggle between the King of England and his Lancastrian cousin. Queen Isabelle, not even 10 years old when her husband was deposed in September 1399, remained in England under honourable house arrest, and in 1401 was sent back to France. She later married her first cousin Charles, Duke of Orléans, and died after giving birth to her only child in 1409. Her little sister Katherine, who was born a few weeks after her return to France, would marry Henry of Monmouth – by then King Henry V – in 1420.

A group of noblemen and other supporters of the late king, including Richard II's half-brother John Holland and his nephew Thomas Holland, the Earl of Salisbury John Montacute, and the former Earl of Gloucester Thomas Despenser, plotted to free Richard in late 1399 and early 1400 and restore him to the throne, and to kill Henry IV and his children. Their conspiracy is known as the Epiphany Rising. Edward of York may have been one of the original plotters, and may have betrayed his fellows to his father the Duke of York, though this is not entirely clear. Shakespeare's play about Richard II includes a scene where Edward's mother the duchess harangues him and makes him tell Henry IV about the plot. In fact, Edward's mother Isabel of Castile had been dead for seven years and the Duchess of York was his stepmother Joan Holland, years his junior and sister and niece of two of the plotters. The Epiphany Rising failed completely. John Holland, Earl of Huntingdon, who was married to Henry IV's sister Elizabeth of Lancaster but was loyal to his half-brother Richard, fell into the hands of the redoubtable Joan de Bohun, Dowager Countess of Hereford and Henry IV's mother-in-law, in Essex. She had him beheaded in the presence of her nephew Thomas Fitzalan, son and heir of the Earl of Arundel executed in 1397. Holland's nephew Thomas Holland and John Montacute, Earl of Salisbury, were summarily beheaded in Cirencester and their heads sent to the king in a basket, and Thomas Despenser was beheaded in Bristol after attempting to flee the country from Cardiff. John Holland's widow Elizabeth of Lancaster married her third husband Sir John Cornwall in early April or before, and in July 1400 Thomas Despenser's widow Constance of York gave birth to Thomas' posthumous daughter Isabella, six and a half months after Thomas' death. Isabella Despenser became the Despenser heir when her brother Richard died in 1413, and via her second marriage to Richard Beauchamp, Earl of Warwick, was the mother of Anne Neville (née Beauchamp), Countess of Warwick and mother-in-law of Richard III.

The failed Epiphany Rising sealed Richard of Bordeaux's fate, and he was murdered at Pontefract Castle on or around 14 February 1400, most probably by being starved to death. He was only 33 years old when he died. The former king's body was brought south, and after a public viewing at St Paul's Cathedral in London was buried at Langley Priory in Hertfordshire, where Richard had buried his older brother Edward of Angoulême a few years before. After his accession to the throne in 1413, Henry V had Richard's remains moved to Westminster Abbey next to his beloved wife Anne of Bohemia, where they remain today. Henry IV may have been reluctant to kill his cousin, but accepted that he had no choice and that Richard's continued existence would always be a threat to him. A pretender called Thomas Ward of Trumpington appeared in Scotland some years later claiming to be Richard II and was taken seriously in some quarters, but there is really no doubt whatsoever that Richard died in February 1400.

Richard II was the only legitimate descendant of Edward III's eldest son, and the descendants of the second son had, whether rightfully or not, been set aside in the interests of the Lancastrians, offspring of the third son. By taking the English throne in 1399, Henry IV had unwittingly laid the foundations for war between his descendants and the descendants of his uncles Lionel of Antwerp and Edmund of Langley.

EPILOGUE: 1400–22

The feelings of Edmund of Langley, Duke of York, about his nephew Richard's sudden and highly convenient demise are unrecorded. Edmund made his will, in French, a few months later, on 25 November 1400. If his first wife Isabel of Castile had indeed had an affair with the late John Holland, Edmund had evidently forgiven her, as he asked to be buried 'near my beloved Isabele, formerly my consort'. He appointed 'my beloved son of Rutland' (*moun tresame fitz de Rotteland*), i.e. his elder son Edward of York, as one of his executors, though did not leave specific items to any of his children and did not mention his daughter Constance Despenser or his younger son Richard of Conisbrough.[1] Making his will suggests that Edmund was then seriously ill, though if so, he rallied, and did not die until 1 August 1402 at the age of 61, last of the many children of Edward III and Philippa of Hainault and the only one to live past 1400. He died at Langley in Hertfordshire, his birthplace, and was buried there; his and Isabel of Castile's tombs can still be seen. His widow Joan Holland, half-niece of the late Richard II and sister of the Earl of Kent beheaded after the Epiphany Rising, was still only in her early or mid 20s and married another three times before her death in 1434, though had no children from any of her four marriages. She was pardoned in 1409 for marrying her second husband William, Lord Willoughby of Eresby without

royal permission, and her third husband Henry, Lord Scrope of Masham
was executed in 1415 for his role in trying to put Edmund Mortimer on
the throne.[2] Edmund of Langley's daughter Constance was something of a
free spirit, and had a relationship with Edmund Holland, Earl of Kent and
younger brother of her stepmother Joan, which resulted in an illegitimate
daughter Alianore or Eleanor Holland in about 1405.[3] Edmund Holland
was Alice Fitzalan's second son and a grandson of Eleanor of Lancaster,
and was at least seven years Constance's junior. Although a half-nephew of
Richard II and the brother and nephew of two of the men who plotted to
kill the new king during the Epiphany Rising, Edmund was a staunch supporter of Henry IV. As his short marriage to the Italian noblewoman Lucia
Visconti was childless, the earldom of Kent remained dormant for some
decades after his death until granted to John of Gaunt's grandson William
Neville in 1461.

   Henry IV had lost his wife Mary de Bohun in 1394 when he was only 27,
and in the early 1400s he decided to marry again. (He had an illegitimate son,
Edmund Lebourde, born in 1401, who joined the Church.)[4] His bride was
Juana of Navarre, born in *c.* 1370 as one of the daughters of King Carlos II
'the Bad' of Navarre, and the widow of Duke John IV of Brittany, who
died in November 1399. The last time a King of England had married a
woman of Navarre was all the way back in 1191, when Richard Lionheart
wed Berengaria of Navarre in Cyprus; famously, this Queen of England
never set foot in England, at least not during her husband's lifetime. The
previous Spanish Queen of England before Juana of Navarre was Leonor of
Castile (d. 1290), wife of Edward I and mother of Edward II, and the next
would be Katherine of Aragon, first queen of Henry VIII and a descendant
of John of Gaunt. Juana had to make the difficult decision to leave her
eight or nine children behind in Brittany – her eldest son John, born in
1389, succeeded his father as duke – and married Henry IV at Winchester
Cathedral on 7 February 1403. Although the couple were only in their
30s when they married and had at least fifteen children between them,
they had none with each other, rather curiously (though one chronicler
thought they may have had two stillborn children). After the lavish and
expensive royal wedding, the couple retired to the Palace of Eltham in
Kent for eight weeks.[5] The king's elder daughter Blanche of Lancaster
had already married, in July 1402 when she was only 10 years old. She
wed the elector Palatine of the Rhine, Ludwig von Wittelsbach, and died

childless in 1409 at the age of 17. Her younger sister Philippa married Erik of Pomerania, King of Sweden, Denmark and Norway, and a first cousin of the late Anne of Bohemia, Richard II's queen. Philippa and Erik had no surviving children, and although Henry IV had six legitimate children he had only one legitimate grandchild, Henry V's son Henry VI. (His sons also fathered several of the illegitimate kind.)

Henry IV's stepmother Katherine Swynford, Dowager Duchess of Lancaster, died on 10 May 1403 and was buried at Lincoln Cathedral, where her son Henry Beaufort ruled as bishop (he was moved to Winchester in 1404 and later became a cardinal). Katherine's youngest child Joan Neville (née Beaufort), Countess of Westmorland, was buried with her many years later. Whether Henry IV was fond of Katherine is hard to say; although it is sometimes stated that because he chose to call her 'the king's mother' in the early 1400s after his father's death he must have been close to her, this was a purely conventional way of referring to one's stepmother and says nothing about their personal relationship. Henry also often called his mother-in-law Joan de Bohun 'the king's mother', and in 1404 referred to his first stepmother Constanza of Castile as 'the king's mother Constance'.[6] It is surely revealing that Henry IV's sister Elizabeth of Lancaster chose to name two of her four daughters after her first stepmother Constanza, one of them born in the early 1400s a few years after Constanza's death, but none after her second stepmother, who had been her governess in childhood. There is no doubt, however, that Katherine Swynford's story is a remarkable one. Plenty of medieval noblemen had mistresses and relationships with them that resulted in illegitimate offspring, but for such a high-ranking nobleman as John of Gaunt to marry his mistress and make their children legitimate was unique in medieval England. This says a great deal about Katherine's character and about John's strong feelings for her, which endured for decades. Katherine and John were the great-grandparents of Edward IV and Richard III, and the great-great-grandparents of Henry VII, the first Tudor king.

Henry Percy, Earl of Northumberland, his younger brother Thomas, Earl of Worcester, and his son and heir Henry 'Hotspur' fought against a Scottish army at the Battle of Homildon Hill in the county of Northumberland in September 1402, and captured a number of Scottish noblemen. They wished to profit from their ransoms, as was their right. Henry IV – perpetually short of cash despite the vast lands he personally owned –

refused and demanded the ransoms for himself, to the absolute fury of the Percys. On top of Henry's breaking of his sacred oath not to harm Richard II and his failure to reward their support of him in 1399 with lands or pay them the large sums of money he owed them, this was the final straw. Northumberland's son Hotspur, besides, had an interest in promoting the claim to the throne of the child Edmund Mortimer, Lionel of Antwerp's great-grandson and heir, who was his wife Elizabeth's nephew. The two Percy brothers and Hotspur renounced their homage to the king.

At Shrewsbury on 21 July 1403, Hotspur and his uncle Worcester with their forces met an army led by Henry IV and his eldest son Henry of Monmouth, Prince of Wales, who was not yet 17. Although the prince suffered a terrible face wound, and despite the loss of the Earl of Stafford (husband of Edward III's granddaughter Anne of Gloucester) who died fighting for the king, the royalist side won. Hotspur was killed during the battle and was buried, but Henry IV had his body dug up, salted, and publicly displayed seated upright at the High Cross in Shrewsbury, where Dafydd ap Gruffudd had been executed by Edward I 120 years before. Hotspur's uncle Thomas Percy, who was 60 or almost, suffered the awful traitor's death of hanging, drawing and quartering, and his head was later placed on London Bridge. Hotspur's body was also quartered and displayed in London, Bristol, Newcastle and Chester.[7] Hotspur's son Henry was 10 years old when he was killed, and the boy spent a few years in exile in Scotland, where his grandfather Northumberland took him in 1405. Young Henry's mother Elizabeth Mortimer was the eldest grandchild of Edward III's second son Lionel of Antwerp, which gave Henry a potential claim to the throne after his Mortimer cousins. In 1416, Henry V allowed the young man his grand-father's earldom of Northumberland, and he married the king's cousin Eleanor Neville, one of the many children of John of Gaunt's daughter Joan Beaufort. No fewer than four of Henry Percy and Eleanor Neville's sons would be killed in battle during the Wars of the Roses.

Constance of York attempted to free Henry Hotspur's nephews, the sons of the late Roger Mortimer, Earl of March (d. 1398), in early 1405. Edmund Mortimer (b. 1391) and his younger brother Roger – as was the case with all medieval noble families, the Mortimers were not creative with names for their sons – were being held in close captivity at Windsor Castle. Constance was almost certainly attempting to take them to their uncle Edmund Mortimer (b. 1376) in Wales, where he was allied with the Welsh lord and rebel Owain Glyn Dŵr.[8] It failed. Constance blamed her brother Edward, Duke of York since their father Edmund of Langley's death in 1402; evidently little love was lost between the York siblings. Edward was imprisoned for several months at Pevensey Castle and Constance at Kenilworth (where she might have given birth to her illegitimate daughter Alianore Holland), and the locksmith who had made duplicate keys so that Constance could gain entry to Windsor Castle was beheaded. After Edward of York's release from Pevensey, he was restored to his lands and royal favour, and set about making an English translation of Gaston de Foix's great work about hunting written in the late 1380s, the *Livre de Chasse*. It is now known as *The Master of Game* and is the first book on hunting in English. Constance, meanwhile, although a first cousin of Henry IV, remained hostile to him and devoted to the memory of her other cousin Richard II.

Maud de Vere (née Ufford), Dowager Countess of Oxford, was another noblewoman antagonistic to Henry IV. She distributed badges with Richard II's emblem of a hart in Essex, to make it look as though the former king – who had treated Maud's only son Robert de Vere with such great affection and favour – was still alive. Maud went so far as to join a conspiracy to depose Henry in 1404, and was imprisoned for a while in the Tower of London. Queen Juana asked her husband to show clemency, and perhaps because of Maud's age (almost 60) and because she was of high birth and his mother Blanche of Lancaster's first cousin, Henry agreed. In December 1404, Countess Maud was pardoned 'for all treasons, felonies, rebellions, misprisions, negligences and trespasses'.[9]

Another rebellion against Henry IV's rule in 1405 led to the execution of an archbishop, Richard Scrope of York, and of 19-year-old Thomas Mowbray, Earl of Norfolk (whose father of the same name had been Henry of Lancaster's adversary in the duel of 1398), on 8 June 1405. The young nobleman and his allies were taken outside York to a field of barley, and beheaded beneath a windmill.[10] Mowbray's heir was his brother John Mowbray, and on 14 November 1407 Henry IV gave custody of the young man to his mother-in-law Joan de Bohun, Dowager Countess of Hereford, who happened to be Mowbray's great-aunt. She was granted £200 a year for his sustenance. On 8 March 1410, the king brought John into the royal household and increased his allowance to £300 a year.[11] Another of Mowbray's great-aunts, Joan of Lancaster's daughter Blanche Poynings (née Mowbray), died on 21 or 24 July 1409; she had been married five times but had no children or at least no surviving children, and John Mowbray, her brother's grandson, was her heir.[12] In January 1312 Mowbray married the king's niece Katherine Neville, another of the many children of Joan Beaufort and the Earl of Westmorland, and their only son, inevitably called John and his father's successor as Duke of Norfolk, was born in September 1415. Katherine Mowbray (née Neville) was born in the late 1390s or 1400 at the latest, and, remarkably, lived long enough to attend her nephew Richard III's coronation in the summer of 1483. The third of her four husbands was John, Lord Beaumont, a few years her junior and Eleanor of Lancaster's great-great-grandson, and the fourth, notoriously, was Edward IV's brother-in-law Sir John Woodville, who was close to half a century her junior.

On 19 February 1408, Henry Percy, Earl of Northumberland, and his ally Thomas, Lord Bardolf fought against a royalist army at the Battle of Bramham Moor in Yorkshire. Bardolf was badly wounded and died soon afterwards, and the great Earl of Northumberland himself, son of Mary of Lancaster and a close relative of the king he spent years fighting against, fell during the battle, aged 66. Like his son's and his brother's in 1403, his head was set on London Bridge. Edmund Holland, Earl of Kent, was also killed in battle in 1408; his heirs were his nephew Edmund Mortimer, Earl of March, son of his late eldest sister Alianore (d. 1405), and his surviving sisters Joan the Dowager Duchess of York, Margaret the Countess of Somerset, Eleanor the Countess of Salisbury, and Elizabeth, daughter-in-law of the Earl of Westmorland.[13]

Anne Mortimer (b. 1390), sister of Edmund, Earl of March, married Edward of York and Constance Despenser's brother Richard of Conisbrough early in 1408, and the marriage was validated on 23 May 1408 by papal dispensation. They had a daughter, Isabella, and their son Richard of York was born on 21 September 1411. Anne died shortly after giving birth to her son and was buried at Langley Priory with her parents-in-law, Edmund of Langley and Isabel of Castile. Richard of Conisbrough would be made Earl of Cambridge in 1414, by which time he was already in his late 20s, perhaps older.

Maud de Vere (née Ufford), Dowager Countess of Oxford and a granddaughter of Henry, Earl of Lancaster (d. 1345), died on 25 January 1413 in her late 60s. She was buried with her long-dead half-sister Elizabeth de Burgh (d. 1363), Duchess of Clarence, at Bruisyard in Suffolk, the abbey founded by Elizabeth's husband Lionel of Antwerp and where their mother Maud of Lancaster had spent the last few years of her life. Maud de Vere had evidently been on good terms with her first cousins Henry Percy, Earl of Northumberland, and Thomas Percy, Earl of Worcester, as in 1402 they and Northumberland's son Hotspur co-signed a petition she presented regarding a manor in Rutland.[14] King Henry IV, to whom the countess had been so hostile – and the Percys' rebellion against the king and their deaths in 1403 and 1408 can hardly have increased her regard for him – outlived her by only a few weeks. The king had already written his will in English on 21 January 1409, calling himself a 'sinful wretch', and died on 20 March 1413 at the age of not quite 46.[15] Henry had survived eight rebellions in thirteen and a half years, and dying of natural causes and passing on his throne to his eldest son Henry of Monmouth was not an insignificant achievement. On 9 July 1412, he had made his second son Thomas of Lancaster the second Duke of Clarence.[16] Clarence married Margaret Beaufort (née Holland), widow of his half-uncle John Beaufort, Earl of Somerset (d. 1410); her six children, his step-children, were his first cousins. Henry IV's younger sons John and Humphrey of Lancaster had to wait until the reign of their brother Henry V to gain titles: Duke of Bedford and Duke of Gloucester respectively. None of the three younger Lancaster brothers had any surviving legitimate children.

Not everyone was happy about Henry V's accession in March 1413: Richard of Conisbrough, Earl of Cambridge, took part in a hare-brained scheme to put his brother-in-law Edmund Mortimer, Earl of March, on the throne, and was beheaded on 5 August 1415. Another man executed after taking part in the plot was Henry, Lord Scrope of Masham, third husband of the Dowager Duchess of York, Joan Holland (her second husband William, Lord Willoughby died in December 1409 just a few months after they were pardoned for marrying without the king's permission, and she married Scrope in September 1410). Scrope was also the nephew of Richard Scrope, Archbishop of York, executed by Henry IV in 1405. Edmund Mortimer was himself not executed and comes across as a born follower, not a leader who might threaten Henry V and the Lancastrian dynasty; evidently Henry V felt the same way. Mortimer had other things on his mind in 1415: he wrote to the Pope asking for a dispensation to marry a woman to whom he was related in the third degree, i.e. second cousins, because he 'desires to have children, but being related to diverse magnates cannot find a wife suitable to his rank whom he can marry without papal dispensation' (an indication of how interrelated the English comital families were).[17] He married Anne Stafford, daughter of the Earl of Stafford and a great-granddaughter of Edward III via the king's youngest son Thomas of Woodstock and his wife Eleanor de Bohun, but sadly for Edmund, given his desire to have children, the marriage did not produce any. Anne had children with her second husband John Holland, Duke of Exeter – born in 1395 as the son of Elizabeth of Lancaster, and a grandson of John of Gaunt – so probably Edmund Mortimer was infertile.

Also in 1415, Henry V resumed the long-standing war against France which had begun when his great-grandfather Edward III claimed the French throne in the 1330s. France was in a dire state, as its king since 1380, Charles VI, was insane and incapable of governing, and the kingdom descended into civil war among the factions battling for power. Edward of York, second Duke of York since 1402, took part in Henry V's invasion of France and wrote his will on 17 August 1415, the day before the king's siege of Harfleur began. It is in French; Edward, like probably all his noble contemporaries, was bilingual, and switched between English and French as he wished. He asked for prayers for Richard II, Henry IV and his own parents Edmund of Langley and Isabel of Castile, and called himself 'of all sinners the most wretched and guilty.' Among the items he left to his wife Philippa (née Mohun) were his 'bed of feathers and leopards' with all the bedding, his white and red tapestries embroidered with garters, falcons and fetterlocks (the badge of the house of York), and a green bed. Edward expressed a wish 'that all my saddles and harnesses be shared equally among my attendants [*henxmen*, in English], except that I wish Rokell to have the best one'.[18] During Henry V's great and famous victory over the French at Agincourt on 25 October 1415, Edward of York was killed, possibly by being smothered to death, and he may have saved Henry V's own life in the process. He was about 42. His widow Philippa Mohun, though many years his senior, outlived him by sixteen years, and his heir was his 4-year-old nephew Richard of York, Richard of Conisbrough's only son.

Alice Holland (née Fitzalan), Dowager Countess of Kent and the younger daughter of Eleanor of Lancaster (d. 1372), lived until 17 March 1416, and died at Beaulieu Abbey a few months before Constance Despenser, who had had an illegitimate child with Alice's son Edmund Holland in about 1405 and was Edward of York's sister, also passed away.[19] Alice's elder sister

Joan de Bohun, Dowager Countess of Hereford and the last surviving grandchild of Henry, Earl of Lancaster (d. 1345) and Maud Chaworth (d. 1322), lived on. On 17 April 1419, Joan finally died at the age of about 72, six years into the reign of her grandson Henry V (who was the eldest child of Joan's younger daughter Mary de Bohun). She had outlived her daughters Mary and Eleanor by twenty-five years and twenty years respectively, and also outlived a number of her grandchildren. Her grandson the king was fond of her: on 10 March 1414 he gave her Leeds Castle in Kent for life, and on 4 April 1416 gave her custody of all the lands of her recently deceased sister Alice.[20] Henry V and his cousin, Joan's granddaughter Anne of Gloucester, Dowager Countess of Stafford and Countess of Eu in France by her third marriage, were her heirs.[21]

Henry V married Katherine de Valois, youngest daughter of Charles VI of France and sister of Richard II's late child-wife Isabelle, in June 1420, and their son Henry VI was born in December 1321. Mere months later, the great Henry of Monmouth was dead in his mid 30s and his baby son succeeded as King of England, becoming King of France as well when his maternal grandfather the unfortunate Charles VI died in December 1422. Henry VI was the third Lancastrian King of England, and the great-great-great-great-grandson of Edmund of Lancaster (1245–96), the dynasty's founder. In 1422 Richard of York was 11, and when his maternal uncle Edmund Mortimer, Earl of March and Ulster, died childless in Ireland in early 1425, Richard was his heir. The son of an executed traitor was lucky enough to have two influential, wealthy and childless uncles, and when Richard came of age he duly inherited the dukedom of York and the earldoms of March and Ulster. Richard also inherited a strong claim to the throne as the senior male descendant of Edward III's second son Lionel of Antwerp, Duke of Clarence, and was also the grandson of the fourth son Edmund of Langley, Duke of York. Henry VI, meanwhile, was descended from the third son John of Gaunt. If King Henry had been the leader his father was, perhaps Richard of York's claim to the throne might never have become an issue; but he was not, and it did.

The stage was set for war between the houses of Lancaster and York, and in the 1450s, when Henry VI became incapacitated and Richard of York claimed the English throne, it came.

ABBREVIATIONS IN NOTES AND BIBLIOGRAPHY

BCM	Berkeley Castle Muniments
C	Chancery (National Archives)
CChR	*Calendar of Charter Rolls*
CCR	*Calendar of Close Rolls*
CCW	*Calendar of Chancery Warrants*
CDS	*Calendar of Documents Relating to Scotland*
CFR	*Calendar of Fine Rolls*
CIM	*Calendar of Inquisitions Miscellaneous*
CIPM	*Calendar of Inquisitions Post Mortem*
CLR	*Calendar of the Liberate Rolls*
Collection	*Collection of All the Wills … of the Kings and Queens of England*
CP	*Complete Peerage, ed. Gibbs*
CPL	*Calendar of Papal Letters*
CPR	*Calendar of Patent Rolls*
CPMR	*Calendar of Plea and Memoranda Rolls*
DL	Duchy of Lancaster (National Archives)
E	Exchequer (National Archives)
FCE	*Fourteenth Century England , ed. Dodd*

Fowler	Kenneth Fowler, *The King's Lieutenant Henry of Grosmont* (1969)
Fowler, thesis	Kenneth Fowler, 'Henry of Grosmont, First Duke of Lancaster', PhD thesis (1961)
'Fragment'	R.B. Pugh, 'A Fragment of an Account of Isabel of Lancaster, Nun of Amesbury'
Goodman	Anthony Goodman, *John of Gaunt The Exercise of Princely Power in Fourteenth-Century Europe*
Howell, *Eleanor*	Margaret Howell, *Eleanor of Provence Queenship in Thirteenth-Century England*
IPM	*Calendar of Inquisitions Post Mortem*
ODNB	*Oxford Dictionary of National Biography*
PP	*Petitions to the Pope 1342–1419*
PW	*Parliamentary Writs*
PROME	*The Parliament Rolls of Medieval England*
Records	*Records of the Borough of Leicester* (2 vols)
Register	*John of Gaunt's Registers*
Rhodes, 'Edmund'	Walter Rhodes, 'Edmund, Earl of Lancaster', *English Historical Review*, vol. 10, no. 37 (1895)
Rhodes, 'Edmund', part 2	Walter Rhodes, 'Edmund, Earl of Lancaster (Continued)', *English Historical Review*, vol. 10, no. 38 (1895)
SC	Special Collections (National Archives)
TV	*Testamenta Vetusta*, vol. 1

NOTES

Chapter 1

1 *CLR 1240–45*, 288, 292; *ODNB*; Margaret Howell, *Eleanor of Provence*, 45.
2 John of Gaunt (d. 1399), husband of Edmund's great-granddaughter and heir Blanche of Lancaster (d. 1368), supposedly raised the story of Edmund's being set aside because of his deformity in 1394 to promote his and Blanche's son Henry of Lancaster's claim to the throne, according to the *Eulogium Historiarum sive Temporis*, vol. 3 (*Continuatio Eulogii*), 369–70. See *Complete Peerage* (hereafter: *CP*), vol. 7, 378, note b, and also below.
3 Four younger sons sometimes assigned to the royal couple by much later writers almost certainly never existed: Howell, *Eleanor*, 45 and note 117, and see her article, 'The Children of Henry III and Eleanor of Provence' in *Thirteenth Century England IV* (1992).
4 *CLR 1245–51*, 77–8.
5 *CLR 1240–45*, 49; *CLR 1245–51*, 49, 83; *CLR 1251–60*, 210.
6 *CPR 1247–58*, 50, 375; *CPR 1258–66*, 376; *CLR 1245–51*, 279.
7 J. R. Maddicott, *Simon de Montfort* (1994), 173–6 (with an image of the will).
8 Michael Prestwich, *Edward I* (1988), 6.
9 *CLR 1245–51*, 106, 151.
10 *CLR 1245–51*, 54, 65, 169; Howell, *Eleanor*, 100–1.
11 Howell, *Eleanor*, 102–3.
12 Howell, *Eleanor*, 101–2.
13 Howell, *Eleanor*, 288–9; Hilda Johnstone, *Edward of Carnarvon 1284–1307* (1946), 24.
14 *CLR 1240–45*, 306; *CLR 1245–51*, 156 (though his careless clerk got their names wrong).
15 Peter Hammond, *Food and Feast in Medieval England* (1993), 125–6.
16 *CLR 1251–60*, 55.
17 Howell, *Eleanor*, 65–9.
18 Howell, *Eleanor*, 126.

19 John Carmi Parsons, 'The Year of Eleanor of Castile's Birth'.
20 Frederick's son with Isabella of England, named Heinrich after his English uncle, was only 12 at his father's death in 1250 and died in 1253.
21 *Oxford Dictionary of National Biography*; Walter Rhodes, 'Edmund, Earl of Lancaster', 23–4 (hereafter: Rhodes, 'Edmund').
22 *CPR 1247–58*, 343–4, 450, 507–8, 567–8; *CPL 1198–1304*, 338, 354, 369; Rhodes, 'Edmund', 27.
23 *ODNB*; Frederick Devon, *Issues of the Exchequer*, 35; Rhodes, 'Edmund', 27.

Chapter 2

1 Cited in Howell, *Eleanor*, 137.
2 *ODNB*; Howell, *Eleanor*, 137.
3 *ODNB*; *CLR 1251–60*, 197.
4 *CLR 1251–60*, 176, 183–4, 196, 270, 289, 379; *Royal and other historical letters illustrative of the reign of Henry III*, ed. Walter Waddington Shirley (1866), vol. 2, 99, for Henry III's letter to Alexander. Marie Lusignan, aka Mariota, was one of the daughters of Henry's half-brother Hugues, Count of La Marche and Angoulême, and married Robert Ferrers, heir to the earldom of Derby, in 1249 when they were both children (*CPR 1247–58*, 54; *CLR 1245–51*, 279).
5 *CLR 1251–60*, 243, 253.
6 *CLR 1251–60*, 373, 376, 385; http://www.westminster-abbey.org/our-history/people/katherine-daughter-of-henry-iii.
7 *ODNB*; Rhodes, 'Edmund', 27, citing *Annales Londonienses*, 53.
8 *CPR 1258–66*, 14, 26.
9 Howell, *Eleanor*, 165–6.
10 *CLR 1251–60*, 513; Rhodes, 'Edmund', 27.
11 *CPR 1258–66*, 90; Howell, *Eleanor*, 102.
12 *Royal and other historical letters*, vol. 2, 99.
13 *CPR 1258–66*, 128.

Chapter 3

1 *Royal and other historical letters*, vol. 2, 197–8.
2 *CPR 1258–66*, 220, 222; Rhodes, 'Edmund', 28.
3 Maurice Powicke, *Henry III and the Lord Edward* (1950), 430.
4 *CPR 1258–66*, 238; *CPR 1266–72*, 736; Howell, *Eleanor*, 190–1.
5 *CPR 1258–66*, 97, 161, 275.
6 J.R. Maddicott, *Simon de Montfort* (1994), 257.
7 *CLR 1251–60*, 107; *CPR 1247–58*, 175.
8 Maddicott, *Montfort*, 325; Powicke, *Henry III and the Lord Edward*, 708.
9 Rhodes, 'Edmund', 28; Robert Somerville, *History of the Duchy of Lancaster*, 1.
10 *CPR 1258–66*, 665.
11 DL 25/2219; *CPR 1258–66*, 612.

12 *CCR 1296–1302*, 497, 571. He was aided by the Archbishop of Canterbury;
    see Andrew Spencer, *Nobility and Kingship in Medieval England* (2013), 252–3.
13 *CPR 1317–21*, 203–4.
14 *Vita Edwardi Secundi*, ed. N. Denholm-Young (1957), 29.
15 *CPR 1324–7*, 36.
16 *CCR 1318–23*, 449.

Chapter 4

1   *CChR 1257–1300*, 78; *CPR 1266–72*, 100.
2   *CChR 1257–1300*, 58, 66, 118–9.
3   *ODNB*.
4   Rhodes, 'Edmund', 29.
5   *CPR 1281–92*, 243; *CPL 1305–41*, 447.
6   *CCR 1318–23*, 697. Sancha's only surviving child was Edmund of Cornwall,
    who died in 1300 without children, siblings, nieces or nephews. His
    earldom of Cornwall passed to his first cousin Edward I as his nearest male
    relative, and to Edward I's son Edward II in 1307. Edward II was thus the
    heir of Edmund and his parents Sancha and Richard.
7   *CPR 1364–7*, 330. Edmund's second son Henry of Lancaster was Blanche of
    Lancaster's grandfather.
8   *CPL 1198–1304*, 435.
9   Howell, *Eleanor*, 248; Sara Cockerill, *Eleanor of Castile: The Shadow Queen*
    (2014), 154–5; *CPR 1266–72*, 411.
10 *CIPM 1272–91*, no. 44.
11 Rhodes, 'Edmund', part 2, 209–10.
12 *CChR 1257–1300*, 121–2; *CPR 1266–72*, 358.
13 Rhodes, 'Edmund', part 2, 210.
14 Powicke, *Henry III and the Lord Edward*, 604.
15 *Flores Historiarum*, vol. 3, 22, cited in Maddicott, *Montfort*, 371.
16 E 101/333/15: *Un cultell dount le Roi Edward estoit naufray en la terre seinte
    en Acres*, 'a knife with which King Edward was wounded at Acre in the
    Holy Land'.
17 Howell, *Eleanor*, 252–3.

Chapter 5

1   *CPL 1198–1304*, 446.
2   Rhodes, 'Edmund', part 2, 211–2.
3   *CPR 1272–81*, 186.
4   *CCR 1272–79*, 7; *CIPM 1272–91*, no. 44, is Aveline's proof of age.
5   *Foedera 1272–1307*, 508.
6   *CPR 1281–92*, 53.
7   Prestwich, *Edward I*, 91.

8 Prestwich, *Edward I*, 90; Rhodes, 'Edmund', part 2, 213.
9 *CPR 1272–81*, 61.
10 *CFR 1272–1307*, 35, says Aveline 'died on the eve of St Martin', i.e.
    10 November; *CIPM 1272–91*, nos 130, 792.
11 The cousins were Ralph Pleys or Plays and the four daughters of Hugh
    Bulebec, namely Philippa, Margery, Alice and Maud.
12 K.B. McFarlane, *The Nobility of Later Medieval England* (1973), 256–9.
13 *CPR 1272–81*, 81, 270.
14 Cited in Howell, *Eleanor*, 291.
15 *CPR 1272–81*, 101, 125; Somerville, *Duchy of Lancaster*, 15, note 1, for the date.
16 Rhodes, 'Edmund', part 2, 213.
17 Rhodes, 'Edmund', part 2, 214.
18 Rhodes, 'Edmund', part 2, 214.
19 Cited in Julian Munby, Richard Barber and Richard Brown, *Edward III's
    Round Table at Windsor* (2008), 95.
20 Richard Barber, *Edward III and the Triumph of England* (2013).
21 *CPR 1272–81*, 165; C 47/27/2/8.
22 *CPR 1272–81*, 156–8, 160, 251–4; Rhodes, 'Edmund', part 2, 217.
23 *CPR 1272–81*, 199; Rhodes, 'Edmund', part 2, 217–8.
24 *CCR 1296–1302*, 174. In July 1297, Thomas' late father's tenants were
    ordered to do homage to do him although he was underage: *CPR
    1292–1301*, 291.
25 *Records of the Borough of Leicester* (hereafter: *Records*), vol. 1, 178.
26 *CIPM 1307–17*, no. 279.
27 *CPR 1272–81*, 251–4, 296; Rhodes, 'Edmund', part 2, 219.
28 *CPR 1272–81*, 370, 440–1; Rhodes, 'Edmund', part 2, 220–3.
29 *CPR 1281–92*, 243. This was the occasion when their grandmother Eleanor
    of Provence, the dowager queen, bequeathed her rights in the county
    of Provence to them. Rhodes, 'Edmund', part 2, 235, says Edmund and
    Blanche also had a daughter, who in some modern books is named as Mary.
    I am unaware of the primary sources which prove her existence, and if she
    did exist she must have died young.
30 *CPR 1272–81*, 306.
31 *CPR 1272–81*, 306, 350, 371; *CCR 1272–79*, 492 ('count of Champagne').
32 Rhodes, Edmund', part 2, 216–7.
33 Rhodes, 'Edmund', part 2, 219.

Chapter 6

1 *Calendar of Ancient Correspondence Concerning Wales*, ed. J. Goronwy Edwards
   (1935), 75.
2 *CPR 1281–92*, 49.
3 *CCR 1302–07*, 298; *CCR 1323–07*, 400.
4 *CPR 1281–92*, 120, 180.

5   Rhodes, 'Edmund', part 2, 225.
6   *Foedera 1272–1307*, 651; Rhodes, 'Edmund', part 2, 225.
7   *CPR 1281–92*, 235, 238–40.
8   Nottinghamshire Archives, DD/FJ/4/25/1.
9   *CPL 1198–1304*, 506.
10   *CPR 1281–92*, 278, 293, 324–5.
11   *CPR 1281–92*, 324–5.
12   *Foedera 1272–1307*, 738; *CPR 1281–92*, 382.
13   *CPR 1281–92*, 374.
14   *CChR 1257–1300*, 427; J. R. Maddicott, *Thomas of Lancaster* (1970), 3.
15   *CPR 1281–92*, 464.
16   *CPR 1301–7*, 208; *CIPM 1272–91*, nos 51, 310, 477.
17   *CPR 1266–72*, 440; M.T.W. Payne and J.E. Payne, 'The Wall Inscriptions
     of Gloucester Cathedral House and the de Chaworths of Kempsford',
     Transactions of the Bristol and Gloucestershire Archaeological Society, 112 (1994),
     94, 97.
18   See http://fmg.ac/Projects/MedLands/chambarsein.htm; *Jean de Joinville et
     les Seigneurs de Joinville*, ed. Henri-François Delaborde (1894), 409.

Chapter 7
1   *CPR 1281–92*, 393, 409.
2   Cited in Marc Morris, *A Great and Terrible King*, 231.
3   *CCR 1288–96*, 179–80.
4   Howell, *Eleanor*, 310–11.
5   *CPR 1281–92*, 463.
6   *CPR 1281–92*, 426, 433.
7   Johnstone, *Edward of Carnarvon*, 17, 28; Devon, *Issues of the Exchequer*, 108–11.
8   Joseph Burtt, ed., 'An Account of the Expenses of John of Brabant and
     Thomas and Henry of Lancaster, AD 1292–3'.
9   *CPR 1281–92*, 483, 508.
10   *CChR 1257–1300*, 427.
11   *CChR 1257–1300*, 423; DL 10/191.
12   *CPR 1292–1301*, 24.
13   LR 14/1071 and 1083 (Office of the Auditors of Land Revenue); 'Friaries:
     The Minoresses without Aldgate' on British History Online; *CPR
     1292–1301*, 106.
14   *CPR 1292–1301*, 24, 30.
15   McFarlane, *Nobility of Later Medieval England*, 256–9.
16   SC 8/20/973; SC 8/143/7118.
17   *CPR 1381–85*, 22.
18   SC 8/64/3163, and see also below, 16.
19   Morris, *Great and Terrible King*, 264–5; Bertie Wilkinson, *The Later Middle
     Ages in England*, 100.

20 *CPR 1292–1301*, 14–16, 27, 33.
21 *CPR 1292–1301*, 16.
22 Prestwich, *Edward I*, 380.
23 Cited in Malcolm Vale, *The Origins of the Hundred Years War* (1996), 196.
24 Vale, *Origins*, 196, 199–200.

Chapter 8

1 *Foedera 1272–1307*, 809.
2 *Ancient Correspondence Concerning Wales*, 154.
3 *Foedera 1272–1307*, 824; *CCR 1288–96*, 450.
4 *Foedera 1272–1307*, 836; *CCR 1288–96*, 507.
5 Prestwich, *Edward I*, 382–3.
6 *CCR 1288–96*, 456; Rhodes, 'Edmund', part 2, 231; Prestwich, *Edward I*, 384.
7 *Foedera 1272–1307*, 832–3.
8 *CCR 1296–1302*, 174; SC 1/19/148.
9 *CIPM 1291–1300*, no. 423.
10 *The Chronicle of Lanercost*, ed. Maxwell, 146.

Chapter 9

1 *CDS 1272–1307*, no. 822 (p. 190). At the same time, a chaplain of Edinburgh was arrested for 'excommunicating the king [Edward] with bell and candle'.
2 *Foedera 1272–1307*, 842; *CIPM 1291–1300*, no. 423.
3 Morris, *Great and Terrible King*, 291–2.
4 *CPR 1292–1301*, 211, 228; C 47/27/3/14.
5 *CCR 1296–1302*, 116; *CIPM 1291–1300*, no. 423.
6 *CPR 1292–1301*, 239, 464, 465; *CFR 1272–1307*, 384–5; see also *CChR 1257–1300*, 423. His mother Blanche seems to have still held Grosmont and Skenfrith in April 1299: *CPR 1292–1301*, 465–6.
7 *CPR 1292–1301*, 239; *CCR 1302–07*, 483; *CPR 1327–30*, 419; *CFR 1327–37*, 144.
8 *CPR 1292–1301*, 307.
9 *Records*, vol. 1, 260, and see also below.
10 *CCR 1296–1302*, 265.
11 *CPR 1292–1301*, 291.
12 *CDS 1272–1307*, 259.
13 *Parliamentary Writs*, vol. 1, 693–4.
14 *CCR 1343–46*, 368.
15 Edmund was not buried on 24 March 1301, as one chronicle cited in Rhodes, 'Edmund', part 2, 234, claims: Edward I was in Evesham, Worcestershire on this date, 100 miles from Westminster. See Henry Gough, *Itinerary of King Edward the First Throughout his Reign* (1900), vol. 2, 199. The Chancery Rolls confirm this; see *CPR 1292–1301*, 581–2, 587, 626 etc. The king was at Westminster for almost all of March 1300.

16 Rhodes, 'Edmund', part 2, 234.

17 *Liber Quotidianus Contrarotulatoris Garderobae, anno regni regis Edwardi primi vicesimo octavo*, ed. John Topham (London, 1787), xxxi–xxxii.

18 *The Roll of Arms of the Princes, Barons and Knights Who Attended King Edward I to the Siege of Caerlaverock*, ed. T. Wright (1864), 42–3, 46–9.

19 *CDS 1307–57*, no. 822, p. 190; also *CFR 1272–1307*, 384 (March 1297). The name was de Lancastre in French and de Lancastria in Latin.

20 *CPR 1292–1301*, 521; *CFR 1272–1307*, 399.

21 *CPR 1313–17*, 441. On the other hand, this same entry on the Patent Roll gives Edmund of Lancaster's date of death as 4 June, when he died on the 5th.

22 *CPR 1301–07*, 117.

23 J.F. Baldwin, 'The Household Administration of Henry Lacy and Thomas of Lancaster', *English Historical Review*, 42 (1927), 194; DL 25/257; DL 25/329; *CPR 1313-17*, 441 (with the 4 June error); *CPR 1317–21*, 203–4; *CPR 1327–30*, 268; *Reports from Commissioners*, vol. 32 (1874), 34, 40; Maddicott, *Thomas of Lancaster*, 320.

24 *CDS 1272–1307*, 392–4; Howell, *Eleanor*, 290.

25 *CPR 1301–07*, 208, 468.

26 Hilda Johnstone, *The Letters of Edward, Prince of Wales 1304–1305* (1931), 70; my translation.

27 G.O. Sayles, *Functions of the Medieval Parliament of England* (1987), 302.

28 Maddicott, *Thomas of Lancaster*, 332; *Adae Murimuth Continuatio Chronicarum*, 271–6 (where Thomas' long letter is cited in full in French and English translation).

29 Maddicott, *Thomas of Lancaster*, 346–7.

30 *The True Chronicles of Jean le Bel, 1290–1360*, 28, 78, 147; *ODNB*.

31 Her *ODNB* entry, for example, says she was the fourth daughter.

32 *Burke's Guide to the Royal Family* (1973), 196, states that Eleanor was born on 11 September 1318, but I am unaware of the primary source which states her date of birth.

33 Joan's date of birth is not known, but her brother William Martin was born in about 1294, and her second husband Nicholas Audley in about 1292. Henry de Lacy was born in 1250 or 1251 and his daughter Alice in 1281.

34 *CPR 1301–07*, 495.

35 C 53/94; Maddicott, *Thomas of Lancaster*, 341–2.

36 *CPR 1307–13*, 68.

37 *Records*, vol. 1, 260: 'To a certain messenger of the lady countess who brought the news that she was pregnant, 1s [shilling].'

38 *CCR 1307–13*, 51.

Chapter 10

1 C 53/95, nos 38, 43, 46, 49; C 53/96, nos 5, 6, 7, 9, 12.
2 Andy King, 'Thomas of Lancaster's First Quarrel with Edward II', *FCE III*, ed. Mark Ormrod (2004), 31–45; Maddicott, *Thomas of Lancaster*, 92–4.
3 King, 'First Quarrel', 33; *CChR 1300–26*, 123, *CCW*, 281; *Foedera 1307–27*, 75.
4 *CPR 1307–13*, 206.
5 Hallam, *Itinerary of Edward II*, 49, 53, 63; *CCR 1307–13*, 226 (Bek gave Edward II his Lincolnshire castle of Somerton and the lands around it).
6 *CCR 1307–13*, 253.
7 J.S. Hamilton, *Piers Gaveston, Earl of Cornwall: Politics and Patronage in the Reign of Edward II* (1988), 85; Maddicott, *Lancaster*, 115; *Lanercost*, 192.
8 Fowler, 27, for the knighting.
9 *CIPM 1347–52*, no. 107.
10 DL 25/1193. Henry was also in Wales, at Kidwelly 75 miles from Grosmont, on 19 May 1309: *CPR 1313–17*, 222.
11 *Records*, vol. 1, 345; the 'Sir' here was a courtesy title given to a nobleman, and Henry had not yet been knighted.
12 Cited in T.F. Tout, *The Place of the Reign of Edward II in English History* (second edition, 1936), 13, note 2.
13 *Vita*, 23.
14 *Vita*, 28.
15 *Vita*, 36; *Trokelowe*, 79–80; *Scalacronica*, ed. Maxwell, 51.

Chapter 11

1 *Foedera 1307–27*, 191–2; *CPR 1307–13*, 516–7; *Annales Londonienses*, 221–25; *Vita*, 43.
2 *CPR 1313–17*, 23; DL 10/214.
3 DL 25/2328/2021; DL 25/1193/930; DL 25/2341/2030; C 53/101, no. 19.
4 C 53/94; C 53/101.
5 *CDS 1307–57*, no. 204.
6 Thomas' household and income from C.M. Woolgar, *The Great Household in Late Medieval England* (1999), 12.
7 *Vita*, 28–9.
8 Baldwin, 'Household Administration', 194; Maddicott, *Lancaster*, 32–4; *Records*, vol. 2, 300, 306, 317.
9 *Vita*, 75.
10 *CCW*, 437, 439–40; *CPR 1313–17*, 384, 432–3.
11 *Testamenta Vetusta* (hereafter: *TV*), vol. 1, 80.
12 Maddicott, *Lancaster*, 187.
13 *CPR 1313–17*, 621 (Buntingford); Thomas Stapleton, 'A Brief Summary of the Wardrobe Accounts of the Tenth, Eleventh and Fourteenth Years of King Edward the Second', *Archaeologia*, 26 (1836), 320 (messenger).

14 *CIPM 1291–1300*, no. 597; *CPR 1313–7*, 553. Thomas Wake was a great-great-grandson of Llywelyn ab Iorwerth, Prince of Gwynedd, and his wife Joan, illegitimate daughter of King John.

15 *CIPM 1317–27*, no. 10.

16 *CPR 1317–21*, 43, 251–2; *CCR 1313–18*, 413. Henry was at Clarendon in Wiltshire with Edward and Queen Isabella on 10 and 14 February 1317: C 53/103, nos 19, 35; *CChR 1300–26*, 339–40.

17 Frances Underhill, *For Her Good Estate*, 18, 135; E 101/377/2.

18 *Anonimalle Chronicle*, 92; *Gesta Edwardi de Carnarvon*, 54.

19 *Vita*, 80.

20 Maddicott, *Lancaster*, 319.

21 C 53/106, nos 26, 31 (York).

22 *Petitions to the Pope 1342–1419* (hereafter: *PP*), 65, 271.

23 A. Tomkinson, 'Retinues at the Tournament of Dunstable, 1309', *English Historical Review*, 74 (1959); *Collectanea Topographica et Genealogica*, vol. 4, eds. F. Madden, B. Bandinel and J.G. Nichols (1837), 67–70.

24 *Adae Murimuth*, 275.

25 *Vita*, 87.

26 J.R.S. Phillips, 'The "Middle Party" and the Negotiating of the Treaty of Leake: A Reinterpretation', *Bulletin of the Institute of Historical Research*, 46 (1973), 17.

27 *CPL 1305–41*, 415, 431, 434, 438–9, 444.

28 Maddicott, *Lancaster*, 207–8; Roy Martin Haines, *King Edward II: His Life, His Reign, and Its Aftermath, 1284–1330* (2003), 107–8.

29 *CPR 1317–21*, 46; *CCR 1313–18*, 575; *Foedera 1307–27*, 345–6; Stapleton, 'Brief Summary of the Wardrobe Accounts', 329, for the surrender of Knaresborough; *CIM 1308–48*, 98–9: Lilburn held Knaresborough from 5 October 1317 to 29 January 1318.

30 *CFR 1307–19*, 225, 316.

31 *CFR 1307–19*, 346–7; *Foedera 1307–27*, 345–346; *CCR 1313–18*, 575.

32 E 40/351; Somerville, *Duchy of Lancaster*, 337.

33 *Foedera 1307–27*, 479.

34 *Flores Historiarum*, vol. 3, 180–1; Maddicott, *Lancaster*, 210; Haines, *Edward II*, 109.

35 *Vita Edwardi Secundi*, 81–2.

Chapter 12

1 *Foedera 1307–27*, 334. Why Henry and not Thomas was John's heir to the French lands is not clear, but as noted above, Edmund of Lancaster was probably trying to split his large inheritance to benefit all his sons, and Thomas as the eldest son and recipient of the greater part of the inheritance had no real need of the French lands.

2 *CPR 1317–21*, 145–6, 153, 217.

3 C 53/105, nos 26, 31; *CPR 1317–21*, 271, 329, 343.

4 *CPR 1317–21*, 262, 271; *CCR 1313–18*, 123.

5 *CPR 1317–21*, 503, 524, 548; *CPR 1321–24*, 69.

6 Haines, *Edward II*, 113; *Vita*, 88.

7 *Vita*, 97, 104.

8 C 53/105, nos 13, 14, 77–80, 82–4, etc; C 53/106, nos 29–31; *CPR 1317–21*, 341; DL 10/232.

9 *Vita*, 97–9, 102.

10 SC 8/204/10172 and 3.

11 *CPR 1317–21*, 440; SC 8/87/4346.

12 *CPR 1317–21*, 531. For Meldon, see Maddicott, *Thomas of Lancaster*, 20–21.

13 *CPR 1317–21*, 524, 548.

14 *CCR 1318–23*, 515–6.

15 *CDS 1307–57*, no. 746; *CCR 1318–23*, 525–6.

16 *CPR 1321–24*, 69.

17 *The Brut or the Chronicles of England*, 216–7.

18 Maddicott, *Lancaster*, 296, 311.

19 *Brut*, 216–21.

20 *Anonimalle*, 106.

21 *Vita*, 125.

22 *CDS 1307–57*, no. 747.

23 *Brut*, 222; *Vita*, 126; *Livere de Reis*, 341–2.

24 *Lanercost*, 234; *Anonimalle*, 108; *Brut*, 222; *Vita*, 126; *Scalacronica*, 67.

25 *Brut*, 223; *Vita*, 126.

26 *Brut*, 223; *Gesta*, 77.

Chapter 13

1 *CPR 1327–30*, 126.

2 *CPR 1327–30*, 124, 125, 194, 317; *CPR 1330–34*, 334.

3 *Foedera 1327–44*, 726.

4 *PP*, 271; *CPR 1345–48*, 350.

5 *Collection of All the Wills*, 54.

6 Maddicott, *Lancaster*, 329.

7 *Foedera 1327–44*, 695.

8 T. Wright, ed., *The Political Songs of England* (1839), 268–72.

9 Maddicott, *Lancaster*, 329–30.

10 *CIM 1308–48*, no. 2103.

11 *Brut*, 230.

12 *CPL 1342–62*, 357.

13 *PP*, 271, 346. Uttoxeter had belonged to the Ferrers family and passed to Edmund of Lancaster in 1269.

14 *PP*, 65, 193, 383; in the first entry, John is wrongly called John de Cornubia, i.e. 'John of Cornwall'.

15 William Arthur Shaw, *The Knights of England: A Complete Record from the Earliest Time*, vol. 1 (1906), p. 6 of the section called 'Knights Bachelors'.

16 *PP*, 262. He is also mentioned in *CCR 1346–49*, 545, and *CPR 1345–48*, 408, 487.

17 *CIPM 1327–36*, no. 82.

18 *CPR 1321–24*, 98.

19 *PP*, 253, for the burial; Paul Dryburgh, 'The Career of Roger Mortimer, First Earl of March', Univ. of Bristol PhD thesis (2002), 102 note 283, citing BL MS Stowe 553, fo. 25r, for the date.

20 *Records*, vol. 1, 353.

21 *PP*, 253.

22 SC 8/124/6156; SC 8/56/2776; SC 8/332/15791A and B.

23 *CCR 1318–23,* 711. The same men were executors of Maud Chaworth's will: *CCR 1318–23*, 686–7. Her will does not survive.

24 *CFR 1319–27*, 268–9, 284.

25 E 101/380/4, fo. 22v.

26 *Vita*, 136–7.

27 *Vita*, 137–8.

28 *Vita*, 140.

29 *CPR 1324–27*, 167, 168, 170.

30 C 53/112, nos 11, 13.

31 *CPR 1324–27*, 283–4, 288.

32 *CPR 1324–27*, 284. Henry's close adherents Thomas Blount and Henry Ferrers were also appointed: *CPR*, 238, 283.

33 C 53/112, nos 3, 5, 6; *CPR 1324–27*, 261.

34 E 326/8707.

35 C 53/111, nos 1, 3, 4, 5, 13, 15, 16, dated 11 November 1324, 26 June 1325, 1 July and 4 July 1325, all at Westminster (Henry's son-in-law Thomas Wake was with him on 1 July) and all during parliament.

36 *Records*, vol. 1, 353; Jennifer Ward, *Elizabeth de Burgh, Lady of Clare (1295–1360)*, 2.

37 *CFR 1319–27*, 418; *CPR 1324–27*, 332.

38 *Records,* vol. 1, 380; *Knighton's Chronicle 1337–96*, ed. G.H. Martin, 435.

39 *Anonimalle*, 129–30.

40 *CCR 1323–27*, 655.

41 *Records*, vol. 1, 353.

42 *Annales Paulini*, 317.

43 *CCR 1327–30*, 445.

44 *CPR 1324–27*, 337.

Chapter 14

1 *CPR 1327–30*, 8, 26.

2 *CCR 1323–27*, 569; *CCR 1330–33*, 99. The constable of Tickhill in 1326 was William Aune, friend and ally of Edward II.

3   *CIPM 1327–36*, no. 250.

4   Fowler, 256, note 16; *Complete Peerage*, vol. 12B, 179.

5   R.B. Pugh, 'Fragment of an Account of Isabel of Lancaster, Nun of Amesbury, 1333–4', 487; *A History of the County of Wiltshire*, vol. 3, ed. R.B. Pugh and Elizabeth Crittall (1956), 250. Henry of Lancaster was a generous benefactor to Amesbury Priory, and gave the prioress £9 annually. 'Fragment', 493; *Wiltshire*, 250.

6   Fowler, 27.

7   'Fragment of Account', 490–1, 495–8.

8   Fowler, 27; Fowler, thesis, 19, 542–4; DL 25/966/751; DL 25/2184; DL 25/2061; DL 25/966.

9   William was in Ireland in October 1329 and February and June 1331: *CPR 1327–30*, 448; *CPR 1330–34*, 119; *CCR 1330–33*, 294; Fowler, 28, for 1328. He was knighted in London in May 1328: *CP*, vol. 12B, 178.

10 Fowler, thesis, 18, note 2.

11 Fowler, thesis, 20, 155, note 2; DL 25/964/749.

12 'Fragment', 489, 492, 496, 497 (curiously, Isabella's account calls Eleanor a countess, though she did not become one until 1345); SC 1/39/143.

13 'Fragment', 491.

14 *PP*, 31.

15 'Fragment', 493 ('sincere affection'); Fowler, thesis, 590–1, *CPR 1345–48*, 96, 372, 401, 449–50, 470, and *CPR 1348–50*, 97 (helping Maud); DL 25/330 (Haltemprice); *Collection of Wills*, 86 (Blanche as executor).

16 Fowler, 216.

17 *PP*, 282 (Beaumont); *ODNB* (Percy); *Register of John of Gaunt*, vol. 1, 268, *CPL 1342–62*, 585 (Mowbray; there are other examples).

18 Cited in Kris Towson, 'Hearts Warped by Passion: The Percy-Gaunt Dispute of 1381', *FCE III*, ed. W.M. Ormrod (2004), 143, note 3.

19 Underhill, *For Her Good Estate*, 95 and 185, note 47. In March 1331 Isabella's mother Elizabeth de Burgh gave her a present for her purification, which usually took place forty days after birth. Henry Ferrers of Groby was much older than his wife, born before 1304 and perhaps in the 1290s.

20 Fowler, 28; *CPR 1330–34*, 265, 397.

21 *CPR 1338–40*, 49; *CPR 1324–27*, 258. Henry had gone through a legal battle with Maud Holland, widow of Sir Robert Holland who was murdered by his men in 1328, over Melbourne: Joe W. Leedom, 'Lady Matilda Holland, Henry of Lancaster and the Manor of Melbourne', *American Journal of Legal History*, 31 (1987).

22 *CPR 1327–30*, 474; *CPR 1334–38*, 553; 'Fragment', 489; Fowler, thesis, 589.

23 John Aberth, *An Environmental History of the Middle Ages* (2012), 199.

24 N.B. Lewis, 'A Certificate of the Earl of Lancaster's Auditors, 1341', *English Historical Review*, 55 (1940), 101–2.

Chapter 15

1   *CFR 1327–37*, 33.

2   *Knighton's Chronicle 1337 to 1396*, 447.

3   *Vita*, 137; *True Chronicles*, 28, 78.

4   *Parliament Rolls of Medieval England (PROME)*, September 1327.

5   *Knighton's Chronicle*, 444.

6   *Annales Paulini*, 337.

7   Natalie Fryde, *The Tyranny and Fall of Edward II 1321–1326* (1979), 224.

8   *CPR 1327–30*, 249, 290.

9   G.W.S. Barrow, *Robert Bruce and the Community of the Realm of Scotland* (second edition, 1976) 367, 369.

10 V.B. Redstone, 'Some Mercenaries of Henry of Lancaster, 1327–1330', *Transactions of the Royal Historical Society*, 7 (1913), 160–1.

11 *CIM 1308–48*, no. 1039.

12 *CPR 1327–30*, 17; *CCR 1327–30*, 192; *Rotuli Parliamentorum; ut et Petitiones, et Placita in Parliamento Tempore Edwardi R. III* (1783), vol. 2, 18; SC 8/57/2806.

13 *CIM 1308–48*, no. 1093; *Annales Paulini*, 342; *Knighton's Chronicle*, 449; *Brut*, 257; J.R. Maddicott, 'Thomas of Lancaster and Sir Robert Holland: A Study in Noble Patronage', *English Historical Review*, 86 (1971), 469–70. In July 1336 and June 1341, Holland's eldest son and heir Robert the younger acknowledged a debt of 250 marks to Henry of Lancaster: *CCR 1333–37*, 685; *CCR 1341–43*, 261.

14 *CIM 1308–48*, no. 1111; 'Fragment of Account', 491.

15 *CFR 1327–37*, 116–7.

16 *Knighton*, 450–1.

17 *CCR 1327–30*, 425; DL 25/3468; Jules Viard, *Documents parisiens du règne de Philippe VI de Valois, 1328–1350* (1900), vol. 1, 84–5.

18 *Knighton*, 451; *CCR 1327–30*, 528, 530–1, 593–4; *CCR 1330–33*, 286–7; *CPR 1330–34*, 26.

19 *Galfridi le Baker de Swinbroke Chronicon*, ed. J.A. Giles, 106; A.R. Myers, *English Historical Documents 1327–1485*, 52; *Knighton*, 460.

20 The *ODNB* entry on Henry, for example, says that by 1329 he was 'old and weak'.

21 E 101/310/24; *CCR 1333–37*, 99; *CCR 1339–41*, 660; *CCR 1341–43*, 275; *CCR 1343–46*, 368; *CPR 1338–40*, 141, 365, 493; *CPR 1343–45*, 487.

22 Henry was at Kenilworth in January, May, June and September 1338, April 1339 and February 1340, Leicester in December 1338, July, August and November 1339, February 1340 and November 1341, Kempsford and possibly Northampton in April 1342, Kenilworth in November 1342, Liverpool in July 1343, Lincoln sometime in 1343, Leicester in March 1344, Higham Ferrers in April 1344, Tutbury in August 1344, Leicester in November 1344 and January 1345, Kenilworth in May and July 1345, and died in Leicester that September. DL 25/2183; DL 25/3576; DL 25/982/759; DL 25/346/288; DL 25/2255/1956; DL 25/334/279; DL 25/1219/951; DL

25/1220/952; DL 25/2302/1996; R 10/63; SC 1/41/50; SC 1/50/174; DL 25/3460; CR 162/238; *Records*, vol. 2, 45–6, 60–2; *Register of John of Gaunt, 1371–75*, vol. 1, 236; *CPR 1361–64*, 200.

23 DL 25/3460.

24 *CCR 1327–30*, 433, 457.

25 DL 25/2305/1999; DL 25/2307/2001.

26 *Records*, vol. 2, 8–9.

27 *CPR 1327–30*, 442, 474, 482; *CCR 1327–30*, 504.

28 *CPL 1305–41*, 411–12; *CPR 1327–30*, 474, 482, 491, 503.

29 *CPL 1305–41*, 318, 411–12.

30 *Records*, vol. 2, 15.

31 *CPMR 1323–64*, 72.

32 *CFR 1327–37*, 175; *CCR 1330–33*, 288.

33 *CPR 1330–34*, 16.

34 BCM/A/1/1/85.

35 Louis Brienne's much older half-sister Yolande (1212–28), from his father John's first marriage to Marie, Queen of Jerusalem, was, like her mother, queen of Jerusalem in her own right. She was the second wife of the Holy Roman Emperor Frederick II (1194–1250), mother of his son Konrad, king of Germany (1228–54) and grandmother of the 16-year-old Konradin beheaded by Charles of Anjou.

36 Johnstone, *Letters of Edward, Prince of Wales*, 73–4 (my translation).

37 *Vita*, 57–8.

38 *CFR 1319–27*, 431 (grant of Atholl's marriage to Beaumont); Brad Verity, 'Isabel de Beaumont', *Foundations* (journal of the Foundation for Medieval Genealogy), 1.5 (2004), 312 and note 14.

39 *CPR 1330–34*, 20, 270.

40 Fowler 256, notes 14 and 15.

41 *CIPM 1336–46*, no. 271, gives John's date of birth.

42 *Adae Murimuth*, 256; *CCR 1330–33*, 147, 151; *CPR 1327–30*, 544, 563, 570–72.

43 *CPR 1338–40*, 457; *CPR 1345–48*, 87.

44 *CPR 1327–30*, 571.

45 *CPR 1330–34*, 227.

46 *English Historical Documents 1327–1485*, 51. At this point, Baker states that Henry was blind.

47 Fryde, *Tyranny and Fall of Edward II*, 224.

48 Caroline Shenton, 'Edward III and the Coup of 1330', *The Age of Edward III*, ed. J. Bothwell (2001), 26–9; Fryde, *Tyranny and Fall of Edward II*, 224; Fowler, 25–6; W.M. Ormrod, *Edward III* (2012), 90; *CPR 1330–34*, 4, 16.

49 Ormrod, *Edward III*, 90; Fowler, 25–6.

50 *English Historical Documents 1327–1485*, 52.

51 *CChR 1327–41*, 199.

52 *CPR 1330–34*, 20, 36. Wake was back by 21 December, p. 36.

Chapter 16

1 *CPR 1330–34*, 41–2, 48; *Foedera 1327–44*, 805–6; E 101/310/24.

2 Jules Viard, 'Itinéraire de Philippe VI de Valois', *Bibliothèque de l'école des chartes*, 74 (1913), 102.

3 *CPR 1330–34*, 90–95, and *Foedera 1327–44*, 813, for the envoys; Ormrod, *Edward III*, 179–80, 613, and Ian Mortimer, *The Perfect King: The Life of Edward III* (2006), 91–3, for Edward III's visit; E 101/310/24 is Henry of Lancaster's expenses and itinerary; Fowler, thesis, 19, for Grosmont.

4 *Foedera 1327–44*, 814.

5 *CPR 1330–34*, 265, 397. Edward III was Blanche of Artois' great-grandson from her first marriage and Henry her grandson from her second, and they were also second cousins, both great-grandchildren of Henry III and Eleanor of Provence.

6 DL 27/192.

7 Fowler, 28.

8 *CCR 1333–37*, 99; *Foedera 1327–44*, 855.

9 *CPR 1330–34*, 484, 486. Sir Nicholas Gernoun, presumably a relative, was given permission in August 1382, in old age, to dwell at Maud and her son-in-law Lionel of Antwerp's foundation of Bruisyard Abbey: *CPR 1381–85*, 161.

10 *CIPM 1327–36*, no. 537.

11 Devon, *Issues of the Exchequer*, 143; *CPR 1330–34*, 490; *CPR 1334–38*, 31; *CPR 1338–40*, 21, 305, 458; *CCR 1337–39*, 85; SC 8/80/3971.

12 *CPR 1338–40*, 115.

13 For example, *CPR 1338–40*, 305, 458; *CPR 1340–43*, 187, 189; *CPR 1350–54*, 495; *CCR 1333–37*, 244, 324.

14 *CPR 1338–40*, 445.

15 *CIPM 1327–36*, no. 537.

16 Underhill, *For Her Good Estate*, 94, 109, 189, note 92; Ward, *Elizabeth de Burgh, Lady of Clare*, 46. Elizabeth was a granddaughter of Henry's uncle Edward I, and thus his first cousin once removed.

17 *CCR 1333–37*, 248.

18 *CCR 1337–39*, 170.

19 *CPR 1334–38*, 6, 41; Fowler, 256, note 16; *CCR 1333–37*, 318, 490; DL 10/273.

20 Henry was '30 years and more' when his father died in February 1352: *CIPM 1352–60*, no. 43. Henry Senior was born in Leconfield, Yorkshire on 6 February 1301: *CIPM 1307–17*, no. 536; *CIPM 1317–27*, no. 435.

21 'Fragment', 488, 492, 497.

22 *Testamenta Eboracensia*, vol. 1, 57.

23 *CFR 1327–37*, 431–2.

24 *Records*, vol. 1, 353; vol. 2, 12, 14–16, 26.

25 *CPR 1334–38*, 206.

26 Linda E. Mitchell, *Portraits of Medieval Women: Family, Marriage and Politics in England, 1225–1350* (2003), 116, 121

27 *CPL 1305–41*, 544, for the vow. The writ for Eble Lestrange's IPM was issued on 17 September 1335; his heir was Roger Lestrange, either his brother or nephew (the IPM states both). *CIPM 1327–36*, no. 681.

28 *Complete Peerage*, vol. 5, 572. Frene's identity is uncertain, but *Complete Peerage* speculates that he may have been a son or younger brother of John de Frene, whose father Hugh died in 1303. Sir John de Frene, Lord of Moccas in Herefordshire, appears in record in early January 1347, when another John Freyne who held land from him died (*CIPM 1336–46*, no. 679); probably the John who held Moccas was Hugh de Frene's older brother or father. The older Hugh de Frene (d. 1303) also owned Moccas: *CPR 1292–1301*, 23. Hugh de Frene the younger (the man who abducted Alice) participated in a jousting tournament which took place in Dunstable in Edward III's seventh regnal year, probably in January 1334: *Collectanea Topographica et Genealogica*, eds. F. Madden, B. Bandinel and J.G. Nichols, vol. 4 (1837), 395. He was appointed custodian of Cardigan Castle, South Wales on 18 December 1330, and two years later was made its constable for life: *CPR 1330–34*, 31, 365; *CCR 1330–33*, 104. He appears to have had connections to Ireland, as a royal servant called Elias Asseburn or Ashburn included him in a list of men to be prayed for daily in the chapel of St Laud in Dublin in 1332, and a Fulk Freyn, presumably a relative, was 'lord of the castle of Faytheli' in Ireland in 1334: *CPR 1330–34*, 303; *CPR 1334–38*, 424; *CPL 1305–41*, 404.

29 *CPR 1334–38*, 282; *CFR 1327–37*, 473; *CCR 1333–37*, 561.

30 SC 8/64/3163 is the petition; it talks about the *traisoun de son frere sire John de Lacy*. As Alice was her father's heir she must have been his only surviving legitimate child, and therefore John de Lacy must have been Earl Henry de Lacy's illegitimate son, and her half-brother. He may have been a clerk in her household. Michael Prestwich suggests in *The Three Edwards: War and State in England 1272–1377* (1980), 138, that Alice 'was not a wholly unwilling victim' of Hugh de Frene's abduction of her and that Frene was attracted more by her lands than her 'physical charms'. In fact, Alice's petition to Edward III makes it all too painfully apparent how frightened, distressed and angry she was about the matter and about her close confinement in the Tower (*en tiele destresse q' nul de ses amys ne bien voillauntz lui puissent approcher ne parler*); she was most certainly an unwilling victim. Although Prestwich states that she had voluntarily taken a vow of chastity after her second husband's death, he does not mention that this reveals she clearly did not wish to marry again. Prestwich also claims that Alice was allowed to go up to her chamber at Bolingbroke to collect her things, but on realising the gravity of her situation tried to escape by deliberately falling from her horse when Frene and his men took her from Bolingbroke to Somerton,

and that Frene subsequently put her back on the horse and had a groom sit behind her to hold her on. These details, which put an unpleasantly farcical spin on Alice's ordeal, are not in her petition nor in any of the Chancery Roll entries pertaining to the abduction, and I have been unable to locate Prestwich's source (he fails to cite one).

31 *CPR 1305–41*, 544.
32 *Complete Peerage*, vol. 5, 572–4; vol. 7, 687.
33 *CCR 1337–39*, 18–20, 25 (lands): *CPR 1334–38*, 450 (attack). See Mitchell, *Portraits of Medieval Women*, 121, for more information.

Chapter 17

1 *CPR 1334–38*, 400; *CChR 1327–41, 390*.
2 Edward's claim to the French throne and Philip's objections are set out in *CPL 1305–41*, 586–8.
3 *CPR 1338–40*, 313, for Lionel's birth.
4 *CPR 1340–43*, 50, 175.
5 At Antwerp in July 1339, Mowbray alienated some of his lands to a clerk called Henry Dale, who worked for the Lancasters, especially Eleanor's sisters Maud, countess of Ulster and Isabella the nun, and their father. DL 10/282 and *CPR 1338–40, 389* for the alienation; *CPR 1334–38*, 553, *CPR 1338–40*, 368, 467, *CCR 1339–41*, 175, *Records*, vol. 2, 45, and 'Fragment', 496, for Dale's association with the Lancasters; he spent Christmas 1338 in Leicester with Henry, earl of Lancaster. Peculiarly, the *Complete Peerage* (vol. 7, 401, note b) says that Dale married Henry's second daughter Isabella the nun.
6 *Records*, vol. 2, 45–6; DL 25/1869; DL 25/964/749.
7 Henry was of full age, i.e. 21, by 14 January 1361: *CCR 1360–64*, 91.
8 *CPR 1340–43*, 72–3.
9 *CIPM 1347–52*, no. 415.
10 *CPR 1350–54*, 63.
11 *CPR 1338–40*, 440; *CFR 1337–47*, 187.
12 *CIPM 1361–65*, 92–116, 231–6. Henry IV's biographer Chris Given-Wilson (*Henry IV*, 24) says that Blanche was, implausibly, only 21 when she died in 1368, which would make her barely 13 when she gave birth to her first child Philippa in March 1360. A date of birth in 1344 or 1345 seems about right.
13 *CPR 1340–43*, 75, 268, 276, 281, 285; DL 25/983; DL 25/75; Fowler, 35–6.
14 Fowler, 215–6.
15 *Records*, vol. 2, 46.
16 Cited in Fowler, 191–2.
17 Cited in Verity, 'Isabel de Beaumont', 314.
18 *CPR 1401–05*, 397.
19 *Livre de Seyntz Medicines* on anglo-norman.net, 27–8, 72, 78.

Chapter 18

1 Ormrod, *Edward III*, 212, 225, 618.
2 *CCR 1341–43*, 467.
3 W.M. Ormrod, 'The Royal Nursery: A Household for the Younger Children of Edward III', *English Historical Review*, 120 (2005), 414; *CPR 1345–48*, 55; Goodman, *John of Gaunt*, 29.
4 *CIPM 1361–65*, no. 144: in October 1361 John was 'aged 21 years about Midsummer last'.
5 *CPL 1342–62*, 305; PP, 151; *CPR 1348–50*, 373; *CCR 1349–54*, 51.
6 *CIPM 1352–60*, nos 116, 121.
7 BCM/D/5/9/4.
8 BCM/D/1/1/9 and 10.
9 BCM D/1/19/2.
10 For the date, Mortimer, *Perfect King*, 183, 467, note 4; Ormrod, 'Royal Nursery', 406, note 34; *CP*, vol. 12B, 895.
11 Ormrod, 'Royal Nursery', 402; *CPR 1340–43*, 569.
12 *CPR 1334–38*, 243; *CPR 1345–48*, 72; *CPR 1348–50*, 108; *CPR 1358–61*, 168; *CPR 1364–67*, 185.
13 *CP*, vol. 12B, 895–6, note i.
14 See http://www.warrenfamilyhistory.com/Download/Earls%20Willl.pdf.
15 *CPR 1358–61*, 117.
16 SC 8/246/12284.
17 John Evans, 'Edmund of Langley and his Tomb', *Archaeologia*, 46 (1881). For Edward III, see Ormrod, *Edward III*, 578, and for Edward I, Prestwich, *Edward I*, 567.
18 *CPL 1305–41*, 585; Mortimer, *Perfect King*, 182.
19 *CPL 1305–41*, 585.
20 Mortimer, *Perfect King*, 183–5, 434.
21 *CChR 1327–41*, 300, is the grant of Chester to Edward of Woodstock; *CChR 1341–1417*, 9, Richmond to John of Gaunt.
22 *CP*, vol. 7, 404.
23 *CPR 1340–43*, 187; Munby, Barber, Brown, *Edward III's Round Table at Windsor*, 36.
24 Ormrod, *Edward III*, 130, 140; Ormrod, 'Royal Nursery', 411 note 74; *CPMR 1323–64*, 153.
25 *CPR 1345–48*, 87.
26 *Foedera 1344–61*, 45.
27 *Adae Murimuth*, 142; Munby, Barber and Brown, *Round Table*, 35, 36, for the tournament. Jean Le Bel says that Henry, earl of Lancaster was there, though he was at Kempsford, Gloucestershire on 2 and 17 April: DL 25/346, 334 and 1215.
28 *CPR 1340–43*, 428.
29 *True Chronicles*, 146–7.

30 *CIPM 1336–46,* no. 381, is John's IPM, though it does not give the date of his death; *CFR 1337–47,* 288, 386; *CCR 1341–43,* 578; *CPR 1340–43,* 506.

31 *CCR 1341–43,* 578, 622, 626.

32 Michael Burtscher, *The Fitzalan Earls of Arundel and Surrey* (2008), 67.

33 CFR 1337–47, 141, 347, 386; *CPR 1338–40,* 312; *CPR 1343–45,* 557; *CPR 1348–50,* 483–4; *CIPM 1336–46,* no. 381.

34 *PP,* 282; a *donsel* was a young man not yet knighted.

35 *CPR 1334–38,* 466; *CPR 1340–43,* 302.

36 *CPR 1338–40,* 95, 99, 116–7; *CCR 1337–39,* 466, 506; *CCR 1339–41,* 421–2, 569–70.

37 *CPR 1334–38,* 430; *CPR 1340–43,* 425, 499; *CCR 1343–46,* 517.

38 Devon, *Issues of the Exchequer,* 144.

39 *ODNB,* 'Thomas Wake'.

40 For example: *CPR 1343–45,* 563, 565; *CPR 1345–48,* 8; 1354–8, 313; *CPR 1374–77,* 251; *PP,* 120, 276, 277.

41 *CPR 1338–40,* 108–9.

Chapter 19

1 *CChR 1341–1417,* 9, 12.

2 Fowler, 45.

3 Timothy Guard, *Chivalry, Kingship and Crusade: The English Experience in the Fourteenth Century* (2013), 53–4; *True Chronicles of Jean le Bel,* 98.

4 Fowler, thesis, 155–6.

5 *Records,* vol. 2, 60–2.

6 Goodman, 30.

7 *CPL 1342–62,* 112, 137.

8 *CPR 1343–45,* 197.

9 *PP,* 74.

10 *CChR 1341–1417,* 20.

11 *Issues of the Exchequer,* 144; 'Fragment', 489, 490, 492, 498.

12 *Knighton, Chronica,* ed. Martin, vol. 2, (1995), 30; *CPR 1343–45,* 366, 384; DL 25/2184.

13 DL 27/36, cited in Fowler, thesis, 68–9.

14 *CIPM 1347–52,* no. 56; *CCR 1346–49,* 344–5.

15 *True Chronicles,* 157.

16 Ormrod, *Edward III,* 302; Fowler, 46; *CP,* vol. 1, 243–4. The Medieval Lands project on www.fmg.ac claims that 'While her first husband was alive, she lived with her second husband'. There is no evidence that Eleanor and Arundel's relationship began while John Beaumont was alive, and no reason to think that it did.

17 *CPR 1343–45,* 224; *Foedera 1344–61,* 8–11.

18 Michael Burtscher, *The Fitzalan Earls of Arundel,* 43 (quotation).

19 *CPL 1305–41,* 164; *PP,* 75, 81.

20 Burtscher, *Fitzalan Earls*, 43.

21 *Foedera 1344 61*, 30–31.

22 *PP*, 75, 81, 99.

23 *CPL 1342–62*, 164, 188, 254.

24 *CPL 1342–62*, 254; *PP*, 75, 81, 99; Burtscher, *Fitzalan Earls*, 44–5.

25 Burtscher, *Fitzalan Earls*, 45.

26 *CPR 1374–77*, 492–3; *CCR 1374–77*, 413, 511, 551. The earl had given the manors to Edmund's mother Isabella Despenser in 1344 for her sustenance.

27 *PP*, 99.

28 Arundel granted a charter at Leicester on that day, and Henry's steward, Sir Edmund Trussell, was one of the witnesses. Warwickshire County Record Office, CR 162/238. William Clinton's wife Juliana née Leyburne was the widow of the Lancastrian adherent and Henry's attorney Sir Thomas Blount (d. 1328), and Clinton himself had been one of Henry of Lancaster's two envoys to Edward III in late 1328 shortly before Henry openly rebelled against Edward's mother.

29 *CPR 1343–45*, 487.

30 *Early Lincoln Wills: An Abstract of All the Wills and Administrations Recorded in the Episcopal Registers of the Diocese of Lincoln, 1280–1547*, ed. Alfred Gibbons, 17–18.

31 Mortimer, *Perfect King*, 217; Ormrod, *Edward III*, 268.

32 *PP*, 151.

Chapter 20

1 Cited in Clifford J. Rogers, 'The Bergerac Campaign (1345) and the Generalship of Henry of Lancaster', *Journal of Medieval Military History*, ed. Bernard S. Bachrach et al, (2004) 89. Grosmont's 1345/46 campaign is discussed in detail in Nicholas A. Gribit, *Henry of Lancaster's Campaign to Aquitaine, 1345–46* (2016).

2 *True Chronicles of Jean Le Bel*, 78, 88.

3 *CCR 1346–49*, 65; *CPR 1345–48*, 558.

4 *CPR 1345–48*, 87.

5 *Records*, vol. 2, 67–8.

6 *CPR 1345–48*, 328–9 (first mention of the younger Richard, 1347), 595 for John and Eleanor; *ODNB* for Thomas; *CFR 1413–22*, 166–7, lists the five Arundel siblings in what must be birth order: Joan, Richard, Alice, John, Thomas.

7 *CPR 1360–64*, 320, 408; *CPR 1364–67*, 28. He died on 25 July 1369, before his mother: *CIPM 1365–69*, no. 321.

8 *ODNB*; Robin Frame, 'The Justiciarship of Ralph Ufford: Warfare and Politics in Fourteenth-Century Ireland', *Studia Hibernica*, 13 (1973), 36, note 165.

9 *CIPM 1336–46*, no. 629. The Dorset jurors stated, 'On what day he [Ralph Ufford] died the jurors know not, because he did not die within the four seas of England, nor who his next heir is or of what age, because he had

no one begotten of him in the county [Dorset].' Maud de Vere née Ufford's IPM in Rutland in March 1413 (*CIPM 1405–13*, no. 1045) confusingly and incorrectly calls her mother 'Elizabeth' and states also incorrectly that this Elizabeth had a sister called Alice.

10 *CPR 1345–48*, 449; *CPR 1370–74*, 463.
11 *CPR 1345–48*, 96.
12 Cited in *ODNB*.
13 *CPR 1348–50*, 86.
14 *CPR 1345–48*, 130, 372, 401, 449–50.
15 *CPR 1345–48*, 96, 372, 401, 449–50, 470; *CPR 1348–50*, 97.
16 Fowler, thesis, 543–4.
17 *CPR 1354–58*, 484–6.
18 *PP*, 488; *CPL 1362–1404*, 37–8.
19 *CPL 1362–1404*, 38, 56; *PP*, 531. Urban called Eleanor 'Eleanor de Lancastre' and Maud 'Matilda de Lancastria'.
20 Michael Robson, ed., *The English Province of the Franciscans (1224–c. 1350)*, 443; *TV*, vol. 1, 182; *Collection*, 111.
21 William Arthur Shaw, *The Knights of England: A Complete Record from the Earliest Time*, vol. 1 (1906), p. 6 of part 2, 'Knights Bachelors'.
22 BCM/D/5/101/8.
23 *CIPM 1352–60*, no. 116.
24 *CPR 1354–58*, 93, 325; *CCR 1354–60*, 27; C 49/7/27.
25 *CIPM 1370–73*, no. 148 (she was 'aged 17 on the eve of St James last' in January 1372).
26 *TV*, vol. 1, 85.
27 *TV*, vol. 1, 80.
28 *CChR 1341–1417*, 63; *CPR 1348–50*, 161, 164.
29 *CCR 1346–49*, 569, 610; *CChR 1341–1417*, 118; *CIPM 1347–52*, 95–100.
30 *CCR 1346–9*, 428, and *CCR 1349–54*, 5, for Isabella; *CP*, vol. 9, 383, for Joan. The *ODNB* entry for Joan's husband John Mowbray (1310–61) says that she was dead by August 1344 when Mowbray was married to another woman, called Elizabeth (not the Elizabeth de Vere whom he later married), apparently on the basis of document BCM D/1/1/7, which dates correctly to 1354 but a scribe wrote '1344' on it by error. A petition was presented to Edward III in early 1348 by 'John Mowbray and Joan his wife', so Joan of Lancaster was certainly alive then; SC 8/167/8311. Joan is mentioned in her father's will of 8 September 1345 when he left her a bequest: *Early Lincoln Wills*, 18. Her obituary of 7 July, though without a year, appears in the Sarum Missal, ed. J. Wickham Legg (1916), 515: *Translacio sancti Thome Martyris: Obitus domine Iohanne domine de Moubray filie Comitis Lancastriae*.
31 *CPL 1342–62*, 375, 385.
32 *CPR 1348–50*, 511.
33 Underhill, *Good Estate*, 95, calling Maud 'Margaret'.

34 *CPL 1342–62*, 385.

35 *ODNB*; *CPR 1367–70*, 244; BCM/D/1/1/4.

36 BCM/D/1/1/13 and 14; *CPL 1342–62*, 585.

37 BCM/D/1/1/5.

38 *TV*, vol. 1, 179–80.

39 Fowler, 93–5.

40 Goodman, 30–31.

41 *CPR 1350–54*, 60.

42 Fowler, 104, citing *Foedera 1344–61*, 5 (*qui in actibus militaribus delectatur*).

43 Timothy Guard, *Chivalry, Kingship and Crusade: The English Experience in the Fourteenth Century*, 73.

44 Guard, *Chivalry*, 74, 126; Fowler, thesis, 548–9.

45 *Register 1371–75*, vol. 1, 158.

46 Fowler, 105–6, and Guard, *Chivalry*, 74–5, for this paragraph.

47 Fowler, 106–7.

48 *CPR 1350–54*, 317; *Foedera 1344–61*, 248; Fowler, 108.

49 Fowler, 108–10.

50 *Foedera 1344–61*, 235; *Knighton*, vol. 2, 69.

51 *True Chronicles*, 107–8.

52 Fowler, thesis, 453; Verity, 'Isabel de Beaumont', 315, 319.

53 *True Chronicles*, 108. Later his brother Albrecht took over.

Chapter 21

1 Patrick Ball, "Mercy Gramercy': A Study of Henry of Grosmont', BA thesis, Univ. of Tasmania (2007), 16.

2 *Testamenta Eboracensia*, vol. 1, 202: *cum libro Gallico de Duce Lancastriae*.

3 *CPL 1342–62*, 585–6; *PP*, 273.

4 Edward of Woodstock, Prince of Wales, had an illegitimate son named Edward, mentioned in 1349 when his father, still only nineteen, bought a pony for him: George-Frederick Beltz, *Memorials of the Order of the Garter*, 383–4. Philippa of Clarence proved her date of birth and that she had come of age, 14, on 24 August 1369: *CIPM 1365–69*, 370–71.

5 *CPR 1354–58*, 352.

6 Devon, *Issues of the Exchequer*, 172; W.M. Ormrod, 'Edward III and his Family', *Journal of British Studies*, 26 (1987), 410, note 46.

7 Bridget Wells-Furby, 'Marriage and Inheritance: The Element of Chance in the Development of Lay Estates in the Fourteenth Century', *FCE X*, ed. Gwilym Dodd (2018), 125.

8 Roger Mortimer, second Earl of March and the grandson of the Earl of March who was executed in 1330, died on 26 February 1360 in his early 30s; his son and heir Edmund was born about 25 January or 2 February 1352: *CIPM 1352–60*, no. 640. Edmund and Philippa's son Roger Mortimer, fourth Earl of March, was born in April 1374.

9   *CPR 1354–58*, 269.
10 Goodman, 34–5.
11 *PP*, 337.
12 *Records*, vol. 2, 108–9.
13 *Issues of the Exchequer*, 172; E 101/393/10. Margaret and Mary, daughters of Edward III and Philippa of Hainault, both died in 1361 in their teens.
14 Cited in Goodman, 34, though my translation differs somewhat.
15 *CPL 1342–62*, 607.
16 Cited in 'Mercy Gramercy', 30–1.
17 Goodman, 35; SC 1/50/124.
18 Ormrod, *Edward III*, 399.
19 *CPR 1358–61*, 437; *ODNB*.

Chapter 22

1   *TV*, 56–9; *Collection*, 22–43.
2   *TV*, 64–6; *Collection*, 83–7. Somerville, *Duchy of Lancaster*, 47, Fowler, 217, and 'Fragment', 492, all assume that 'our very dear cousin of Walkington' meant Sir William Walkington, but it appears in the female form, *nostre tres chiere cosyne de Walkynton*, and William had been dead since February 1357 or earlier anyway: *CPR 1354–58*, 506. In 1343, Blanche Wake called Master Robert Walkington and his sister Agnes, wife of Sir John Mauduit, her kinsfolk, and in the same year her sister Maud also acknowledged Robert as her kinsman (*PP*, 29, 74). I am unaware of the precise relationship between the Lancasters and Walkingtons, but perhaps it was via the Lancasters' mother Maud Chaworth (d. 1322). Robert was a clerk of the older Henry, earl of Lancaster: DL 25/334/279.
3   Fowler, 218; *Records*, vol. 2, 124.
4   Fowler, 216; *Collection of Wills*, 83.
5   *CFR 1356–68*, 159.
6   *CFR 1356–68*, 157, 158, 194.
7   *CCR 1360–64*, 201–11; *CFR 1356–68*, 163–6.
8   For Juliane, see Douglas Richardson's posts in www.soc.genealogy.medieval.
9   *CPR 1367–70*, 237; *CIPM 1365–69*, no. 397.
10 *CIPM 1370–73*, no. 125, for Robert's date of birth.
11 *CIPM 1361–65*, no. 118.
12 *CIPM 1361–65*, no. 299.
13 *Knighton*, vol. 2, 116.
14 *PP*, 453; *CPL 1362–1404*, 60; Andrew Villalon and Donald Kagay, *To Win and Lose a Medieval Battle: Najera (April 3, 1367), A Pyrrhic Victory* (2017), 201.
15 *CPR 1361–64*, 167.
16 *CChR 1341–1417*, 174.
17 *CPR 1361–64*, 44.

Chapter 23

1 Laura Tompkins, 'Mary Percy and John de Southeray: Wardship, Marriage and Divorce in Fourteenth-Century England', *FCE X*, ed. Gwilym Dodd (2018), 132–56 (145 for the quote).

2 Nigel Saul, *Richard II* (1997), 18.

3 *Issues of the Exchequer*, 87; *CPR 1364–67*, 53; *ODNB*.

4 Goodman, 45–6.

5 Chris Given-Wilson, *Henry IV*, 12.

6 *Issues*, 190–1. Ingelram Falconer had previously served Blanche's father, and was still in John of Gaunt's service with his wife Amye in April 1372: Fowler, thesis, Appendix J; *Register 1371–75*, vol. 2, 34.

7 *CIPM 1377–84*, no. 656, is her proof of age, wrongly calling her 'Mary daughter and heir of John Orby', who was her grandfather.

8 *CIPM 1365–69*, nos 242, 402, 406; *CIPM 1377–84*, nos 571–4. After her short marriage to Edward III's illegitimate son John de Southeray was annulled (they had married in early 1377 when they were both underage), Mary Percy married John, Lord Ros of Helmsley in Yorkshire, a grandson of Ralph Stafford, earl of Stafford and Margaret Audley, before June 1382.

9 Cited in *ODNB*.

10 Mary Ros née Percy, Lady Ros and Oreby, died childless in 1394 at the age of 26; her will is in *Testamenta Eboracensia*, vol. 1. 201–3. She refers to her half-brother Henry Percy as 'my dearest brother the lord earl of Northumberland', her mother-in-law Beatrice née Stafford and sister-in-law Elizabeth Clifford as her mother and sister respectively, and also left bequests to her nephews Hotspur and Ralph Percy, but Isabella Percy is not identified.

11 *CIPM 1365–69*, no. 397.

12 *CCR 1369–74*, 370.

13 SC 8/163/8116. Lionel of Antwerp was called 'Leo' on the Patent Roll in November 1342 and May 1343 (*CPR 1340–43*, 569; *CPR 1343–45*, 42), so perhaps 'Leo Mowbray' was just a mix-up by a clerk.

14 Ian Mortimer, *The Fears of Henry IV*, 26; *ODNB*, 'Henry IV'; *Register 1371–75*, part 2, 35–6, 154–5.

15 *TV*, vol. 1, 70–1. He himself had received a palfrey horse called Bayard Juet from his brother the Prince of Wales when he was 10: Beltz, *Memorials of the Order of the Garter*, 384.

16 *TV*, vol. 1, 73–4.

17 Goodman, 46–7; *CP*, vol. 7, 415 note g; Thomas Wright, *Feudal Manuals of English History* (1872), 151.

18 *Register 1371–75*, vol. 2, 24–5, 37, 72, 94, 106, 269 298, etc.

19 *CIPM 1370–73*, no. 125, p. 103.

20 *TV*, vol. 1, 87.

21 *CPR 1370–74*, 463.

Chapter 24

1   *Register 1371–75*, vol. 2, 30–31, 112–3.
2   *Anonimalle 1333 to 1381*, 69, 153.
3   *Register 1371–75*, vol. 2, 55, 321; Goodman, 50.
4   *Issues of the Exchequer*, 195; *Register 1371–75*, vol. 1, 169–70.
5   *Register 1371–75*, vol. 2, 56. John Beaufort's *ODNB* entry gives his date
    of birth as *c.* 1371, as does the *Complete Peerage* (vol. 12A, 39–40), which
    seems a little early though is certainly not impossible. John was knighted
    by 6 December 1391 (*CPR 1391–96*, 15), and according to Jean Froissart
    took part in the Crusade of Louis, Duke of Bourbon, to Barbary in May
    to September 1390 (though I have been unable to find any safe conduct
    issued to Beaufort before he supposedly travelled abroad in 1390).
    Complete Peerage, vol. 12A, 40, note d, cites an entry on the Patent Roll
    (*CPR 1391–96*, 63) which states that John Beaufort was granted 100 marks
    a year to stay with the king on 7 June 1392. A later memorandum
    underneath this entry adds that the grant was cancelled because
    Richard II had granted Beaufort issues and profits from the lordship
    of Berkhamsted instead on '10 September in his twenty-first year'. This
    means Richard II's twenty-first regnal year which ran from 22 June 1397
    to 21 June 1398, not John Beaufort's twenty-first year of life as *Complete
    Peerage* implies, and does not necessarily mean that John was 21 or shortly
    to become 21 at the time of the grant in June 1392.
6   *Records*, vol. 2, 155, 171. The king in question was John's nephew Richard II.
7   *Register*, vol. 1, 136–8.
8   *Records*, vol. 2, 170; Goodman, 361–2.
9   *The Chronica Maiora of Thomas Walsingham* (2005), trans. David Preest, 292.
10 *Register 1371–75*, vol. 2, 22–23, 107–8.
11 *Register 1371–75*, vol. 2, 248, 256, 260–1, 276–7, 280; *Register 1379–83*, vol. 2, 259.
12 Given-Wilson, *Henry IV*, 24, 31 note 38.
13 *CIPM 1370–73*, no. 239.
14 *CIPM 1370–73*, no. 148; *CIPM 1374–77*, no. 148.
15 *Register 1371–75*, vol. 2, 51, 155.
16 Cited in *ODNB*.
17 *CPR 1377–81*, 440–1.
18 *ODNB*. The 1909 edition of his book *Master of Game*, which has a foreword
    by none other than Theodore Roosevelt, gives his name as Edward
    of Norwich.
19 *Register 1371–75*, vol. 1, 104; vol. 2, 96, 119, 165.
20 Anthony Tuck, 'Richard II and the House of Luxembourg', in Goodman,
    Anthony, and Gillespie, James L., eds., *Richard II: The Art of Kingship*, 224.
    This Wilhelm was the nephew of Wilhelm of Bavaria, who had been
    married to Gaunt's sister-in-law Maud of Lancaster.
21 *Register 1371–75*, vol. 2, 191–3.

22 *CIPM 1370–73*, no. 167. Eleanor was 'of age', i.e. 14, on 8 May 1380. *CPR 1377–81*, 502.
23 *CPR 1374–77*, 337.
24 *TV*, 94–6.
25 Chris Given-Wilson, 'Wealth and Credit, Public and Private: The Earls of Arundel, 1306–1397', *English Historical Review*, 106 (1991), 1.

Chapter 25

1 *Anonimalle*, 114.
2 *CPR 1377–81*, 105, 343.
3 *CPR 1377–81*, 125, 416, 594.
4 *CCR 1381–85*, 493–4.
5 *CIPM 1377–84*, nos 438–46; *Early Lincoln Wills*, 83.
6 *Register 1379–83*, vol. 2, 259, 280, 282 etc.
7 *Register 1379–83*, vol. 2, 297.
8 *Register 1379–83*, vol. 1, 50; *CPR 1377–81*, 186.
9 *CPR 1381–85*, 364.
10 Given-Wilson, *Henry IV*, 27.
11 *CPR 1377–81*, 537; Given-Wilson, *Henry IV*, 27 note 17.
12 *CPR 1381–85*, 95; *Register 1379-83*, vol. 2, 309.
13 Mortimer, *Fears of Henry IV*, 370–71.
14 Kathryn Warner, *Richard II: A True King's Fall*, 105–6.
15 *Anonimalle 1333 to 1381*, 152–3.
16 *Register 1379–83*, vol. 2, 362, 366.
17 Printed in *Register 1379–83*, vol. 2, 410–11.
18 Kris Towson, 'Hearts Warped by Passion: The Percy-Gaunt Dispute of 1381', *FCE III*, ed. W.M. Ormrod (2004), 150.
19 Walsingham, *Historia Anglicana*, vol. 2, 33, cited in Towson, 'Hearts Warped', 143.
20 *CPR 1381–85*, 79.

Chapter 26

1 *CIPM 1377–84*, nos 819–29.
2 *CChR 1341–1417*, 281, 301; *CPR 1381–85*, 236; *CCR 1381–85*, 493.
3 *Register 1379–83*, vol. 2, 258–60.
4 *CPR 1381–85*, 574; *CPR 1385–89*, 24, 51, 62.
5 *CPR 1389–92*, 407.
6 Mortimer, *Fears*, 371–2.
7 *CCR 1392–96*, 318; *CPL 1362–1404*, 391–2.
8 *TV*, 129.
9 *CPR 1399–1401*, 414–5, 519.
10 *CPR 1391–96*, 213.
11 *CPR 1391–96*, 598.

12 *CCR 1389–92*, 235, 242, 299 etc; *CCR 1392–96*, 234, 307, 387; *CPR 1385–88*, 475; *CPR 1391–96*, 342, 435.

13 *TV*, 134–5.

14 The 1408 IPM of Edmund Holland, earl of Kent, gives his sisters' birth order: Alianore, Joan, Margaret, Eleanor, Elizabeth (Alianore and Eleanor were the same name; I have used the medieval spelling and the modern spelling for clarity and to differentiate the sisters). *CIPM 1405–13*, no 622, and see also their mother Alice née Fitzalan's, *CIPM 1413–18*, no. 608.

15 Given-Wilson, *Henry IV*, 96–7; *CP*, vol. 7, 378, note b.

16 Cited in Paul Strohm, *England's Empty Throne: Usurpation and the Language of Legitimation 1399–1422* (1998), 4.

17 Goodman, 361.

18 *CPR 1399–1401*, 247; Given-Wilson, *Henry IV*, 86–7.

Chapter 27

1   *CPR 1385–89*, 412.

2   *CPR 1389–92*, 499.

3   *CPR 1396–99*, 46, 60, 286, 290, 319 etc.

4   *CPR 1396–99*, 211.

5   *Foedera 1373–97*, 528, 530.

6   *PROME*, Appendix to the September 1339 parliament.

7   Cited in *ODNB*.

8   *Collection*, 118; *TV*, 139.

9   *CPR 1396–99*, 408.

10 Katherine's son William Montacute the younger, tragically killed jousting by his own father in 1382, was one of the eleven boys knighted with Richard of Bordeaux and Henry of Lancaster in 1377, which implies that he was born in the 1360s, as all the others except Thomas of Woodstock were.

11 Given-Wilson, *Henry IV*, 116–7.

12 Michael Bennett, *Richard II and the Revolution of 1399*, 143.

13 *TV*, 140–5; *Collection*, 145–76.

Chapter 28

1   Devon, *Issues of the Exchequer,* 269.

2   *Chronicque de la Traison et Mort de Richart Deux Roy Dengleterre*, ed. Benjamin Williams, 63–6.

3   *TV*, 146–9; *Collection*, 177–85.

4   *CPR 1399–1401*, 280, 541.

5   *Chronicles of the Revolution*, 166, 186; Bennett, *Richard II and the Revolution*, 184.

6   *CChR 1341–1417*, 384, 387.

7   *CPR 1399–1401*, 69, 507; *CPR 1405–08*, 83, 84, 106.

8   *CPR 1401–05*, 108.

9   K.B. McFarlane, *The Nobility of Later Medieval England,* 243–4.
10 McFarlane, 244.
11 Edward II was also Henry IV's great-grandfather, but Richard was Edward's heir.

Epilogue

1   *Collection,* 187–9.
2   *CPR 1408–13,* 75, for the pardon.
3   The date of Alianore Holland's birth is not known, though Brian Wainwright, in a personal communication with the author, has suggested that she may have been born in 1405 when Constance was imprisoned at Kenilworth Castle. Edmund Mortimer was given permission to marry 'whomsoever he will of the king's allegiance' on 10 January 1405 (*CPR 1401–05,* 478), so perhaps his affair with Constance which resulted in her pregnancy with Alianore had already taken place (and ended) by then.
4   Mortimer, *Fears of Henry IV,* 372; Given-Wilson, *Henry IV,* 421, note 63.
5   Given-Wilson, *Henry IV,* 421.
6   *CPR 1399–1401,* 34, 58, 60; *CPR 1401–05,* 397; *CPR 1408–13,* 419.
7   Given-Wilson, *Henry IV,* 228.
8   Edmund Mortimer (b. 1376) was the fourth child of Philippa of Clarence, and the younger brother of Roger, earl of March (1374–98). His sister-in-law, the Mortimer boys' mother Alianore Holland, dowager countess of March and now the wife of Lord Charlton, a granddaughter of Eleanor of Lancaster, died later in 1405.
9   *CPR 1401–05,* 391, 480.
10 Given-Wilson, *Henry IV,* 269.
11 *CPR 1405–08,* 375; *CPR 1408–13,* 167–8, 220. Joan was the sister of Mowbray's maternal grandfather Richard Fitzalan, Earl of Arundel.
12 *CIPM 1405–13,* no. 604; *CPR 1408–13,* 167–8.
13 *CIPM 1405–13,* no. 622. The young Edmund Mortimer was also heir to his paternal aunt Philippa, Countess of Pembroke and Arundel (d. 25 September 1400).
14 *CPR 1401–05,* 69–70, 512.
15 *Collection,* 203–7.
16 *CChR 1341–1417,* 447.
17 *CPL 1404–15,* 456.
18 *Collection,* 217–22.
19 *CIPM 1413–18,* nos 608, 621.
20 *CPR 1413–16,* 168, 171; *CPR 1416–22,* 2.
21 *CPR 1416–22,* 389–90.

SELECT BIBLIOGRAPHY

PRIMARY SOURCES

An Account of the Expenses of John of Brabant and Thomas and Henry of Lancaster, AD 1292–3, ed. Joseph Burtt (London, 1953)

Adae Murimuth Continuatio Chronicarum, ed. E.M. Thompson (London, 1889)

Annales Londonienses 1195–1330, in W. Stubbs, ed., *Chronicles of the Reigns of Edward I and Edward II*, vol. 1 (London, 1882)

Annales Monastici, ed. H.R. Luard, 5 vols (London, 1864–69)

Annales Paulini 1307–1340, in Stubbs, *Chronicles of the Reigns*, vol. 1

Annales Ricardi Secundi et Henrici Quarti, in J. de Trokelowe et Anon., *Chronica et Annales*, ed. H.T. Tiley (London, 1866)

The Anonimalle Chronicle 1307 to 1334, ed. W.R. Childs and J. Taylor (Leeds, 1991)

The Anonimalle Chronicle 1333–1381, ed. Vivian Hunter Galbraith (Manchester, 1927; reprinted with minor corrections 1970)

The Antient Kalendars and Inventories of the Treasury of His Majesty's Exchequer, 3 vols, ed. Francis Palgrave (London, 1836)

The Brut or the Chronicles of England, parts 1 and 2, ed. F.W.D. Brie (London, 1906–08)

Calendar of Ancient Correspondence Concerning Wales, ed. J. Goronwy Edwards (Cardiff, 1935)

Calendar of Ancient Petitions Relating to Wales, ed. William Rees (Cardiff, 1975)

Calendar of Chancery Warrants 1244–1326 (London, 1927)

Calendar of the Charter Rolls, 4 vols, 1257–1417 (London, 1906–16)

Calendar of the Close Rolls, 42 vols, 1242–1413 (London, 1916–32)

Calendar of Documents Relating to Scotland, 3 vols, 1272–1509, ed. Joseph Bain (Edinburgh, 1887–88)

Calendar of Entries in the Papal Registers Relating to Great Britain and Ireland: Papal Letters, 5 vols, 1198–1415, ed. W.H. Bliss and J.A. Tremlow (London, 1893–1903)

Calendar of the Fine Rolls, 13 vols, 1272–1413 (London, 1911–33)

Calendar of Inquisitions Miscellaneous, 7 vols, 1219–1422 (London, 1916–68)

Calendar of Inquisitions Post Mortem, 20 vols, 1236–1418 (London, 1904–95)

Calendar of the Liberate Rolls, 6 vols, 1226–1272 (London, 1916–64)

Calendar of Memoranda Rolls (Exchequer), Michaelmas 1326–Michaelmas 1327 (London, 1968)

Calendar of the Patent Rolls, 41 vols, 1216–1422 (London, 1901–11)

Calendar of Select Plea and Memoranda Rolls, 3 vols, 1323–1412, ed. A.H. Thomas (London, 1926–32)

Calendar of Various Chancery Rolls, 1277–1326 (London, 1912)

Cartae et Alia Munimenta quae ad Domimium de Glamorgancia Pertinent, vol. 3 (Cardiff, 1910)

The Chronica Maiora of Thomas Walsingham, 1376–1422, trans. David Preest (Woodbridge, 2005)

The Chronicle of Adam Usk, 1377–1421, ed. Chris Given-Wilson (Oxford, 1997)

The Chronicle of Bury St Edmunds, 1212–1301, ed. Antonia Gransden (London, 1964)

The Chronicle of Geoffrey le Baker of Swinbrook, trans. David Preest (Woodbridge, 2012)

The Chronicle of Lanercost 1272–1346, ed. Herbert Maxwell (Glasgow, 1913)

The Chronicle of Pierre de Langtoft, vol. 2, ed. Thomas Wright (London, 1868)

The Chronicle of Walter of Guisborough, ed. Harry Rothwell (London, 1957)

Chronicles of the Reigns of Edward I and Edward II, 2 vols, ed. W. Stubbs (London, 1882–83)

Chronicles of the Revolution, 1397–1400: The Reign of Richard II, ed. Chris Given-Wilson (Manchester, 1993)

Chronicon Henrici Knighton, Monachi Leycestrensis, vol. 1, ed. Joseph Rawson Lumby (London, 1889)

Chronicque de la Traison et Mort de Richart Deux Roy Dengleterre, ed. Benjamin Williams (London, 1846)

Chronicon Galfridi le Baker de Swynebroke, ed. E.M. Thompson (Oxford, 1889)

Chronique Métrique de Godefroy de Paris, ed. J.A. Buchon (Paris, 1827)

Collectanea Topographica et Genealogica, vol. 4, eds F. Madden, B. Bandinel and J.G. Nichols (London, 1837)

A Collection of All the Wills Now Known to be Extant of the Kings and Queens of England, ed. John Nichols and Richard Gough (London, 1780)

Croniques de London, ed. G.J. Aungier (London, 1844)

Davies, James Conway, 'The First Journal of Edward II's Chamber', *English Historical Review*, 30 (1915)

A Descriptive Catalogue of Ancient Deeds, ed. H.C. Maxwell, 6 vols (London, 1890–1915)

The Diplomatic Correspondence of Richard II, ed. Edouard Perry (London, 1933)

Documents Illustrating the Crisis of 1297–98 in England, ed. Michael Prestwich (London, 1980)

Early Lincoln Wills: An Abstract of All the Wills and Administrations Recorded in the Episcopal Registers of the Diocese of Lincoln, 1280–1547, ed. Alfred Gibbons (Lincoln, 1888)

English Historical Documents, vol. 3, 1189–1327, ed. Harry Rothwell (second edition; London, 1995)

English Historical Documents, vol. 4, 1327–1485, ed. A.R. Myers (London, 1969; reprinted 1996)

Eulogium Historiarum sive Temporis, vol. 3 (*Continuatio Eulogii*), ed. F. Hayden (London, 1863)

Flores Historiarum, ed. H.R. Luard, 3 vols (London, 1890)

Foedera, Conventiones, Literae, 8 vols, 1272–1413, ed. T. Rymer (London, 1816–29)

'A Fragment of an Account of Isabel of Lancaster, Nun of Amesbury, 1333–4', ed. R.B. Pugh, in *Festschrift zur Feier des zweihundertjährigen Bestandes des Haus-, Hof- und Staatsarchivs*, vol. 1, ed. Leo Santifaller (Vienna, 1949)

Froissart, Sir John, *Sir John Froissart's Chronicles of England, France and the Adjoining Countries*, trans. Thomas Johnes, 2 vols (London, 1855)

Gesta Edwardi de Carnarvon Auctore Canonico Bridlingtoniensi, in W. Stubbs, ed., *Chronicles of the Reigns of Edward I and Edward II*, vol. 2 (London, 1883)

Gough, Henry, *Itinerary of King Edward the First Throughout His Reign, A.D. 1272–1307*, 2 parts, 1272–1285 and 1286–1307 (Paisley, 1900)

Grosmont, Henry of, first Duke of Lancaster, *The Book of Holy Medicines*, trans. and ed. Catherine Batt (Tempe, Arizona, 2014)

Hallam, Elizabeth, *The Itinerary of Edward II and his Household, 1307–1327* (London, 1984)

Haskins, G.L., 'A Chronicle of the Civil Wars of Edward II', *Speculum*, 14 (1939)

Histoire de St Louis par Jean Sire de Joinville, ed. Natalis de Wailly (Paris, 1848)

Historia Anglicana, vol. 1, ed. T.H. Riley (London, 1863)

Historia Vitae et Regni Ricardi Secundi, ed. George B. Stow (Philadelphia, 1977)

The Household Book of Queen Isabella of England: For the Fifth Regnal Year of Edward II, ed. F.D. Blackley and G. Hermansen (Edmonton, 1971)

Inquisitions and Assessments Relating to Feudal Aids 1284–1431, 6 vols (London, 1899–1920)

Issues of the Exchequer, ed. Frederick Devon (London, 1837)

Jean Froissart: Chronicles, trans. and ed. Geoffrey Brereton (London, 1978)

Johannis de Trokelowe et Henrici de Blaneforde Chronica et Annales, ed. H.T. Riley (London, 1866)

John of Gaunt's Register, vol. 1, 1371–1375, ed. Sydney Armitage-Smith (London, 1991)

John of Gaunt's Register, vol. 2, 1379–1383, ed. Eleanor C. Lodge and Robert Somerville (London, 1937)

Knighton's Chronicle 1337–1396, ed. G.H. Martin (Oxford, 1995)

Le Livere de Reis de Britanie e le Livere de Reis de Engletere, ed. John Glover (London, 1865)

Le Livre de Seyntz Medicines: The Unpublished Devotional Treatise of Henry of Lancaster,
 ed. A.J. Arnould (Oxford, 1940) (available on www.anglo-norman.net)
Letters of Edward, Prince of Wales, 1304–1305, ed. Hilda Johnstone (London, 1931)
Letters of the Kings of England, vol. 1, ed. J.O. Halliwell (London, 1848)
Liber Quotidianus Contrarotulatoris Garderobae, anno regni regis Edwardi primi
 vicesimo octavo, ed. John Topham (London, 1787)
Matthaei Parisensis, Monachi Sancti Albani, Chronica Maiora, 7 vols, ed. H.R. Luard
 (London, 1872–83)
Matthaei Parisensis, Monachi Sancti Albani, Historia Anglorum, 3 vols, ed. F. Madden
 (London, 1866–9)
National Archive records, especially BCM (Berkeley Castle Muniments), C
 (Chancery), DL (Duchy of Lancaster), E (Exchequer), SC (Special Collections)
The Parliament Rolls of Medieval England, ed. Brand, Curry, Given-Wilson,
 Horrox, Martin, Ormrod and Phillips (Scholarly Editions, 2005)
Parliamentary Writs and Writs of Military Summons, 3 vols, 1273–1328, ed. Francis
 Palgrave (London, 1827–34)
Petitions to the Pope 1342–1419, ed. W.H. Bliss (London, 1896)
Polychronicon Ranulphi Higden, monachi Cestrensis, vol. 8, ed. Joseph Rawson
 Lumby (London, 1865)
Records of the Borough of Leicester, vol. 1, 1103–1327 and vol. 2, 1327–1509, ed. Mary
 Bateson (London, 1899–1901)
Records of the Wardrobe and Household, 1285–86 and 1286–89, ed. Benjamin F.
 Byerly and Catherine Ridder Byerly (London, 1977–86)
Recueil de Lettres Anglo-Françaises 1265–1399, ed. F.J. Tanqueray (Paris, 1916)
The Reign of Richard II From Minority to Tyranny 1377–1397, ed. A.K. McHardy
 (Manchester, 2012)
The Roll of Arms of the Princes, Barons and Knights Who Attended King Edward I to
 the Siege of Caerlaverock, ed. T. Wright (London, 1864)
Royal and Other Historical Letters Illustrative of the Reign of Henry III, ed. Walter
 Waddington Shirley, 2 vols (London, 1862–6)
Royal Charter Witness Lists for the Reign of Edward II, 1307–1326, ed. Jeffrey S.
 Hamilton (London, 2001)
Scalacronica: The Reigns of Edward I, Edward II and Edward III as Recorded by Sir
 Thomas Gray of Heton, knight, ed. Herbert Maxwell (Glasgow, 1907)
Scalacronica: By Sir Thomas Gray of Heton, Knight. A Chronicle of England
 and Scotland from A.D. MLXVI to A.D. MCCCLXII, ed. J. Stevenson
 (Edinburgh, 1836)
Society of Antiquaries of London Manuscript 122
Stapleton, Thomas, 'A Brief Summary of the Wardrobe Accounts of the Tenth,
 Eleventh and Fourteenth Years of King Edward the Second', *Archaeologia,*
 26 (1836)
Statutes of the Realm, vol. 1: 1100–1377 (London, 1810)
Testamenta Eboracensia, or Wills Registered at York, vol. 1 (London, 1835)

Testamenta Vetusta: Being Illustrations from Wills, vol. 1, ed. Nicholas Harris
  Nicolas (London, 1826)
Thomas Walsingham, Quondam Monachi S. Albani, Historia Anglicana, ed. Henry
  Thomas Riley (London, 1864)
True Chronicles of Jean le Bel, 1290–1360, trans. and ed. Nigel Bryant
  (Woodbridge, 2011)
Vita Edwardi Secundi Monachi Cuiusdam Malmesberiensis, ed. N. Denholm-Young
  (London, 1957)
*The War of Saint-Sardos (1323–1325): Gascon Correspondence and Diplomatic
  Documents*, ed. Pierre Chaplais (London, 1954)
The Westminster Chronicle 1381–1394, ed. L.C. Hector and B.F. Harvey
  (Oxford, 1982)

SELECTED SECONDARY SOURCES

Baldwin, J.F., 'The Household Administration of Henry Lacy and Thomas of
  Lancaster', *English Historical Review*, 42 (1927)
Barber, Richard, *Edward, Prince of Wales and Aquitaine: A Biography of the Black
  Prince* (Woodbridge, 1978)
Barker, Juliet, *England, Arise: The People, the King and the Great Revolt of 1381*
  (London, 2014)
Beltz, George Frederick, *Memorials of the Most Noble Order of the Garter from Its
  Foundations to the Present Time* (London, 1841)
Bennett, Michael, *Richard II and the Revolution of 1399* (Stroud, 1999)
Biggs, Douglas, 'The Reign of Henry IV: The Revolution of 1399 and
  the Establishment of the Lancastrian Regime', *FCE I*, ed. Nigel Saul
  (Woodbridge, 2000)
Cockerill, Sara, *Eleanor of Castile: The Shadow Queen* (Stroud, 2014)
Denholm-Young, N., *Richard of Cornwall* (Oxford, 1947)
Dodd, Gwilym, ed., *The Reign of Richard II* (Stroud, 2000)
Dodd, Gwilym, and Biggs, Douglas, eds, *Henry IV: The Establishment of the
  Regime, 1399–1406* (Woodbridge, 2003)
Dodd, Gwilym, and Musson, Anthony, eds, *The Reign of Edward II: New
  Perspectives* (York, 2006)
Fowler, Kenneth, 'Henry of Grosmont, First Duke of Lancaster 1310–1361',
  PhD thesis, University of Leeds, 1961
Fowler, Kenneth, *The King's Lieutenant: Henry of Grosmont, First Duke of
  Lancaster 1310–1361* (London, 1969)
Frame, Robin, 'The Justiciarship of Ralph Ufford: Warfare and Politics in
  Fourteenth-Century Ireland', *Studia Hibernica*, 13 (1973)
Gibbs, Vicary, *The Complete Peerage of England, Scotland, Ireland, Great Britain*

and the United Kingdom: Extant, Extinct, or Dormant, by G.E.C., 13 vols in 14 parts (second edition, London 1910–59)

Gillespie, James L., ed., *The Age of Richard II* (Stroud, 1997)

Given-Wilson, Chris, 'Wealth and Credit, Public and Private: The Earls of Arundel, 1306–1307', *English Historical Review*, 106 (1991)

Given-Wilson, Chris, 'Richard II, Edward II, and the Lancastrian Inheritance', *English Historical Review*, 109 (1994)

Given-Wilson, Chris, *Henry IV* (New Haven and London, 2016)

Goodman, Anthony, *The Loyal Conspiracy: The Lords Appellant Under Richard II* (Coral Gables, Florida, 1971)

Goodman, Anthony, *John of Gaunt: The Exercise of Princely Power in Fourteenth-Century Europe* (Harlow, 1992)

Goodman, Anthony, and Gillespie, James L., eds, *Richard II: The Art of Kingship* (Oxford, 1999)

Gribit, Nicholas A., *Henry of Lancaster's Campaign to Aquitaine, 1345–46* (Woodbridge, 2016)

Haines, Roy Martin, *King Edward II: His Life, His Reign and Its Aftermath, 1284–1330* (Montreal, 2003)

Hamilton. J.S., *Piers Gaveston, Earl of Cornwall 1307–1312: Politics and Patronage in the Reign of Edward II* (Detroit, 1988)

Hamilton. J.S., 'Charter Witness Lists for the Reign of Edward II', *FCE I*, ed. Nigel Saul (Woodbridge, 2000)

Howell, Margaret, 'The Children of Henry III and Eleanor of Provence', *Thirteenth Century England IV*, ed. P.R. Coss and S.D. Lloyd (Woodbridge, 1992)

Howell, Margaret, *Eleanor of Provence: Queenship in Thirteenth-Century England* (Oxford, 2001)

Johnstone, Hilda, *Edward of Carnarvon 1284–1307* (Manchester, 1946)

King, Andy, 'Thomas of Lancaster's First Quarrel with Edward II', *FCE III*, ed. W.M. Ormrod (Woodbridge, 2004)

Leedom, Joe W., 'Lady Matilda Holland, Henry of Lancaster and the Manor of Melbourne', *American Journal of Legal History*, 31 (1987)

Lewis, N.B., 'A Certificate of the Earl of Lancaster's Auditors, 1341', *English Historical Review*, 55 (1940)

Maddicott, J.R., *Thomas of Lancaster 1307–1322: A Study in the Reign of Edward II* (Oxford, 1970)

Maddicott, J.R., 'Thomas of Lancaster and Sir Robert Holland: A Study in Noble Patronage', *English Historical Review*, 86 (1971)

Maddicott, J.R., *Simon de Montfort* (Cambridge, 1994)

McFarlane, K.B., *The Nobility of Later Medieval England* (Oxford, 1973)

Mitchell, Linda E., *Portraits of Medieval Women: Family, Marriage and Politics in England, 1225–1350* (New York, 2003)

Moor, Charles, *Knights of Edward I*, 5 vols (London, 1929–32)

Morris, Marc, *A Great and Terrible King: Edward I and the Forging of Britain* (London, 2008)

Mortimer, Ian, *The Perfect King: The Life of Edward III, Father of the English Nation* (London, 2006)

Mortimer, Ian, *The Fears of Henry IV: The Life of England's Self-Made King* (London, 2007)

Mortimer, Ian, *Medieval Intrigue: Decoding Royal Conspiracies* (London, 2010)

Munby, Julian, Barber, Richard and Brown, Richard, *Edward III's Round Table at Windsor* (Woodbridge:, 2007)

Ormrod, W.M., 'The Personal Religion of Edward III', *Speculum*, 64 (1989)

Ormrod, W.M., 'The Royal Nursery: A Household for the Younger Children of Edward III', *English Historical Review*, 120 (2005)

Ormrod, W.M., *Edward III* (New Haven and London, 2011)

Oxford Dictionary of National Biography, online edition, at www.oxforddnb.com

Parsons, John Carmi, 'The Year of Eleanor of Castile's Birth and her Children by Edward I', *Mediaeval Studies*, 46 (1984)

Parsons, John Carmi, *Eleanor of Castile: Queen and Society in Thirteenth-Century England* (Basingstoke, 1995)

Payne, M.T.W. and Payne, J.E., 'The Wall Inscriptions of Gloucester Cathedral House and the de Chaworths of Kempsford', *Transactions of the Bristol and Gloucestershire Archaeological Society*, 112 (1994)

Phillips, J.R.S., *Aymer de Valence: Baronial Politics in the Reign of Edward II* (Oxford, 1972)

Phillips, J.R.S., 'The "Middle Party" and the Negotiating of the Treaty of Leake: A Reinterpretation', *Bulletin of the Institute of Historical Research*, 46 (1973), 17

Phillips, Seymour, *Edward II* (London and New Haven: Yale University Press, 2010)

Powicke, Maurice, *Henry III and the Lord Edward: The Community of the Realm in the Thirteenth Century* (Oxford, 1950)

Prestwich, Michael, *The Three Edwards: War and State in England 1272–1377* (London, 1980)

Prestwich, Michael, *Edward I* (London, 1988)

Prestwich, Michael, 'The Court of Edward II', *The Reign of Edward II: New Perspectives*, ed. Gwilym Dodd and Anthony Musson (York, 2006)

Pugh, T.B., 'The Marcher Lords of Glamorgan and Morgannwg, 1317–1485', *Glamorgan County History, III: The Middle Ages*, ed. T.B. Pugh (1971)

Pugh, T. B., *Henry V and the Southampton Plot of 1415* (Southampton, 1988)

Rhodes, Walter, 'Edmund, Earl of Lancaster', *English Historical Review*, vol. 10, no. 37 (1895)

Rhodes, Walter, 'Edmund, Earl of Lancaster (Continued)', *English Historical Review*, vol. 10, no. 38 (1895)

Saul, Nigel, 'Richard II and the Vocabulary of Kingship', *English Historical Review*, 110 (1995)

Saul, Nigel, *Richard II* (New Haven and London, 1997)

Sayles, George Osborne, *The Functions of the Medieval Parliament in England* (London, 1988)

Shaw, William Arthur, *The Knights of England: A Complete Record from the Earliest Time*, vol. 1 (London, 1906)

Somerville, Robert, *History of the Duchy of Lancaster, vol. 1: 1265–1603* (London, 1953)

Strohm, Paul, *England's Empty Throne: Usurpation and the Language of Legitimation 1399–1422* (1998)

Tompkins, Laura, 'Mary Percy and John de Southeray: Wardship, Marriage and Divorce in Fourteenth-Century England', *FCE X*, ed. Gwilym Dodd (Woodbridge, 2018)

Tout, T.F., *Chapters in the Administrative History of England*, 6 vols (Manchester, 1920–37)

Tout, T.F., *The Place of the Reign of Edward II in English History* (second edition, Manchester, 1936)

Towson, Kris, 'Hearts Warped by Passion: The Percy-Gaunt Dispute of 1381', *FCE III*, ed. W.M. Ormrod (2004)

Underhill, Frances, *For Her Good Estate: The Life of Elizabeth de Burgh* (New York, 1999)

Vale, Malcolm, *The Origins of the Hundred Years War: The Angevin Legacy 1250–1340* (Oxford, 1990)

Vale, Malcolm, *The Princely Court: Medieval Courts and Culture in North-West Europe* (Oxford, 2001)

Verity, Brad, 'The First English Duchess: Isabel de Beaumont, Duchess of Lancaster (c. 1318–c. 1359)', *Foundations*, 1.5 (2004) (Journal of the Foundation for Medieval Genealogy)

Wainwright, Brian, *Frustrated Falcons: The Three Children of Edmund of Langley, First Duke of York* (2013)

Ward, Jennifer, *English Noblewomen in the Later Middle Ages* (London and New York, 1992)

Ward, Jennifer, *Women of the English Nobility and Gentry, 1066–1500* (Manchester and New York, 1995)

Ward, Jennifer, *Women in England in the Middle Ages* (London and New York, 2006)

Ward, Jennifer, *Elizabeth de Burgh, Lady of Clare (1295–1360)* (Woodbridge, 2014)

Warner, Kathryn, 'The Adherents of Edmund of Woodstock, Earl of Kent, in March 1330', *English Historical Review*, 126 (2011)

Warner, Kathryn, *Edward II: The Unconventional King* (Stroud, 2014)

Warner, Kathryn, *Isabella of France: The Rebel Queen* (Stroud, 2016)

Warner, Kathryn, *Long Live the King: The Mysterious Fate of Edward II* (Stroud, 2017)

Warner, Kathryn, *Richard II: A True King's Fall* (Stroud, 2017)

Warner, Kathryn, 'Bought by the King Himself': Edward II, his Chamber, his Interests and his Family in 1325–26', *FCE X*, ed. Gwilym Dodd (Woodbridge, 2018)

Wells–Furby, Bridget, 'Marriage and Inheritance: The Element of Chance in the Development of Lay Estates in the Fourteenth Century', *FCE X*, ed. Gwilym Dodd (Woodbridge, 2018)

Woolgar, C.M., *The Great Household in Late Medieval England* (Yale University, 1999)

Wright, Thomas, *The Political Songs of England* (London, 1839)

INDEX

(Women appear under their maiden names, and people's highest titles are the only ones given)

The History Press
The destination for history
www.thehistorypress.co.uk